BRITAIN AND THE ECONOMIC PROBLEM OF THE COLD WAR

Modern Economic and Social History Series

General Editor: Derek H. Aldcroft

Titles in this series include:

Studies in the Interwar European Economy
Derek H. Aldcroft

Arms and the State
Sir William Armstrong and the Remaking of British Naval Power, 1854–1914
Marshall J. Bastable

Whatever Happened to Monetarism?
Economic Policy Making and Social Learning in the United Kingdom Since 1979
Michael J. Oliver

Disillusionment or New Opportunites?
The Changing Nature in Offices, Glasgow 1880–1914
R. Guerriero Wilson

Raleigh and the British Bicycle Industry
An Economic and Business History, 1870–1960
Roger Lloyd-Jones and M.J. Lewis

Battles for the Standard
Bimetallism and the Spread of the Gold Standard in the Nineteenth Century
Ted Wilson

The British Footwear Industry
Peter R. Mounfield

Trade Unions and the Economy: 1870–2000
Derek H. Aldcroft and Michael J. Oliver

The British Electronics Industry
Technical Promise and Market Failure, 1930–2000
John F. Wilson

Britain and the Economic Problem of the Cold War

The Political Economy and the Economic Impact of the British Defence Effort, 1945-1955

TILL GEIGER

ASHGATE

Published by
Ashgate Publishing Limited
Gower House
Croft Road
Aldershot
Hampshire GU11 3HR
England

Ashgate Publishing Company
Suite 420
101 Cherry Street
Burlington, VT 05401-4405
USA

Ashgate website: http://www.ashgate.com

British Library Cataloguing in Publication Data
Geiger, Till
Britain and the economic problem of the Cold War : the political economy and the economic impact of the British defence effort, 1945-1955. – (Modern economic and social history)1. Cold War – Economic aspects – Great Britain 2. Defense industries – Great Britain – History – 20th century 3. Great Britain – Armed forces – Procurement – History – 20th century – 4. Great Britain – Defenses – Economics aspects – History – 20th century 5. Great Britain – Military policy 6. Great Britain – Economic policy – 1945-1964 7. Great Britain – Economic conditions – 1945-1964 8. Great Britain – Foreign relations – 1945-1964 9. Great Britain – Relations – United States 10. United States – Relations – Great Britain I. Title
330.9'41085

Library of Congress Cataloging-in-Publication Data
Geiger, Till.
Britain and the economic problem of the Cold War : the political economy and the economic impact of the British defence effort, 1945-1955 / Till Geiger.
p. cm. – (Modern economic and social history series) Includes bibliographical references and index.
ISBN 0-7546-0287-7 (alk. paper)
1. Great Britain – Defenses – Economic aspects. 2. Great Britain – Economic conditions – 1945-1964. 3. Cold War – Economic aspects. I. Title. II. Series.
HC260.D4G44 2004
330.941'0854–dc22

2003025800

ISBN 0 7546 0287 7

Printed and bound in Great Britain by Antony Rowe Ltd, Chippenham, Wiltshire

Contents

Part III: The economic impact of British defence expenditure

List of Tables, Graphs and Equations

List of Graphs

List of Equations

List of Abbreviations

AACP	Anglo-American Council on Productivity
AMP	Additional Military Production
BEA	British European Airways
EPU	European Payments Union
FBI	Federation of British Industry
GDCF	Gross Domestic Capital Formation
GNP	Gross National Product
IFF	Identification, Friend or Foe
MAAG	Military Assistance Advisory Group
MDAP	Mutual Defense Assistance Program
MoS	Ministry of Supply
MTDP	Medium Term Defence Plan
NAC	North Atlantic Council
NATO	North Atlantic Treaty Organisation
OED	Oxford English Dictionary
OEEC	Organisation for European Economic Co-operation
OSP	Offshore Procurement
ROF(s)	Royal Ordnance Factories
SBAC	Society of British Aircraft Constructors
TCC	Temporary Council Committee
UNECE	United Nations Economic Commission for Europe
WSEG	Weapons Systems Evaluation Group

List of Abbreviations of Archival Sources and Published Documents

BLM	Papers of Field Marshall Viscount Montgomery of Alamein
BT	Board of Trade
CAB	Cabinet Office
CP	Records of the British Communist Party
DBPO	Documents of British Policy Overseas
FRUS	Foreign Relations of the United States
H.C. Deb	House of Commons, *Official Report*, Parliamentary Debates (Hansard)
IOR	India Office Library and Records
IWM	Imperial War Museum, Department of Documents
JRULM	John Rylands University Library Manchester
LPA	Labour Party Archive
M-O A	Tom Harrison Mass-Observation Archive
NARA	National Archives and Record Administration
NMLH	National Museum of Labour History
PRO	Public Record Office
RG	Record Group
SCDI	Scottish Council (Development and Industry)
SRO	Scottish Record Office
T	Treasury
WO	War Office

Modern Economic and Social History Series General Editor's Preface

Economic and social history has been a flourishing subject of scholarly study during recent decades. Not only has the volume of literature increased enormously but the range of interest in time, space and subject matter has broadened considerably so that today there are many sub-branches of the subject which have developed considerable status in their own right.

One of the aims of this new series is to encourage the publication of scholarly monographs on any aspect of modern economic and social history. The geographical coverage is world-wide and contributions on the non-British themes will be especially welcome. While emphasis will be placed on works embodying original research, it is also intended that the series should provide the opportunity to publish studies of a more general thematic nature which offer a reappraisal or critical analysis of major issues of debate.

Derek H. Aldcroft
University of Leicester

Preface

This book has been in gestation for a long time. During my research, I have greatly benefited from the help of archivists who assisted my search for material on the impact of the British defence effort during the first cold war in numerous government, university and private archives in England, Scotland and the United States. Without their advice and suggestion, I might not have discovered some important sources. I would particularly like to thank Dr. Michael Moss of the University of Glasgow Archive who drew my attention to the recently catalogued records of the Scottish Council (Development and Industry). I would also like to thank the librarians of the Queen Mother Library at the University of Aberdeen, the Main Library at the Queen's University of Belfast, the British Library of Political and Economic Science, the John Rylands University Library Manchester and the British Library for their help and assistance. I am grateful to the Controller of Her Majesty's Stationery Office for granting permission to cite Crown Copy material held at the Public Record Office.

Some of its ideas have been previously published and been incorporated in this book. I would like to thank Anthony Gorst, Lewis Johnman, Scott Lucas, and the Institute of Contemporary British History for the permission to reprint chapter 4[1] and Dominique Barjot for permission to republish parts of chapter 6.[2]

Over the years, I have benefited tremendously from the comments and suggestions from numerous friends, colleagues, audiences at conferences and seminars, and my students. I am particularly grateful to Larry Butler, Helen Mercer, Peter Payne, Duncan Ross, Lorenza Sebesta, Richard Toye, Tim Whisler, and John Wilson for their insights and willingness to read and comment on most or some of the chapters. I would also like to thank Hilary Owen for patiently listening to my ideas, encouraging me, and reading all the chapters at various stages. All the comments and suggestions have made this a

---

1 Till Geiger, "'The next war is bound to come': Defence production policy, supply departments and defence contractors in Britain, 1945-57," in *Contemporary British History, 1931-61: Politics and the limits of policy*, ed. Anthony Gorst, Lewis Johnman, and W. Scott Lucas (London: Pinter, 1991), 95-118.

2 Till Geiger, "The British state, defence industry and the influence of American technology, 1945-65," in *Catching up with America: Productivity missions and the diffusion of American economic and technological influence after the second world war*, ed. Dominique Barjot (Paris: Presses de l'Université de Paris-Sarbonne, 2002), 157-70.

much better book than it otherwise would have been. However, this work and its errors remain entirely my own.

Finally, I would like to dedicate this book to my wife, Hilary, and to the memory of Pepper.

Introduction

Britain and the economic problem of the cold war: Themes and questions

Many accounts of British development since 1945 are directed at finding an explanation for the slower economic growth rate which Britain experienced compared to that of other Western European countries. In this context, some analysts have attributed the slower economic growth rate to the relatively high British defence expenditures. These accounts reflect two empirical observations: firstly that Britain spent more on defence than other countries and secondly that the British economy grew less rapidly than other western economies. The implication of these analyses is that Britain's relative economic decline could have been prevented, if policy-makers had not spent so much on defence. By implication, the casual comparisons of growth rates and defence efforts suggests that British society could have grown as rapidly as other Western European countries in the post-war period. However, such comparisons do not establish a causal link between Britain's defence effort and slow economic growth.[1] Authors tend to present only scant evidence for such a causal relationship between defence expenditure and economic development suggesting that their readers are willing to accept this assertion as an *a priori* assumption.[2] Therefore, the link between the two empirical observations is essentially discursive rather than causal. By attaching such significance to this discursive link, such narratives emplot[3] the start of Britain's decline in terms of the decision of British governments to spend a larger proportion of national income on defence after 1945 than had been the case prior to rearmament in the 1930s. In a sense, the discursive link between high defence expenditure and

---

[1] Roger Middleton provides a good summary of the existing literature; see Roger Middleton, *Government versus the Market: Growth of the public sector, economic management and British economic performance* (Cheltenham: Edward Elgar, 1996), 614-17.

[2] The reactionary critiques of the welfare state often rely on a similar *a priori* assumption linking the ungovernability of western democracies to growing social provision; see Albert O. Hirschman, *The Rhetoric of Reaction: Perversity, futility, jeopardy* (Cambridge: Harvard University Press, 1991), 118-24.

[3] The term 'emplot' is borrowed from Hayden White and refers to "… the way by which a sequence of events fashioned into a story is gradually revealed to be a story of a particular kind"; see Hayden White, *Metahistory: The historical imagination in nineteenth-century Europe* (Baltimore: Johns Hopkins University Press, 1973), 5-11 (quote:7).

slow economic growth only makes sense if the process of decline started at the moment that a British government increased the proportion of the national income spent on defence in peacetime. Therefore, historians of this period have read the end of their narrative – Britain's relative economic decline – into the beginning – the historical situation, which prompted this action – and vice versa, thereby establishing Britain's decline as an inevitable plot within our memory of the origins of the cold war.[4]

The key question emerging from this analysis is, when and why did this discursive link between Britain's defence effort and relative economic decline emerge. This explanation formed an important element in the declinist accounts, which began to appear in the late 1950s. These accounts reflected the growing concern among policy-makers as well as the informed public about the apparent differential in British and Western European growth rates.[5] An outstanding example of this literature is Andrew Shonfield's critique of British post-war economic policy, which blamed excessive defence expenditure for exacerbating the strain on the economy in this period. Shonfield argued that high overseas defence expenditure contributed to the repeated balance of payments crises, which forced the government to adopt restrictive measures to curb overall demand for imports. Throughout his book, he argued that such measures disproportionately affected industrial investment. In this context, he suggested that the decision to rearm during the Korean War slowed the rate of capital formation, because of a cut in the initial allowances for business investments.[6] However, Shonfield offers no empirical evidence for his assertion that government intervention reduced the rate of industrial investment or that higher investment would have led to higher economic growth.[7] Moreover, he provides no proof that British industrialists would have invested more if the government had spent less on defence. His claims, that too many resources were devoted to the development of military technology, were mainly supported by anecdotal evidence. Nevertheless, policy-makers used this suggestion to justify their decision to scale down Britain's defence effort as the result of a comprehensive review of military strategy.[8]

---

4 This point draws on Paul Ricœur, "Narrative Time," *Critical Inquiry* 7 (1980): 180.

5 Jim Tomlinson, "Inventing 'decline': the falling behind of the British economy in the postwar years," *Economic History Review* 49 (1996): 731-57.

6 Andrew Shonfield, *British Economic Policy since the War* (Harmondsworth: Penguin, 1958).

7 Later empirical studies on economic growth and investment behaviour found no evidence to substantiate such a relationship, see for example R. C. O. Matthews, Charles H. Feinstein, and J. C. Odling-Smee, *British Economic Growth, 1856-1973* (Oxford: Oxford University Press, 1982), 393.

8 Ministry of Defence, *Defence: Outline of future policy*, Cmnd. 124 (London: Her Majesty's Stationery Office, 1957).

At first sight, policy-makers seemed to accept the criticisms about British economic performance voiced outside government. However, this discourse arguably reflected continuous conflicts over the size of the defence budget in the immediate post-war period. While never cast in terms of foregoing economic growth, most defence white papers referred to the difficult decisions faced by the government over the allocation of public expenditures. British policy-makers insisted that reducing Britain's defence effort might jeopardise the fruits of victory in the Second World War. The 1947 Defence White Paper captured this conviction that the British defence effort represented a necessary sacrifice.

> [H]owever, admirable ... the aim of lightening the national burden [may be, h]is Majesty's Government are fully resolved to strike a considered balance between the needs of defence of this country and the urgent requirement of the post-war national economy as a whole.[9]

The quote suggests that a majority of British policy-makers tended to regard defence expenditure not merely as a "regrettable necessity", but as an economic burden.[10] Therefore, most policy-makers perceived the existence of some ill-defined conflict between the needs of national security and those of economic reconstruction. This perception implicitly assumed that defence expenditures would reduce the resources available for economic reconstruction. By extension, defence expenditure would slow the pace of economic recovery. Arguably, this perceived trade-off between national security and economic development already encapsulates in embryonic form the discursive link between supposedly excessive defence expenditure and slow economic growth, which became common currency in the late 1950s. However, it is important to stress that Britain's relative economic decline did not enter the decision-making process about the size of the British defence effort before the 1957 Defence Review.[11] Nevertheless, policy-makers believed that the British defence effort deprived the civil economy of necessary resources. Throughout this period, policy-makers disregarded the potential for positive effects from defence expenditure in terms of economic development, employment creation, and stabilisation of economic demand. For the most part, economists and economic policy-makers disregarded the impact of defence expenditure on the civilian economy. For example, the former economic

---

9 Ministry of Defence, *Statement relating to Defence 1947*, Cmd. 7042 (London: His Majesty's Stationery Office, 1947), 2-4 (quote: 4).

10 Economists often refer to defence expenditure as a "regrettable necessity"; see Wilfred Beckerman, *An introduction to National Income Analysis*, 3rd ed. (London: Weidenfeld and Nicholson, 1980), 44.

11 On this point, see John Saville, *The Politics of Continuity: British foreign policy and the Labour government, 1945-46* (London: Verso, 1993), 8-9.

adviser to the wartime government, James Meade, argued that in contrast to the war, peacetime economic planning was primarily concerned with the civilian economy. He noted as an exception to this rule that peacetime governments might take military considerations into account when planning the location and preservation of strategic industries. Nevertheless, he decided to ignore these military aspects in his discussion of economic planning in his influential book *Planning and Price Mechanism* published in 1948.[12] If an economic adviser commented on the economic impact of defence expenditure, they argued that due to chronic over-employment of the civil economy, military production should be reduced further to free additional labour for the civilian economy.[13] Arguably, this perception biased the interpretation of the economic impact of British defence expenditure throughout the immediate post-war period. As a consequence, policy-makers did not conceive of military expenditure as potentially wealth-creating in the conditions of post-war reconstruction.[14]

The foregoing analysis shows that discussion of economic policy rarely considered the economic impact of British military expenditure. Nevertheless, foreign policy-makers realised that Britain's financial position had deteriorated due to the Second World War and circumscribed the government's room for manoeuvre in terms of defence and foreign policy. As a consequence, the British government depended to a increasing degree on American financial assistance.[15] Despite this realisation, policy-makers tended to reduce the question of striking the right balance between the defence burden and economic reconstruction to an issue of fiscal policy. In this context, the problem for the political decision-makers is to know how much defence is enough? Too much defence can stunt economic development, too little can lead to war and potentially defeat. The answer depends on an assessment of the military situation and the economic sustainability of the defence effort.[16] In

[12] James Edward Meade, *Planning and the Price Mechanism: The liberal-socialist solution* (London: George Allen and Unwin, 1948), 2.

[13] On this point, see the discussion at the beginning of chapter 4.

[14] As Paul Kennedy points out in the introduction to his study on *The Rise and Fall of the Great Powers*, military expenditure can in certain situations contribute to wealth creation and therefore to the rise of great powers; see Paul Kennedy, *The Rise and Fall of Great Powers: Economic change and military conflict from 1500 to 2000* (London: Fontana, 1989), xv-xviii. Long-term empirical studies confirm that the relationship between defence efforts, investment and wealth creation is contingent on the level of economic development and military technology; see Walter G. Hoffmann, "Der Anteil der Verteidigungsausgaben am Bruttosozialprodukt - Ein internationaler und intertemporaler Vergleich," *Kyklos* 23 (1970): 80-97. Despite growing faster, more developed countries spent a higher proportion of their national income on defence in the period from 1945 to 1970 than between the two world wars. This analysis points towards a more complex relationship between defence and wealth creation than suggested by the claims that excessive postwar defence expenditures caused British economic decline.

[15] On this point, see Saville, *Politics of continuity*, 75-80.

[16] Meade, *Planning*, 22.

peacetime, this decision cannot be reduced to a simple economic problem as it can in wartime when the problem becomes what is the maximum share of national income which can be allocated to the war effort.[17] In this sense, there is no one answer to the question: How much defence expenditure can the country afford? This fact is often obscured in the annual battle over the budget, which centres around a set of unanswerable questions: Are the planned expenditures enough to assure national security? Is it prudent to reduce defence expenditure? Can we afford this level of defence expenditure? Indeed, defence economists emphasise the political nature of this allocation decision and the importance of who gets to make the decision about the level of defence expenditure.[18] As the government's economic adviser, Robert Hall, observed during the budget discussions in 1957:

> It is a matter of choice between spending the national income in various ways, and if we say we can only afford a certain amount, it means we prefer other things.[19]

Hall argued that since "other forms of [g]overnment expenditure are more or less fixed," the government had increasingly no option but to reduce defence expenditure in order to increase welfare expenditure or reduce taxes. However, another senior Treasury official, Roger Makins, used Hall's answer to argue in a personal memorandum to the Chancellor, Peter Thorneycroft, for further increases in the defence budget, because there was no compelling economic reason why Britain could not spare more money to fund its military more adequately. As this episode shows, policy-makers at times held different views about the level of defence expenditure Britain could (or ought to) afford. In some cases, such differences of opinion could even trigger the resignation of ministers as happened during the Korean War, when Aneurin Bevan and Harold Wilson resigned over a small reduction in social welfare expenditure to finance rearmament.[20] As the quotes show, British policy-makers did discuss the defence budget in terms of what the country could afford, which reflected their acute awareness that Britain's precarious financial position might not

---

[17] E. A. G. Robinson, "The Overall Allocation of Resources," in *Lessons of the British War Economy*, ed. D. N. Chester (Cambridge: Cambridge University Press, 1951), 34-57.; Meade, *Planning*, 2.

[18] Todd Sandler and Keith Hartley, *The Economics of Defense* (Cambridge: Cambridge University Press, 1995), 52-3.

[19] Public Record Office, Kew, Treasury (hereafter: PRO T) PRO T 171/483: memorandum Hall - Makins, 26 February 1957.; PRO T 171/483: "Defence and the Budget", memorandum Makins - Thorneycroft, 28 February 1957.

[20] On this episode, see Kenneth O. Morgan, *Labour in Power, 1945-1951* (Oxford: Oxford University Press, 1985), 441-63.; and the analysis in chapter 3 of this book.

permit the country to continue bearing the expense of its defence effort.[21] The exchange between Hall and Makins revealed the internal battle between the economic policy-makers who favoured further cuts and the foreign policy-makers who insisted that Britain should maintain its role as a global power. At the same time, the dispute between Hall and Makins also highlights the fact that economic theory provides little guidance for policy-makers on how much the government should spend on defence. Economists can, however, offer some advice on the likely economic impact of a certain level of defence expenditure.

Aware of the political nature of the decision about public expenditures, economic advisers tend to be reluctant to offer advice on how large the defence budget should be. This professional reticence is frustrating for ministers looking for guidance on how much can be afforded. In turn, ministers turn to their military planners for an answer on how much is needed for the defence of the realm. Such questions often take the form of what represents the absolute minimum military requirements to achieve national security. Given their own interests, military planners may offer disingenuous advice by representing certain expenditure, military bases or weapons as essential to meet a military threat. However, military planners lack any objective criteria by which to determine what represents the minimum defence effort to deter an adversary. In this sense, strategic theory does not offer any more reliable answers on the problem of national defence than economic theory. Therefore, the strategic theorist, Bernard Brodie, argued in the late 1940s that military planners should be asked to utilise the available budget as effectively as possible to maximise the country's military strength. Indeed, economic theory may provide useful tools for determining the allocation of the available financial resources. For example, cost-benefit analyses or operations research might help military planners to decide between different weapons systems.[22] However, the inescapable conclusion remains that when it comes to determining the size of the national defence effort, policy-makers can hardly expect military planners to offer unbiased expert advice.

Regarded in this light, the cold war was arguably an unsolvable economic and military problem. As such it presented decision-makers with a difficult political problem, the intractable nature of which also gives rise to serious epistemological problems for historians of this period. In line with the dominant discourse about British decline, an analysis of the economic impact

---

[21] As early as 1946, the Prime Minister of the first Labour government, Clement Attlee, raised serious doubts in these terms about the affordability of the British defence effort and military presence in the Middle East; see Saville, *Politics of continuity*, 112-48.

[22] Bernard Brodie, "Strategy as a Science," *World Politics* 1 (1949): 476-8. On this point, see also Charles Hitch, "Economics and Military Operations Research," *Review of Economics and Statistics* 40 (1958): 199-209.

of the cold war might argue that the British defence effort had a detrimental effect on economic growth. However, former decision-makers may criticise such an account insisting that the negative impact may have been regrettable, but unavoidable given the serious military threat.[23] While the fact that no war had actually broken out might suggest that the scale of military effort was excessive, military planners rejected such suggestions citing uncertainty about the scale of the military threat in the late 1940s and early 1950s.[24] Pointing out that absolute security might be impossible to achieve, Field-Marshal Bernard Montgomery argued that the only way in which western countries could reduce their defence budgets would be by integrating their armed forces and thereby eliminating the duplication of national military efforts and command structures.[25] These typical justifying discourses reflect the contemporaneous warnings of governments throughout the cold war that spending less on defence might jeopardise national security. As the quote from the 1947 Defence White Paper illustrates, government ministers regarded defence expenditure as an important (first) claim on national resources. As the cold war intensified, policy-makers used the Soviet military threat to justify the relatively large British defence efforts. At the same time, most western foreign policy-makers acknowledged that the Soviet Union was hardly in a position to fight another global conflict in the foreseeable future having sustained massive casualties and physical damage during the war. Therefore, the Soviet military threat did not really exist in the first years after the Second World War.[26]

To some extent, the curious history of the term *cold war* illustrates the changing perception of the relations between the victorious powers in the immediate post-war period.[27] The compilers of the Oxford English Dictionary (OED) attribute the first use of the term to George Orwell in an article for *Tribune* in 1945. The reference in the article, however, does not directly refer to the cold war as the ideological confrontation between the Soviet Union and the western powers.[28] In March 1946, *The Observer* described recent changes

---

[23] For example, see Edwin Plowden, *An Industrialist in the Treasury: The post-war years* (London: Andre Deutsch, 1990), 119-20.

[24] Ministry of Defence, *Defence: outline*, 1-3.

[25] Bernard L. Montgomery, *The Memoirs of Field-Marshal the Viscount Montgomery of Alamein, K.G.* (London: William Collins, Sons & Co., 1958), 506-29.

[26] On this point, see Saville, *Politics of continuity*, 208-11.; and the analysis in chapter 3.

[27] The following analysis draws on the entry for *cold war* in the Oxford English Dictionary; see J. A. Simpson and E. S. C. Weiner, *The Oxford English Dictionary*, 2nd ed. (Oxford: Clarendon Press, 1989), volume 3, 462-3.

[28] The essay argues that the emergence of atomic weapons will lead to a world dominated by three or four oligarchic states each possessing nuclear weapons and therefore "undefeatable". Orwell predicted that this situation would lead to an international structure in which each nuclear power would be locked "in a permanent state of 'cold war' with its neighbours."; see George Orwell, "You and the Atom Bomb," in *Collected Essays, Journalism*

in Soviet foreign policy towards Britain as starting "... to make a 'cold war' on Britain and the British Empire."[29] However, the term entered common usage in the American public debate through Walter Lippmann's book on current American foreign policy entitled *Cold War* and published in early 1947.[30] Indeed, the next British usage cited by the compilers of the OED occurs in a speech by Anthony Nutting, the Conservative Member of Parliament for Melton, during a debate on foreign affairs in the House of Commons on 22 January 1948, which attributed the term to American commentators.[31] The manner in which the usage of the term evolved suggests that British policy-makers became convinced much earlier than did their American counterparts that the Soviet government had become impossible to deal with. As D. C. Watt has suggested, British policy-makers formed this conviction by early 1946 which coincides with the reference to the cold war in *The Observer* article in March of the same year.[32] To some extent, the learning process of British foreign policy-makers reflected not only Soviet actions, but also the open anti-communism of the Foreign Secretary, Ernest Bevin, and the majority of Foreign Office officials at the time.[33] The present analysis underlines the fact that the cold war emerged after 1945 but drew on a much older historical conflict between the East and the West.[34]

Since the cold war only came to be accepted as a justification for higher defence expenditure in early 1948, the question arises whether British government decided to increase defence expenditure before or after the cold war had become an accepted reality. As Graph I:1 shows, British defence remained just below the £800 million level throughout the late 1940s.[35] Not

---

and Letters of George Orwell: volume 4: In Front of Your Nose, 1945-1950, eds. Sonia Orwell and Ian Angus (London: Secker and Warburg, 1968), 6-10, quote: 9 (quotation marks in the original). While one might be struck by the accuracy of the prediction, the discovery of nuclear weapons did not immediately lead to a world of nuclear stalemate.

29 *The Observer*, 10 March 1946, 4.

30 Walter Lippmann, *Cold War: A Study in American Foreign Policy* (London: Hamish Hamilton, 1947).

31 House of Commons, *Official Report*, vol. 446, Parliamentary Debates (Hansard), Fifth Series (London: His Majesty's Stationery Office, 1948), col. 411.

32 Donald C. Watt, "Britain, the United States and the opening of the cold war," in *The Foreign Policy of the British Labour Governments, 1945-1951*, ed. Ritchie Ovendale (Leicester: Leicester University Press, 1984), 43-60.

33 Saville, *Politics of continuity*, 40-64 and 93-111.

34 On this point, see Eckart Conze, "Konfrontation und Détente: Überlegungen zur historischen Analyse des Ost-West-Konflikts," *Vierteljahreshefte für Zeitgeschichte* 46 (1998): 269-82.; Paul Dukes, *The Last Great Game: USA versus USSR: Events, conjectures, structures* (London: Pinter, 1989).

35 The defence estimates for financial year 1947/48 include terminal charges of £118.5 million for the demobilisation of British servicemen after the Second World War. If these terminal charges are taken out of the estimates, the planned defence expenditures amounted to £780.5 million, which corresponds closely to the amounts set aside for defence in

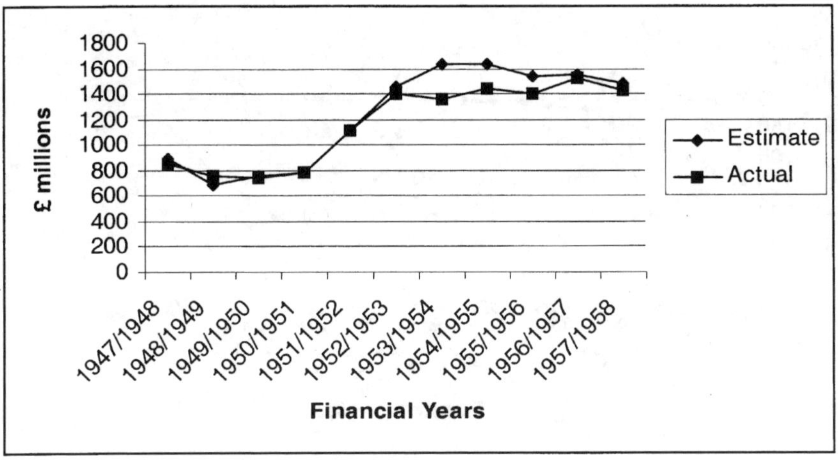

Graph I:1 British Defence Estimates and Expenditure, 1947–58

Note: The dates refer to the British financial year (1 April – 31 March).
Source: Ministry of Defence, *Statement on Defence*, (London: Her Majesty's Stationery Office, various years); Central Statistical Office, *Annual Abstract of Statistics* (London: Her Majesty's Stationery Office, various years).

only did British defence expenditure remain stable, but the armed services did not spend the full amount allocated to military purposes in the defence estimates in this period. The increase in cold war tensions did not lead to sudden increases in defence expenditure prior to the Korean War (see Graphs I:1 and I:2). The only notable exception is the financial year 1948/49, when the costs of the Berlin airlift forced the government to overspend its defence budget.[36] Graphs I:1 and I:2 show that the decision to increase British defence expenditure after the end of the Second World War pre-dated the cold war. Therefore, the increased British defence effort in the immediate post-war period reflected historical contingencies at the time rather than being intrinsically linked to regaining the Empire or the increased cold war tensions after 1948.

It becomes apparent from Graph I:1 that the outbreak of the Korean War on 25 June 1950 led to a massive expansion of the British defence effort. After several years of a large-scale military build-up, successive Conservative governments then started to reduce defence spending from the mid-1950s. To some extent, these reductions were initially achieved by under-spending the provisional defence budget (see Graph I:2). The deep cuts in military

the financial estimates for the next three financial years; see Ministry of Defence, *Statement relating to Defence 1947*.

[36] The first four months of the Berlin airlift cost the British taxpayer roughly £2.3 million, see Ann Tusa and John Tusa, *The Berlin Blockade* (London: Coronet, 1989), 363-6.

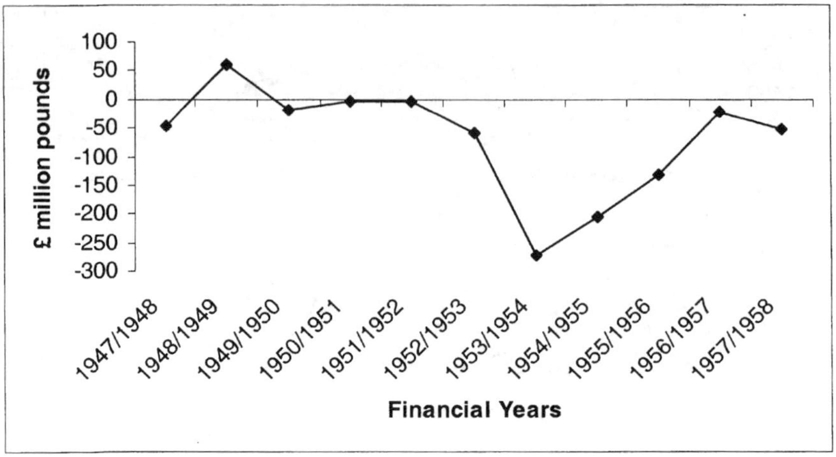

Graph I:2 Difference between Defence Estimates and Defence Expenditure, 1947–58

Source: see Graph I:1

expenditure in the 1952/53 financial year reflected the outcome of a defence review, which had been initiated by the Conservative Government to reduce the balance of payments deficit by increasing engineering exports.[37] Despite the reductions, Conservative ministers stated in the 1954 Defence White Paper that Britain's defence effort "continued to impose a heavy burden on our economy in terms both of the budget and the balance of payments."[38] Nevertheless, this review marked the beginning of a serious reconsideration of the structure of Britain's armed forces. After the 1953 review, policy-makers adopted a more capital-intensive defence posture in order to improve the firepower, but reduce the overall cost of defence. In many ways, these decisions paved the way for the changes in defence procurement policy announced in the 1957 Defence White Paper.[39] Graphs I:1 and I:2 suggest the massive structural shifts in British defence expenditure after the end of the Second World War and the outbreak of the Korean War respectively. Therefore, it is hardly surprising that many accounts focus on these two moments as turning points with far-reaching consequences for British economic development. For this reason, chapters 1 and 3 of this book analyse

---

37 Ministry of Defence, *Statement on Defence 1953*, Cmd. 8768 (London: His Majesty's Stationery Office, 1953), 3-4.

38 Ministry of Defence, *Statement on Defence 1954*, Cmd. 9075 (London: Her Majesty's Stationery Office, 1954), 4.

39 On the development of British defence policy in this period, see Michael Dockrill, *British Defence Policy since 1945* (Oxford: Basil Blackwell, 1988), 41-81.; William Jackson, *Britain's Defence Dilemma: An inside view* (London: B. T. Batsford, 1990), 49-72.

the decisions, which led to the major increases in British defence spending after 1945 and June 1950.

On balance, historians have appraised records of post-war governments positively arguing that policy-makers did remarkably well given the constraints they faced. These accounts invariably treat Britain's economic and military capabilities as a factor which circumscribed the actions of British policy-makers. However, these historical studies tend to analyse one particular aspect of the defence equation, often in isolation. Therefore, the emphasis is almost exclusively on the intricacies of decision-making about foreign, defence or economic policy. In this context, historians may refer to military, diplomatic or financial considerations entering into the decision-making process, but these are rarely directly related to one another.[40] As a consequence, this literature rarely explores for example the impact of the defence effort on the economy or of economic performance on military capability. Nevertheless, the literature implicitly accepts the realist assumption that military (and by implication) political power is to some extent a function of economic strength.[41] In this sense, historians share the sense of most contemporary decision-makers that Britain had emerged weakened from the latest war, and that maintaining its political influence as a medium power therefore represented a remarkable achievement. Due to this emphasis on historical circumstances, this group of historians is rather sceptical of the suggestion that policy-makers could realistically have pursued a different national security policy and hence spent less on defence in this period.[42] Sceptical accounts tend to reject the declinist claims, because their own detailed analyses emphasise the constraints operating at the time. Nevertheless, sceptical accounts fail to dismiss the claims made in

[40] An exception are Tony Gorst's studies of the inter-relations between military planning and defence budget in the late 1940s; see Anthony Gorst, "British military planning for post-war defence, 1943-1945," in *Britain and the First Cold War*, ed. Anne Deighton (Basingstoke: Macmillan, 1990), 91-108.; Anthony Gorst, "Facing Facts?: The Labour Government and defence policy 1945-1950," in *The Attlee Years*, ed. Nick Tiratsoo (London: Pinter, 1991), 190-209.; and Anthony Gorst, "'We must cut our coat according to our cloth': the making of British defence policy 1945-1948," in *British Intelligence, Strategy and the Cold War*, ed. Richard Aldrich (London: Routledge, 1992), 143-65.

[41] The realist paradigm dominated International Relations in the immediate postwar period, see Torbjørn L. Knutsen, *A History of International Relations Theory*, 2nd ed. (Manchester: Manchester University Press, 1997), 231-58.

[42] This categorisation of the majority of historical studies as "sceptical accounts" follows Hayden White's use of the term to describe those narrative accounts of human development which defend the achievements of historical actors and are critical of the potential for further progress. Besides declinist accounts, White used the term "progressive" for historical studies, which emphasise the potential for further development and at times criticise historical actors for their failure to fully exploit such opportunities; see Hayden White, "The Politics of Historical Interpretation: Discipline and de-Sublimation," in *Content of the Form: Narrative Discourse and Historical Interpretation* (Baltimore: Johns Hopkins University Press, 1987), 64-5.

the declinist literature, however unsubstantiated they are, because of their limited scope. For the most part, sceptical historians ignore rather than engage with declinist discourse.

However, some historians have been disturbed by the persuasiveness of declinist accounts, which seem to find their way into mainstream history without serious challenge.[43] One of the methodological flaws of declinist accounts is the extent to which its agenda is informed by hindsight. The assertion that high defence expenditure caused slower economic growth in Britain since 1945, illustrates this point about over-relying on knowledge about the past to establish a narrative of historical developments. Firstly, the accounts are invariably informed by the knowledge that the cold war confrontation never led to a hot war. Secondly, such an assertion could also be based on recent studies, which showed that western assessments of the Soviet military threat tended to exaggerate the overall strength of the Warsaw Pact's armed forces.[44] Thirdly, other western governments spent less on defence without this relative neglect of national security leading to an armed confrontation with the eastern bloc. Therefore, declinist accounts can safely imply that British post-war governments could safely have spent less on defence. A similar string of arguments can be used to suggest to readers that slower economic growth in Britain can be attributed to a lower investment rate. Exploiting the reader's familiarity with the subsequent history, declinist authors create the illusion of potential for an alternative history based on a different set of policy choices. While it might be worthwhile to investigate alternative histories through counterfactuals or experiments in "virtual history",[45] declinist accounts never

---

[43] In an article on declinist literature, Tomlinson criticises his fellow economic historians for being obsessed with the question of British economic decline, while overlooking its narrative construction in the late 1950s; see Tomlinson, "Inventing 'decline'." Both David Edgerton and Jim Tomlinson have attempted to reveal the deep historical and methodological flaws in Correlli Barnett's declinist accounts of wartime and postwar Britain; see David Edgerton, "The Prophet Militant and Industrial: The Peculiarities of Correlli Barnett," *Twentieth Century British History* 2 (1991): 360-79.; and Jim Tomlinson, "Correlli Barnett's History: The case of Marshall aid," *Twentieth Century British History* 8 (1997): 222-38. These articles challenge respectively Correlli Barnett, *The Audit of War: The illusion and reality of Britain as a great nation* (Basingstoke: Macmillan, 1986).; and Correlli Barnett, *The Lost Victory: British dreams, British realities, 1945-1950* (Basingstoke: Macmillan, 1995).

[44] Matthew A. Evangelista, "Stalin's Postwar Army Reappraised," *International Security* 7 (1982): 110-38.

[45] Niall Ferguson has suggested that historians might learn more about the past by constructing realistic alternative "virtual" histories derived from documented prognostication by contemporary observers. Through this method, he argues that historians can write history from the unique perspective of the historical actor to whom the future course of events is uncertain; see Niall Ferguson, "Introduction - Virtual History: Towards a 'chaotic' theory of the past," in *Virtual History: Alternatives and Counterfactuals*, ed. Niall Ferguson (London: Picador, 1997), 79-90. However, it remains unclear in what way Ferguson's approach differs from previous pleas for the use of counterfactual analysis in (economic) history nor whether he really overcomes the shortcomings of counterfactual speculation; see Peter D. McClelland,

establish the empirical basis for their assertions that an alternative course of action would have led to higher growth. Most declinist authors argue that the policies of the post-war Labour government alternatively led to perverse results, proved futile, or jeopardised Britain's achievements during the Second World War.[46] This line of argument is mirrored in the progressive literature, which argues that the Labour government would have achieved more had ministers been more determined to push through their reformist agenda by pursuing a more socialist foreign policy or planning the economy more rigorously.[47] Arguably, declinist or progressive accounts compare historical developments against an implied counterfactual course of events suggesting that an alternative outcome would have been possible. Due to this intricate relationship between historical fact and narrative, the task of historian involves disentangling historical developments from their narration in contemporaneous as well as historical studies.

Previous interpretations provide a catalogue of ready-made hypotheses about historical developments, which can serve as a starting point for examining the documentary evidence. If the implied alternative histories of previous studies have shaped the discourse about the relationship between the British defence effort and relative economic decline, then these interpretations provide the logical points of departure for an attempt to analyse the impact of defence on British society. By examining the potential alternative histories of this period, this book seeks to provide a better understanding of precisely how Britain's defence effort affected economic development.[48] To achieve this objective, this study focuses on different key interpretations of important episodes such as Korean war rearmament. In this respect, therefore, this book necessarily revisits the answers previous authors have proposed to the following questions: why British policy-makers spent more on defence than did other countries; why Britain did not use defence procurement more effectively; and, whether high defence expenditure contributed to Britain's relative

---

Causal Explanation and Model Building in History, Economics and the New Economic History (Ithaca: Cornell University Press, 1975), 146-68, particularly 152.

[46] Albert Hirschman has argued that reactionary discourse can be considered as adhering to one of three basic arguments: perversity, futility or jeopardy thesis. The argument in the text accepts this categorisation for declinist literature, see Hirschman, *Rhetoric*, 1-10.

[47] On the general point about progressive literature, see Hirschman, *Rhetoric*, 149-63. On the specific point, such a line of argument underlies for example, Saville, *Politics of continuity.*; or Teddy Brett, Steve Gilliatt, and Andrew Pople, "Planned Trade, Labour Party policy and US intervention: the successes and failures of post-war reconstruction," *History Workshop* 13 (1982): 130-42.

[48] Reinhart Koselleck argues that an idea of the potential histories is needed for a proper understanding of historical records; see Reinhart Koselleck, "Standortbindung und Zeitlichkeit: Ein Beitrag zur historiographischen Erschließung der geschichtlichen Welt," in *Vergangene Zukunft: Zur Semantik geschichtlicher Zeiten* (Frankfurt/Main: Suhrkamp, 1979), 206-7.

economic decline. Arguably, these three aspects – the political context and the international situation, economic impact of military expenditure, and the relative cost of the British defence burden – determined the overall impact of British defence policy on economic development. To do justice to the multi-faceted nature of the subject matter, the book takes an eclectic approach drawing on a variety of previous historical studies and social science theories.[49] Arguably, the key limitation of this approach is that it privileges the questions of past authors and thereby disregards to some extent other potential outcomes. For example, this study's focus on declinist accounts may overlook the possibility that the British defence effort significantly contributed to economic stability and even to growth in the immediate post-war period. Nevertheless, by revisiting and testing previous interpretations, this book offers a more considered analysis of the British defence effort and its economic impact during the period of the first cold war.

Following this approach, this book examines aspects of the political economy of British defence expenditure in Part 1, British defence production policy in Part 2, and the economic impact of British defence expenditure in Part 3. Each part of the book itself consists of three self-contained studies, which examine some facet of the impact of the British defence effort during this period. The examination of political economy in Part 1 starts by asking how the post-war British state attempted to reform the capability of its defence establishment to deal with the challenges of defence in the post-war world. Chapter 2 examines the Anglo-American relationship in the latter half of the 1940s. This analysis is followed in chapter 3 by a re-examination of whether American pressure compelled the Attlee government to rearm during the Korean War and thus brought about its downfall in November 1951. Part 2 assesses the impact of British defence procurement on industry and the economic structure of Britain. Chapter 4 analyses whether British defence procurement policy contributed significantly to the strain on the economy during the first decade after the war. Using contemporary newspaper reports, chapter 5 examines the relationship between the British government and the domestic aircraft industry in the first post-war decade. The following chapter analyses the attempts to improve productivity in the British ammunition industry in the 1950s. Part 3 discusses whether the British defence effort placed an undue burden on the economy. Chapter 7 analyses the relationship between Britain's defence effort and economic development during the conversion from a war to a peace economy. The next chapter re-examines the economic crisis of 1951 in order to establish to what extent the Korean War rearmament

[49] On the advantages of such an eclectic approach for historians, see Hans-Jürgen Puhle, "Theorien in der Praxis des vergleichenden Historikers," in *Theorie und Erzählung in der Geschichte*, eds. Jürgen Kocka and Thomas Nipperdey (München: Deutscher Taschenbuchverlag, 1979), 132-6.

programme contributed to the economic downturn and ended the rapid economic expansion of the late 1940s. The last chapter assesses the impact of the defence effort on investment and long-term economic development. The conclusion discusses the book's findings in the framework of modern endogenous growth theory showing that Korean war rearmament led to a loss of momentum which arguably hampered economic development, but did not cause the relatively slower growth of the British economy during the Great Boom from 1950 to 1973. By probing the subject matter from these different directions, this book attempts to add to our understanding of the impact of the post-war defence effort on British politics, economy and society.

Part I

The political economy of British defence expenditure

Chapter 1

Securing the People's Peace: Reflections on the anachronistic nature of the British warfare state in the early cold war, 1945–55

In his book *The Lost Victory*, Correlli Barnett accused the first Attlee government of being complacent about the harsh economic realities faced by Britain at the end of the war. He claims that British politicians should not have deluded themselves about Britain's continued great power status or the country's ability to afford what he describes as a lavish welfare state. Barnett argues that this spirit of complacency arose from a belief "... that in Britain's war record lay the assurance that in every way she was, and would remain, a first class world power."[1] Barnett suggests that the general attitude of complacency therefore prevented the fundamental reforms of British government and industry needed to revive the country's fortunes by failing to develop a comprehensive development strategy in order to compete successfully with its rivals. This criticism reflects the underlying premise for his analysis of the decline of British power, the concept of total strategy, which he conceives "... as encompassing all factors relevant to preserving or extending the power of a human group in the face of rivalry from other groups." In line with this premise, Barnett tries to understand the phenomenon of "the decay of British power" as a multifaceted process involving a broad spectrum of social factors "ranging from religion to technology, from education to foreign policy, from literature to grand strategy."[2] The concept of total strategy implies that in the struggle between nation states, governments and societies should aim to improve a nation's ability to project power and suggests that the primary objective of government economic policy should be to extend the military capabilities of the nation. However, the very vagueness of his concept of total strategy allows Barnett to imply that the Attlee government contributed to the decay of British power through its policies

---

1 Correlli Barnett, *The Lost Victory: British dreams, British realities, 1945-1950* (Basingstoke: Macmillan, 1995), 178.

2 Correlli Barnett, *The Collapse of British Power* (Gloucester: Alan Sutton, 1984), xi.

without examining whether this relative decline reflected the changes in the world arising from the Second World War. Nor indeed does he analyse the extent to which the Attlee government could redress this decline given the available resources. The real problem with Barnett's thesis is its circularity: British politicians deluded themselves about the decline of British power and therefore they did not do enough to address these problems, but the changed international environment and the available resources might not have permitted the radical improvements in British power which Barnett imagined the Attlee government should have achieved.

In contrast to Barnett, the evidence indicates that far from being complacent, the British state reformed the institutional basis for its war-making capacity in the immediate post-war period. While no radical reform of central government machinery was attempted, several innovative aspects of wartime government led to the partial reform of administrative structures and the decision-making process in Whitehall.[3] As part of these partial reforms, the government set up a central organisation for defence and military procurement recognising that Britain had been ill-prepared for the Second World War.[4] At an institutional level, all public procurement became the responsibility of the Ministry of Supply creating the potential for a more interventionist approach by the government. Reform extended to government decision-making. For example, the increased reliance on cabinet committees reduced the burden on individual ministers after 1945. Despite the cult of the generalist civil servant in central government, government retained many specialists recruited during the Second World War. For example, the Ministry of Supply retained most of the scientific research community built up during the Second World War in newly formed government research establishments. At the same time, David Edgerton has pointed out that these interventionist policies in the defence industrial sector ran counter to the more laissez-faire approach in other sectors of the economy.[5] Despite this contradiction, this active policy to maintain and strengthen the defence production base shows that the Attlee government did not neglect the need to extend the country's ability to project power in the post-war world. Therefore, Barnett's accusation of complacency seems hard to sustain.

Indeed, Britain not only spent more on defence than any western European state in this period, but it also spent more than half of central government's expenditure on goods and services for defence (see Table 1.1). Therefore, the post-war British state should be regarded as a warfare state which prioritised

---

3 In general, see Peter Hennessy, *Whitehall* (London: Fontana, 1990), 120-68.

4 Ministry of Defence, *Central Organisation for Defence*, Cmd. 6923 (London: His Majesty's Stationery Office, 1946), 4-6.

5 David Edgerton, "Whatever happened to the British warfare state? The Ministry of Supply, 1945-1951," in *Labour Governments and Private Industry: The Experience of 1945-1951*, eds. Helen Mercer, Neil Rollings, and Jim Tomlinson (Edinburgh: Edinburgh University Press, 1992).

Table 1.1

The British Warfare State, 1945–55

Military Defence Expenditures as percentage of total current public expenditure on goods and services in £ million

	Defence Expenditures	Current Public Expenditures on Goods and Services	Defence expenditures as percentage of current public expenditure on goods and services
1948	740	1,223	60.5
1949	770	1,437	53.6
1950	820	1,508	54.4
1951	1,090	1,815	60.1
1952	1,450	2,211	65.6
1953	1,540	2,320	66.4
1954	1,554	2,356	66.0
1955	1,524	2,372	64.3
1956	1,624	2,541	63.9
1957	1,534	2,523	60.8

Source: Central Statistical Office, *National Income and Expenditure 1958* (London: Her Majesty's Stationary Office, 1958), 41, Table 44.

the development of its military capabilities. These figures do not include other central government expenditures such as transfer payments and grants to local authorities. Nevertheless, Table 1.1 provides a rough indication of the relative (and potential) importance of the warfare aspect of the British state in the immediate post-war period, since the government as monosponist effectively controlled the defence production base through its purchases of military hardware and sponsorship of weapon development projects.[6]

Given the apparent importance attached by policy-makers to maintaining Britain's military power base, the question arises why did this commitment to the warfare state become such an integral part of the post-war British state. This question is particularly intriguing since commitment to the warfare state potentially limited the scope of the Labour government's domestic reform programme. The first section of this chapter will examine the interrelationship

[6] John Rylands University Library Manchester, Labour Party Archive (hereafter: JRULM LPA): JRULM LPA Research Department. folder: Aircraft Industry.: R.222, "Nationalisation of Aircraft Industry", Memo submitted to National Executive by the Rt. Hon. G. R. Strauss, M. P., February 1953.

between the commitment to the post-war reforms for both the British warfare state and the British welfare state. These two policy objectives amounted to two sides of securing a people's peace for Britain. The following section will therefore examine in more detail the anachronistic nature of the reforms of the British warfare state. On the one hand, the experiences of the Second World War informed these reforms to the machinery of central government and its relationship to the armed services and the defence industry. On the other hand, defence policy-makers faced a considerable degree of uncertainty about the future at the end of the war. The development of the atomic bomb had the potential to change the nature of warfare. Given their destructive power, atomic weapons might convince humankind of the necessity for international disarmament and world government. In the absence of such an international security agreement, the nuclear revolution underlined the importance of science and technology in the development of new weapons. At the same time, limited financial resources constrained defence policy-making and military procurement in the immediate post-war period. Securing the people's peace became a balancing act between learning from the experiences of the Second World War and anticipating the impact of these ponderables: the role of science in modern war, financial constraints, defence policy-making, and military procurement.

"If, they say, this is a people's war, then it must issue a people's peace."[7]

In this sentence written in 1943, the prominent Labour Party thinker, Harold Laski, attempted to sum up the profound change in the views of ordinary Britons brought about by the war effort. Aware that the country had come close to defeat, Laski argued that ordinary people felt that they had saved the country, if not civilisation, through their efforts. Through their collective sacrifice, they had rescued the country from the brink of defeat resulting from the failed policy of appeasement instigated by the ruling classes in order to protect their wealth and position within British society. As a consequence, ordinary people demanded substantial changes to British society after the end of the war. Indeed, they felt entitled to be sure that the collective sacrifice would not lead to a return to the mass-unemployment and widespread social deprivation of the interwar period. Without social reform, such sentiments might easily turn to social strife and lead potentially to a violent revolution unless change could be accomplished through democratic means. The war therefore opened up the possibility of changing British society by consent.[8]

---

[7] Harold Laski, *Reflections on the Revolution of our Time* (London: George Allen and Unwin, 1943), 160.

[8] Laski, *Reflections*, 160-61.

Laski's programmatic statement reflected the potential political implications for conceiving of the British war effort as a people's war. This discursive construction reflected the importance of the individual contribution to the war effort. Reflecting on the period 1936 to 1948, E. P. Thompson suggested that the wartime experience instilled in individuals a sense that history depended on their actions, their heroism on the battlefield, their endurance living under the bombs, and their work in the war factories. This experience instilled a sense in many left-wing activists that they were shaping the course of history.[9] Wartime experience convinced those on the Left about the desirability of political change, but the experience of the Blitz did little to restore the public's faith in local authorities, central government or democracy. Despite post-war claims, the war did not politicise the population in any definable direction.[10]

At the same time, the displacement of normal life tested not only the individual, but also the state, the economy and society.[11] The early defeats called into question many of the existing institutional arrangements for wartime mobilisation. At the time, the author Nigel Balchin captured this prevailing feeling of great vulnerability, not only from invasion and bombing, but also from economic and financial collapse, in his novel *Darkness falls from the Air*. In the first pages, the novel paints a bleak picture of Britain after Dunkirk. Besides contemplating the military situation, the novel launches into an exposition of the financial predicament and the inflationary gap. After a long night touring London bars in the early days of the Blitz, the main protagonist, the civil servant Bill, reflects that all this frivolity:

> '... is pretty disgraceful in wartime.'
> 'You mean we can't afford it?' said Marcia.
> 'God knows. I have given up reckoning whether I could afford things. But even if I can afford it the country can't.'

After a protracted debate about the merits of 'living a little' given the constant threat of immanent death, Bill settles the bill which "... hadn't helped the inflationary gap a bit."[12] In a way, wartime Britain could not afford to live a little. From the fall of France in 1940, Britain's ability to resist Nazi Germany depended crucially on material and financial assistance not only from the United States, but also from the Dominions and other countries such as India and Egypt. As the economic adviser to the Treasury, John Maynard Keynes

---

9 Edward P. Thompson, *The Poverty of Theory: or an orrery of errors* (London: Merlin Press, 1978), 97-101.

10 Tom Harrison, *Living through the Blitz* (Harmondsworth: Penguin, 1976), 312-14.

11 Arthur Marwick, *Britain in the Century of Total War: War, peace and social change, 1900-1967* (Harmondsworth: Penguin, 1970), 12-13.

12 Nigel Balchin, *Darkness Falls From the Air* (originally published in 1942), (London: Sphere, 1969), 5-11 (quote: 11).

pointed out at the end of the war, this financial assistance allowed Britain to mobilise its own manpower and industrial resources without having to export goods in order to pay for its imports or maintain its armed forces overseas. However, with the war coming to an end the country faced a "financial Dunkirk" unless Britain expanded its exports massively, reduced its government overseas expenditure, and could secure additional financial assistance to cover its import bill during the transition from war to peace.[13]

With collapse a real possibility, the war called into doubt whether the structure of the British state would endure the struggle against Nazism. To some extent, this fear reflected the unsettling effect which the disenfranchised masses had had on the political life of the interwar period. Given these apprehensions about the masses, the questioning of existing political structures led to calls for a far-reaching reform of democratic institutions extending political rights to social and economic entitlements.[14] For example, the economist Joseph Schumpeter noted in 1943 that British society

> would be confronted at the end of this war with an economic situation, a social atmosphere, a distribution of political power substantially different from those of 1918.

At the same time, state bureaucracy would be unlikely to relinquish full control over the economy after the end of the war as it had in 1918.[15] As a consequence, many contemporary observers believed that the Second World War created a situation in which a radical transformation of society seemed possible, or even inevitable. In this sense, the concept of the people's war included a rejection of the past and opened a window to a brighter future, a people's peace.

Despite this general sense that changes were necessary, there remained considerable uncertainty about how change should be accomplished and secured. To some extent, the process of normal politics was suspended during the war. Given the political differences within the coalition government, ministers had difficulties agreeing on a reform agenda. Regarding reconstruction as a secondary concern, Churchill would have preferred to postpone all major decisions on social reform until after the war. At the same time, the government found itself outmanoeuvred by the efforts of the social

---

[13] Roger John Bullen and M. E. Pelley, eds., *Documents on British Policy Overseas, series 1, volume 3: Britain and America: Negotiations of the United States loan, 3 August - 7 December 1945* (London: Her Majesty's Stationery Office, 1986), (hereafter: DBPO) 1iii, 27-37: note by Mr. Dalton, 14 August 1945.

[14] Laski, *Reflections*.; Karl Mannheim, "The Crisis of Culture in the Era of Mass-Democracies and Autarchies," *Sociological Review* 26 (1934): 105-29.

[15] Joseph A. Schumpeter, *Capitalism, Socialism and Democracy* (originally published in 1943), (London: Unwin Hyman, 1987), 374.

reformer William Beveridge who published proposals on a comprehensive social welfare system as well as employment policy. In response, the government published its own proposals committing a post-war government to the pursuit of full employment, some form of national insurance and education reform. While these promises of domestic reform were only made in the later stages of war, they belatedly legitimised the increase in citizenship obligations by offering the extension of social rights after the end of hostilities.[16] Indeed, Attlee regarded this social reform programme as a revolution for working-class people.[17] For convinced socialists, the reforms stopped short of the *real* democratisation of society, but reflected the wide-spread demand to prioritise democratic (social) claims over others.[18] Its unexpected election victory in 1945 resulted from the commitment of the Labour Party to social reform and domestic reconstruction.[19]

Using Reinhart Koselleck's metahistorical categories, the impetus behind the reforms reflected not only the field of experience (*Erfahrungsraum*) of the interwar period and the war, but also the horizon of expectation (*Erwartungshorizont*) about the post-war world. In periods of structural change (i.e. 1945), the people may press for change, whilst having only limited actual experience of the new reformed society. Since they do not know what to expect, popular expectations will be guarded, but relatively open about the nature of the new society.[20] While the *Erfahrungsraum* of the new society is still limited, the open *Erwartungshorizont* allows for radical changes in the institutional structure of a society. At one level, decision-makers have considerable scope for decisive intervention during these periods of transition after a revolution or war. However, their decisions are often influenced by an analysis of the previous failed system.[21] In 1945, the proposals for reform

---

16 Colin Hay, "The Structural and Ideological Contradictions of Britain's Post-War Reconstruction," *Capital and Class* 34 (1994): 25-59.

17 Paul Addison, *The Road to 1945: British Politics and the Second World War* (London: Quartet Books, 1982), 272.

18 G. D. H. Cole, *The Intelligent Man's Guide to the Post-War World* (London: Victor Gollancz, 1947), 644-5.

19 Steve Fielding, "What did 'The People' want? The meaning of the 1945 General Election," *Historical Journal* 35 (1992): 623-39.

20 This analysis draws on Reinhart Koselleck's study of the influence of experience on expectations for future development; see Reinhart Koselleck, "'Erfahrungsraum' und 'Erwartungshorizont' - zwei historische Kategorien," in *Vergangene Zukunft: Zur Semantik geschichtlicher Zeiten* (Frankfurt/Main: Suhrkamp, 1979), 349-75.

21 On this point, see Robert W. Cox, "Towards a post-hegemonic conceptualization of world order: reflections on the relevancy of Ibn Khaldun," in *Governance without Government: Order and Change in World Politics*, eds. James N. Rosenau and Ernst-Otto Czempiel (Cambridge: Cambridge University Press, 1992), 132-59.; Till Geiger, "Believing in the Miracle Cure: Economic transition in Germany and East-Central Europe," in *Germany Since Unification: The Domestic and External Consequences*, ed. Klaus Larres (Basingstoke: Macmillan, 1998), 174-202.

reflected the experiments of limited nationalisation in the interwar period, economic planning of wartime mobilisation, state provision of social services during the war and the influence of Russian state socialism, as well as a rejection of mass-unemployment, slums, poverty and social insecurity.[22]

Beyond the domestic sphere, contemporary reformers regarded the reform of international relations as an essential precondition for the success of democratic social reform at home. In the preface to his book *The Price of Peace*, William Beveridge linked his crusade for full employment and social welfare to the need for lasting peace. For the architect of the British welfare state, attainment of military security remained the most important, if most difficult objective.[23] Reflecting his liberal convictions, the book argues for a form of world government and security arrangement. If such a plan failed, Beveridge favoured the establishment of a regional security arrangement as a second best solution and a first step toward a world-wide organisation for peace. In his reasoning, Beveridge explicitly linked such a security arrangement to his suggestions for the regulation of the world economy arising from his proposed domestic economic settlement. While realists dismissed the liberal dream of abolishing war, Beveridge argued that Britain should be prepared to pay the price for peace through the partial surrender of sovereignty to a world or regional security arrangement.[24]

Whatever its merits, *The Price of Peace* reflected the *Zeitgeist* which saw a close connection between democracy, economic security and peace. From a different political perspective, Harold Laski argued that the success of any domestic reform depended on an international economic system committed to world-wide economic expansion. Since economic planning in the Soviet Union allowed for the uninterrupted expansion of domestic economic activity, the major threat to post-war international stability potentially emanated from the United States. The longer the war lasted, the greater the economic power of the United States would become thus increasing the power of capitalist interest groups which might oppose supporting European recovery if European countries contemplated the adoption of socialist reform programmes. Therefore, the viability of any ambitious domestic reform programme by a post-war British Labour government depended on President Franklin Delano Roosevelt or at least a Democratic administration committed to a continuation of the New Deal retaining power in the United States. Indeed, Laski feared that any major economic contraction of the American economy might lead to the rise of fascist dictatorship in the United States.[25] Reviewing Laski's book, George Orwell agreed with him about the urgency of resolving the economic

---

22 For example, see Laski, *Reflections*.; Cole, *Intelligent Man's Guide*.
23 William Beveridge, *The Price of Peace* (London: Pilot Press, 1945), vii.
24 Beveridge, *Price of Peace*, 83–9.
25 Laski, *Reflections*, 192-4 and 219-24.

problems faced by Britain and the wider world, but took him to task for his failure to acknowledge the "totalitarian possibilities" of socialism. Therefore, Orwell stressed that resolving the economic problems would like the defeat of Nazism only be one step towards creating a more free and equal society.[26]

Reflecting the *Zeitgeist* favouring post-war international co-operation, the overwhelming majority of the British public favoured a form of world government as well as putting the British armed forces under the authority of the United Nations provided that other nations did likewise. Labour activists and voters in particular, were strongly committed to some form of internationalism.[27] In this context, the destruction of Hiroshima and Nagasaki in August 1945 underlined for many the need for some form of international security arrangement. Hearing the news of the atomic bomb, many British people expressed their profound shock and dismay at the arrival of the nuclear age and its inherent dangers for the future. The Scottish novelist, Naomi Mitcheson, wrote about the bomb in the diary she kept for Mass-Observation on 10 August 1945:

> All the time one keeps on thinking of this bomb, and what it may make the future look like. A perpetual menace over everything but may be as salutary as hell fire was in its time. I wonder. The Soviet Union of course should have it. Probably the world is in for a period of communism. It will be unpleasant in some ways but it won't destroy other values nearly as badly as Nazi-ism. I intend that my children shall survive.[28]

Many people responded similarly to the news of the first nuclear attacks. The horror led to a feeling that Armageddon was inevitable unless permanent peace could be achieved. Many people initially hoped that the use of the bomb would rule out another war. Over the next year, this sentiment slowly gave way to a feeling that the existence of atomic weapons might prevent another global war and thus be justifiable despite the potential horrors.[29] After the initial shock passed, nearly 50 per cent of people expected another global war within 25 years, a statistic which clearly reflects a growing sense of international tension.[30]

---

[26] George Orwell, "Revolt in the Urban Desert," *The Observer*, 10 October 1943.

[27] Mass-Observation, *Peace and the Public* (London: Longmans, Green & Co., 1947), 24-55.

[28] Diary entry, 10 August 1945; reprinted in Dorothy Sheridan, ed., *Among You Taking Notes ...: The wartime diary of Naomi Mitchison, 1939-1945* (Oxford: Oxford University Press, 1986), 337.

[29] Mass-Observation, *Peace*, 8-9.

[30] Mass-Observation, *Peace*, 14-19. The writers of this report suggested that these opinions reflected the recent experience of the Second World War during which neither strategic bombing nor poisoned gas had played the decisive role many had predicted between the wars. This finding reflects the wartime Mass-Observation reports on the impact of the Blitz; see Harrison, *Living*.

Much to the dismay of many Labour supporters, the Attlee government's foreign policy soon resembled that of Churchillian realism.[31] However, this development reflected the realities confronting the incoming Labour Foreign Secretary, Ernest Bevin. After the attacks on Hiroshima and Nagasaki had led to the end of the Second World War, officials of the British Embassy in Washington reported to the Foreign Office that most American observers no longer regarded Britain as a superpower on a par with the United States and the Soviet Union. Therefore, many American policy-makers suggested that any international settlement depended primarily on reaching an accord with the Soviet Union. Since Britain would require continued financial assistance, some American observers reasoned that the Labour government would have to follow the American lead in establishing a new international order. Given its atomic monopoly, the American political establishment would not see the election of a Labour government in Britain as diminishing its preponderant power in the world. Indeed, the change of government might make it more difficult to obtain further financial assistance from the United States. While few American observers believed that a socialist Britain would become communist, Embassy staff reported that

> [a]t the same time warnings are heard in financial and business circles that America should beware of countenancing any proposal to grant extensive credits to a Britain which would be likely to employ them to underwrite State Socialism.[32]

Given the serious financial situation facing the country, Labour ministers felt that despite some misgivings, they had little choice but to agree to enter into negotiations about a major loan with the Truman administration. Keynes and other officials left Labour ministers in no doubt that obtaining a loan from the American government would be contingent on acceding to the Bretton Woods agreements and making concessions over the preferential trading relations within the British Commonwealth and Empire.[33] At the same time, British interests were challenged by the Soviet Union in Greece, Turkey, and Iran. During the war, many left-wing Labour activists believed that British socialism could act as a bridge between capitalist America and communist Russia. However, Stalin not only did not regard the British Labour government as truly socialist, but also remained deeply suspicious of British and American foreign

---

[31] Konni Zilliacus, *I Choose Peace* (Harmondsworth: Penguin, 1949), 275-337.; Cole, *Intelligent Man's Guide*, 1019-32. On this point, see also Till Geiger, "Opposition in the Shadows of an Emerging Conflict: The Aberdeen Trades Council, government policy and voicing dissent in the cold war, 1945-1955," *Northern Scotland* 13 (1993): 103-35.

[32] DBPO 1iii, 10-22 (quote: 19-20): Balfour - Bevin, 9 August 1945.

[33] DBPO 1iii, 72-7: Record of a meeting of ministers, 23 August 1945.

policy.[34] While Stalin pursued an opportunistic expansionist foreign policy in Eastern Europe, he accused Britain of being imperialist by assisting the Greek government and clinging to its Empire.[35] After Bevin challenged Stalin and his foreign minister, Molotov, over Greece, Turkey, and Iran, the Soviet leadership quietly gave into an increasingly united front of the two western powers.[36] Throughout his time in office, Bevin remained determined to maintain Britain's status as an independent major power in a world order based on three spheres of influence (or the three Monroes in his words). However, he soon found that given its vulnerability Britain would find it difficult to defend its sphere of influence based on western Europe, the Mediterranean, the Middle East, the British Empire and the Commonwealth. Therefore, Britain would be forced to take sides in the developing confrontation between the two dominant super-powers.[37] Given the strong anti-British sentiments in the Soviet Union and the United States, even some of his critics acknowledged that there seemed few realistic alternatives to Bevin's foreign policy in the immediate post-war period.[38] Arguably, the events of 1945 almost immediately narrowed the choices available to British foreign policy-makers and seemed to rule out the expectations of utopian internationalism. From mid-1946 onwards, the foreign policy-making community expected a cold war rather than some form of international security arrangement based on the United Nations.[39] Determined to uphold Britain's role as a major power, the Attlee government remained intent upon maintaining Britain's military capabilities and defence production base.

The imperatives of the scientific and technological arms race

At the end of the Second World War, the explosion of the first atomic bombs demonstrated beyond any doubt that science had revolutionised modern warfare. Even on the battlefield, the contribution of scientists to the war effort

---

[34] Milovan Djilas, *Conversations with Stalin* (Harmondsworth: Penguin, 1963), 90.

[35] Extracts from the proceedings of the Moscow Conference of Foreign Ministers, 16-26 December 1945.; reprinted in Graham Ross, ed., *The Foreign Office and the Kremlin: British Documents on Anglo-Soviet Relations, 1941-45* (Cambridge: Cambridge University Press, 1984), 267-81.

[36] John Lewis Gaddis, *We Now Know: Rethinking cold war history* (New York: Oxford University Press, 1997), 30-33.

[37] Alan Bullock, *Ernest Bevin: Foreign Secretary, 1945-51* (Oxford: Oxford University Press, 1985), 191-5.; Robin Edmonds, *Setting the Mould: The United States and Britain, 1945-1950* (Oxford: Clarendon Press, 1986), 26-30.

[38] Cole, *Intelligent Man's Guide*, 1029-31.

[39] On this point, see Donald C. Watt, "Britain, the United States and the opening of the cold war," in *The Foreign Policy of the British Labour Governments, 1945-1951*, ed. Ritchie Ovendale (Leicester: Leicester University Press, 1984), 43-60.

underscored the increased importance of modern technology to the military. During the Second World War, massive funding for military research and development advanced military technology in several areas. For example, jet engines had been conceived in the 1930s and developed during the war leading to the first operational jet fighters by the end of the war. The innovations in jet engine and air frame design opened the path to supersonic flight in the immediate post-war period. Apart from the technological innovations, the application of scientific methods such as operations research transformed the nature of warfare in the air and at sea. In the case of radar, operations research significantly improved the effectiveness of the original technological innovation. Operations research enabled another major breakthrough in anti-submarine warfare by initiating a change in the setting of depth charges for mines. Indeed, these success stories led to the widespread application of operations research as a management tool in industry after 1945.[40] Another example is the refinement of statistical quality control techniques in the manufacture of ammunition. After the war, the Ministry of Supply disseminated these new techniques for use in industry.[41]

Given the nature of scientific progress, a former government adviser, Sir Henry Tizard, warned that governments had to pursue a pro-active military research and development policy in the nuclear age. To develop such a policy, governments would come to depend on scientific advice about future technological developments.[42] In the United States, for example, the Air Force commissioned a study forecasting the likely development of aircraft and rocket technology. To keep up with the state of military technology, this study concluded that the government would have to devote a quarter of the annual air force budget to research and development after the war.[43] In contrast to the Air Force, the American Navy adopted a problem-driven approach reflecting its operational requirements. On balance, this approach seemed less successful as officials often failed to identify requirements correctly.[44] Despite major cuts in the military research and development budget, the American government expanded its close relationship with several key research laboratories at the

---

[40] Maurice W. Kirby and Rebecca Capey, "The origins and diffusion of operational research in the UK," paper presented at the Annual Conference of the Economic History Society, Lancaster University, 29-31 March 1996, 150.

[41] Ministry of Supply. Directorate of Royal Ordnance Factories. Explosives, *Industrial Experimentation* (London: His Majesty's Stationery Office, 1946).

[42] Henry T. Tizard, "Science and the Services," *Journal of the Royal United Service Institution* 91 (1946): 333-46.

[43] Michael H. Gorn, *Harnessing the Genie: Science and Technology Forecasting for the Air Force, 1944-1986* (Washington: Office of Air Force History, 1988), 11-50.

[44] David K. Allison, "U.S. Navy Research and Development since World War II," in *Military Enterprise and Technological Change: Perpectives on the American Experience*, ed. Merritt Roe Smith (Cambridge: MIT Press, 1985), 295-307.

Massachusetts Institute of Technology, Stanford, Berkeley and the California Institute of Technology.[45]

On the other side of the Atlantic, the British government accepted the overriding importance of continued military research and development.[46] In its reform of the central organisation of defence, the Attlee government created a Committee of Defence Research Policy to advise the Chiefs of Staff and the Defence Committee on matters of research and development. The Defence Research Committee was to be chaired by an eminent scientist and consist of officials directly involved in research and development in the Service Departments and the Ministry of Supply.[47] This proposal fell far short of the suggested organisation outlined by Tizard in an address to the Royal United Service Institution in 1946

> The retention of scientific advisers on the Staffs of all three Services is a step in the right direction, but it is not enough in itself. What is needed is a scientific staff attached to the central Chiefs of Staff organisation that will devote its whole time to the study of the influence of advancing scientific knowledge on the problems of defence. This is a branch of strategical study that needs just as much attention and forethought as any other branch of military strategy; indeed, it requires more. If we neglect it I see no chance whatsoever that our great country will survive another world war.[48]

In contrast to the United States Air Force forecast of technological development, the British Defence Research Committee lacked the time and remit to chart future research and development plans. The absence of an independent scientific staff proved to be a major handicap for the Committee in appraising development projects.[49]

A report of the Select Committee on Estimates in 1956 exposed these shortcomings in the arrangements governing research and development contracts. In particular, the report criticised the fact that most officials in Services Departments tended to be officers on secondment from the services rather than scientists. As a consequence, research policy concentrated on ongoing weapons development and production contracts. Defence contractors found this constant rotation of staff very disruptive.[50] The appraisal of any new

---

[45] Stuart W. Leslie, *The Cold War and American Science: The military-industrial-academic complex at MIT and Stanford* (New York: Columbia University Press, 1993), 1-43.

[46] Ministry of Defence, *Statement relating to Defence*, Cmd. 6743 (London: His Majesty's Stationery Office, 1946), 7.

[47] Ministry of Defence, *Central organisation*, 9.

[48] Tizard, "Science," 343.

[49] House of Commons, *Second Report from the Select Committee on Estimates, Session 1956-57: The Supply of Military Aircraft*, Parliamentary Papers (London: Her Majesty's Stationery Office, 1956), xviii-xix.

[50] House of Commons, *Supply of Military Aircraft*, xx-xxxi.

idea fell to these officials in the Service Departments and the Ministry of Supply. One example of this concerns the Chief Designer of Vickers, Barnes Wallis, who outlined a radical new proposal for a multi-role aircraft, code-named Swallow, in the mid-1950s. Based on an analysis of the diverse needs of the Royal Air Force, Wallis suggested an air frame with variable geometry or movable wings. This design would have allowed the aircraft to perform deep interdiction bombing raids, fighter patrols and reconnaissance missions while operating from improvised airfields.[51] One remarkable aspect is its similarity to the Tornado (or the Multi-Role Combat Aircraft) developed by a western European consortium in the 1970s for the air forces of Britain, West Germany and Italy.[52] Given the radical nature of the proposal, most officials rejected the project as unworkable but meriting further discussion.[53] This reaction confirmed concerns of the head of Bomber Command, Arthur Harris, at the end of the war that if decisions regarding research and development were left to military men rather than scientists, their inherent conservatism would stifle innovative ideas for future weapons.[54] However, in defence of the civil servants assessing this project, it is important to remember that the whole project relied on radically new ideas about aircraft design and control. Moreover, its multi-role application as fighter, bomber, or reconnaissance aircraft represented a major departure in military aircraft design. Ahead of its time in terms of technology and application, the pursuit of design excellence arguably prevented the early development of a military aircraft incorporating variable wing geometry in this particular case.[55]

As this example suggests, government relied primarily on the expertise of service departments for military procurement decisions. After the Second World War, the government concentrated a significant share of the research efforts in several government research establishments in order to have a source of independent scientific advice.[56] At the same time, senior policy-makers of the Ministry of Aircraft Production encouraged several universities to establish chairs of aeronautical engineering and were instrumental in setting up

---

[51] Public Record Office, Kew (hereafter: PRO) Air Ministry (hereafter AIR) PRO AIR 20/7578: Barnes N. Wallis, "The Air Defence of Great Britain: A New Approach", Vickers-Armstrong Ltd., Research and Development Department, Weybridge1953.

[52] N. W. Boorer, "Barnes Wallis, Designer (1887-1979): A memorial lecture," paper presented at the British Aerospace Factory, Weybridge, 4 March 1981. Boorer worked with Barnes Wallis on the Swallow project at the Aeronautical Research and Development Department of Vickers-Armstrong at Weybridge. See also Mary Kaldor, *The Baroque Arsenal* (London: Abacus, 1983), 141-2.

[53] PRO AIR 20/7578: Minute Ivelaw - Chapmann, 24 July 1953.; PRO AIR 20/7578: Minute Chapman - Ivelaw, 18 August 1953.

[54] Arthur Harris, *Bomber Offensive* (London: Collins, 1947), 269-80.

[55] Boorer, "Barnes Wallis."

[56] David Edgerton, *England and the Aeroplane: An Essay on a Militant and Technological Nation* (Basingstoke: Macmillan, 1991), 103.

Cranfield College of Aeronautics as "... a specialised postgraduate institution outside the university system."[57] While these universities received some research contracts, the public funding of higher education ensured that British universities did not become as dependent on military contracts as some American universities.[58] While relying on the public sector for fundamental research, the British government turned to private aircraft constructors in order to develop new aircraft technology. As Edgerton has pointed out, this policy of giving priority to the private sector in the development and production of weapons not only ran counter to long-standing Labour policy but also to its plans to nationalise a substantial proportion of industry.[59]

In his address to the Royal United Services Institution Tizard predicted, on the basis of publicly available information, that most major powers would acquire atomic weapons by the end of the 1940s. Tizard went on to draw a remarkably accurate picture of the nuclear war age. Given the tremendously destructive power of atomic bombs, nations would have to build up a stockpile of atomic bombs which could be used at any time with little or no prior warning. In all likelihood, World War Three would be a short nuclear exchange instead of another global war of attrition. Therefore, defence policy ought to take into account the challenges of the atomic age. At one level, this meant the continued refinement of conventional weapons systems in order to improve military preparedness. The increased vulnerability of the national industrial base in a nuclear war situation demanded that governments continuously equip their armed forces with the most advanced weapons systems. In the nuclear war age, governments could no longer rely on their superior economic strength delaying full mobilisation until the outbreak of another global war.[60]

In the first two decades after the war, military technology advanced qualitatively more rapidly than in any other period. Supersonic flight, thermonuclear weapons and rocket technology changed the armoury of modern super-powers beyond recognition. By the mid-1960s, most new weapons development concentrated on the further refinement of existing weapons technology.[61] In line with this development, the economics of weapons acquisition changed profoundly. Pound for pound, the destructive capability of

57 Manchester, Queen's Belfast, Queen Mary College London, Hull, Bristol, and Southampton; see Edgerton, *England and the aeroplane*, 97.

58 Seymour Melman, *The Permanent War Economy: American Capitalism in Decline*, rev. ed. (New York: Touchstone, 1985), 224-5.

59 David Edgerton, "Public ownership and the British arms industry, 1920-50," in *The Political Economy of Nationalisation in Britain, 1920-50*, eds. Robert Millward and John Singleton (Cambridge: Cambridge University Press, 1995), 164-88.; Edgerton, "Whatever happened," 105-8.

60 Tizard, "Science," 340-42.

61 Harvey Brooks, "The Military Innovation System and the Qualitative Arms Race," in *Arms, Defense Policy, and Arms Control*, eds. Franklin A. Long and George W. Rathjens (New York: W. W. Norton & Company, 1976), 78.; Kaldor, *Baroque arsenal*, 170-4.

nuclear weapons cost a fraction of the equivalent amount (in terms of TNT) of conventional explosives. Hydrogen bombs would also be far more economic than conventional bombs as they are less cumbersome and can be delivered by small aircraft or even missiles.[62] By the mid-1950s, the explosion of a single thermo-nuclear device "... *would release far more explosive energy than the total explosive energy released by mankind in all its history*."[63] In the immediate post-war period, the rapid development of military technology reinforced the increased scientific effort to ensure military preparedness. In turn, the increased scientific effort contributed to the technological arms race.[64] In this competition, Britain could not compete on equal terms particularly with the United States as it lacked the financial, technical and human resources.

Limited economic resources

Most contemporary observers agreed that Britain's limited resources restricted its war potential after 1945.[65] International relations analysts broadly defined a country's war potential as the capability of a society to mobilise for war taking into account population, natural resources, industrial and scientific base, and military capabilities. Despite being widely used, Klaus Knorr noted that the concept of war potential defied clear definition and therefore measurement given the changing nature and vagaries of modern warfare. For example, the advent of nuclear warfare reduced the importance of a strong industrial base for mobilisation in a global war of attrition. In this sense, continuous efforts to maintain the readiness of the armed forces would be more important in the age of the cold war.[66] Economists have used a narrower concept defining war potential as the maximum share of economic output which could be diverted to the war effort. During the Second World War, Britain devoted in excess of 50 per cent of the Gross National Product (GNP) to the war effort. Given its limited domestic resources, Britain had relied heavily on American Lend-Lease

---

[62] Tizard, "Science," 341.; Defence Science Organisation, *Nuclear Explosions and their Effects* (Delhi: Ministry of Information and Broadcasting, Publications Division, 1958), 21-2.

[63] Defence Science Organisation, *Nuclear explosions*, 7 (Italics in the original). An atomic or thermonuclear bomb fritters away a considerable proportion of the explosive energy released in its detonation; see Defence Science Organisation, *Nuclear explosions*, 6-7.

[64] Brooks, "Military innovation system," 93-6.; Defence Science Organisation, *Nuclear explosions*, 12-13.

[65] For example, see Nicholas Mansergh, "Britain, the Commonwealth and Western Union," *International Affairs* 24 (1948): 491.; Charles Webster, Ian Jacob, and Austin Robinson, *United Kingdom Policy: Foreign, strategic, economic* (London: Royal Institute of International Affairs, 1950), 10-12.

[66] Klaus Knorr, *The War Potential of Nations* (Princeton: Princeton University Press, 1956), 4-15.

aid and borrowing from the Sterling Area. External finance and material support contributed an additional 10-17 per cent of national income to the British war effort.[67] In addition to the accumulated sterling liabilities of £3,700 million, Britain owed the United States large sums for the Lend-Lease Aid it received.[68] During the war, the British government had also built up considerable domestic debts thus inflating the money supply.[69] For the incoming Attlee government, the problem of "how to pay for the war" became the problem of how to pay for reconstruction while paying off the war. The sudden end to the war in the Far East exacerbated the financial problems by prematurely ending the flow of Lend-Lease supplies. Directly after the end of the war, additional military commitments and the shortage of shipping space slowed the pace of British demobilisation. As a direct consequence, British government expenditure overseas remained a substantial added burden to the economy. Concerned about Britain's status as a major power, the government did not drastically reduce overseas expenditures until after the convertibility crisis in the summer of 1947. To finance the balance of payments deficit, Britain further increased its borrowing from the United States and the Sterling Area after 1945.[70] As Charles Webster noted, the changed economic circumstances reduced the country's ability to sustain a degree of mobilisation in a future war which would be similar to that of the Second World War. In a short study, R. C. Tress estimated that Britain's capacity to mobilise for all-out war would only be about 37 per cent of GNP in 1948-49.[71] Therefore, the domestic war potential of the British economy would have been 10 per cent of GNP less than it was at the height of mobilisation during the Second World War.[72]

In Whitehall, the intensification of the cold war also led to a re-examination of the economic war potential of the British economy. Early in 1950, a committee of senior officials, chaired by the Cabinet Secretary Sir Norman Brook, examined the likely position of the British economy during a future

---

67 Mark Harrison, "Resource Mobilisation for World War II: the U.S.A., U.K., U.S.S.R. and Germany, 1939-1945," *Economic History Review* 41 (1988): 189-90.

68 Central Statistical Office, *Fighting with Figures: A Statistical Digest of the Second World War* (London: Her Majesty's Stationery Office, 1995), 218-26.

69 The ratio of broad money M3 to GNP rose from 0.54 in 1938 to 0.79 in 1946; see Susan Howson, *British Monetary Policy, 1945-51* (Oxford: Clarendon Press, 1993), 177, Table 4.4.

70 Thomas Balogh, "The International Aspect," in *The British Economy, 1945-1950*, eds. G. D. N. Worswick and P. H. Ady (Oxford: Oxford University Press, 1952), 476-510.

71 R. C. Tress, "Defence and Public Finance," *London and Cambridge Economic Service* 27 (1949): 2-6.

72 Taking only domestic resources into account, the level of mobilisation in terms of GNP during the Second World War peaked at 47 per cent in 1943 and 1944; see Harrison, "Resource mobilisation," 184, Table 3.

war.[73] As a first step, the committee agreed to base its deliberations on the assumption that another global war might occur as early as 1955. Departing from the implicit ten-year rule adopted after the Second World War, this assumption added to the urgency of the committee's deliberations. Given the difficulties of predicting the shape of a future war economy, officials agreed to base their forecast on the distribution of manpower[74] at the height of the Second World War. Any tentative forecast would include an estimate of the drop in productivity due to war damage. To some extent, the mobilisation of labour would be a secondary consideration to the question of finance. In the light of the experience of the Second World War, the committee agreed that "... from the outset [Britain] should be dependent on [financial] assistance ..." to pay for essential imports. Therefore, any projection of the likely shape of a future war economy would have to be based on far-reaching assumptions about the degree of Anglo-American co-operation. In all likelihood, the United States and Canada would again become the arsenals of the western powers. As during the Second World War, Britain would have to reduce its exports while relying on external finance for its imports. "In spite of the weakness of [its] bargaining position, ..." the British government had to obtain a guarantee from the Americans regarding the long-term prospects of British exports. From the perspective of the British government, the Allies should agree the extent to which resources would be pooled and jointly allocated. To that end, the necessary machinery would have to be established preferably prior to western rearmament. Given the weakness of the British bargaining position, the timing of any approach to the American government would be crucial as an unfavourable agreement might prejudice the long-term economic recovery of the British economy after another global conflict. While senior officials had no illusions about the war potential, the committee assumed that economic mobilisation would resemble in broad terms the war economy during the Second World War. Judging from previous experience, the accumulation of sufficient stockpiles of weapons and material would require several years depending on the requirements of the armed forces and the likely rate of

[73] The following discussion is based on PRO CAB 130/59: Minutes of the 1st Meeting of a Cabinet Committee (Gen 317: The National Economy at War), 21 March 1950. All quotes are taken from this document.

[74] The minutes only speak of "manpower" in contrast to earlier official documents which openly acknowledged the contribution of women to the British war economy; for example see Ministry of Reconstruction, *Employment Policy*, Cmd. 8195 (London: His Majesty's Stationery Office, 1944). The potential conflicts and difficulties of mobilising womanpower for another global war did not feature in the committee's deliberations. Given the experience of the Second World War, this remains an intriguing omission; on this point, see Harold L. Smith, "The effect of the war on the status of women," in *War and Social Change: British Society in the Second World War*, ed. Harold L. Smith (Manchester: Manchester University Press, 1986), 208-29.; Penny Summerfield, *Women Workers in the Second World War: Production and patriarchy in conflict* (London: Routledge, 1989).

conversion to war production. Assuming another global war might break out any time after 1955, the decision to rearm would have to be faced sooner rather than later. At their second meeting in June 1950, officials acknowledged that such a decision to rearm would be politically unpopular, because rearmament might lead to cuts in private consumption.[75] A month later in response to the North Korean invasion of South Korea, the Attlee government decided to rearm despite concerns over the potential economic impact.[76]

The committee's deliberations highlighted the financial constraints on British defence capabilities in this period. Throughout the discussions, the experience of economic mobilisation during the Second World War informed the committee's conclusions. Given the events of the recent past, the overarching problem would be how to pay for another war before the bill for the last war had been settled. Undoubtedly, the accumulated debts of the Second World War significantly reduced the British war potential.[77] Indeed, limited financial resources severely restricted Britain's ability to sustain its overseas military commitments and any large-scale rearmament.[78] This conclusion begs the question whether the British government could have prevented this predicament. Arguably, two controversial measures could have solved this problem. Firstly, a capital levy could have reduced the domestic debt and the inflationary potential in the economy.[79] Secondly, Britain should have demanded that the countries holding sterling balances assume a considerable share of the cost of the war. Both measures would have amounted to a declaration of bankruptcy. A capital levy had been tentatively debated by the economic advisers to the wartime coalition, but economic policy-makers did not seriously consider such a controversial measure in the summer of 1945.[80] After Stafford Cripps became Chancellor, the imposition of a capital levy was contemplated on the suggestion of his predecessor Hugh Dalton, but shelved due to the administrative problems of its implementation.[81] Similarly,

---

75 PRO CAB 130/59: Minutes of the 2nd Meeting of a Cabinet Committee (Gen 317: The National Economy at War), 21 June 1950.

76 Bullock, *Bevin*, 796-801.

77 Tress, "Defence," 2-6.

78 Anthony Gorst, "Facing Facts?: The Labour Government and defence policy 1945-1950," in *The Attlee Years*, ed. Nick Tiratsoo (London: Pinter, 1991), 190-209.; Anthony Gorst, "'We must cut our coat according to our cloth': the making of British defence policy 1945-1948," in *British Intelligence, Strategy and the Cold War*, ed. Richard Aldrich (London: Routledge, 1992), 143-65.

79 In his pamphlet "How to Pay for the War" originally published in 1940, John Maynard Keynes suggested a capital levy could discharge the liabilities arising from deferred pay and forced savings; see John Maynard Keynes, "How to Pay for the War," in *Essays in Persuasion*, ed. Royal Economic Society (Basingstoke: Macmillan, 1984), 406-8.

80 Alec Cairncross and Nita Watts, *The Economic Section: A Study in Economic Advising* (London: Routledge, 1989), 79-80 and 208-9.

81 Cairncross and Watts, *Economic Section*, 246.; Howson, *British monetary policy*, 217-19.

the unilateral annulment of the sterling balances would have undermined the position of the City of London as a major financial centre and sterling as the world's second most important reserve currency. Maintaining the sterling area presented the only viable strategy for limiting the hegemonic ambitions of the United States.[82] Arguably, American financial assistance might not have been as forthcoming if Britain had abandoned its role as a major power. Whenever Britain faced serious financial problems, American policymakers considered extending additional economic aid dreading the possibility of fighting the cold war on their own.[83] With hindsight, this decision to maintain its position as a major power may have been misguided given its long-term consequences, but the strategy proved successful in the short term.[84]

Having fallen on hard times, Britain arguably could not afford the increased post-war defence effort. Indeed, these financial difficulties hampered Britain's preparations for another global war. In the immediate post-war period, the lion's share of the British defence effort was spent on maintaining the manpower levels of the British armed forces. Only with great reluctance did ministers consent to cutting overseas military expenditures.[85] This priority deflected from another objective of post-war British defence policy which was re-equipping the armed forces with the most modern weapons in time for another global conflict. To save money ministers decided to concentrate resources on basic research into military technology and the development of new weapon systems. Therefore, this defence procurement strategy relied on there being sufficient time for rearmament.[86]

However, the military commitments of the immediate post-war period were larger than expected and this meant that Britain could not afford to finance this defence strategy, as a comparison between the wartime expenditure plans and post-war defence budgets shows. The wartime expenditure plans called for defence expenditure of £550 million (in 1942 prices) in 1948. £220 million of this was to be spent on the procurement of new equipment. Converted to 1948 prices, these wartime plans suggested that the British government intended to spend £850 million in total on defence and £369 million on military

---

[82] Peter Burnham, *Political Economy of Postwar Reconstruction* (Basingstoke: Macmillan, 1990), 180-88.

[83] National Archives and Record Administration, Washington (hereafter NARA) Record Group (hereafter RG) 218. NARA RG 218. Box 19: Memorandum Ohly - Gruenther, "Need for an Assessment of the Full Implications to American Security of the Current British Dollar Crisis", 1 September 1949. This thesis is further explored in chapter 2.

[84] Burnham, *Political economy*.

[85] George C. Peden, "Economic Aspects of British Perceptions of Power on the Eve of the Cold War," in *Power in Europe? Great Britain, France, Italy and Germany in a Postwar World, 1945-1950*, eds. Josef Becker and Franz Knipping (Berlin: Walter de Gruyter, 1986), 248-50.

[86] Ministry of Defence, *Statement relating to Defence*. See also chapter 4.

procurement in 1948.[87] Actual expenditure did not quite reach these levels. The overall defence budget envisaged expenditure of £770 million in 1948 or roughly 90 per cent of the expenditure envisaged in the wartime expenditure plans. The procurement budget had, however, been severely pruned. The 1948 defence budget set aside £188 million for military procurement including research and development.[88] Measured against national output, the wartime expenditure plans envisaged that 6.8 per cent of Gross National Product (GNP) would be spent on defence. In 1948, actual expenditure accounted for 7.1 per cent of GNP. The share of military procurement was planned to be 2.7 per cent of GNP. However, the actual ratio of military procurement to GNP reached only 1.8 per cent.[89] This different emphasis in the defence budget reflected a shift in military, political and economic priorities. Militarily, the incoming Labour government decided to maintain Britain's global military presence and its status as a major world power. Economically, ministers prioritised reconstruction over defence procurement.

Compared to the United States, Britain devoted relatively more resources to maintaining its defence production capacity. In the United States, the Truman administration swiftly reduced defence expenditure after 1945 to just over $13 billion or 5 per cent of GNP.[90] As part of this general demobilisation, the American government drastically reduced its budget for military research and development thus ignoring the scientific community's advice. An influential study for the Army Air Force Chief of Staff, General Arnold, estimated in late 1945 that to maintain American technological leadership, the Air Force should spend 5 per cent of its annual wartime budget on research and development.[91] Assuming this suggestion had been implemented, the United States government would have had to spend in the order of $4,370 million per annum (in 1944 prices) in the post-war period. In the fiscal year 1947/48, actual research and development expenditure for all three services was just $469 million (in 1947 prices) or less than 10 per cent of the expenditure deemed necessary in 1945.[92] This much reduced research and development budget still

---

87 PRO T 160/1407/F.18876: "Post-war expenditure", memorandum Gilbert - Bridges, 7 November 1942.

88 Ministry of Defence, *Statement related to Defence 1948*, Cmd. 7327 (London: His Majesty's Stationery Office, 1948).

89 The ratios are calculated from the figures in the text and the following additional statistical sources: Central Statistical Office, *Fighting with figures*, 229, Table 11.3.; Central Statistical Office, *National Income and Expenditure 1958* (London: Her Majesty's Stationery Office, 1958), 7, Table 1.

90 Robert A. Pollard, *Economic Security and the Origins of the Cold War, 1945-1950* (New York: Columbia University Press, 1985), 257, Table A.2.

91 Gorn, *Harnessing the genie*, 36.

92 These figures have been calculated on the basis of: Bureau of the Census, *The Statistical History of the United States: From Colonial Times to the Present* (New York: Basic Books, 1976), 230 and 966.

amounted to £116.4 million at the prevailing exchange rate or to more than half of the British defence procurement budget in this period (£188 million).[93]

It is more difficult to compare the British defence effort with that of the Soviet Union, because of the lack of contemporary comparable national income estimates. Based on the estimates published in *The Economist* in December 1948, the Soviet Union spent between 12.5 and 14 per cent of its GNP of $80 billion on defence.[94] Converted at the prevailing exchange rate, the defence budget of the Soviet Union was roughly £2,500 million or more than three times as large as the British defence expenditure in 1948. According to American national security analysts, the Soviet Union invested heavily in improving its war potential in addition to its defence budget. In this context, one report claimed that this expenditure of an additional 7 per cent included outlay on research and development and stockpiling for military purposes.[95] If the Soviet Union spent only 1 per cent of its GNP on military research and development, its military research and development expenditure would have been larger than the British defence procurement budget in this period.

---

[93] This figure has been calculated using the official exchange rate which overvalued sterling. Therefore, the official exchange rate of $4.03 to £1 did not reflect the relative purchasing power of the British defence budget. If the exchange rate after the devaluation of sterling in 1949 (£1 = $2.80) is used, American military research and development amounted to £167.5 million nearly matching British procurement expenditures. However, this figure will be an over-estimate given the higher purchasing power of British defence spending (1.40) relative to that of the United States. If the different purchasing power is taken into account, the American military research and development budget roughly equalled the figure based on the official exchange rate (£119.6 million). On the different purchasing power of British and American defence expenditures, see Milton Gilbert and Irving B. Kravis, *An International Comparison of National Products and the Purchasing Power of Currencies: A Study of the United States, The United Kingdom, France, Germany and Italy* (Paris: Organisation for European Economic Co-operation, 1954), 43, Table 16.

[94] Special Correspondent, "Russia's Economic Revival - II," *The Economist*, 18 December 1948, 1022-3. The dollar figure is taken from Howard S. Ellis, *The Economics of Freedom: The Progress and Future of Aid to Europe* (New York: Harper & Brothers, 1950), 18 Table 2. The article in *The Economist* contains several estimates of Soviet national income in roubles drawing attention to the massive problems associated with Soviet national income statistics in this period. As far as it is possible to reconstruct, Howard Ellis and his collaborators based their figure of $80 billion for Soviet GNP on the article's suggestion that Russian national income was less than 30 *per cent* of that of the United States; see Special Correspondent, "Russia's Economic Revival - II," 1022.

[95] Department of State, ed., *Foreign Relations of the United States, 1952-1954, volume ii: National Security Affairs* (Washington: Government Printing Office, 1984), 89-113.: Annex to a Report to the National Security Council by the Executive Secretary (Lay), 22 August 1952. *The Economist*'s special correspondent noted in his article in 1948 that the Soviet Union devoted roughly 6 per cent of its national income to building up strategic stockpiles of food and raw materials to ensure continued production in case of a disruption of the transport system due to severe winter weather or war; see Special Correspondent, "Russia's Economic Revival - II," 1023. Therefore, the American interpretation of Russian national income statistics may be an incorrect attribution of these expenditures as serving military objectives.

Table 1.2

Indicators of the Economic War Potential of the United Kingdom, the United States and Soviet Union, 1948

	Production of coal (million of tons)	Production of Pig-Iron and Ferro-Alloys (million of tons)	Production of Crude Steel (million of tons)	Production of Electrical Power (Thousand millions of kilowatt hours)
United Kingdom	210.8	9.5	15.1	47 β
United States	581.9	55.0	80.3	356
as per cent of United Kingdom	*276*	*582*	*532*	*757*
Soviet Union	203.8	14.0	16.7 α	63
as per cent of United Kingdom	*97*	*148*	*111*	*134*

Notes: α estimate by Steel Division of the United Nations Economic Commission for Europe; β Great Britain.

Sources: United Nations. Economic Commission for Europe. Research and Planning Division. *Economic Survey of Europe in 1948*. (Geneva: United Nations. Department of Economic Affairs, 1949), 11, Table 8, 280, Table IV, 10, Table 7 and 278, Table II.

Despite the unreliability and limited comparability of contemporary GNP estimates, these comparisons illustrate the relative disadvantage at which the British warfare state found itself in competing with the other superpowers. Discussing Britain's position as a major power in 1950, Charles Webster noted that Britain

> ... is much inferior to armed strength and war potential to the United States. She is greatly inferior to the Soviet Union in land forces, but this is a position which she has often held before as regards the Great Powers of the Continent. The difference today lies in the fact that the defeat of Germany and Italy, the disappearance of the Austro-Hungarian Empire, and the weakness of France has overthrown the balance of power in Europe. Moreover, Britain's economic position has been so strained by the war that, though still the second greatest producer of manufactures, she no longer has the relative potential that she once possessed.[96]

This relative weakness is reflected by the indicators of Britain's economic war

96 Webster, Jacob, and Robinson, *United Kingdom policy*, 12.

Table 1.3

Increase in Defence Budgets of the United Kingdom, the United States and Soviet Union, 1948–55

	Increase in Defence Budget, 1949–53$^{\alpha}$ (in per cent)	Defence Expenditures as percentage of UK, 1949	Defence Expenditures as percentage of UK, 1952
United Kingdom	70.5		
United States	227.2	495	967
Soviet Union at official exchange rates	64.4 $^{\beta}$	262	221
at Benoit-Lubbell exchange rates[97]	64.4 $^{\beta}$	562	473

Notes: $^{\alpha}$ at constant 1960 $ prices
$^{\beta}$ 1948–52

Source: Defence Expenditures: Stockholm International Peace Research Institute. *SIPRI Yearbook of World Armaments and Disarmament, 1968/69*. (Stockholm: Almqvist & Wiksell, 1970), 200-201, Table 1 A.1. and Table 1 A.2.

potential in Table 1.2. Moreover, many western observers feared that the economic war potential of the Soviet Union would grow more rapidly due to the higher proportion of national income the country invested particularly in heavy industry.[98] However, these figures hide the fact that Britain's defence effort probably imposed a greater burden on its economy than that of the two other superpowers on their economies, because the size of the British armed forces exacerbated the severe manpower constraint in the domestic economy. As the cold war arms race of the next five years after 1948 showed, Britain lacked the scope for enlarging and modernising its armed forces on a comparable scale to the other two superpowers.[99] While Britain matched the increase in Soviet defence expenditure in this period, its own effort was dwarfed by the massive expansion of the American military effort (see Table 1.3). In response to the deepening cold war, the Soviet Union and the United

[97] Benoit-Lubbell's exchange rate estimates provide defence-purchasing-power-parity exchange rates for the Soviet Union in an attempt to correct the disparities in the official and commercial exchange rates. On the problem of exchange rates relating to Russian defence expenditure estimates, see Stockholm International Peace Research Institute, *SIPRI Yearbook of World Armaments and Disarmament, 1968/69* (Stockholm: Almqvist & Wiksell, 1970), 198-9.

[98] Special Correspondent, "Russia's Economic Revival - II," 1022-3.

[99] On the size and modernisation of Soviet armed forces in this period, see Thomas W. Wolfe, *Soviet Power and Europe, 1945-1970* (Baltimore: Johns Hopkins University Press, 1970), 9-12 and 38-44.; on NATO forces in general, see Hastings Lionel Ismay, *NATO: The first five years, 1949-1954* (Paris: North Atlantic Treaty Organisation, 1954), 101-11.

Table 1.4

Increased Military Mobilisation of the United Kingdom, the United States and Soviet Union, 1948–55

	Strength of the Armed Forces (in 1,000) 1948	1950	1952	1955	Increase in the size of armed forces 1948–55 (in per cent)	Increase in the size of armed forces 1950–52 (in per cent)
United Kingdom	808	666	848	784	-3.0	27.4
United States	1,446	1,460	3,636	2,935	103.0	149.0
Soviet Union	2,874			5,763	100.5	

Source: United Kingdom: Central Statistical Office. *Annual Abstract of Statistics*, vol. 93 (London: Her Majesty's Stationery Office, 1956), 116, Table 136.; United States: Bureau of the Census. *The Statistical History of the United States: From Colonial Times to the Present* (New York: Basic Books, 1976), 1141, Series 904-16.; Soviet Union: Thomas W. Wolfe, *Soviet Power and Europe, 1945-1970* (Baltimore: Johns Hopkins University Press, 1970), 9-10.

States more than doubled the strength of their armed forces between 1948 and 1955.[100] Managing to increase its armed forces by a quarter during the Korean war, the acute labour shortage forced the British government to slightly reduce the size of its armed forces in the same period (see Table 1.4). This analysis suggests that Britain was falling behind the other two superpowers in terms of overall strength, a finding confirmed by a comparison of the war potential of the three major powers as measured by the Correlates of War Index (see Table 1.5). As a consequence of the country's limited mobilisation potential, British military planners accepted that the country would depend on outside military and economic assistance in case of a future global war. Therefore, they acknowledged the necessity of a more capital-intensive defence posture and argued for the build-up of Britain's nuclear arsenal just prior to the outbreak of the Korean war in June 1950.[101] Given the country's relative weakness, British policy-makers regarded maintaining the links with the Commonwealth and the Empire as crucial to enhancing Britain's war potential. For this reason, British policy-makers largely ignored the threats to these links by the rise of nationalism in the colonies, Britain's declining capability to protect far-flung dominions militarily and the ascendancy of American power.[102]

---

[100] 1948 and 1955 are the only years for which manpower figures for the Soviet Union are available; see Wolfe, *Soviet power*, 9-12.

[101] DBPO 2iv, 411–31: "Defence Policy and Global Strategy", Report by the Chiefs of Staff, 7 June 1950.

[102] A. P. Thornton, *The Imperial Idea and its Enemies: A study in British power*, 2nd ed. (Basingstoke: Macmillan, 1985), 316-24.

Table 1.5

Correlates of War Index[103] for the United Kingdom, the United States and Soviet Union, 1945–55

	1945	1950	1955
United Kingdom	17.5	14.1	12.2
United States	42.9	38.7	41.2
Soviet Union	25.5	37.6	39.4

Source: G. John Ikenberry, *After Victory: Institutions, strategic restraint and the rebuilding of order after major wars* (Princeton: Princeton University Press, 2001), 279.

Presentism versus the Future in British defence policy

Despite Britain's limited resources, the British defence effort remained symbolic of national independence. In this context, the acquisition of an independent nuclear deterrent became the ultimate symbol of major power status in the nuclear age. As David Ellwood has pointed out, the British decision to build an atomic bomb has a certain ironic quality with hindsight:

> [At] the very time when the Labour government was taking the portentous decision to develop its own atomic bomb, in order – among other things – to guarantee Britain's long-term status as a Great Power and avoid dependence on the unpredictable Americans, [...] Attlee and Bevin [were] obliged to admit that the country's financial position was so grave that they were forced to abandon an area [– Greece and Turkey –] which the British government had always insisted was vital to national security.[104]

The retrospective juxtaposition of these two decisions implies a lack of coherence in British foreign and defence policy-making. With hindsight, it is tempting to suggest that the decision to develop a British atomic bomb necessitated the retrenchment of Britain's overseas military commitments or vice versa. In reality, the British government had been committed to both

[103] The Correlates of War index measures a state's war potential based on military personnel, military expenditure, energy production, iron and steel production, urban population, and total production. On the Correlates of War index, see J. David Singer and F. Diehl Paul, eds., *Measuring the Correlates of War* (Ann Arbor: University of Michigan Press, 1990).

[104] David Ellwood, *Rebuilding Europe: Western Europe, America and postwar reconstruction* (London: Longman, 1992), 68.

policies – the nuclear weapons programme and Britain's economic and military assistance to Greece and Turkey – for several years.

In late 1945, the Truman administration refused to share nuclear technology with Britain despite the British involvement in the Manhattan Project. At the time, the British government had already authorised the construction of a nuclear weapons establishment at Harwell. Therefore, the wheels had already been set in motion, when fifteen months later a small group of ministers decided to go ahead with the development of a British bomb.[105] To some extent, American reticence to share nuclear technology contributed to the British decision to build a bomb in January 1947. Totally unrelatedly, ministers reconsidered overseas military expenditures in response to a growing drain on dollar reserves in the Spring of 1947. In ending British economic and military assistance to Greece and Turkey, ministers prioritised the future capacity to project power over the ongoing demonstration of power in a protracted conflict. Moreover, this move shrewdly predicted that the Americans would fill the breech left by the withdrawal of British aid providing substantial economic assistance and military support from 1947 onwards.[106] Having followed the crises along the Northern Tier of the Middle East (Iran, Turkey, Greece) with growing apprehension, the American national security community decided to step in.[107] As this analysis shows, the causal link between the two decisions, suggested by Ellwood, did not exist. The withdrawal from Greece and Turkey never had the symbolic importance of the loss of India and Palestine or indeed the acquisition of the bomb. Indeed, Bevin barely mentioned the British government's decision to end its financial and military assistance to Greece. In the end, the real importance of the withdrawal from Greece derived from the resulting American commitment in western European security.[108] Abandoning the nuclear bomb project would have offered similar savings of foreign currency reserves, but no similar improvement of western European security. However, American assistance did not automatically extend the American nuclear umbrella to western Europe and hence did not undermine the case for a British bomb.

Despite Britain's resource constraints, the acquisition of an atomic capability nevertheless made sense in terms of cost and effect:

---

[105] Bullock, *Bevin*, 185-9 and 245-6.

[106] In the end, British soldiers remained in Greece until the end of the civil war there; see Bullock, *Bevin*, 369-71.

[107] Pollard, *Economic security*, 107-32.

[108] Bullock, *Bevin*, 369-71.

> For the same money and effort nuclear weapons, as compared with conventional weapons, give thousands of times (if not more) larger yields in terms of target damage.[109]

Given this economic rationale, any country with the necessary scientific base would at least be tempted to acquire atomic weapons particularly in the absence of any security guarantee. Through the British participation in the Manhattan Project, British nuclear scientists had acquired the basic knowledge required to proceed with the construction of a British bomb. Given these favourable circumstances, Britain's nuclear programme proved comparatively inexpensive and its overall economic impact relatively small. Labour and steel shortages delayed the British bomb project and the development of a strategic bomber capable of delivering the bomb. Despite the importance of the bomb project, ministers did not force the pace of its development by granting the nuclear programme priority over economic reconstruction.[110] Arguably, the decision to acquire atomic weapons paved the way for the adoption of a more capital-intensive defence strategy. Over the next decade, the British defence policy community recognised that scientific advance had radically changed the basis of all military planning. Based on this (by now obvious) conclusion, the government decided to reshape British defence policy in 1957. In the 1957 Defence White Paper, ministers embraced a military posture based on a national deterrent and collective defence arrangements in western Europe.[111]

In the immediate post-war period, debates on British defence policy tended to focus on resource allocation rather than strategy. In 1945, Attlee himself initiated a potentially wide-ranging debate about future British defence policy when he questioned the need for British military bases in the Middle East. Instead of a fruitful reassessment of the strategic objectives, a protracted battle ensued between the defence planning community and the Treasury over the resources needed to meet the ambitious objectives set out by the Chiefs of Staff.[112] Discussing the future shape and size of the armed forces, ministers failed to decide the extent to which resources should be allocated to "fighting the cold war" and "preparing for a possible shooting war". In the end, ministers decided to resolve their dilemma by fixing a ceiling for the defence budget

[109] Defence Science Organisation, *Nuclear explosions*, 21-2.

[110] On the atomic bomb project, see Margaret Gowing, *Independence and Deterrence: Britain and atomic energy, 1945-1952, vol. 2: policy execution* (Basingstoke: Macmillan, 1974), 36-90 and 343-50.

[111] Ministry of Defence, *Defence: Outline of future policy*, Cmnd. 124 (London: Her Majesty's Stationery Office, 1957), 1.

[112] Despite considerable indigenous opposition to the continued British presence in the region, ministers decided against a withdrawal from its bases in the Middle East. These debates have been chronicled by Gorst, "Facing Facts?.".; Gorst, "We must cut our coat."

taking into account the needs for economic reconstruction.[113] Given the shortage of industrial manpower, ministers reduced the size of the armed forces and the length of national service.[114] While setting the main parameters of British defence efforts, ministers left the final allocation of expenditure to the Chiefs of Staff and the individual services.[115] Without clear ministerial guidance, the defence policy-making community engaged in across-the-board cuts rather than assessing the cost-benefits of individual expenditure programmes. Despite the Attlee government's intention to improve the co-ordination of defence policy, each service strove to maintain its independence under the new institutional arrangements. Given the divergent interests of the different services, the military leadership seemed reluctant to agree an overall defence strategy which would have optimised the financial resources available to meet the large number of strategic objectives British defence policy envisaged in this period.[116]

In the immediate post-war period, the new central organisation for defence created by the incoming Labour government drew on the experience of the Second World War. Given the legacy of appeasement, ministers deferred to the military planners for guidance on the best defence strategy. When Attlee questioned certain overseas commitments, the military leadership insisted that the Middle East and the Empire remained vital to British defence. This initial defeat prompted the Prime Minister and successive Chancellors to concentrate their efforts on containing the escalating defence budget. The divergent interests of the Treasury and the defence policy-making community shaped British defence policy, thus postponing strategic decisions about the objectives, size and shape of the British defence effort in the dawning nuclear age. The policy-makers' indecision reflected the growing tensions between the superpowers rather than any weakness in the institutional arrangements. In the immediate post-war period, most policy-makers perceived Soviet foreign policy as unduly antagonistic to British interests. Afraid of appeasing Stalin, ministers remained set on holding the line in the emerging cold war. Aware of their own vulnerability in terms of economic resources, ministers decided to maintain a large military presence overseas and an increased degree of defence preparedness. Arguably, Britain's relatively limited potential to compete in another rearmament race restricted the scope for withdrawals from overseas bases in the immediate post-war period. At the same time, as Britain attempted

[113] PRO CAB 130/41: Minutes of the 1st Meeting of a Cabinet Committee (Gen 254: Size of the Armed Forces in the Years 1949, 1950 and 1951), 25 October 1948.

[114] Alec Cairncross, *Years of Recovery: British Economic Policy, 1945-51* (London: Methuen, 1985), 386-93.

[115] PRO CAB 130/41: Minutes of the 1st Meeting of a Cabinet Committee (Gen 254: Size of the Armed Forces in the Years 1949, 1950 and 1951). 25 October 1948.

[116] Bernard L. Montgomery, *The Memoirs of Field-Marshal the Viscount Montgomery of Alamein, K.G.* (London: William Collins, Sons & Co., 1958), 487-97.

to maintain a world-wide military presence commensurate with its status as a major world power, ministers searched for allies to contain Soviet expansionism in Europe. Given the poor state of western European armed forces, British policy-makers became convinced that a western European military alliance would not prove sufficient to defend western Europe and Britain against any Soviet incursion westward. In this sense, British attempts to preserve an independent role as a major power on the world stage contributed to the emergence of two rival military blocs.[117] In this context, the British atomic bomb became an important symbol reassuring ministers and the country of Britain's continued importance as a major player in the unfolding cold war arms race.

Reforming military procurement: the case of tank procurement

The reforms of British defence establishment reflected lessons of wartime mobilisation. This is particularly true for the post-war organisation of British defence procurement. Despite some real success stories, some areas of wartime production were plagued by persistent problems arising from misguided procurement decisions, flawed designs, and weak project management. There remains general agreement that British wartime tank procurement suffered from all these problems since the early stages of rearmament. Some of the blame must rest with the General Staff for failing to develop a forward-looking policy for tanks in the 1930s or after Dunkirk.[118] As a consequence of this failure, the British army had to rely on American-built Sherman tanks. At the same time, the shortcomings of wartime tank procurement convinced policy-makers of the need for a far-reaching reform of the procurement process.

To overcome the wartime problems, the new post-war supply organisation for tanks and armoured vehicles was "... based on two fundamental principles": centralised control of the whole procurement process and standardisation of components across types. [119] By centralising control in the hands of a Director

---

[117] Wilfried Loth, *Die Teilung der Welt: Die Geschichte des Kalten Kriegs, 1941-1955*, 7th rev. ed. (München: Deutscher Taschenbuch Verlag, 1989), 348-50.

[118] House of Commons, *War-Time Tank Production: Reports by the Select Committee on National Expenditure and the Replies to these Reports by the Government of the day*, Cmd. 6865 (London: His Majesty's Stationery Office, 1946).; J. D. Scott and Richard Hughes, *The Administration of War Production* (London: Her Majesty's Stationery Office, 1955), 281-3. On the problems of British wartime tank production, see G. MacLeod Ross, *The Business of Tanks: 1933 to 1945* (Elms Court: Arthur H. Stockwell, 1976).; A. J. Smithers, *Rude Mechanicals: An account of tank maturity during the Second World War* (London: Grafton, 1989).; Correlli Barnett, *The Audit of War: The illusion and reality of Britain as a great nation* (Basingstoke: Macmillan, 1986), 161-5.

[119] This paragraph is based on the summary of the post-war supply organisation for fighting vehicles in the British Library, India Office Library and Records (hereafter IOR)

General (Fighting Vehicles), the Ministry of Supply hoped to address the difficulties that had resulted from the separation of design and production management in the early stages of the war. Post-war reorganisation called for the amalgamation of the different design departments for tanks and wheeled vehicles into one newly created research establishment based at Chobham outside London. At Chobham, staff not only designed new vehicles, but also carried out applied research into special problems of vehicle design as well as materials and instruments. Despite financial constraints, the Ministry of Supply modernised the new research establishment by buying the latest machinery such as a German machine for cutting bevel gears in 1946.[120] In order to carry out elaborate tests of new designs, the Proving Department would provide important military feedback on new weapons, guns and armaments at an early stage. In the new organisational structure, the co-ordination and supervision of fighting vehicles production rested with the Production Department. While they came under the control of the Director General, both the Proving Department and the Inspection Department also reported directly to the General Staff on whether new designs met the specifications laid down by the military.

On the production side, the government converted a Royal Ordnance factory in Barnbow (Leeds) into the first government tank factory at the end of the war. Through this conversion, the Directorate of Fighting Vehicles could now turn to a government-owned establishment for the construction of prototypes rather than turning to private manufacturers.[121] In the light of the private firms' poor performance, wartime officials favoured the centralisation of research and development as well as the creation of tank production capacity in the public sector. Additionally, the Directorate for Fighting Vehicles attempted to enter into long-term relationships with three private tank manufacturers in order to preserve a nucleus of tank production capacity for a future war. Given the limited prospects for large production orders, two firms (Vauxhall, Leyland) rejected the advances of the Ministry of Supply preferring to supply the lucrative private market for vehicles.[122] In contrast to the third firm, Vickers, neither Leyland nor Vauxhall had traditionally engaged in defence work to a significant degree. Had Vickers, as a major defence contractor, refused to co-operate this might have undermined its ability to compete for other defence

---

L/WS/1/835: RAC Conference Report, Appendix E: New Ministry of Supply Organisation for the Provision of Vehicles, 12-17 November 1945. On the importance of the wartime experience, see also Scott and Hughes, *Administration*, 281-8.

[120] Tobias Kampmann, *Vom Werkzeughandel zum Maschinenbau: Der Aufstieg des Familienunternehmens W. Ferd. Klingelnberg Söhne, 1900-1950* (Stuttgart: Franz Steiner, 1994), 256.

[121] IOR L/WS/1/835: RAC Conference Report, Appendix E: New Ministry of Supply Organisation for the Provision of Vehicles, 12-17 November 1945.

[122] This episode is analysed in more detail in chapter 4

contracts.[123] Vickers could sustain a loss arising from tank production as long as profits from other defence contracts absorbed any shortfall. The incentive for Vickers was the prospect of obtaining large defence production contracts as the price for cooperation with the government.[124] Nevertheless, this public-private sector partnership remained a remarkable aspect of the post-war supply organisation for tanks. Intriguingly, one of the strongest advocates of a government tank factory had been the future chairman of Vickers-Armstrong, Robert Micklem, in his capacity as Director General (Fighting Vehicles) during the last two years of the war.[125]

However, the new organisational structure for tank procurement left the relationship between the War Office and the supply organisation unresolved. Indeed, the organisational structure had been drawn up prior to making any decision as to whether the supply organisation would remain a separate Ministry of Supply or return to the War Office.[126] Placing the supply organisation in a separate government department might have stored up problems for the future. During the Second World War, the disappointing performance of British built tanks had to be attributed to the failure of the General Staff to develop "... a forward policy for tanks up to the end of 1942."[127] In the reformed institutional structures, the General Staff remained isolated from the technological expertise and scientific advice needed to plan future weapons development.[128] Instead, the General Staff relied on military officers to oversee the procurement process for the War Office.[129] To some extent, the separation of functions obscured the process of drawing up the initial specifications for a new weapons system. Therefore, the post-war reforms only addressed the problems arising from the management of wartime tank procurement and production, while neglecting those relating to drawing up the specifications for new weapon systems.

With the war drawing to a close, the War Office attempted to learn from the wartime experience. Based on his experiences on the battlefield, Field-Marshall Bernard Montgomery stressed that the British Army should adopt a

---

[123] A refusal would have amounted to a rejection of the unwritten rules of government-defence industry relations. Hence, Vickers might become an outcast finding it impossible to obtain further defence contracts. This analysis is drawn from George A. Akerlof, "The economics of caste and of the rat race and other woeful tales," in *An Economist's Book of Tales* (Cambridge: Cambridge University Press, 1984), 23-44, particularly 42-3.

[124] On this point, see William P. Rogerson, "Economic Incentives and the Defense Procurement Process," *Journal of Economic Perspectives* 8 (1994): 65-90.

[125] Smithers, *Rude mechanicals*, 196.

[126] IOR L/WS/1/835: RAC Conference Report, Appendix E: New Ministry of Supply Organisation for the Provision of Vehicles.12-17 November 1945.

[127] Scott and Hughes, *Administration*, 283.

[128] Ross, *Business*, 314-21.

[129] Kenneth Macksey, *The Tanks: The History of the Royal Tank Regiment, 1945-1975* (London: Arms and Armour Press, 1979), 69-70.

main battle tank in future. Such a tank would have to serve two purposes as infantry support in close combat and in armoured formations in hot pursuit. To fulfil this dual role, the main battle tank would have to be equipped with a powerful gun, engine and armour.[130] Among these characteristics, Montgomery repeatedly stressed the importance of adequate firepower for a main battle tank:

> in the contest between gun and armour, the gun can always win in the end – but if it is to do so experiments must always continue searching for better guns.[131]

Against this advice, the General Staff decided to develop a heavy tank (F.V. 201) to compensate for the lack of fire-power of the newly developed Centurion tank. Despite the positive field trials of the Centurion, General Staff insisted that, even with a 20 pounder gun, it would be no match for the newest Russian heavy tank, the Josef Stalin III. However, technical problems delayed the development of the F.V. 201. Due to financial pressures, the War Office decided to adopt the Centurion as main battle tank in the interim. Fortunately, further field trials established that the Centurion performed remarkably well against standard Russian tanks due to its superior fire control system. During the Korean war, the Centurion tank proved to be the "... outstanding tank of the war" due to its "... thick armour, superior firepower and mechanical reliability".[132] On the battlefield, the Centurion's armour withstood direct hits leading to relatively few losses. Describing a direct hit on a tank, a young lieutenant observed that "everyone flapped quite unnecessarily".[133] However, given the ongoing F.V. 201 project, the War Office made no effort to improve the 20 pounder tank gun of the Centurion. Arguably, the Centurion remained under-gunned until the introduction of a purpose-built 105 mm tank gun in 1959, which virtually eliminated the need for a heavy tank.[134] At the same time, the absence of overall co-ordination meant that other ways of increasing the Centurion's firepower, such as the development of high explosive shells, were not sufficiently explored.[135]

---

130 Imperial War Museum, Department of Documents (hereafter IWM), Papers of Field Marshall Viscount Montgomery of Alamein (hereafter BLM): IWM BLM 129/2: Memorandum on Future Design of Capital Tank, 24 October 1944.

131 IWM BLM 129/1: Memorandum on British Armour, 6 July 1944.

132 Simon Dunston, *Modern Combat Vehicles 2: Centurion* (Shepperton: Ian Allan, 1980), 107.

133 IWM 86/61/1: Lieutenant L. G. G. Smith: Letter from Korea, 25 December 1951.; see also Macksey, *Tanks*, 75-84.

134 R. M. Ogorkiewicz, *Design and Development of Fighting Vehicles* (London: Macdonald, 1968), 42-4.; Dunston, *Centurion*, 7-18 and 41-58.; but for a different view, see Macksey, *Tanks*, 70-72.

135 "Obituaries: Maj-Gen Derrick Wormald," *The Daily Telegraph*, 31 March 1994, 27.

At one level, the priority accorded to a new heavy tank is surprising. In the closing stages of the Second World War, the tank seemed to loose its ability to dominate the battlefield owing to the emergence of infantry anti-tank weapons (i.e. Bazooka, Panzerfaust), more effective anti-tank guns and low flying fighter bombers. Moreover, any mass concentration of armoured formations would, in the future, constitute an ideal military target for an atomic bomb. While arguing for caution, some military planners suggested that the future role of tanks had to be radically rethought. A major strand of opinion favoured equipping airborne formations with light tanks in order to maintain their mobility in the interlude before the likelihood of a nuclear war.[136] Citing the high survivability of tanks during American atomic tests in the Nevada desert, other military thinkers insisted that tanks remained the only effective weapon with which to oppose the large Soviet tank formations in central Europe. To restore an element of surprise to the battlefield, J. F. C. Fuller argued for improving the night fighting capabilities of tanks.[137] Obsessed with the perceived superiority of Soviet armoured formations, military procurement officers argued for the development of more and more sophisticated battle tanks such as the F.V. 201, but delayed improvements in the existing main battle tank.

Just as in the case of tanks, government officials overhauled the supply organisation for other weapon systems such as military aircraft. The reforms for each aspect of the supply organisations reflected the specific problems relating to the wartime production of a particular weapons system. Given the relative success of wartime aircraft production, the government continued to rely after the end of the war on the expertise of private firms for the development and production of military aircraft. Indeed, the government rejected the nationalisation of the aircraft industry despite the important contribution of state-owned factories and Power Jets during the war.[138] In contrast to tank procurement, the government restricted its direct involvement in the aircraft industry to fundamental research.[139] To that end, several research establishments engaged in fundamental research diffusing the results to the whole industry (e.g. Royal Aircraft Establishment, National Physical Laboratory, National Gas Turbine Establishment). The actual development and design work remained in the hands of private industry. To retain the expertise of the design teams, the government engaged the industry in a considerable

---

[136] A. J. Wilson, "The future of armour as the arm of mobility," *Royal United Services Institute Journal* 91 (1946): 396-400.; C. Paddock, "Future Wars and the Use of Armour," *Brassey's Annual* 67 (1956).

[137] J. F. C. Fuller, "The Tank in Future Warfare," *Brassey's Annual* 63 (1952): 262-72.

[138] Edgerton, "Whatever happened," 105-8.

[139] PRO T 225/653: "Future of Aircraft Production", note Gilbert - Eady and Barlow, 17 December 1943.

number of aircraft development projects in the immediate post-war period. On the surface, these government-sponsored development efforts seemed to maintain the British aircraft industry's lead in jet aircraft design.[140] However, the division of the research effort between government research facilities and private aircraft manufacturers lacked direction, co-ordination and proper management. From the start, basic research and aircraft development projects competed for limited funds. After the devaluation of the pound in 1949, further cuts led to the cancellation of several projects. Before most development projects had come to fruition, the unexpected emergency of the Korean war exposed the inherent risks of this strategy. Left without a modern jet fighter, the government ordered aircraft off the drawing board in a manner reminiscent of the Churchill tank order during the Second World War.[141] Due to the mixed record of British defence procurement strategy, Britain acquired a reputation as "a nation of prototype builders" rather than reliable aircraft manufacturers.[142] The British experience in the immediate post-war period is hardly an endorsement for a deliberate policy of "investing in research and development until a threat materialises". In the end, only large production orders allowed firms to recoup their overheads such as those incurred by maintaining a large design team for development work.[143]

At best, the post-war reforms of the British supply organisation can be characterised as contingencies addressing some of the wartime deficiencies. In 1945, the incoming Attlee government inherited plans which had been drawn up during the last two years of the war by the service and supply departments. Despite the stated emphasis on research and development, the structures did not facilitate technological excellence. Decision-makers who were at the centre remained removed from scientific advice. In order to maintain an independent industrial base for defence, the supply departments initiated a profusion of new weapons projects thus complicating the control and oversight of individual projects. At the same time, the supply departments encouraged their established defence contractors to retain as large a production capacity as possible in order to preserve the war potential of the defence industry. Due to a lack of production contracts, the major defence firms, however, struggled to maintain their cash flow and profits.

---

[140] JRULM LPA Research Department. folder: Aircraft Industry.: R.221 (revised), "The Aircraft Industry", February 1953.

[141] House of Commons, *Supply of Military Aircraft.*; Ministry of Defence, *The Supply of Military Aircraft*, Cmd. 9388 (London: Her Majesty's Stationery Office, 1955).

[142] JRULM LPA Research Department. folder: Aircraft Industry.: Brief A232(a), Some notes on Supply of Military Aircraft, 5 December 1953.

[143] House of Commons, *Supply of Military Aircraft*, xxix-xxxiii.

Conclusion

By 1957, the contingencies of the immediate post-war period crystallised into the enduring structures which govern the British defence effort to this day. However, the birth pangs of the British warfare state (described in previous sections in this chapter) remain integral to the current policy. British defence policy-makers are still striking the balance between seemingly endless defence objectives and limited (and diminishing) financial resources.[144] Surprisingly, the British warfare state has not been seriously contested in sharp contrast to the attacks made on the other aspects of the post-war settlement (e.g. the welfare state, nationalisation of public services, public housing, full employment policies).[145]

In the immediate post-war period, ministers linked Britain's defence policy with the recent experience of total war. By enlisting the collective memory "... of those who had fought and died in the common cause", politicians translated recent experience into a coherent discourse for increased military preparedness, meeting international commitments and war prevention in the late 1940s.[146] As the cold war intensified, most Britons increasingly approved of the government's resolute foreign policy.[147] After the outbreak of the Korean war, most Britons interviewed dreaded the prospect of yet another war, but at the same time most supported the government's policy of sending troops to Korea, because they were tired of "... constantly living on the edge".[148] At the same time, this emerging discourse had an unfortunate consequence. Since British society owed a debt to those who fought in the war, politicians seemed inclined to leave many decisions to the military planners and supply departments.[149] Therefore, ministers never thoroughly questioned military

---

[144] John Baylis, *British Defence Policy: Striking the Right Balance* (Basingstoke: London, 1989), 72-80.; David Greenwood, "Defence and National Priorities since 1945," in *British Defence Policy in a Changing World*, ed. John Baylis (London: Croom Helm, 1977), 174-207.

[145] Brian Bond, *War and Society in Europe, 1870-1970* (London: Fontana, 1984), 222-3.; Edgerton, *England and the aeroplane*, 83-5.

[146] The quote is taken from the 1946 Defence White Paper; see Ministry of Defence, *Statement relating to Defence*, 3. For a later example of this discourse, see also Emmanuel Shinwell's statement on defence policy in May 1950, see House of Commons, *Official Report*, vol. 472, Parliamentary Debates (Hansard), Fifth Series (London: His Majesty's Stationery Office, 1950). (hereafter 472 H.C. DEB. 5s.), columns 1264-80.

[147] For such claims, see for example A. V. Alexander in May 1947, 437 H.C. DEB. 5s., col. 2538-9; and Stafford Cripps in April 1949, PRO T 171/399: Budget Broadcast - as delivered, 6 April 1949.

[148] Tom Harrison Mass-Observation Archive, University of Sussex, Brighton, (hereafter MOA) MOA Box: Korea 1950: Public Opinions of the Korean War, June-July 1950.

[149] The Treasury in particular hoped to induce a radical review of defence policy by imposing deep cuts in the defence budget; see PRO T 225/73: memorandum Bridges - Dalton, 10 January 1947.; PRO T 225/74: minute Gilbert - Bridges, 13 January 1949. On these

manpower requirements, weapon development projects and other aspects of the British warfare state.

The remainder of this concluding discussion will highlight some of the more anachronistic aspects of the British defence effort. In addition to providing the motivation for the large defence effort, the experience of the Second World War shaped decision-making about British defence policy between the end of the war and the 1957 Defence White Paper. For example, wartime experience informed the reform of institutional structures leading to the creation of a Ministry of Defence and a Ministry of Supply. Significantly, these plans first evolved during the war taking into account past neglect, failures and achievements. Having faced the threat of invasion and military defeat, British policy-makers remained aware of the contingent nature of the British defence effort. Given its straightened circumstances, British post-war defence relied on a future collective security arrangement preferably under the umbrella of the United Nations or alternatively a western alliance involving the United States. In this respect, expectations about a future war mirrored recent experience.

Due to the dominant influence of the wartime experience, the expectations of the defence policy-making community did not necessarily take account of the advances in weapons technology and the nuclear revolution. Indeed, the 1957 Defence White Paper started with the admission that "[i]t ha[d] been clear for some time ..." that the nuclear revolution had radically changed the nature of warfare. Citing the uncertainty about the capabilities of emerging weapons technology, the military leadership admitted delaying a reappraisal of future British defence policy until the time when

> the future picture is becoming sufficiently clear to enable a comprehensive reshaping of policy to be undertaken with any degree of confidence.[150]

For the same reason, the Chiefs of Staff resisted attempts to plan for a future global war. This resistance undermined efforts to draw up a realistic rearmament and mobilisation programme for a potential British war economy in the future. Given the problems in the early days of the Second World War, economic policy-makers regarded such contingency planning as helpful, if not essential.[151] As Robert Hall observed in his diary in 1950,

---

occasions, the service chiefs and the Minister of Defence opposed such moves vigorously, see for example the discusssions of PRO CAB 130/41: Minutes of a Cabinet Committee (Gen 254: Size of the Armed Forces in the Years 1949, 1950 and 1951)., 25 October 1948, 1 November 1948, 5 November 1948.

[150] The quotes are taken from Ministry of Defence, *Defence: outline*, 1. On the position of the Chiefs of Staff, see Montgomery, *Memoirs*, 435-6.

[151] E. A. G. Robinson, "The Overall Allocation of Resources," in *Lessons of the British War Economy*, ed. D. N. Chester (Cambridge: Cambridge University Press, 1951), 56-7.

> [i]t was rather depressing because all the civilians seemed to understand the problem very well and the soldiers, because they felt that if they made forecasts these would be unreliable, felt that forecasts were no use. They could not see that to a civilian planner, who needed up to 3 years to do anything, all one did implied a forecast and it might as well be looked at.[152]

This conflict of cultures raises the question whether a detailed study of military trends might have led to a more appropriate British defence policy for the dawning nuclear age.[153] As the discussion of post-war procurement policy showed, the supply departments endeavoured to maintain the war potential of the British economy in terms of a large defence production base, which could be quickly expanded in a future war of attrition. At a meeting discussing the future size and shape of the aircraft industry in 1950, the Ministry of Supply representative acknowledged that if a future war were brief no war potential would need to exist.[154] To some extent, the outbreak of the Korean war prevented an early re-thinking of post-war supply policy. Firmly wedded to the war potential policy, the supply departments expanded defence production capacity during Korean war rearmament, even though the existing defence production capacity would have sufficed to carry out most of the rearmament programme.[155] In the existing decision-making structures, too many decisions remained solely in the hands of the military and were not subject to wider scrutiny. Moreover, scientific advice remained peripheral to procurement decisions. Despite the contribution of operations research to the war effort, new weapons development projects were not assessed in terms of military requirements and needs, nor were they subjected to a cost-benefit analysis.[156] Arguably, a certain degree of duplication could have been avoided if they had been. For example, the question should have been asked whether the up-gunning of the Centurion tank did not make more sense than developing a new heavy tank. It should also have been asked whether the country really needed three strategic bombers. As several parliamentary inquiries showed, the weapons procurement process could have benefited from tighter project

---

[152] Diary entry, 26 June 1950; reprinted in: Alec Cairncross, ed., *The Robert Hall Diaries, 1947-53* (London: Unwin Hyman, 1989), 119.

[153] William Wallace, "World Status without Tears," in *The Age of Affluence, 1951-1964*, eds. Vernon Bogdanor and Robert Skidelsky (London: Macmillan, 1970), 196-201. In this period, British decision-makers seemed to rely on their intuition rather than on scientific analysis; see Greenwood, "Defence and national priorities," 180.

[154] PRO T 225/369: Note of a meeting to consider draft paper on the Size and Shape of the Aircraft Industry, 20 April 1950.

[155] See chapter 4.

[156] On the potential contribution of operations research and economics to defence planning, see Charles Hitch, "Economics and Military Operations Research," *Review of Economics and Statistics* 40 (1958): 199-209.

management, scientific advice and economic appraisal of projects in the immediate post-war period.

Lacking an independent source of scientific or economic advice on defence policy, politicians generally accepted military advice concerning the future requirements of the armed services.[157] Arguably, ministers contented themselves with overseeing the British warfare state from the "commanding heights" of the Defence Committee rather than appreciating the need for proper scrutiny of all aspects of the defence effort.[158] In 1945, the Foreign Secretary, Ernest Bevin, argued that the economic and financial situation had to be reviewed carefully before the Cabinet decided on the size of armed forces. Indeed, "[w]ith the coming of the atomic bomb ...", Bevin questioned whether the provisional post-war defence budget of £500 million "... is needed or can be afforded".[159] Early in 1946, the Treasury attempted to curb Britain's extensive overseas commitments questioning the rationale that justified a continued military presence around the globe in terms of retaining bases for a future war with the Soviet Union.

> We simply cannot afford to make our plans on the basis of being ready for an immediate war with Russia.[160]

However, the stabilisation of British power and prestige overseas soon dominated the agenda for British defence policy-makers. Short-termism perpetuated contingencies. In extending national service, ministers insisted that this regrettable necessity would be revoked once the international situation improved and the build-up of regular forces was completed.[161] Given the perceived temporary nature of this measure, the government ignored calls for the democratisation or reform of the armed forces.[162] At the same time, service chiefs blamed ministers for the

---

[157] After the outbreak of the Korean war, the government sought economic advice on how to plan the British defence effort for the first time. As a consequence, the Economic Section played a major part in the preparation of the British rearmament programme; see Cairncross and Watts, *Economic Section*, 144-5.

[158] Ministry of Defence, *Central organisation*, 6-7. The Labour Party's similarly half-hearted approach to economic planning was criticised by some observers, see for example Michal Kalecki, "The Minimum Essentials for Democratic Planning," in *Socialism: Functioning and Long-Run Planning (Collected Works of Michal Kalecki, vol. 3)*, ed. Jerzy Osiatynski (Oxford: Clarendon Press, 1992), 269-74. On the contemporary planning debate, see also Richard Toye, "Gosplanners versus Thermostatters: Whitehall planning debates and their political consequences, 1945-49," *British Contemporary History* 14 (Winter, 2000): 81-106.

[159] PRO CAB 127/38: Note Bevin - Attlee, 3 September 1945.

[160] PRO T 247/71: memorandum Waley - Keynes, 4 February 1946.

[161] 433 H.C. DEB. 5s., col. 1959-61; 437 H.C. DEB. 5s.; col. 2539-41.

[162] 437 H.C. DEB. 5s.; col. 2571-2, 2576-7.

> parlous state of the Army [arising] from heavy and continued pressure [...] to reduce the manpower ceiling and the money ceiling, while heavy commitments still remain. We cannot run a good show on the manpower allotted, and *at the same time preserve our essential structure and training machinery*; the latter two are essential so that we could handle a big scale emergency. (emphasis in the original)[163]

But if the armed forces were so overstretched, the national interest might have been better served by a reduction of military commitments. For example, considerable savings could have been achieved by a withdrawal from contentious bases such as Egypt. Arguably, the absence of strong public opposition to the British defence effort strengthened the hand of the service chiefs.[164] In the area of defence procurement, the post-war supply organisation mirrored the sectional interests of the defence industry which had been intimately involved in drawing up the institutional arrangements during the war.[165]

As the foregoing analysis shows, the structures of the British defence establishment were reformed after 1945, in ways which generally reflected the experience of the Second World War. As the cold war intensified, the scope for radical reform of the armed forces and supply organisation became progressively smaller since the emerging discourse associated neglecting national security with recent history. Britain's excessive defence effort during the cold war could always be justified with appeals to the collective national memory of the Second World War. After 1945, war prevention could hardly be regarded as an optional extra in an increasingly antagonistic (and initially anti-British) world. Empowered by the electorate to secure the people's peace, ministers felt obliged to defend the achievements of Britain's democratic revolution.[166] Therefore, the Minister of Labour, George Isaacs, was able to justify the unprecedented step of peace-time military service in May 1947.

> The state, rightly or wrongly, has a duty to perform. [...] We believe that if we do not do something of this sort there is a greater risk that the forces of danger, reaction, misery and greed will become more rampant in the world unless we take our place [among the peace-loving nations] It is the responsibility of all citizens to defend the state. At the same time, it is the supreme duty of the State to defend its citizens [...], we wish it were

---

[163] IWM BLM 206/14: memorandum by Montgomery, CIGS/BM/31/2626, 12 September 1948.; see also IWM BLM 206/12: "Staff Conference with the Minister of Defence", note by Montgomery, 10 September 1948.

[164] During the debate of the National Service Bill, the main opposition came from the Labour backbenches; see Bullock, *Bevin*, 395.

[165] On this point, see the general warning of Laski, *Reflections*, 309.

[166] Even critics of the government's foreign policy agreed with this sentiment; for example, see Cole, *Intelligent Man's Guide*, 642 and 1027-8.

> possible to wander along in the world without arms, but the world being as it is, we must face the occasion as it is.[167]

Throughout the cold war, British governments and a majority of the electorate did their duty and supported the British defence effort with all its anachronisms. Indeed, to this day this discourse has lost some, but by no means all, of its original political potency. In contrast to its welfare state incarnation, the British warfare state has remained almost unquestioned as a "one nation" project arising from the people's war.[168]

---

[167] 437 H.C. DEB 5s., col. 2614.

[168] On the idea of "one nation" projects, see Bob Jessop, *State Theory: Putting Capitalist States in their Place* (University Park: Pennsylvania State University Press, 1990), 211-12.

Chapter 2

An antagonistic partnership: Britain and American economic assistance, 1945–50

In March 1950, the Foreign Secretary, Ernest Bevin, made one of his rare appearances in the House of Commons to defend his foreign policy during the debate of the Consolidated Funds Bill following the 1950 budget. Before he rose to speak, his Conservative opposite number, Anthony Eden, urged the Labour government to provide political leadership in western European affairs in an effort to resolve the German problem. Indeed, Eden went further arguing for the creation of a western European military force within the military organisation of the North Atlantic alliance.[1] Responding to Eden's speech, Bevin emphasised the degree of bipartisanship over foreign policy between the recently re-elected Labour government and the Conservative opposition. Despite the large areas of agreement, Bevin rejected the Conservative advocacy of a common western European army, because the limited military co-operation under the Brussels Treaty had convinced him that western Europe lacked the economic and military resources to successfully deter the Soviet threat in Europe. Moreover, Bevin reminded the Conservative front-bench that they would also reject any proposals for European integration which would infringe parliamentary sovereignty. Therefore, he argued that the best way forward lay in seeking an Atlantic partnership through wider integration within the North Atlantic Treaty Organisation (NATO). Indeed, he suggested that the forthcoming North Atlantic Council meeting scheduled for May would deepen military as well as politico-economic integration within the alliance and lead to a new relationship between Britain, Europe and the United States. He concluded by expressing his hope

> that before long, instead of aid from America in the way we have known and instead of pressure upon us to integrate, we shall evolve in such a way that wider integration will take place.

---

[1] House of Commons, *Official Report*, vol. 473, Parliamentary Debates (Hansard), Fifth Series (London: His Majesty's Stationery Office, 1950), (hereafter 473 H.C. Deb. 5s.) col. 316-18.

Given the "great power and potentiality of the West", if western statesmen were to succeed in their attempt to bring about this wider integration among western nations, then the improved military capability of the alliance would assure long-term peace in Europe and for Britain. However, Bevin stressed that by integration he meant "not so much union, [but] unity of spirit, unity of action and the comradeship between" the western nations.[2] Wider integration within the Atlantic alliance appealed to the British foreign policy-making community, because such a development would they hoped end Britain's status as just another recipient of American aid, but might allow for the revival of a special relationship with the United States within the western alliance.[3]

Implicitly, Bevin's statement acknowledged that the Labour government's attempts to restore Britain's position as a major independent power after 1945 had failed against their expectations.[4] As chapter 1 shows, it soon became obvious that Britain had emerged from the Second World War as the weakest of the three major powers vulnerable to pressure from both the Soviet Union and the United States. Aware of the country's vulnerability in the immediate post-war period, British defence and foreign policy-makers devoted their energies to regaining a certain degree of independence as an actor on the international stage. In order to achieve this objective, British policy-makers felt they had little choice but to approach the American government for financial assistance in autumn 1945, while maintaining Britain's global military presence. This dependency exposed the British government to considerable American pressure over an early return to convertibility and trade liberalisation. The reluctance of British policy-makers to agree to the American conditions originated from their concern that such a commitment would undermine their ability to pursue an independent economic policy to maintain domestic full employment. In their eyes, American officials misunderstood the severity of Britain's economic problems and the multilateral nature of the Sterling Area. However, British attempts to re-establish sterling as a major currency arguably undermined the working of the new international financial institutions created at Bretton Woods in the immediate post-war period.[5]

---

2 473 H.C. Deb. 5s., col. 318-30 (quotes: 330).

3 On this point, see also Alan Bullock, *Ernest Bevin: Foreign Secretary, 1945-51* (Oxford: Oxford University Press, 1985), 757-65.; Ritchie Ovendale, *The English-Speaking Alliance: Britain, the United States, the Dominions and the Cold War, 1945-51* (London: George Allen and Unwin, 1985), 284-5.

4 Anthony Clayton, "'Deceptive Might': Imperial Defence and Security, 1900-1968," in *The Oxford History of the British Empire, volume 4: The Twentieth Century*, eds. Judith M. Brown and Wm. Roger Louis (Oxford: Oxford University Press, 1999), 294-5.

5 Harold James, "The IMF and the Creation of the Bretton Woods System," in *Europe's Post-War Recovery*, ed. Barry Eichengreen (Cambridge: Cambridge University Press, 1995), 105-9.

Shaken by the failure of sterling convertibility in August 1947, the British government resisted American pressure for more far-reaching economic co-operation among the European recipients of Marshall aid. In spring 1948, British ministers undermined the attempts of American officials and other western European governments to endow the Organisation for European Economic Co-operation with real powers to co-ordinate western European economic recovery.[6] At the same time, Bevin initiated the creation of a military alliance between Britain, France and the Benelux countries in order to counter the growing Soviet threat in Europe. Some American observers initially perceived this move as a revitalisation of the European integration process started by the Marshall Plan initiative. However, they were sceptical about the request for military aid by the members of the newly formed Western Union.[7] While Bevin and British policy-makers continued to resent being treated as just another European country by the American aid administration, they hoped that by providing leadership in the area of European military co-operation they could obtain an American security guarantee for western Europe.[8] However, British military planners soon became disillusioned about the military capabilities of their western European allies.[9] As a consequence, British foreign policy-makers together with the Canadian government approached the Truman administration to widen the existing military arrangement between the western European nations to include the United States and Canada after the Communist putsch in Prague in February 1948.[10]

This indicates that while the Attlee government shared American objectives in creating a new liberal international economic order, it remained apprehensive that these new arrangements would force an early removal of economic controls thus endangering full employment at home. Despite resisting American pressure over foreign economic policy, British ministers sought military co-operation with the United States in the immediate post-war period. As this analysis shows, the British government tried to escape its dependency on American financial assistance and sought to rebuild its wartime partnership with the United States against the background of the emerging cold war in Europe. Indeed, a discussion paper for the Communist Party of Great Britain conference in October 1951 cited approvingly the historian, Palme

---

6 Alan S. Milward, *The Reconstruction of Western Europe, 1945-51* (London: Methuen, 1984), 168-95.

7 John H. Williams, *Economic Stability in a Changing World: Essays in economic theory and policy* (New York: Oxford University Press, 1953), 91-2.

8 John Baylis, *The Diplomacy of Pragmatism: Britain and the Formation of NATO, 1942-1949* (Basingstoke: Macmillan, 1993), 65-75.

9 Bernard L. Montgomery, *The Memoirs of Field-Marshal the Viscount Montgomery of Alamein, K.G.* (London: William Collins, Sons & Co., 1958), 499-503.

10 Baylis, *Diplomacy of pragmatism*, 92-7.

Dutt, who characterised the Anglo-American relationship as "one of subordination alongside conflict, of *antagonistic partnership*, with the US in the dominant position."[11] This chapter will analyse the antagonistic nature of the Anglo-American relationship in the immediate post-war period. The first section examines the contribution of American financial aid to Britain's economic recovery, the second section discusses the motivation of the Truman administration to extend financial and military assistance to Britain in the late 1940s. The final two sections assess the emergence of a renewed Atlantic partnership between the two countries in the first six months of 1950.

Britain and American economic assistance, 1945–50

As chapter 1 showed, Britain emerged from the Second World War as the weakest of the three remaining major powers. Indeed, its war-making capabilities continued to decline compared to the United States and the Soviet Union. That analysis underlined that in terms of economic power, the United States had acquired a predominant position due to the massive expansion of its economy during the Second World War. In contrast, British economic output increased only marginally during the Second World War and fell below its 1940 level for the last years of the war.[12] While the volume of imports decreased by roughly a quarter during the war, Britain had reduced her exports to 30 per cent of their prewar total.[13] In the absence of sufficient export earnings, the British government had been forced to sell a major proportion of British overseas assets to finance its war effort. At the same time, the government borrowed heavily from her dominions and colonies to sustain its fight against the Axis powers.[14] As a consequence of this massive borrowing, Britain had become financially dependent on the United States, India and its colonies by 1941 or 1942.[15] This financial dependency left the newly elected Attlee government with the monumental task of securing additional external financial assistance to finance the country's reconstruction. Indeed, Lord

11 John Rylands University Library Manchester (hereafter JRULM), Records of the British Communist Party (hereafter: CP), JRULM CP/CENT/ECON/1/2: "New Features of Imperialism after the Second World War", discussion paper for conference, 6 October 1951. (italics in the original).

12 Mark Harrison, "Resource Mobilisation for World War II: the U.S.A., U.K., U.S.S.R. and Germany, 1939-1945," *Economic History Review* 41 (1988): 189, Table 4.

13 Central Statistical Office, *Fighting with Figures: A Statistical Digest of the Second World War* (London: Her Majesty's Stationery Office, 1995), 207, Table 9.4.

14 Central Statistical Office, *Fighting with figures*, 225, Table 10.8.

15 William Roger Louis, "American anti-colonialism and the dissolution of the British Empire," *International Affairs* 61 (1985): 402-3.

Keynes and the Treasury warned that the country faced a "financial Dunkirk" unless it could obtain such financial assistance.[16] Nevertheless, the British foreign policy-making community assumed that the British economy would recover "a dominating place in the economic world" after a short period of transition.[17] While being aware of the country's vulnerability in the immediate post-war period, British defence and foreign policy-makers devoted their energies to re-establishing Britain as a major power and thereby regaining a certain degree of independence as an actor on the international stage. In order to achieve this objective, British policy-makers felt they had little choice but to maintain Britain's global military presence and therefore had to approach the American government for financial assistance in autumn 1945.

However, this financial dependency allowed the American government to use its economic power in order to ensure British co-operation in creating the new international economic order the American government envisaged. When deciding to approach the Truman administration in the autumn of 1945 for additional financial assistance, Keynes and the newly elected Labour ministers hoped the American government could be persuaded to offer Britain a large grant or at least an interest free loan. Much to the dismay of the British delegation, American negotiators only held out a loan of 4 billion dollars at 2 per cent interest tied to a string of political conditions including early convertibility of sterling, co-sponsoring an international trade conference, and ending the discrimination of dollar imports.[18] These conditions prompted Otto Clarke, a civil servant in the Treasury's Overseas Finance Division, to denounce the Anglo-American loan agreement as a de facto sell-out:

> Our right to be bilateral, to exploit our buying power and debtor position to expand our exports, would have been well sold for $5 billion grant in cash. But not for $4 billion at 2% interest.[19]

His sentiments were shared by many cabinet ministers including the Minister of Health and the government's leading left-winger, Aneurin Bevan. After

---

[16] Roger John Bullen and M. E. Pelley, eds., *Documents on British Policy Overseas, series 1, volume 3: Britain and America: Negotiations of the United States loan, 3 August - 7 December 1945* (London: Her Majesty's Stationery Office, 1986). (hereafter DBPO 1iii), 27-37: note by Mr. Dalton, 14 August 1945.

[17] PRO FO 371/45694: "Effect of Britain's External Financial Position on Foreign Policy", 9 February 1945., as cited by Jim Tomlinson, "The Attlee Government and the Balance of Payments, 1945-1951," *Twentieth Century British History* 2 (1991): 55. See also Clayton, "Deceptive might," 294-5.

[18] Alec Cairncross, *Years of Recovery: British Economic Policy, 1945-51* (London: Methuen, 1985), 100-109.

[19] "The Loan Negotiations in Washington", minute by R. W. B. Clarke, 23 October 1945; reprinted in: Richard Clarke, *Anglo-American Economic Collaboration in War and Peace, 1942-1949*, ed. Alec Cairncross (Oxford: Clarendon Press, 1982), 137-9.

some wrangling, both governments agreed a slightly smaller loan of $3.75 billion, but largely on the terms of the American government.[20]

Given the strong reservations of many British policy-makers and parliamentarians, it remains surprising that the Attlee government accepted these stringent terms.[21] To some extent, the conditions imposed in the Anglo-American loan agreement reflected commitments entered into by the wartime coalition government under the Atlantic charter and Article VII of the Mutual Aid Agreement. However, these commitments had been made at a time when Britain's survival depended on American material and financial assistance and therefore the British government was hardly in a position to refuse. While the conditions seemed incompatible with Labour's commitment to economic planning, Keynes persuaded key Labour politicians, following the initial wartime discussion of a new post-war international economic order, that Britain would benefit from a multilateral trade regime after the war.[22] Despite some misgivings, the Attlee government reluctantly agreed to the conditions tied to the American $3,750 million loan, because the majority of ministers accepted the judgement of Keynes and other Treasury officials that a trading bloc based on the Sterling Area would not prove a viable alternative as long as British industry could not satisfy the penned-up import demand of other countries.[23] Indeed, internal contingency plans showed that Britain could have financed essential imports out of its remaining reserves provided that overseas military expenditures had been pared to the bone. According to the British chief negotiator, Lord Keynes, this analysis demonstrated that "... the American loan is primarily required to meet the political and military expenditure overseas."[24] However, the implications of such radical cuts proved politically unacceptable to a majority of British policy-makers. In their eyes, Britain's home strength derived to a significant degree from the Empire. Moreover, as one of the victorious powers, ministers believed Britain should play a constructive role in the post-war settlement. The loan seemed the only way to (re)assert Britain's rightful place as a major power.[25]

---

[20] Cairncross, *Years of recovery*, 109-12.

[21] On this debate, see Cairncross, *Years of recovery*, 108-11.; but also Wilfried Loth, *Die Teilung der Welt: Die Geschichte des Kalten Kriegs, 1941-1955*, 7th rev. ed. (München: Deutscher Taschenbuch Verlag, 1989), 38-41.

[22] Richard Toye, "The Labour Party's External Economic Policy in the 1940s," *The Historical Journal* 43 (2000): 189-215.

[23] DBPO 1iii, 27-37: note by Mr. Dalton, 14 August 1945. See also Cairncross, *Years of recovery*, 90-93.

[24] "If Congress rejects the Loan", minute Keynes - Clarke, 22 February 1946; reprinted in Clarke, *Anglo-American economic collaboration*, 151-2 (quote: 152).

[25] Bullock, *Bevin*, 121-6.; Tomlinson, "Balance of payments," 50-58. On this point, see also the analysis in chapter 1.

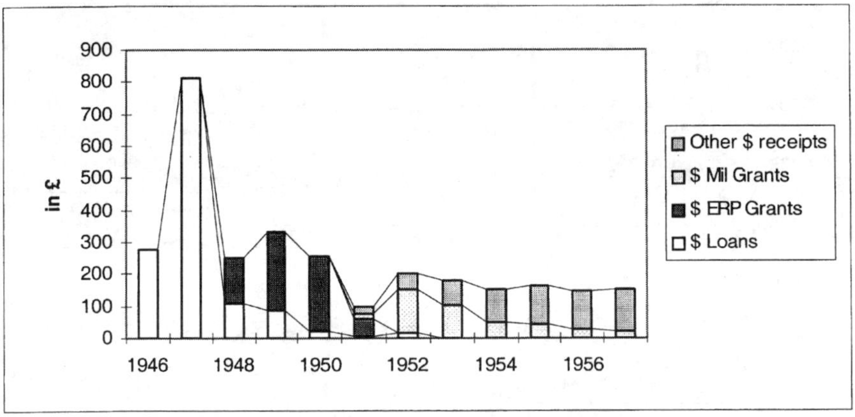

Graph 2.1: Special Dollar Receipts from Government Loans, Grants and Other Receipts, 1946–57

Notes: *$ Loans*: United States and Canadian governments loans; *$ ERP Grants*: United States government grants under the European Recovery Program; *$ Mil Grants*: United States government grants under the Mutual Security Program; *Other $ receipts*: Expenditures by American and Canadian military forces stationed in Britain and Offshore Procurement contracts by the United States government

Source: Treasury, *United Kingdom Balance of Payments, 1946-1957* (London: Her Majesty's Stationery Office, 1959), 54, Table 15.

If the American loan (and a smaller Canadian loan) are placed in the wider context of American financial assistance in the immediate post-war period, it becomes obvious that these loans far exceeded grants and material assistance provided to Britain under the European Recovery Program and Mutual Security Program (see Graph 2.1). In order to assess the relative importance of American financial assistance, these dollar receipts have to be set in relation to the three crucial aspects of economic development: gross domestic capital formation, British overseas government expenditures, and the balance of current payments with the dollar area. As Graph 2.2 shows, the American and Canadian loans and financial assistance financed British overseas government expenditure between 1947 and 1950. If only overseas military expenditures are taken into account, foreign financial assistance covered these expenditures for the period 1947 to 1955 except during the economic crisis in 1951. Therefore, the criticisms of high overseas military expenditure ignore to some extent the fact that in 1946 most overseas military expenditures arose as a direct consequence of the Second World War and were thus unavoidable. The overall increase in overseas government expenditure reflected substantial increases in

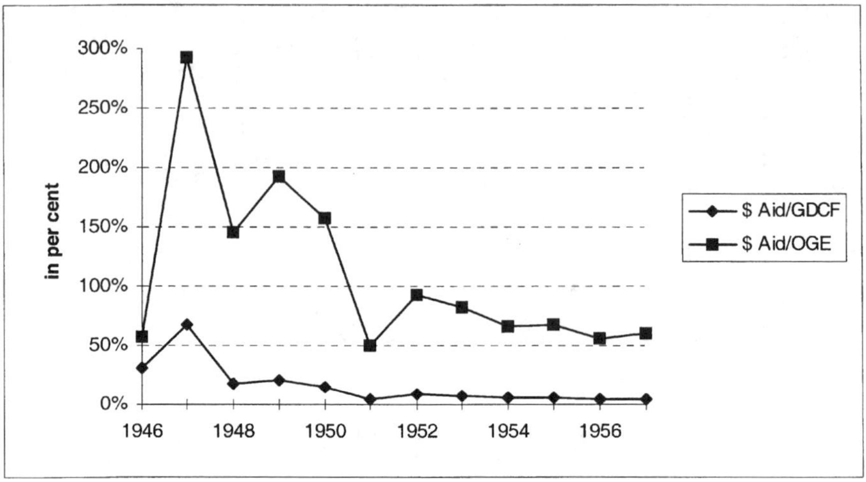

Graph 2.2: The Relative Importance of Dollar Loans and Grants to Britain, 1946–57

Notes: *$ Aid*: total special dollar receipts from the American and Canadian governments; *GDCF*: Gross Domestic Capital Formation; *OGE*: Overseas Government Expenditure by the British government.

Sources: *$ Aid* and *OGE*: Treasury, *United Kingdom Balance of Payments, 1946-1957* (London: Her Majesty's Stationery Office, 1959), 54, Table 15 and 50, Table 14.; *GDCF*: Central Statistical Office, *National Income and Expenditure 1968* (London: Her Majesty's Stationery Office, 1968), 2–3, Table 1.

grants to colonies and for the diplomatic service.[26] At the same time, the American loan funds amounted to over 60 per cent of British gross domestic capital formation in 1947. In terms of overall investment, Marshall aid proved much less important than the American loan during the previous year. However, as Cairncross has shown, a considerable proportion of available funds for investment was actually invested overseas primarily in the dominions in order to re-establish sterling as a major international currency.[27] Moreover, the special dollar receipts contribute to economic reconstruction by financing the import of food and machinery from the United States. In Graph 2.3, each line represents the contribution which American financial assistance made to the British balance of payments; the lower point of each line represents the current balance of payments[28] with the dollar area and the upper data point indicates the improvement after taking into account the financial assistance

[26] Treasury, *United Kingdom Balance of Payments, 1946-1957* (London: Her Majesty's Stationery Office, 1959), 50, Table 14.

[27] Cairncross, *Years of recovery*, 152-64.

[28] The current balance of payments includes the balance of trade and current payments, but excludes capital movements.

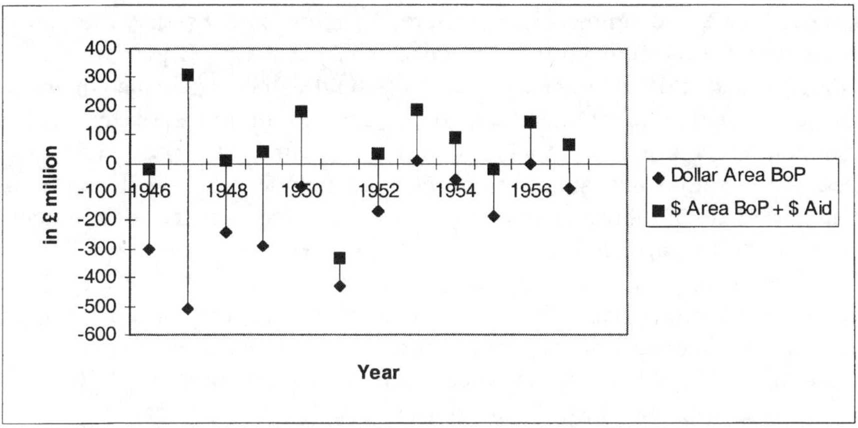

Graph 2.3: Special Dollar Receipts and the Dollar Gap, 1946–57

Notes: *$ Aid*: total special dollar receipts from the American and Canadian governments; *Dollar Area BoP*: Current Balance of Payments with the Dollar Area.

Sources: Treasury, *United Kingdom Balance of Payments, 1946-1957* (London: Her Majesty's Stationery Office, 1959), 54, Table 15 and 22, Table 4.

from the United States and Canada. Since most of the upper data points are above the line, this demonstrates that American and Canadian financial assistance for the most part closed Britain's dollar gap in the immediate post-war period. Again, the crisis year of 1951 is the only exception.[29]

Between 1945 and 1947, the American loan therefore allowed the Attlee government not only to pursue domestic reconstruction, but also to re-establish its position as a major power. Most importantly, the loan paid for British imports of food and machinery from the United States during 1946 and 1947. Subconsciously, British policy-makers appear to have assumed that the American government would provide further financial assistance once the loan ran out.[30] As Graph 2.2 shows, British overseas government expenditures did not absorb all financial assistance in the immediate post-war period. While remaining a major burden, Britain's military presence abroad did not represent an unbearable load on the British economy.[31] At the same time, Britain continued to increase the substantial debts it owed to its colonies.[32] Without its

[29] The economic crisis of 1951 is examined in more detail in chapter 9.

[30] Milward, *Reconstruction*, 47-55.

[31] For such claims, see Andrew Shonfield, *British Economic Policy since the War* (Harmondsworth: Penguin, 1958), 104-7.; W. A. P. Manser, *Britain in Balance: The Myth of Failure* (Harmondsworth: Penguin, 1973), 30-36.

[32] Thomas Balogh, "The International Aspect," in *The British Economy, 1945-1950*, eds. G. D. N. Worswick and P. H. Ady (Oxford: Oxford University Press, 1952), 482-3 and 481, Table 2.

massive overseas government expenditure, Britain could not have obtained such additional finance from its dependencies. By allowing Britain to sustain its Empire and this additional source of funds, the American financial assistance provided more than the crucial margin in terms of the Attlee government's reconstruction policies during the first two post-war years. Indeed, the government managed to balance the economic cost of its domestic welfare reforms with those arising from its world-wide military commitments in the years following 1945. Through good macro-economic management, the Attlee government almost succeeded in its attempts to stabilise the economy on the eve of the Korean war.[33] Despite its relative success, the question remains whether or not spending so much of Britain's limited economic resources on maintaining a large military presence overseas merely postponed Britain's eventual loss of its status as a major power.[34] As this analysis has shown, the economic crisis of 1951 revealed the frailty of this strategy. When American financial assistance failed to materialise, Britain's economic position became unsustainable leaving the government the option of cutting either social welfare expenditure or the rearmament programme.

If the American loan merely postponed the decline of Britain as a major power, what alternative policy could the Attlee government have pursued? Some British politicians, such as the Conservative politician and wartime minister, Leo Amery, advocated robust independence by forming an economic bloc based on the sterling area.[35] However, Keynes warned that such bilateralism would disrupt the recovery of export trade and the operation of the sterling area. Indeed, the advocates of an independent British economic bloc may have deluded themselves about the willingness of other Commonwealth and European countries to adopt the type of common austerity programme that such a course would have required. In many ways the appeal of the sterling area to member states lay primarily in the access to the London capital market and the dollar pool which it afforded. Moreover, the alternative regime would have relied heavily on state trading and bulk purchasing, but such policies would not been attractive to other sterling area countries. For example, the Irish government in this period constantly complained about the low prices the Ministry of Food was prepared to pay for Irish agricultural exports.[36] While

[33] Alec Cairncross, *The British Economy since 1945* (Oxford: Blackwell, 1992), 85-6.

[34] Balogh, "The International Aspect," 480.; Clarke, *Anglo-American economic collaboration*, 70.

[35] John Barnes and David Nicholson, eds., *The Empire at Bay: The Leo Amery Diaries, 1929-1945* (London: Hutchinson, 1988), 1051-3.

[36] Till Geiger, "Why Ireland needed the Marshall Plan but did not want it: Ireland, the Sterling Area and the European Recovery Program, 1947-1948," *Irish Studies in International Affairs* 11 (2000): 205-6.

British bulk-purchasing stimulated Canadian exports of primary products[37], the Canadian government insisted that the British government paid for at least half of its agricultural imports from Canada in transferable sterling rather than drawing on the Canadian loan. This Canadian position reflected the fact that the United States had displaced Britain as the hegemonic economic power in Canada in the first half of the twentieth century.[38] The limited flow of hard currency allowed the Canadian government to stave off the country's developing a dollar shortage. Given Canada's growing integration in the American market, the inconvertibility of sterling and other European currencies severely restricted the ability of Canada to finance vital imports from south of the border.[39] The other alternative would have been to radically reduce overseas military expenditure and withdraw from many parts of the colonial empire in order to rebuild the economy.[40] However, all these alternative policies would have required a small loan on commercial terms from American banks. The question is whether such a loan would have been forthcoming on the scale required to kick-start the economy.[41] Even though the withdrawal from overseas bases and rapid demobilisation would have released much needed manpower for the government's reconstruction effort, many on the left of the Labour Party rejected such a step at the time.[42] Moreover, if Britain had adopted a neutralist foreign policy, it is unlikely, as the next section shows, that the United Kingdom would have received the American loan in 1946 and financial assistance during later economic crises.[43]

The strategic dimension of American financial support for the British socialist project, 1945-48

For the American government, the British loan represented the opportunity costs of advancing its vision of a multilateral international economic order.

---

[37] Tim Rooth, "Britain's Other Dollar Problem: Economic Relations with Canada, 1945-50," *Journal of Imperial and Commonwealth History* 27 (January, 1999): 86.

[38] Harold Adams Innes, "Great Britain, the United States and Canada," in *Essays in Canadian Economic History* (Toronto: Toronto University Press, 1956), 404-12.

[39] Rooth, "Britain's other dollar problem," 83-92.

[40] Balogh, "The International Aspect," 480.

[41] Cairncross, *Years of recovery*, 109-13.

[42] Bullock, *Bevin*, 125-8.

[43] Clayton, "Deceptive might," 294-5. For example, American military planners pressed for additional financial aid for Britain during the devaluation crisis of 1949; see National Archives and Record Administration, Washington (hereafter: NARA), Record Group (hereafter: RG) NARA RG 218. Box 19: Memorandum Ohly - Gruenther, "Need for an Assessment of the Full Implications to American Security of the Current British Dollar Crisis", 1 September 1949.

When the Anglo-American loan agreement reached Capitol Hill, many American legislators opposed the agreement, because they felt the money would be squandered on the establishment of a British welfare state and on bailing out the Empire. As the Labour government's socialist agenda was seen as a major obstacle to a speedy recovery, final acceptance of the Anglo-American loan agreement reflected the fact that many American observers continued to regard Britain as a valuable partner in their attempt to secure a liberal world order.[44] While Anglo-American military co-operation had been reduced to informal contacts in the immediate post-war period, American military planners continued to assume the availability of British bases throughout the Empire in the event of another global war.[45] This implicit reliance on British military power led to tensions between the two governments, because American policy-makers over-estimated Britain's economic capabilities to sustain its continued military presence in western Europe, the Mediterranean and the Middle East.[46] The economic burden of these military commitments threatened economic viability in early 1947. When the Attlee government turned to the United States threatening to withdraw from Greece, the Truman administration hurriedly announced a $400 million aid programme for Greece and Turkey in order to contain the Soviet threat in Europe.[47]

Opposing the economic rationale of the Marshall Plan, American military planners argued that economic assistance should be distributed according to the relative importance of a given country to American national security rather than solely according to economic need. Given the limits of American military, political and economic power around the world, a strong stabilised western Europe enhanced the military capabilities of the United States for containing

---

[44] Robert A. Pollard, *Economic Security and the Origins of the Cold War, 1945-1950* (New York: Columbia University Press, 1985), 66-73.; Melvyn P. Leffler, *A Preponderance of Power: National security, the Truman administration, and the cold war* (Stanford: Stanford University Press, 1992), 61-3.

[45] Elizabeth Barker, *Britain between the Superpowers* (Basingstoke: Macmillan, 1983), 54-5.; Eisenhower - Ismay, 28 December 1946, reprinted in: L. Galambos, ed., *The Papers of Dwight David Eisenhower: The Chief of Staff* (Baltimore: Johns Hopkins University Press, 1978), volume 7, 1344-5. On the strategic importance of Britain in American war plans, see JCS 1725/1, "Strategic Guidance for Industrial Mobilisation Planning", 1 May 1947, reprinted in: Thomas H. Etzold and John Lewis Gaddis, eds., *Containment: Documents on American policy and strategy, 1945-1950* (New York: Columbia University Press, 1978), 302-11. At one point during the Anglo-American loan negotiations, American officials tried to obtain base rights in Britain and on British overseas bases in return for the loan; see DBPO 1iv (1945-46), 319-21: Bevin - Balfour, 29 May 1946.

[46] Leffler, *Preponderance of power*, 62.

[47] Pollard, *Economic security*, 114-32.

the Soviet Union.[48] After the convertibility crisis of 1947, the Attlee government further reduced defence expenditures in the 1947 autumn budget making an American security guarantee increasingly essential for British defence plans.[49] After the Czech coup and the Berlin crisis of 1948, British foreign policy-makers redoubled their efforts to entangle the United States in a defensive alliance.[50] As a first step, Foreign Secretary Ernest Bevin pushed for the creation of a western European alliance. After signing the Brussels Treaty, Britain committed itself to providing half the additional forces of the Western Union's military expansion programme in the hope of receiving American military assistance.[51] British policy-makers entered the additional defence commitment in order to obtain a lasting American security guarantee for the defence of western Europe. This continental commitment represented the opportunity costs Britain incurred in achieving the North Atlantic Treaty.

After the formation of the Brussels Pact, American policy-makers insisted that reconstruction should take priority over rearmament, because only economic stability could create a sound basis for military defence in the long run.[52] American policy-makers feared that rather than improving their defensive capabilities, Brussels Pact countries would use military aid to regain their colonial empires as the French government did in Indochina.[53] To limit such abuse, Brussels Pact countries received military assistance grants in the form of American surplus equipment or end-items subject to the condition that

---

[48] Based on a combination of both criteria, the Joint Chiefs of Staff put forward the following list in order of priority for financial assistance: Great Britain, France, Germany, Italy, Greece, Turkey, Austria, Japan, Belgium, Netherlands, ...; see JCS 1769/1, "United States assistance to other countries from the standpoint of national security", 29 April 1947, reprinted in: Etzold and Gaddis, eds., *Containment*, 71-83.

[49] At the time, the Chancellor, Hugh Dalton, pressed for significant cuts in defence expenditures; see his diary entries for mid-September, 18 September, 20 September and 2 October 1947, reprinted in: Ben Pimlott, ed., *The Political Diary of Hugh Dalton, 1918-40, 1945-60* (London: Jonathan Cape, 1986), 412-15. Even before the convertibility crisis of the summer, the British Chiefs of Staff considered obtaining American and western European assistance essential; see DO(47)44, 'Future Defence Policy', report by the Chiefs of Staff, 22 May 1947, reprinted in J. Lewis, *Changing Direction: British military planning for post-war strategic defence, 1942-1947* (London: Sherwood Press, 1988), 370-87.

[50] Baylis, *Diplomacy of pragmatism*, 67-75.

[51] Lawrence Kaplan, *A Community of Interests: NATO and the Military Assistance Program, 1948-1951* (Washington: Government Printing Office, 1980), 16-34.; Bert Zeeman, "Der Brüsseler Pakt und die Diskussion um einen westdeutschen Militärbeitrag," in *Vom Marshallplan zur EWG: Die Eingliederung der Bundesrepublik Deutschland in die westliche Welt*, eds. Ludolf Herbst, Werner Bührer, and Hanno Sowade (München: R. Oldenbourg, 1990), 411-16.

[52] Pollard, *Economic security*, 223-8.

[53] Ronald H. Spector, *Advice and Support: The Early Years of the U.S. Army in Vietnam, 1941-1960* (New York: Free Press, 1985), 97-104.; Lloyd C. Gardner, *Approaching Vietnam: From World War II through Dienbienphu* (New York: W. W. Norton, 1988), 66-87.

recipient countries could not transfer end-items to other countries or use such weaponry outside NATO without the consent of the American government. To administer and monitor military assistance, the American government approached recipient governments about establishing Military Assistance Advisory Groups (MAAG) in their countries.[54] When the American government presented a draft bilateral agreement to all North Atlantic Treaty signatories in November 1949, the British government initially objected to some of the proposed conditions for military aid. Given the rather secretive attitude of Whitehall, British officials resisted the American demand for extensive detailed information about British defence programmes in return for minimal assistance for the British defence effort. Another stumbling bloc that developed was the British position that the country could not afford to increase defence production without more substantial assistance from the United States. Worried by such views, American negotiators raised these issues with senior Foreign Office officials. After this intervention, the outstanding problems were resolved and a bilateral agreement was signed removing the last obstacle for the creation of the MAAG in Britain.[55] As this episode shows, by the late 1940s, the paramount consideration of British foreign policy had become ensuring, if necessary at considerable opportunity cost, a continued American contribution to the defence of western Europe.

During the 1950 fiscal year, American military assistance officials planned to deliver seventy B-29 bombers for the Royal Air Force.[56] In addition to this end-item aid, MAAG supported an array of additional military production (AMP) projects to finance the purchase of machinery and raw materials vital to British defence production.[57] Before approving an AMP project, MAAG scrutinised each application carefully. As part of this process, members of the MAAG would visit factories regularly to assess whether or not the requested equipment or raw materials contributed to an expansion of defence

---

[54] Till Geiger and Lorenza Sebesta, "National Defense Policies and the Failure of Military Integration in NATO: American Military Assistance and Western European Rearmament, 1949-54," in *The United States and the Integration of Europe: Legacies for the Postwar Era*, eds. Francis H. Heller and John R. Gillingham (New York: St. Martin's Press, 1996), 256-7.

[55] NARA RG 59. Box 3530: 741.5-MAP/1-1850: telegram, Holmes - Secretary of State, 18 January 1950.; NARA RG 59. Box 3530: 741.5-MAP/3-2950: despatch Bruins - Department of State for MAP, 29 March 1950.; see also William Adams Brown, Jr. and Redvers Opie, *American Foreign Assistance* (Washington: Brookings Institution, 1953), 478-81.

[56] The 1950 fiscal year refers to the American fiscal year: 1 July 1949 - 31 June 1950.

[57] NARA RG 59. Box 3530: 741.5-MAP/5-1150: telegram Douglas - Secretary of State (for MAP), 11 May 1950.

production.[58] Despite British reluctance to accept military aid, the Truman administration argued that British participation was politically vital for the success of the Mutual Defense Assistance Program (MDAP).[59] After the American military assistance programme for Britain had been announced, British officials did not hide their disappointment at only receiving seventy B-29 bombers rather than more financial assistance through AMP projects.[60] In making such a small allocation, American policy-makers rejected the British position that the over-stretched British economy could not support a further increase of the defence production. In British eyes, American policy-makers failed to appreciate that Britain already contributed more than its fair share to the western defence effort.[61] Many British officials felt misled over military assistance by the vague promises of their American counterparts. Despite this initial indignation, British participation in the Mutual Defense Assistance Program paved the way for a deeper American involvement in the defence of western Europe.

NATO Reform, the European Payments Union and the Schuman Plan, May 1950 [62]

As this analysis suggests, the over-riding priority of entangling the United States in the defence of western Europe permeated foreign policy decisions including those of an economic nature. In the late 1940s, American foreign policy-makers hoped Britain would play a more active leadership role in Europe. This American stance annoyed those British ministers who were convinced that Britain presented a special case due to its links to the Commonwealth and its military interests outside western Europe. To some extent, American policy-makers did assuage Britain's aspirations for a privileged status within the Alliance. However, American indulgence on this

---

[58] NARA RG 59. Box 3530: 741.5-MAP/3-3150: MAAG-UK Progress Report, despatch Bruins - Department of State for FMACC, 31 March 1950.

[59] NARA RG 319. Box 96: ORS 091 Gr. Britain (5 May 1950), Position Papers for the FY1951 MDAP (Current Situation in the United Kingdom and the Relationship to MDAP) (FMACC D-16/1), 5 May 1950.

[60] NARA NARA RG 59. Box 3530: 741.5-MAP/7-750: Political report on development of the MDAP program in the United Kingdom, despatch Bruins - Department of State for MAP, 7 July 1950.7 July 1950.

[61] Diary entries, 27, 28 April and 26 May 1950, reprinted in Alec Cairncross, ed., *The Robert Hall Diaries, 1947-53* (London: Unwin Hyman, 1989), 111-12 and 114-15.

[62] I am grateful to Richard Toye for letting me draw on our joint work on Britain's decision to join the European Payments Union for this section.

occasion masked the latent conflict between two different visions and cultures regarding western defence and European integration.[63]

In the spring of 1950, the Foreign Office hoped to convince American officials of the advantages of an Anglo-American special relationship, potentially also comprising Canada, within the framework of the North Atlantic Treaty. Through this type of close working relationship, British policy-makers hoped that the combined pressure of an Anglo-Saxon troika would induce the western European member states of the Alliance to increase their defence efforts. During their preliminary discussions, American diplomats initially agreed to formalise a special relationship of this nature with their British counterparts. When the American Secretary of State, Dean Acheson, learned about it he insisted that all evidence of this Machiavellian arrangement be destroyed.[64] Despite this note of discord, these discussions revealed that both American and British policy-makers regarded western rearmament as a growing priority.[65]

For some analysts, this emerging consensus on western rearmament ended the process of (re-)negotiating the post-war Anglo-American relationship.[66] However, the apparent consensus masked crucial differences in their respective positions. Having been concerned about western military weakness for years, British officials welcomed the change in the American position expecting that the Truman administration would assume a larger share of the defence burden thus allowing Britain to reduce its defence effort. Across the Atlantic, American national security policy-makers became increasingly concerned about the perceived gap between the growing Soviet military potential and the failure of the West to keep pace with this expansion.[67] While the American side pressed for an expansion of western European defence efforts, the British government remained equally interested in the equitable distribution of the defence burden.[68] Despite these different objectives, both governments favoured the reform of NATO institutions and decision-making mechanisms to

---

[63] Michael J. Hogan, *The Marshall Plan: America, Britain, and the reconstruction of Western Europe* (Cambridge: Cambridge University Press, 1987), 274-9.

[64] Dean Acheson, *Present at the Creation: My Years in the State Department* (New York: W. W. Norton and Company, 1969), 387-8.

[65] DBPO 2ii (1950), 267-76: Record of the First Bipartite Ministerial Meeting held in the Foreign Office on 9 May 1950 at 11.30 a.m.; Notes on a Conversation after Lunch at 1 Carlton Gardens on 9 May 1950.

[66] Robin Edmonds, *Setting the Mould: The United States and Britain, 1945-1950* (Oxford: Clarendon Press, 1986), 203-5.

[67] John Lewis Gaddis, *Strategies of Containment: A critical appraisal of post-war American national security policy* (New York: Oxford University Press, 1982), 89-109.

[68] Peter Foot, "Defence Burden-Sharing in the Atlantic Community, 1945-1954," (Aberdeen Centre for Defence Economics: Aberdeen Studies in Defence Economics, 1981).

ensure the implementation of the Medium Term Defence Plan (MTDP), which the alliance's Military Committee approved in April 1950.

During the discussions in the spring of 1950, one remaining contentious issue between British and American policy-makers concerned the negotiations about the creation of the European Payments Union (EPU). Throughout the spring, the head of the Economic Cooperation Administration (ECA), Paul Hoffman and his staff pressurised the British government to join this scheme. To prepare the ground for a stronger American commitment to the defence of western Europe, Bevin stressed to the cabinet that the Americans wanted the British "... to give more of a lead in Europe, particularly in such matters as the ..." EPU.[69] On the eve of Acheson's arrival, the Chancellor, Stafford Cripps, indicated that the negotiations for an EPU agreement were proceeding well and therefore this issue should not be an obstacle to an agreement with the Americans on Atlantic security.[70] To some extent, the British decision to join the EPU has to be seen in the historical context of the on-going negotiations to strengthen military and economic co-operation within the Alliance. Despite seemingly irreconcilable differences between the ECA and the British Treasury, the newly re-elected Labour government stressed its determination to conclude an agreement on a new European payments arrangements.[71] Not only Bevin, but also the Chancellor, Stafford Cripps, acknowledged that the failure to conclude a new European payments agreement would cause a major rift in Anglo-American relations potentially undermining western defence co-operation.[72]

Due to Cripps' deteriorating health, the Minister of State for Economic Affairs, Hugh Gaitskell, assumed responsibility for the last stages of the negotiations in March 1950. Firmly opposed to convertibility, he remained rather apprehensive that the American proposals for a multilateral clearing union would mark the return to the gold standard. Therefore, it is rather surprising that he went on to negotiate Britain's entry into the European Payments Union successfully paving the way for the limited liberalisation of

[69] DBPO 2ii (1950), 203-6 (quote: 204): C.P. (50) 92, "Conversations with United States and French Officials", memorandum by the Secretary of State for Foreign Affairs, 2 May 1950.

[70] DBPO 2ii (1950), 301-3: Note of an Informal meeting of Ministers held at 1 Carlton Gardens on Thursday, 11 May 1950, at 9.30 a.m.; DBPO 2ii (1950), 352-4: Note of an Informal meeting of Ministers held at 1 Carlton Gardens on Thursday, 15 May 1950, at 9.45 a.m.

[71] 472 H.C. Deb. 5s., col. 37-40.

[72] At a crucial point in the negotiations of the second Intra-European Payments Agreement in summer 1949, Cripps stated "with a touch of exaggeration, that failure in these circumstances would mean the end of European cooperation in the OEEC, but also in the Western European Union and the Atlantic Alliance"; see Robert Marjolin, *Architect of European Unity: Memoirs, 1911-1986* (London: Weidenfeld and Nicolson, 1989), 218-20.

European payments and thereby for the de facto restricted convertibility of European currencies.[73] A newcomer to the European stage, Gaitskell found much to his surprise that leading ECA officials, particularly Harriman's deputy, Milton Katz, thought along similar lines to himself on the issue of international convertibility. In order to break the ice between the two sides, the British Representative at the Organisation for European Economic Co-operation (OEEC), Edmund Hall-Patch arranged a first meeting between Gaitskell, Harriman and Katz before a dinner party he gave in Paris in March 1950. During the dinner, the Secretary General of the OEEC, Robert Marjolin, persuaded Gaitskell that most European governments resented Britain's attempts to maximise its economic power in western Europe by discriminating against them through its bilateral payments agreements.[74] While these dinner conversations broke the ice, American foreign policy-makers remained disappointed by the lack of progress in reaching a final agreement. In order to put pressure on the British government, Acheson presented an aide-memoire to Bevin stressing the vital importance the Truman administration attached to successful conclusion of an EPU agreement.[75] Eager to secure a far-reaching American commitment to Western defence, the Attlee government informed the Americans during their discussions in May of their willingness in principle to join the EPU subject to an agreement about additional financial aid. In June, the Katz-Gaitskell Agreement removed the last outstanding hurdles to British membership.[76]

The link between these two issues is underlined by the obvious difference in the case of the third major proposal for Western co-operation which coincided with the North Atlantic Council meeting in May 1950, the Schuman Plan. The French foreign minister, Robert Schuman, announced his famous proposals for

---

[73] Philip Maynard Williams, *Hugh Gaitskell: a political biography* (London: Jonathan Cape, 1979), 218-21.; Scott Kelly, "Ministers Matter: Gaitskell and Butler at odds over convertibility, 1950-52," *British Contemporary History* 14 (2000): 27-53. In their seminal account, Kaplan and Schleiminger claim that Gaitskell continued as late as June 1950 to see the EPU proposals as a return to the gold standard; see Jacob Kaplan and Günther Schleiminger, *The European Payments Union: Financial Diplomacy in the 1950s* (Oxford: Clarendon Press, 1989), 77. However, a closer reading of the records suggests that Gaitskell confronted Katz with this reason for the British reluctance to join the EPU during their initial meeting in March; see Till Geiger and Richard Toye, "Britain, America and the origins of the European Payments Union: A reassessment," (unpublished manuscript, 2003).

[74] Document 6: "Paris dinner on E.P.U., 25.3.50", 27 March 1950, and diary entries, 26 May (continued) and 11 August 1950; reprinted in: Philip M. Williams, ed., *The Diary of Hugh Gaitskell, 1945-1956* (London: Jonathan Cape, 1983), 178-82, 185-7 and 189-91. See also, Williams, *Hugh Gaitskell*, 221-2.

[75] Department of State, ed., *Foreign Relations of the United States, 1950, volume iii: Western Europe* (Washington: Government Printing Office, 1977), (hereafter: FRUS (1950) iii), 655-7.: Acheson - Bevin, 11 May 1950.

[76] Williams, *Hugh Gaitskell*, 222-4.

a European Coal and Steel Community on the day of Acheson's arrival in London. Having been sworn to secrecy, Acheson felt unable to tell his hosts about the immanent French initiative. Taken by surprise, Bevin reacted with extreme annoyance that the French foreign minister had not given him any advance notice of his proposals. In his memoirs, Acheson speculates whether the British reaction might have been different, if Schuman had "... authorised (him) to run what risks there were in trying to persuade Bevin and Attlee to give the plan their support."[77] While Americans welcomed Schuman's initiative as a historic step towards European integration, Labour politicians opposed to subjugating the British economy to a supranational authority ruled out British membership. Such opposition, however, did not undermine Anglo-American co-operation, because American foreign policy-makers needed British support for their plans to strengthen the North Atlantic alliance. The British response to the Schuman Plan forced the Americans to assume a neutral position on the unfolding dispute between its two major European allies.

As presented by the Attlee government, the Schuman Plan proposals demanded an unacceptable abrogation of national sovereignty.[78] However, the Attlee government did indicate its willingness to make some concessions in this regard on the issue of military defence. As one leading commentator, Barbara Ward, noted the Attlee government's position could hardly be described as consistent over the issue of pooling national sovereignty.[79] In contrast to the concept of an Atlantic community, western European integration held little attraction for British policy-makers and commentators.[80] Given British reservations about the liberalisation of intra-European payments, only considerable American hegemonic pressure could persuade the British government to join the EPU and thereby formally abandon the option of creating an independent economic bloc based on the sterling area.[81] Reassured that this step would not mean an early return to convertibility, the British government decided to accept the American proposals for a multilateral intra-European payments system in order to avert an open rift within the western

---

[77] Acheson, *Present at the creation*, 382-9 (quote:385).

[78] Edmund Dell, *The Schuman Plan and the British Abdication of Leadership in Europe* (Oxford: Clarendon Press, 1995).; Milward, *Reconstruction*, 380-417.

[79] Barbara Ward, *Policy for the West* (Harmondsworth: Penguin, 1951), 236-7.

[80] On the preference for an Atlantic community, see for example Lionel Robbins, "Towards the Atlantic Community," *Lloyds Bank Review* New Series (1950): 1-24.; Nora Beloff, *The General Says No: Britain's exclusion from Europe* (Harmondsworth: Penguin Books, 1963), 52-3.

[81] This interpretation follows Peter Burnham in arguing that the Attlee government changed the regime of accumulation governing the British economy from a neo-bilateral strategy based on the sterling area to a strategy based on regional integration of the non-dollar world; see Peter Burnham, *Political Economy of Postwar Reconstruction* (Basingstoke: Macmillan, 1990), 145-9.

alliance. This episode showed that Britain lacked the economic power to prevent the creation of an intra-European payments system, which it could not dominate, merely by threatening to stay outside the EPU. In this sense, the decision to join the EPU represented a major shift in British foreign economic policy, and it reflected the desire to cultivate the re-emerging Anglo-American partnership in the cold war struggle against the Soviet threat.

From Dependency to Atlantic Partnership

In the immediate post-war period, Bevin and the British foreign policy-making community worked hard to re-establish Britain's position as major power, which they felt she should rightfully occupy as one of victors of the Second World War. In order to achieve this objective, the Attlee government soon realised that they would require substantial financial assistance from the American government. When such financial assistance was only available subject to tough conditions, ministers searched for an alternative to the negotiated loan agreement. However, the government found that domestic recovery depended on the American loan unless the government was prepared to impose severe austerity measures until Britain's export earnings had recovered sufficiently to finance its import bill as well as the costs of its military presence overseas and its economic links with the sterling area. In the absence of any palatable alternatives, the government agreed to the American conditions, partly because the key economic figures in the government thought that Britain would benefit from participation in a multilateral international monetary and trading regime.

In an attempt to re-establish Britain's international economic position, the government attempted to revitalise the sterling area against American opposition. As became obvious during the Anglo-American loan negotiations, American policy-makers saw the sterling area and the imperial preference systems as means by which British government could redirect trade away from the United States to Britain. British negotiators failed to convince their American counterparts that far from discriminating against dollar goods, the sterling area payment arrangements enabled member states to increase their imports from the dollar zone.[82] Having ruled out defaulting on the sterling balances, Britain made considerable amounts of dollars available to members for imports from the United States. While the government continued to borrow substantial sums from its colonies, it took no steps to restrict capital exports to the dominions in order to strengthen the cohesion of the Commonwealth.

---

[82] Cairncross, *Years of recovery*, 105-8.

Table 2.1

Material Capabilities of the White Commonwealth, the United States and Soviet Union, 1948–49

	Population (in million)	Area (in 1000 km^2)	National income (in $ billion)	Defence expenditure (in $ billion)
United Kingdom *UK*	50.2	243	42.0	3.0
South Africa	11.4	1,223	3.8	...
Australia	7.6	7,703	7.3	.2
New Zealand	1.9	267	1.9	.0
Canada	11.8	9,953	13.2	.2
White Commonwealth WC	83.0	19,392	68.3	3.5
WC ÷ UK	*1.7*	*79.5*	*1.6*	*1.2*
USSR	193.0	22,270	65.0	9.0
USA	150.7	7,827	250.0	11.9
UK vs. *USSR*	*0.3*	*0.0*	*0.6*	*0.3*
WC vs. *USSR*	*0.4*	*0.9*	*1.1*	*0.4*
UK vs. *USA*	*0.3*	*0.0*	*0.2*	*0.3*
WC vs. *USA*	*0.6*	2.5	*0.3*	*0.3*
UK vs. *USA & USSR*	*0.1*	*0.0*	*0.1*	*0.1*
WC vs. *USA & USSR*	*0.2*	*0.6*	*0.2*	*0.2*

Source: *White Commonwealth*: United Nations. Department of Economic Affairs. Statistical Office, *Statistical Yearbook 1951*, vol. 3 (New York: United Nations, 1951), 21-33, Table 1, 430-33, Table 156, and 443-522, Table 166 (National income and defence expenditure in $ calculated based on exchange rates in Table 159 (439-42)).;
United States and Soviet Union: "NSC 68: United States Objectives and Programs for National Security", 14 April 1950; reprinted in Thomas H. Etzold and John Lewis Gaddis, *Containment: Documents on American Policy and Strategy, 1945-1950* (New York: Columbia University Press, 1978), 405 and 407.

British foreign policy-makers attached such importance to consolidating its relations with the dominions, because the defence of vital British interests, particularly in the Middle East, depended on the continued willingness of dominion governments to provide armed forces in any future conflict. Indeed, British defence planners continued to assume that they could count on the resources of the dominions to bolster up the metropolis in an emergency. In theory, the population and economic strength of the White Commonwealth would extend Britain's war-making capabilities by around 50 per cent (see

Table 2.1).[83] However, dominion governments became reluctant after 1945 to commit themselves unquestioningly to supporting Britain in a future war. Aware that they could not provide adequate defence for the Empire and the Commonwealth, the British ministers chose not to revive the Committee of Imperial Defence after 1945.[84] Moreover, as the comparison of Table 2.1 shows, the resultant improvement in overall strength proved insufficient to balance the superior material capabilities of the other two superpowers (ratio < 1). In this sense, as Anthony Clayton argues,

> Britain's global presence, indicated by the vast areas of the earth's surface coloured red on the map, created the illusion of global strength which in practise served to obscure realities.[85]

Given the reluctance of the dominion governments to commit themselves to rushing to Britain's aid in an armed conflict against the Soviet bloc, Bevin sought first a defensive alliance with western Europe and later an enduring American security guarantee for western Europe in order to redress the military balance in western Europe. Most western European governments shared the apprehensions about the Soviet military threat, but Table 2.2 shows that western European countries on their own would have found it difficult to mobilise the resources to balance the Soviet threat (ratio < 1). However, the western alliance had an indisputable preponderance of power over the Soviet Union and its allies in the late 1940s.[86] At least on paper, the North Atlantic

---

[83] This estimated improvement in strength does not take into account geographical area which is vastly distorted by the relative size of Canada and Australia as compared to their population.

[84] Ministry of Defence, *Central Organisation for Defence*, Cmd. 6923 (London: His Majesty's Stationery Office, 1946). See also Nicholas Mansergh, *Survey of Commonwealth Affairs: Problems of wartime co-operation and post-war change, 1939-1952* (London: Oxford University Press, 1958), 326-9.; Clayton, "Deceptive might," 294-6.

[85] Clayton, "Deceptive might," 281.

[86] Escott Reid, *Time of Fear and Hope: The making of the North Atlantic Treaty, 1947-1949* (Toronto: McClelland and Stewart, 1977), 9. The ratios of capabilities in Table 2.2 are based on the figures for population and Gross National Product used by American foreign policy-makers in their reappraisal of the Soviet threat in spring 1950; see "NSC 68: United States Objectives and Programs for National Security", 14 April 1950; reprinted in Etzold and Gaddis, eds., *Containment*, 385–442. NSC-68 gives no separate estimates for the respective size of military forces. Therefore, I have taken the force estimate published in the *New York Times* in December 1950; see "Military Strength Around the World," *New York Times*, 10 December 1950, E 5. These force estimates are slightly lower than the American intelligence figures quoted by Matthew A. Evangelista, "Stalin's Postwar Army Reappraised," *International Security* 7 (1982): 113, Table 1. Similarly, the manpower figures for western armies are considerably lower than official American figures; see NARA RG 469. Box 7. folder: European Briefing Book: Mutual Security Agency, European Briefing Book, Revised, 10 June 1952. Therefore, these inaccuracies bias the resulting analysis in favour of exaggerating Soviet military strength. On balance, it seemed preferable to base the table on one

Table 2.2

Ratio of Capabilities Between the Various Potential Alliance Networks, 1948–49

Coalitions	Population	GNP	Size of Armed Forces	Defence Expenditures in $
western Europe vs. *USSR*	0.87	1.29	0.41	0.45
western Europe vs. *USSR & eastern Europe*	0.63	0.98	0.32	0.41
USA & western Europe vs. *USSR & eastern Europe*	1.18	3.88	0.45	2.07
USA vs. *USSR & eastern Europe & western Europe*	0.33	1.47	0.24	1.17

Source: *Population, GNP, Defence Expenditures in $*: "NSC 68: United States Objectives and Programs for National Security", 14 April 1950; reprinted in Thomas H. Etzold and John Lewis Gaddis, *Containment: Documents on American Policy and Strategy, 1945-1950* (New York: Columbia University Press, 1978), 385-442 (figures from 405 and 407).; *Size of the Armed Forces*: "Military Strength Around the World," *New York Times*, 10 December 1950, E 5.

Treaty created a military alliance which outstripped the capabilities of the Soviet bloc in all categories except the size of its armed forces (ratio >1). Moreover, Table 2.2 reveals the preponderance of American economic, but also military, power in this period. From the perspective of the United States, the worst case scenario would be if western Europe became part of the Soviet Union's sphere of influence. But even in this case, the United States would only have been inferior in terms of its population and the size of its armed forces. The figures probably overstate the size of the Soviet armed forces. Indeed, other contemporary estimates suggested a rough balance between the armed forces of the two rival military blocs. Even without allowing for this potential exaggeration, the western position on the eve of the Korean war compared not unfavourably with the Allied position against the Axis powers in1942 except in terms of military forces (see Table 2.3). While this manpower gap caused considerable anxiety among western policy-makers, they also cited as an indication that the Soviet leadership was preparing for war the fact that

source rather than using different potentially incompatible estimates. Nevertheless, the table should still approximate to the military balance as perceived by leading American foreign policy-makers in early 1950.

Table 2.3

A Comparison of Allied and Axis strength in World War II

Allies/Axis (great powers only)	Population	GDP	Size of the Armed Forces	Defence Expenditures in $
1939		2.3	0.9	0.4
1940		2.1	1.5	1.1
1941		2.0	0.9	1.3
1942	1.8	2.1	1.3	2.1
1943		2.5	1.5	2.6
1944		3.3	1.9	
1945		5.1	1.8	

Source: Mark Harrison. "The Economics of World War II: An overview." In Mark Harrison (ed.), *The Economics of World War II: Six great powers in international comparison*. (Cambridge: Cambridge University Press 1998), 1-42. My calculations from Tables 1.2, 1.3, 1.5, and 1.8.

the Soviet Union was spending twice the West's proportion of national income on defence. This discursive construction of the Soviet threat informed the consensus for western rearmament in spring 1940.[87]

International relations theorists have argued that a weaker nation will usually weigh up the opportunity costs of acceptance against the implications of refusing to yield to hegemonic pressure. On the other side of the equation, any attempt to exercise power involves opportunity costs for the hegemon, and the power of a hegemon depends on its willingness to meet the considerable opportunity costs of persuading another state to follow a certain course of action.[88] This analysis suggest that the costs of balancing the potential threat to Britain from any of the other potential alliance formations would have been prohibitive for the country outside a defensive arrangement involving the United States. British defence planners broadly shared this assessment as the British Chiefs of Staff acknowledged in their review of defence policy and global strategy in June 1950:

---

87 Till Geiger, "Studies in the political economy and economic impact of British defence expenditure and American military aid to Britain, 1945-1955," (Ph. D. Dissertation, University of Aberdeen, 1998), 184-192.

88 J. Harsanyi, "The dimension and measurement of social power," in *Power in Economics*, ed. K. W. Rothschild (Harmondsworth: Penguin, 1971), 77-80. For a critical analysis of Harsanyi's attempt to model social power, compare Robert O. Keohane, *After Hegemony: Cooperation and Discord in the World Political Economy* (Princeton: Princeton University Press, 1984), 65-84.

> The British Commonwealth and the Continental Powers, whether individually or collectively, cannot fight Russia except in alliance with the United States: nor could the United States fight Russia without the help of the British Commonwealth.[89]

This statement accurately reflected western Europe's dependence on American military assistance to deter the Soviet threat along the Iron Curtain dividing the continent. At the same time, the Chiefs of Staff argued that a degree of interdependence existed between the United States and Britain including the Commonwealth and its Empire. The formulation implicitly suggested that no similar degree of interdependence existed between the United States and the other signatories to the North Atlantic Treaty. In order to maintain the defensive arrangements with the United States, the Labour government had to balance the benefits of the American security guarantee against the drawbacks of acceding to American demands for economic liberalisation on a European and an international level.

Even if this British perception of being a partner to the United States in the cold war struggle was self-deluding, the growing tensions between the United States and the Soviet Union improved Britain's bargaining position vis-à-vis the Truman administration. Despite the clear asymmetry in terms of economic and military power between the United States and Britain, financial dependency gave way to something more akin to interdependence during the immediate post-war period. This analysis suggests that the relative vulnerability of the weaker state within an asymmetric interdependent relationship depends on the availability of alternative policy choices and their cost implications.[90] In the immediate aftermath of the Second World War, Britain proved vulnerable to American hegemonic pressure over its request for a large-scale loan from the American government. By the time of the Marshall Plan, the Attlee government was able to resist concerted American pressure to abandon the imperial preference system, because of the increasing strategic importance of Britain's global military presence to the United States in its attempt to contain what it saw as Soviet expansionism in Europe and Asia. While no longer facing economic disaster, Labour ministers used Britain's continued economic weakness after the sterling crisis of 1947 to successfully resist American demands at a time when the Truman administration could no

89 DBPO 2iv, 411-31: "Defence Policy and Global Strategy", Report by the Chiefs of Staff, 7 June 1950.

90 Helen Leigh-Phippard, *Congress and US Military Aid to Britain: Interdependence and dependence, 1949-56* (Basingstoke: Macmillan, 1995), 17-18.

longer risk the failure of the Marshall Plan initiative.[91] As the negotiations over NATO reform and EPU in May 1950 show, British foreign policy-makers overcame their aversion to deeper European economic integration in order to strengthen the American commitment to the defence of western Europe. While the British government obtained an American commitment to NATO reform and western rearmament in May 1950, it conceded over the EPU but only after securing additional American economic assistance and by curtailing the powers of the EPU Management Board. Arguably, such intergovernmental bargaining across different multilateral organisations at an international and European level allowed Britain to defend and balance its security and economic interests. In many ways, this type of behaviour became typical for the multi-layered open nature of the emerging international settlement after 1945.[92]

---

[91] On the GATT negotiations, see Richard Toye, "The Attlee government, the Imperial Preference System, and the creation of GATT," *English Historical Review* (forthcoming).

[92] On this point, see Till Geiger, "Embracing Good Neighbourliness: Multilateralism, *Pax Americana*, and European integration, 1945-58," in *Regional Trade Blocs, Multilateralism, and the GATT: Complementary Paths to Free Trade?*, eds. Till Geiger and Dennis Kennedy (London: Pinter, 1996), 56-78. On the multi-layered open nature of the emerging international order, see also G. John Ikenberry, *After Victory: Institutions, strategic restraint and the rebuilding of order after major wars* (Princeton: Princeton University Press, 2001), 170-75.

Chapter 3

'Tied to the Tail of a Kilkenny Cat'?: The Anglo-American relationship, British rearmament and the political crisis of 1951

The first two chapters pursued an analysis of two elements which underpinned the postwar British warfare state: on the one hand, the commitment to securing the people's peace involving the recasting of the British defence establishment, strategy and policy; and on the other hand, the attempts to embed Britain in overlapping military alliances in order to compensate for the country's reduced war potential. This twin strategy seemed to come to fruition in the first half of 1950 with the emergence of a closer working relationship with the American government in terms of western defence co-operation. However, in the event this conflation of British domestic and foreign policy interests with those of the Truman administration in strengthening western defences against the Soviet military threat lasted a matter of weeks only to be overtaken by events in the Far East. The outbreak of the Korean war convinced many American policy-makers of the immanence of another global war and the need for the massive increase of western defence efforts. While British policy-makers accepted the importance of resisting the North Korean invasion, they nevertheless grew concerned that the Truman administration might be drawn into a protracted conflict in Korea which might distract its attention from the more important objective of preventing an invasion of western Europe by Soviet forces. At the same time, American pressure to rearm led to conflicts between the Labour government's domestic reform agenda and its foreign policy strategy. These disagreements over rearmament precipitated a major political crisis over the 1951 budget leading to the resignation of two senior government ministers, the Minister of Labour and National Service, Aneurin Bevan, and the President of the Board of Trade, Harold Wilson in April. Given the government's slender majority, the resignations undermined the Labour government and forced the Prime Minister Clement Attlee to call an early general election. Against the background of the deepening economic and political crisis, the Labour Party lost the election in October. Despite pooling more votes than the Conservatives, the electoral defeat traumatised the Labour movement reinforcing the rift within the party. Moreover, the loss confined the Labour

Party to opposition for over a decade. In the search for an explanation, in previous research attention has therefore focused on the decision to embark on the Korean war rearmament programme and on the question of whether the split in the Labour Party could have been prevented.

The origins of this particular historical interpretation can be traced to Bevan's and Wilson's resignation speeches which called into question the economic feasibility of the United Kingdom defence programme given the growing raw material shortages and price increases caused by the massive American stockpiling programme.[1] To avoid further economic hardship, they argued, the government should have re-examined the rearmament programme and restrained the excesses of American capitalism. Together with a group of left-wing MPs, the two ex-ministers called on the government in a Tribune pamphlet to return to a socialist foreign policy based on equitable economic development at home and abroad.[2] Building on contemporary interpretations, the left-wing historian, Perry Anderson, traced the origins of the British economic decline to a failure to radically reshape British society after the war. According to Anderson's reading, the Attlee government remained stuck within the mould of existing political structures, and adherence to inherited imperial dreams, thus becoming dependent on American government support in order to carry out its programme of social and economic reform. Despite the considerable achievements, this promising experiment ended in an electoral disaster due to its ill conceived agenda and dependence on the United States.

> [Through] the imposition of massive rearmament for war in Korea [...] decisions in Washington [...] closed this cycle of reformism in London. In 1950 Britain's engineering industry and Labour's political unity were sacrificed to the role of imperial subcontractor by the Attlee administration. The first majority Labour government expired under a military budget so large it had to be pruned by the Conservative government that succeeded it.[3]

However, Anderson went further than Bevan and Wilson and argued that American policies had undermined the British domestic socialist project, because the British Labour movement failed to develop a coherent socialist project ultimately causing the downfall of the Attlee government.

The common element to these accounts is the belief that American policies circumscribed the scope of the Attlee government to pursue its socialist

---

[1] House of Commons, *Official Report*, vol. 487, Parliamentary Debates (Hansard), Fifth Series (London: His Majesty's Stationery Office, 1951), (hereafter 487 H.C. Deb. 5s.) col. 34-43 and 228-31.

[2] *One Way Only: A Socialist Analysis of the Present World Crisis*, A Tribune Pamphlet (London: Tribune Publications, 1951).

[3] Perry Anderson, "The Figures of Descent," in *English Questions* (London: Verso, 1992), 121-92 (quote: 165).

programme. This chapter will explore the Anglo-American politico-economic defence relationship during the early stages of the Korean war. Based on the analysis of chapter 2, the following three sections will analyse the political economy of defence co-operation between the British and American governments after the outbreak of the Korean war. In light of this, the final section will assess whether the political crisis of 1951 could in fact have been avoided if the Attlee government had resisted American pressure for further increases in the defence programme.

Korean war and British rearmament

Stunned by the North Korean invasion of South Korea, British officials welcomed the American-led United Nations intervention to oppose this communist aggression. However, policy-makers in London initially feared that the Korean war might distract American attention from the growing Soviet threat in western Europe. Therefore, British officials were relieved to learn that far from abandoning western Europe the Truman administration called for immediate western rearmament. In the weeks after the outbreak of the Korean war, British diplomats in Washington tried to convince policy-makers at home that the American pressure for rearmament represented an opportunity to demonstrate British support for the Truman administration's foreign policy. By supporting the American initiative, the Attlee government could ensure the continued effective leadership of the West by the United States. If the British government dithered, this unique opportunity to secure lasting British influence in western Europe might be missed. Given the shift in American priorities, the Economic Minister to Washington, Leslie Rowan, confirmed "... that [Britain] had a good chance of being treated as a partner if [the British] did their stuff." Moreover, rearmament might provide the potential to earn substantial amounts of American dollars through military assistance and arms exports.[4]

A clear demonstration of resolve demanded an increase in British defence efforts. While convinced of this necessity, economic advisers remained cautious about mobilising the economy for rearmament. In their submission to the American government, British economic policy-makers stressed that the lack of unemployed capacity severely limited the extent to which the defence production could be expanded without endangering the economic recovery.[5] In order to rearm, the British government would have to increase its imports of

4 Diary entry, 18 July 1950; reprinted in Alec Cairncross, ed., *The Robert Hall Diaries, 1947-53* (London: Unwin Hyman, 1989), 124.

5 National Archives and Record Administration, Washington (hereafter NARA) Record Group (hereafter RG) 59. Box 3528: 741.5/8-450: telegram, Douglas - Foster and Bissell, 4 August 1950.

vital materials. An increase of imports required the continued recovery of British exports despite increased defence production. Limiting the likely economic impact of rearmament therefore became the primary concern of economic policy-makers. In their discussions with officials from the Ministry of Supply, the government's chief economic advisers, Robert Hall and Edwin Plowden, stressed the imperative of preserving exports from the engineering industry. Hall also emphasised the need to conserve, if not to build up, the stocks of strategic materials for rearmament. As a consequence, additional defence production would further exacerbate the potentially precarious balance of payments situation. To limit these risks, British policy-makers hoped to persuade the United States to adopt a form of planned trade regime for the duration of the Korean war emergency.[6]

While the British government deliberated over its defence programme, American officials in London became convinced that Whitehall was treating the Korean crisis with a distinct lack of urgency. According to plans emanating from Whitehall, the proposed increases in the British defence effort mostly consisted of already planned weapons production projects. Since the British government did not plan to redirect civilian production to the defence programme, American aid officials thought that the British proposals fell far short of what the British economy could afford. Indeed, for American policy-makers, cuts in private and public non-defence consumption had become the criteria for the Attlee government's determination to rearm.[7] After generous promises of military aid, the British rearmament programme assumed that American financial assistance would cover roughly half of the increased British defence expenditure of £1,100 million.[8] Disappointed by the limited scale of the British proposals, American diplomats rejected the British request of £550 million as being more than the Truman administration had contemplated. Continuing to press for an early announcement of western European rearmament plans, American aid officials emphasised that Washington required several months to reach a final decision on the military assistance requests.[9]

---

6 Diary entries, 5 and 11 July 1950; reprinted in Cairncross, ed., *Robert Hall diaries*, 122-3.

7 NARA RG 59. Box 3528: 741.5/7-2950: telegram, Douglas - Secretary of State, 29 July 1950.; NARA RG 59. Box 3528: 741.5/8-350: telegram, Douglas - Perkins, 3 August 1950.; NARA RG 59. Box 3528: 741.5/8-1150: telegram, Douglas - Secretary of State, 11 August 1950.; NARA RG 59. Box 3530: 741.5-MAP/9-150: MDAP Monthly General Report, despatch Bruins - Department of State, 1 September 1950.

8 NARA RG 59. Box 3528: 741.5/8-1050: telegram, Douglas - Secretary of State, 10 August 1950.; diary entry, 11 August 1950; reprinted in Philip M. Williams, ed., *The Diary of Hugh Gaitskell, 1945-1956* (London: Jonathan Cape, 1983), 194-6.

9 Roger John Bullen and M. E. Pelley, eds., *Documents on British Policy Overseas, series 2, volume 3: German Rearmament, September - December 1950* (London: Her Majesty's Stationery Office, 1989). (hereafter: DBPO 2iii (1950)), 1-4: Bevin - Franks, 2

Without a firm commitment of American military aid, the Attlee government found itself in a quandary over the rearmament programme. For the British government, announcing the enlarged defence effort prior to an agreement on military aid carried the risk of undermining public support for rearmament and of fuelling anti-American sentiments.[10] All initial planning assumed substantial financial assistance. However, the Americans only offered essential end-items conditional on further increases in the western European defence effort. This response threw into doubt the economic viability of the British defence programme.[11] During the discussions of the rearmament programme, the service departments pressed hard for much larger increases in the defence budget. Indeed, the planned British defence programme of £3,600 million fell far short of the estimated £6,000 million needed to meet the British share of the NATO's Medium Term Defence Plan which had been agreed in May 1950.[12] At an early stage in the deliberations, ministers damaged the British case for additional American aid by approving a £200 million increase in soldiers' pay. For the service ministries, the Korean war proved a welcome opportunity to rush through a number of their favourite expenditure projects without proper consultation. Dismayed by the willingness of other ministers to go along with these demands, the Minister for Economic Affairs, Hugh Gaitskell, feared that the decision to increase service pay set a bad precedent.

> (1) It will give the Defence Ministry the idea that they can spend anything they like and get away with it. (2) It will lead to a general feeling money no longer matters.[13]

Despite giving way over service pay, the majority in the cabinet insisted that rearmament should not threaten economic recovery. On 12 September 1950, ministers announced the £3,600 million defence programme in the House of Commons without having received a firm commitment of military aid from the United States. In this context, Attlee reminded his audience and the Americans that Britain spent proportionally more on defence than other North Atlantic Treaty signatories.[14] Shortly after the government's announcement, the frailty of the cabinet consensus became obvious. On the eve of the annual party

---

September 1950.; Calendar i: U.K. 3 year defence programme, 3 August - 7 September 1950; Calendar ii: Conversation between Mr. Bevin and Mr. Stofford, 23 August 1950.

[10] DBPO 2iii (1950), 1-4: Bevin - Franks, 2 September 1950.; diary entry, 5 September 1950; reprinted in Cairncross, ed., *Robert Hall diaries*, 126.

[11] Diary entry, 4 September 1950; reprinted in Cairncross, ed., *Robert Hall diaries*, 125-6.

[12] Diary entries, 20 October and 20 November 1950; reprinted in Cairncross, ed., *Robert Hall diaries*, 132-5.

[13] Diary entry, 11 August 1950; reprinted in Williams, ed., *Diary of Hugh Gaitskell*, 196-7 (quote: 197).

[14] 478 H.C. Deb. 5s col. 365-6.

conference, Bevan threatened to split the Labour Party if the government decided to finance rearmament through cuts in the welfare budget.[15] By the middle of September 1950, conflicting pressures limited the government's policy options. Further increasing defence expenditure in order to influence the Truman administration might necessitate welfare cuts and lead to the fall of the Labour government.

Initially, the government's economic advisers seemed fairly optimistic about the economic situation. On balance, their forecasts suggested that the programme could be sustained by permitting an increase in the cost of living above wage rises. Despite continued uncertainty over American assistance, the government's economic advisers remained confident that the overall impact of rearmament would be restricted to a small reduction in engineering exports. Undeterred by the initial American conditional offer of end-items, British officials reckoned that Britain would receive £350 million in financial assistance.[16] However, when the scale of the American defence programme became known in October 1950, Hall became increasingly concerned about the implications for the British economy. In his eyes, the "greatest threat to the British economy" might be raw material shortages.

> Already the United States have announced a large cut in exports of cotton and if this is persisted in we will soon have unemployment in Lancashire and all our hard work will be undone.[17]

At first, the balance of payments situation remained more stable than the initial forecasts. Over the next few months, the British balance of payments improved due to a smaller than expected rise in imports while exports continued to increase. As a consequence of the continued rapid increase in world raw material prices, the export earnings of British colonies led to a significant rise in Britain's dollar reserves.[18] Wide-spread speculation about a possible revaluation of Sterling further inflated British hard currency reserves.[19] To keep the price increases under control, British officials unsuccessfully sought

---

15 Diary entry, 27 September 1950; reprinted in Cairncross, ed., *Robert Hall diaries*, 128-9.

16 Diary entry, 7 September 1950; reprinted in Cairncross, ed., *Robert Hall diaries*, 126.

17 Diary entry, 8 October 1950; reprinted in Cairncross, ed., *Robert Hall diaries*, 129-31 (quote:131).

18 Diary entry, 20 November 1950; reprinted in Cairncross, ed., *Robert Hall diaries*, 133-5. On the development of the balance of payments, see also Treasury, *United Kingdom Balance of Payments, 1948 to 1951*, Cmd. 8379 (London: His Majesty's Stationery Office, 1951), 5, Table 1.

19 Alec Cairncross, *Years of Recovery: British Economic Policy, 1945-51* (London: Methuen, 1985), 235-8.; diary entries, 5 and 20 February 1951; reprinted in Cairncross, ed., *Robert Hall diaries*, 146-9.

an agreement on raw material allocation to be administered by NATO throughout the autumn of 1950.[20]

In order to advance the British case, Gaitskell visited Washington in October 1951. While in the United States, Attlee appointed him to succeed Stafford Cripps as Chancellor of the Exchequer. During his discussions in Washington, American aid officials started to push for an early termination of ERP assistance to Britain because of the improvement in the British reserve position. At the same time, the American side declined to discuss the British request for additional financial assistance under the contemplated military assistance programme.[21] Given the circumstances, the economic advisers counselled Gaitskell to insist on the continuation of Marshall aid to Britain until the ongoing NATO burden-sharing exercise had reported. To some extent, Britain was paying the price for its "... reluctance to spend dollars to keep [the reserves] from rising."[22] Such a strategy would have reduced the balance of payments surplus strengthening the British case for economic assistance. Indeed, due to the initial delay in the strategic stockpiling programme, the government exacerbated the balance of payments deficit in 1951 by purchasing stocks at inflated prices.[23] Still hoping for an agreement on the allocation of raw materials, the British government neglected to reduce its reserves by building up its strategic stockpiles. More worryingly in the short term, the November elections for Congress cast doubt on whether or not Britain would receive any financial support for its £3,600 million defence programme. During Gaitskell's visit to Washington in October 1950, American officials clarified the position on military aid stressing Congressional opposition to unconditional financial aid. As a potential alternative, the American side proposed to channel dollars to Britain by purchasing weapons through offshore procurement (OSP) contracts. While such additional dollar earnings might help to finance dollar imports, the American government might allocate the weapons to another country thereby limiting the direct benefit to Britain. In any event, the sum offered amounted to merely a fifth of the defence programme rather than half

---

[20] Diary entries, 4, 7, 12, 20, and 26 September, and 8 October 1950; reprinted in Cairncross, ed., *Robert Hall diaries*, 125-31.; Michael J. Hogan, *The Marshall Plan: America, Britain, and the reconstruction of Western Europe* (Cambridge: Cambridge University Press, 1987), 344-8.

[21] Memorandum on Washington visit, 8-12 October 1950; reprinted in Williams, ed., *Diary of Hugh Gaitskell*, 204-11.

[22] Diary entry, 12 October 1950; reprinted in Cairncross, ed., *Robert Hall diaries*, 131.

[23] Leo Pliatzky, *Getting and Spending: Public expenditure, employment and inflation* (Oxford: Basil Blackwell, 1982), 13-14. This counterfactual claim is examined in chapter 8.

the additional expenditure as British policy-makers had assumed during the planning stage.[24]

In October 1950, the bilateral negotiations on the British £3,600 million defence programme and American military aid reached an impasse. To some extent, both sides failed to recognise the extent to which the other side's position was constrained by domestic politics. For example, in order to assure parliamentary support, the Attlee government down-played the expansion in the British defence effort emphasising the re-equipment of existing units rather than the creation of additional divisions. From the perspective of American officials, the Attlee government seemed unwilling to make any substantial sacrifices to defeat the Soviet threat.[25] However, the Attlee government felt Britain had complied far more readily than other NATO partners with American requests for increases in the western defence efforts. As the Truman administration initiated the process, ministers expressed bewilderment about American reticence in discussing military aid.[26] By supporting the American position in NATO, the British government expected to obtain significant concessions in bilateral negotiations with the Truman administration. Against this background, the American intention to terminate ERP aid surprised British ministers. According to the Whitehall rumour mill, Bevan and other left-wing ministers proposed that the government should respond by reducing the defence programme by £600 million.[27] Committed to their £3,600 million defence programme, British policy-makers pinned their hopes on the impending NATO burden-sharing exercise redistributing the defence burden more equitably between member states. Through this strategy, British ministers hoped to progress from the status of a supplicant to that of a partner of the United States on the issue of Western rearmament. At least temporarily, this approach brought the dissidents back into the fold.[28]

---

24 Memorandum on Washington visit, 8-12 October 1950; reprinted in Williams, ed., *Diary of Hugh Gaitskell*, 204-11.

25 NARA RG 59. Box 3528: 741.5/8-350: telegram, Douglas - Perkins and Acheson, 3 August 1950.

26 NARA RG 59. Box 3528: 741.5/9-850: telegram, Katz - Holmes, Bonesteel, Perkins and Harriman, 8 September 1950.

27 Besides Bevan, newspaper reports identified the Minister of War, John Strachey and the Minister of Supply, George Strauss as dissidents within the government. Despite official denials, many MPs suggested there was substance to initial newspaper reports in the United States; see "British deny seeking curb in rearmament," *New York Times*, 21 November 1950.; NARA RG 59. Box 3531: 741.5-MAP/12-550: U.K. Political and Economic Situation as Affecting MDAP (In lieu of usual monthly MDAP general report), despatch Bruins - Department of State, 5 December 1950.

28 NARA RG 59. Box 3528: 741.5/11-1850: telegram, Holmes - Secretary of State, 18 November 1950. See also memorandum on Washington visit, 8-12 October 1950; reprinted in Williams, ed., *Diary of Hugh Gaitskell*, 204-11.

Since the outbreak of the Korean war, British policy-makers had tended to underestimate the strength of domestic criticism of American foreign policy. Given the seriousness of the world situation, the Truman administration expected unquestioned support for its foreign policy from its allies. In this context, some American officials feared that the persistent British demand for equal partner status might undermine its policy on western rearmament. On the other hand, British policy-makers shared American anxieties about agreeing a NATO defence production programme. Such concerns prompted Gaitskell to describe NATO's High Priority Production Program as "chicken-feed."[29] Against this background, one American official suggested that Britain might be persuaded to increase its defence effort substantially in return for preferential treatment. In addition, Britain should assume a leadership role in integrating western European defence efforts. By footing a proportion of the British dollar import bill, the United States would gain "... a full fledged dependable partner in the NATO." In contrast to the other potential partners France and West Germany, such a role was "... not too far ahead of [Britain's] capabilities and prestige."[30] If American attempts to persuade western European countries to rearm failed, the United States would still benefit from a strategic partnership with Britain in waging the cold war.

At the same time, considerable differences between the two governments emerged about the conduct of the Korean war.[31] For the Foreign Office, this minor conflict represented a side-show compared to the confrontation between the two rival military blocs in western Europe. Worried by General MacArthur's aggressive statements, many British observers feared American actions might trigger a global war by attacking the People's Republic of China. In Washington, the continued unease over the conduct of the Korean war in Britain and western Europe was interpreted as an unwillingness to face up to the fact that the world might "... be on the verge of a global war." Therefore, American military planners emphasised the necessity of persuading the Attlee government to expand its £3,600 million defence programme.[32] Perturbed by President Truman's ambiguous comments, Attlee flew to Washington to seek assurances from Truman that the United States would not deploy atomic

---

[29] See footnote 26.

[30] NARA RG 59. Box 3530: 741.5-MAP/11-2850: "UK Production Programs and Defense Efforts", memorandum Bray - Ohly and Bell, 28 November 1950.

[31] On tensions between the two governments over the conduct of the Korean war, see Ra Jong-yil, "Special relationship at war: The Anglo-American relationship during the Korean War," *Journal of Strategic Studies* 7 (1984): 301-17.; Michael J. Dockrill, "The Foreign Office, Anglo-American relations and the Korean War, June 1950-June 1951," *International Affairs* 62 (1986): 459-76.; and William Stueck, *The Korean War: An International History* (Princeton: Princeton University Press, 1995), particularly 130-38.

[32] NARA RG 319. Box 98: G-3 091 Great Britain (4 Dec 50), Over-All Statement of the Problem Involved (JCS 2176/1), 4 December 1950.

weapons without prior consultation. Acting under considerable pressure from British public opinion, senior ministers neglected to examine the likelihood of attaining the British objectives by forcing an unplanned summit on the beleaguered Truman administration.[33] Therefore, Attlee and the British delegation found themselves at a disadvantage in their negotiations with the Truman administration. While the American side pressed for substantial increases in the British defence effort, the British delegation failed to reach an accommodation on raw materials or military aid.[34] In the eyes of British observers, Attlee's intervention contributed to Truman's decision to rule out the use of atomic weapons in the present circumstances.[35] While the communiqué remained rather vague on this point, Truman seemed initially willing to concede that the United States would consult its allies prior to using atomic weapons. However, such an agreement would in all likelihood have been blocked by Congress as undermining its constitutional right to declare war.[36] Despite the unconvincing achievements of the Attlee visit, the summit reaffirmed the common objective of Western military co-operation to contain the Soviet threat.[37]

Apart from this external pressure, the armed services urged the Attlee government to increase the £3,600 million defence programme.[38] For the service chiefs, the British deficiency of jet fighters became top priority in late November 1950. Given the lack of an advanced British jet fighter, the Ministry of Defence argued for the procurement of the 484 American F-86 aircraft. At the same time, the Minister of Defence pressed for a substantial increase in the British jet engine capacity.[39] After their decision, the Attlee government approached the Truman administration to finance the 484 F-86 fighters for the Royal Air Force. Fearing this request might create an undesirable precedent, the Joint American Military Advisory Group accorded this project "very low priority." If Britain received F-86s as end-item aid, other western European

---

33 Dean Acheson, *Present at the Creation: My Years in the State Department* (New York: W. W. Norton and Company, 1969), 478-85.

34 Diary entry, 8 December 1950; reprinted in Cairncross, ed., *Robert Hall diaries*, 135-9. On the American objectives, see also NARA RG 43. Entry Records of Council of Foreign Ministers. Box 52. folder US-UK Talks. Washington. December 1950. Briefing Book. 1 of 2: Briefing Book for Prime Minister Attlee's Visit, December 1950.

35 Dennis Healey, *The Time of my Life* (Harmondsworth: Penguin, 1990), 125-6.; Kenneth Harris, *Attlee* (London: Weidenfeld and Nicholson, 1982), 461-7.

36 Acheson, *Present at the creation*, 478-85.

37 NARA RG 273. NSC 93/1: Report to the National Security Council by the Department of State on Results of the Conversations between the President and the British Prime Minister, 4 January 1951.

38 Diary entries, 20 and 21 October 1950; reprinted in Cairncross, ed., *Robert Hall diaries*, 132-3.

39 Public Record Office, Kew, London (hereafter: PRO), Cabinet Office (hereafter: CAB) 130/65: PRO CAB 130/65: Minutes of an Ad hoc Meeting of Ministers in the Prime Minister's Room at the House of Commons, 23 November 1950.

countries would also demand the most modern American military aircraft rather than increase domestic aircraft production. As an alternative, the Joint American Military Advisory Group suggested that Britain procure the F-86s in Canada requesting AMP assistance for the jet engines.[40] After considerable arm-twisting, the Canadian government provided F-86s for the Royal Air Force as part of Canadian mutual aid to NATO rearmament.[41]

Despite applying for American military assistance for the F-86s, British ministers increasingly accepted that the chances of Britain receiving substantial American military aid were receding. Given the improved reserve position, British ministers now gave way to American pressure and agreed to the termination of ERP aid in late December 1950.[42] Putting on a brave face, ministers presented this decision at home as the country regaining its economic independence.[43] After his return from Washington, Attlee and other senior ministers believed that their continued ability to influence American foreign policy depended on increasing the defence programme.[44] Therefore, the cabinet now faced having to increase the £3,600 million defence programme without American financial aid. Against the background of further reversals in Korea, the Attlee government yielded to the demands of the services departments and the persistent pressure from the Truman administration. To win public approval for an enlarged defence programme, government ministers set out to "educate" the British public about the need to re-arm and to accept some economic hardship.[45] At the same time, ministers remained determined to minimise the economic impact of the defence programme. Therefore, ministers decided against the introduction of controls or preferential allocation of resources for defence production. When he announced the enlarged £4,700 million defence programme, Attlee added an important caveat by emphasising that the British rearmament effort depended on the availability of raw materials and machine

---

40 NARA RG 334. Entry 110. Box 51: telegram Kibler - CSAF, 29 December 1950.

41 Heinz-Werner Würzler, "Die Anfänge kanadischer Militärhilfe für die europäischen NATO-Partner: Probleme und Motivationen (1948/49-1951/52)," in *Das Nordatlantische Bündnis, 1949-1956*, eds. Klaus A. Maier and Norbert Wiggershaus (München: R. Oldenbourg Verlag, 1993), 124-6.

42 Diary entry, 5 January 1951; reprinted in Williams, ed., *Diary of Hugh Gaitskell*, 222-3.

43 Department of State, ed., *Foreign Relations of the United States, 1951, volume iv: Europe: Political and Economic Developments* (Washington: Government Printing Office, 1985), (hereafter FRUS 4i (1951)), 894-9.: Gifford - Secretary of State, 20 January 1951. See also Treasury, *Economic Survey for 1951* (London: Her Majesty's Stationery Office, 1951), 3-4.

44 Harris, *Attlee*, 465.

45 NARA RG 59. Box 3528: 741.5/12-2950: telegram Balwin - Department of State, 29 December 1950.; FRUS 4i (1951), 887-8: Gifford - Secretary of State, 29 December 1950.

tools from the United States.[46] In anticipation of an equitable burden-sharing agreement in NATO, the British government did not ask the Truman administration for general financial support for the increased defence programme.[47]

Despite the cabinet decision to increase the defence programme, ministers remained divided over the urgency of rearmament and the economic implications. Economic considerations mattered little to the military planners pressing for an even larger rearmament drive. The Minister of Defence, Emmanuel Shinwell, staunchly advocated the case of the service departments including the creation of additional defence production capacity.[48] Initially, the Treasury questioned the economic rationale of any expansion of the domestic defence industry. Reluctantly, Gaitskell consented to the service ministries' plans prior to cabinet approval of the increased defence programme.[49] Being convinced of the necessity to support the United States, Gaitskell felt obliged to push the £4,700 million defence programme through the cabinet in the absence of Bevin, Shinwell and the Commonwealth Secretary, Patrick Gordon-Walker.[50] Before the decision on the rearmament programme, Attlee reshuffled his cabinet moving Bevan to the Ministry of Labour to assure his future support for the government's economic measures.[51] Despite supporting some aspects of economic policy such as an agreement with the trade unions on wage restraint, Bevan expressed his apprehensions about American foreign policy in no uncertain terms. By inextricably linking Britain to the American side in the cold war, Bevan feared that the Attlee government risked being dragged into a nuclear confrontation by American belligerence towards the Soviet Union. Hinting at the potential consequences, Bevan described the British position as being "... tied to the tail of a Kilkenny cat."[52] Recalling the fabled Kilkenny cats who fought until only their tails remained, Bevan's comment implied that his reservations about the rearmament programme arose largely from his objections to American foreign policy and hegemonic power,

---

[46] Cabinet Office, *Defence Programme: Statement made by the Prime Minister in the House of Commons on Monday, 29th January, 1951*, Cmd. 8146 (London: His Majesty's Stationery Office, 1951), 6-7.

[47] NARA RG 59. Box 3531: 741.5-MAP/1-2951: letter Franks - Acheson, 29 January 1951.

[48] NARA RG 59. Box 3528: 741.5/1-1751: telegram, McArthur - Perkins, 17 January 1951.; PRO T 229/850: minute Shinwell - Gaitskell, 18 January 1951.

[49] PRO T 229/850: note Plowden - Armstrong, 15 January 1951.; PRO T 229/850: letter Gaitskell - Shinwell, 19 January 1951.; for a more extensive discussion, see chapter 4.

[50] Diary entry, 30 January 1950; reprinted in Cairncross, ed., *Robert Hall diaries*, 146.

[51] Harris, *Attlee*, 469-70.

[52] Diary entry, 2 February 1950; reprinted in Cairncross, ed., *Robert Hall diaries*, 146-7 (quote: 147).

rather than economic considerations.[53] While cabinet unity seemed assured on the surface, the divisions within the cabinet deepened between the so-called pro-American and anti-American factions.

To some extent, the heated debates within the Parliamentary Labour Party (PLP) reflected accurately the differences of opinion within the government. While a majority supported the government's rearmament policy, left-wing MPs criticised the government for caving in to American pressure over German rearmament and for its support of a resolution condemning Chinese aggression in Korea.[54] In these shouting matches, Gaitskell increasingly became the target of the left wing critics.[55]

Just prior to the announcement of the enlarged defence effort, the reluctance of the Attlee government to support an American resolution branding the People's Republic of China as an aggressor soured Anglo-American relations.[56] Against this background, American officials were less than fulsome in their praise of the £4,700 million defence programme. While not disputing the sincerity of the British defence effort, the announced increase in the British defence effort was regarded as a compromise package between different factions within the cabinet. In their assessments, American diplomats in London depicted the £4,700 million defence programme as falling short of the defence contribution which NATO might require of Britain.[57] In the light of the continued criticism of American domination, the embassy, however, counselled the State Department to desist from pressing for further increases in the British defence programme.[58] Despite not requesting American economic aid, British ministers missed no opportunity to reiterate their expectation that Britain would receive some financial support as a result of the on-going NATO burden-sharing exercise.[59] In late March, American policy-makers dashed these British expectations by informing Whitehall that its growing dollar reserves disqualified Britain from receiving economic aid for the time being. Moreover, the ECA proposed to present its economic aid requests to Congress without taking into account national defence efforts.[60] The ECA's unwavering insistence on the reserve principle dismayed British officials who had harboured the illusion that Britain would receive some financial support as a

---

[53] Harris, *Attlee*, 469-70.

[54] Diary entries, 31 January and 8 February 1951; reprinted in Tony Benn, *Years of Hope: Diaries, Papers and Letters, 1940-1960*, ed. Ruth Winstone (London: Arrow Books, 1994), 134-9.

[55] Willie Hamilton, *Blood on the Walls* (London: Bloomsbury, 1992), 70.

[56] FRUS 4i (1951), 903-5: telegram Gifford - Secretary of State, 29 January 1951.

[57] FRUS 4i (1951), 911-14: telegram Gifford - Secretary of State, 31 January 1951.

[58] FRUS 4i (1951), 916-22: telegram Gifford - Secretary of State, 9 March 1951.; telegram Gifford - Secretary of State, 14 March 1951.

[59] NAW RG 59. Box 3528: 741.5/2-1751: telegram Gifford - Secretary of State., 17 February 1951.; FRUS 4i (1951), 916-8: telegram Gifford - Secretary of State, 9 March 1951.

[60] FRUS 4i (1951), 923-5: telegram Batt - Foster, 21 March 1951.

result of the NATO burden-sharing exercise. Moreover, British policy-makers increasingly felt that the American defence effort contributed to the persistent raw material shortages and the limited availability of machine tools which exacerbated the economic strains on the British defence effort. Without some American help, many British economic policy-makers worried that Britain simply would not be able to carry out its enlarged defence programme.[61]

In early April 1951, Hall flew to Washington to confer with senior American officials about Britain's growing economic problems.[62] Both sides agreed in their general appraisal of the British economic position and concentrated on addressing the expected British balance of payments deficit due to increased imports. ECA officials acknowledged that the United States stockpiling programme might adversely affect the economic development in other western economies. In response, the British side insisted that these imports would be essential to meet the projected defence production targets. However, American officials seemed more troubled about the potential policy response to a shortfall in export earnings. The Deputy Administrator of the ECA, Richard Bissell, expressed aloud his concerns that in such an eventuality, the Attlee government might restrict the supply of raw materials from the Sterling Area to western Europe in order to reduce the growing British surplus with other EPU countries. To pre-empt such a step, Bissell offered to support a change in the EPU agreement to increase the proportion of dollar surplus countries would receive. According to Hall, Bissell suggested that deficit countries should settle their balance with the EPU in full. In turn, this change would enable the EPU to reimburse 75 per cent of surplus balances. This suggestion was music to Hall's ears, because the British government was "... very much tempted to break EPU up altogether on present trends."[63] However, other western European countries would probably have opposed an attempt to break up the EPU, because such a move would have ended the liberalisation of intra-European trade. Indeed, the EPU Management Board pursued policies which ran counter to Anglo-American intentions in early 1951. In response to the growing West German deficit, the EPU Management Board had just granted the West German government a temporary bridging facility of $120 million against the opposition of the ECA. This episode underlines the fact that

[61] FRUS 4i (1951), 919-22 and 925-8: telegram Secretary of State and European Cooperation Administration - Batt and Spofford, 30 March 1951.; telegram Acheson - Embassy in the United Kingdom, 30 March 1951.; telegram Gifford - Secretary of State, 5 April 1951.

[62] On Hall's visit, see Till Geiger, "Studies in the political economy and economic impact of British defence expenditure and American military aid to Britain, 1945-1955," (Ph. D. Dissertation, University of Aberdeen, 1998), 206-7.

[63] Diary entry, 7 April 1951; reprinted in Cairncross, ed., *Robert Hall diaries*, 150-53 (quote: 152).; see also FRUS 4i (1951), 930-33: Memorandum of Conversation by Alexander M. Rosenson, 6 April 1951.

the ECA lacked the leverage to influence the operations of the EPU. Bissell's suggestion, therefore, amounted to little more than thinking aloud.[64]

However, these discussions served as a mere prelude to the real difference of opinion. Meanwhile American officials made reassuring noises that Britain might receive some aid directly or through the EPU. The American reassurances failed to address British discontent over the allocation of military assistance. In no uncertain terms, the British representatives pressed their case that military assistance should be granted on the basis of a country's contribution to the Western defence effort. Moreover, the British officials re-emphasised the British position that any economic assessment should not focus merely on Britain's dollar reserves, but also take into account the overall financial position of an economy. As they pointed out, "[i]f this was done, it would be necessary to consider the UK as a special case because of its sterling liabilities." Put on the defensive by the ferocity of the British representations, Bissell chose to hide behind Congress. Suggesting the ECA's hands were tied on this matter, Bissell offered no hope that the Truman administration might be able to depart from the reserve principle in the light of the burden-sharing exercise.[65]

In increasing the British rearmament programme to £4,700 million in January, the majority among the Attlee cabinet had taken considerable political risks. At the time, leading ministers trusted that compliance with American demands would ensure that Britain would receive some military aid as a result of the NATO burden-sharing exercise. In Hall's eyes, the sheer incredibility of America's attitude on this was bound to undermine the supporters of American foreign policy within the Attlee government. As Hall pointed out,

> [i]f [ministers] had known that there would be this arbitrary rule, which as far as the UK is concerned may mean that we can *never* get any help, they may well think twice [about implementing the defence programme].[66] (Italics in the original)

As British ministers were publicly committed to increased defence expenditures, the American decision to renege on unconditional offers of military aid left the former without any credible response. Short of abandoning the rearmament programme, the Labour government might withdraw from the

---

[64] On the ongoing crisis in the EPU, compare Alan S. Milward, *The Reconstruction of Western Europe, 1945-51* (London: Methuen, 1984), 430-55.; Jacob Kaplan and Günther Schleiminger, *The European Payments Union: Financial Diplomacy in the 1950s* (Oxford: Clarendon Press, 1989), 97-153.

[65] FRUS 4i (1951), 930-33: memorandum of conversation by Alexander M. Rosenson, 6 April 1951.; diary entry, 7 April 1951; reprinted in Cairncross, ed., *Robert Hall diaries*, 150-53.

[66] Diary entry, 7 April 1951; reprinted in Cairncross, ed., *Robert Hall diaries*, 150-53 (quote: 151).

NATO burden-sharing exercise. Given American pronouncements on military aid, the Nitze exercise had become a pointless venture from a purely British perspective.[67] Given Whitehall's unease about releasing sensitive information, cynics might even have preferred a belated opt-out from the NATO burden-sharing exercise.

After his return from Washington, Hall sought a meeting with the ECA representative in Britain, William Batt. Acting as an emissary for Gaitskell, the chief economic adviser passed on the Chancellor's concerns about the potential political fall-out from the American position on military aid. In the run-up to the budget, Gaitskell wanted to avoid any open conflict which might raise the domestic political temperature. In no uncertain terms, Hall spelled out the fact that Gaitskell felt betrayed by the American decision to adhere to the reserve principle and disregard the outcome of the Nitze exercise in advance. Prompted by this intervention, Batt advised Washington to indicate publicly that the reserve principle would not serve as the only criterion for the allocation of military aid in future. In the opinion of the staff at the London embassy, the current inflexibility over military aid allocations potentially undermined crucial British support for American policy in multilateral discussions. They concluded, therefore, that the Truman administration should not forget its staunchest advocate in western Europe. In the following months, American diplomats in London continued to press for more flexibility in the administration of American economic and military assistance. Repeatedly, Batt emphasised the need to assist the British defence effort through the provision of raw materials, machine tools and technical expertise.[68] By late April, this concerted campaign started to make an impression on the State Department. Senior officials favoured reducing the Anglo-American tensions by accommodating the Attlee government over raw materials and military aid.[69] To some extent, the Chancellor's intervention contributed to the softening of the American position. However, this change of policy did little to stem the rising tide of anti-Americanism among Labour Party politicians and supporters.[70]

67 The Nitze exercise refers to the ongoing NATO burden-sharing exercise; for a more detailed discussion see Geiger, "Studies," 204-9.

68 FRUS 4i (1951), 933-5: telegram Batt - Foster, 11 April 1951.; NARA RG 59. Box 3528: 741.5/4-551: telegram Batt - Foster, Bissell and Wood, 5 April 1951.

69 FRUS 4i (1951), 935-41: memorandum Perkins - Acheson, 26 April 1951.

70 FRUS 4i (1951), 941-4: telegram Gifford - Secretary of State, 11 May 1951.

The budget and the political crisis, April 1951

In the meantime, domestic political tensions reached crisis point and led to an unbridgeable rift within the Attlee cabinet. To some extent, Gaitskell knowingly risked alienating Bevan through the introduction of prescription charges for certain National Health Service (NHS) prescriptions. Having initially agreed to these charges, Bevan retracted his consent in a speech to dockers in Bermondsey several days before the budget. Despite Bevan's open threats of resignation, the Chancellor insisted on reducing welfare expenditures in the budget.[71] On the day before the budget, Bevan threatened to resign again unless the cabinet over-ruled the Chancellor. Nevertheless, Attlee and the cabinet backed Gaitskell's budget proposals.[72] Fearing the political damage that would be likely to ensue for the Attlee government, a group of junior ministers urged Bevan to reconsider his position.[73] Rather than resigning immediately before the budget, Bevan dithered over whether to remain in the cabinet. After the positive response to the budget, the confrontation shifted to the meetings of the Parliamentary Labour Party. In a stormy meeting, Bevan repeated his plea for a reconsideration of NHS charges in order to preserve party unity. Despite the appeals for party unity from both camps, tempers frayed as senior ministers defended the budget proposals. Interventions degenerated into personal attacks which revealed the deep divisions between the two sides and made a compromise seem increasingly unlikely.[74]

Nevertheless, Bevan procrastinated for nearly two weeks before resigning from the cabinet. At first, Truman's decision to relieve General MacArthur of his command in Korea seemed to have restored the uneasy compromise within the Attlee cabinet.[75] As the left-wing Labour MP, Tom Driberg, confided in his diary:

> A good morning. Bright spring sunshine, a touch of warmth at last; Aneurin Bevan has *not* resigned from the government; and General MacArthur *has* been sacked.
>
> Great relief in the Party about Nye; for it seems to be generally assumed that his resignation, and that of one or two other Ministers with him, would precipitate an election—and at this moment we should almost certainly lose an election.

---

71 Diary entry, 24 April 1951; reprinted in Cairncross, ed., *Robert Hall diaries*, 153-55. See also Peter Hennessy, *Never Again: Britain, 1945-1951* (London: Vintage Books, 1993), 416-8.; Kenneth O. Morgan, *Labour in Power, 1945-1951* (Oxford: Oxford University Press, 1985), 443-61.

72 Patrick Gordon Walker, *The Cabinet* (London: Jonathan Cape, 1970), 133.

73 James Callaghan, *Time and Change* (Glasgow: Collins/Fontana, 1988), 107-15.

74 Diary entry, 11 April 1951; reprinted in Benn, *Years of hope*, 145-8.

75 Morgan, *Labour in power*, 450-52.

> [...] Nobody thought that Truman would have the guts to sack MacArthur. He is that perpetually astonishing phenomenon, the little man who sometimes does the big thing. No doubt the British Government brought some pressure in this direction—but we mustn't say so for the fear of playing into the hands of Truman's enemies. It would be too bad to get rid of MacArthur as Supreme Commander, only to have him turning up as President next time.[76]

Like Driberg, many contemporary British observers attributed this decision to British influence on American foreign policy.[77] Rather than attempting to defuse the smouldering conflict, senior ministers failed to address the mounting criticism of the party's left wing. Arguably, their complacency brought to a head the acrimonious debate over foreign and economic policy within cabinet which had threatened to split the Labour Party for months. Since the outbreak of the Korean war, Aneurin Bevan had opposed any reduction of welfare expenditure to finance rearmament. When Gaitskell's 1951 budget proposed to cut NHS expenditure by £13 million, Bevan faced the dilemma that the small cut did not justify resignation. Indeed, many on the Labour benches almost provoked Bevan's reaction by describing the cuts as trivialities.

Feeling humiliated by the open disregard of his position, Bevan decided to resign on 25 April. The next day, Bevan used his resignation statement to launch a ferocious attack on the government's economic, social and foreign policy describing the proposed cut as the thin end of a wedge which might result in undoing the major achievement of the first Attlee government. In his speech, Bevan accused Gaitskell of sacrificing socialist principles for negligible savings. After all, if Gaitskell found "... it necessary to mutilate, the Health Service for £13 million out of £4,000 million, what will he do next year?"[78] Continuing his attack, Bevan argued that given the planned budget surplus, the budget amounted to the economics of Bedlam relying on whistle-blowing intervention rather than economic planning. He felt that the excessive number of Treasury economists disregarded the underlying economic facts meant and therefore failed to manage the economy or to direct industrial production in a sensible fashion. For Bevan, the lack of realism underlying the government's rearmament programme exemplified the misguided nature of

---

[76] Diary entry, 11 April 1951; reprinted in Tom Driberg, *The Best of Both Worlds: A personal diary* (London: Phoenix House, 1953), 7-8.

[77] For such a view, see diary entry, 11 April 1951; reprinted in Benn, *Years of hope*, 145-8.; Michael Newman, *John Strachey* (Manchester: Manchester University Press, 1989), 124-5.

[78] The remainder of this paragraph is based on Bevan's resignation speech, see 487 H.C. Deb. 5s. col. 34-43 (quote: col. 41). My text alludes to some of Bevan's forceful expressions (the original phrases to which I refer are listed with their location): "arithmetic of Bedlam" (col. 42), "'whistle-blowing' planning" (emphasis in the original) (col. 39), "there are too many economists advising the Treasury" (col. 39), "unrestrained behaviour" (col. 36) and "... to be diverted from our path by the exigencies of the immediate situation" (col. 43).

these economic policies. Due to massive American purchases of vital basic materials and machinery, the rearmament programme had already fallen behind schedule. Indeed, the unrestrained demand of the United States threatened to cause mass-unemployment and economic hardship throughout the western world. Despite the impending economic crisis, the Attlee government chose to persist with an already fictitious rearmament programme. Rather than persevering in adversity, Bevan thought that the government should scale down the rearmament programme. Revising the defence programme downwards would remove the necessity to reduce the welfare budget. Having consented to rapid western rearmament, ministers had embarked on a course which Bevan warned might undermine liberal democracy. By discarding democratic socialism, the government had allowed itself "... to be diverted from [its] path by the exigencies of the immediate situation." Against this background, Bevan conceded that Gaitskell's budget achieved a remarkable feat:

> It united the City, satisfied the Opposition and disunited the Labour Party – all this because we have allowed ourselves to be dragged too far behind the wheels of American diplomacy.[79]

Aside from the fervent criticism of government policy, contemporary public reaction neglected the second recurring theme of the speech – Britain being a victim of "the anarchy of American competitive capitalism."[80] On the Labour benches, the anti-American remarks were seen as mainly rhetorical. Alienating even left-wing Labour MPs, Bevan's contempt for Gaitskell detracted from the substance of his criticisms. To some extent, Bevan and Wilson blunted their message by their continued willingness to compromise over the prescription charges. At one point, Bevan seemed willing to accept fudging the issue by agreeing to an informal ceiling on NHS spending in return for not imposing the prescription charges.[81] Despite the generally unsympathetic reception of Bevan's resignation, the President of the Board of Trade, Harold Wilson, and a junior minister in the Ministry of Supply, John Freeman decided to leave their ministerial posts. As party leaders feared at the time, the resignation row condemned the Labour Party to more than a decade in opposition.[82]

Given the political fall-out from the speech, historians have focused primarily on the domestic implications of the rift within the Labour Party. To

---

[79] 487 H.C. Deb. 5s. col. 38.

[80] 487 H.C. Deb. 5s. col. 39. On the contemporary reaction, see Morgan, *Labour in power*, 452-4.

[81] Diary entries, 30 April and 4 May; 1951; reprinted in Williams, ed., *Diary of Hugh Gaitskell*, 238-57.; Callaghan, *Time and change*, 111-15.

[82] Given his anger and rage, Bevan's speech "reads far better than it sounded" to those present; see diary entries, 23 and 24 April 1951; reprinted in Benn, *Years of hope*, 149-53 (quote: 149). On the political damage of the resignations, see also diary entry, 4 May 1951, reprinted in Williams, ed., *Diary of Hugh Gaitskell*, 248-57.

some extent, the political consequences gave particular poignancy to the disagreement between ministers. Since the disagreements were arguably bridgeable, historical interpretations have attributed the resignations to a mixture of personal reasons ranging from frustrated ambitions and conflicts of personality to shrewd personal calculation.[83] Nevertheless, the resignation row quickly took on the character of a struggle between two different visions of democratic socialism competing for the soul of the party. In a sense, history vindicated Bevan. With the benefit of hindsight, Bevan claimed correctly that the rearmament programme would be unrealisable, a fact conceded by Churchill when he announced a major revision of the defence programme in December 1951.[84] For many supporters, this belated vindication confirmed that the failure of the Attlee government to heed Bevan's warning about rearmament undermined its achievements in terms of social policy and economic recovery. This interpretation furthered the belief that Gaitskell and the majority of Labour MPs sacrificed democratic socialism for the sake of rearmament against a non-existent threat.[85] However, this interpretation remains problematic, because the fault lines it implies did not divide the party neatly into two camps. For example, the Minister of War, John Strachey did not resign despite his affinity to the Keep Left Group.[86] Indeed, his name had been connected with the opposition to any increase in the defence programme during the previous autumn.[87] Moreover, most ministers agreed with Bevan's apprehensions about the economic impact of rearmament.[88] According to the left-wing Labour MP, Tony Benn, Gaitskell agreed in his speech to the PLP with Bevan's analysis describing "... the American attitude on stockpiling as very dangerous indeed." To the same meeting, the Chancellor defended the government's record on social policy pointing to the increase in welfare

---

[83] See footnote 71. On the personal motivations of the key protagonists, see also Brian Brivati, *Hugh Gaitskell* (London: Richard Cohen, 1996), 113-23.; Ben Pimlott, *Harold Wilson* (London: HarperCollins, 1992), 156-72.

[84] Morgan, *Labour in power*, 455-61.; Hennessy, *Never again*, 416-18.

[85] *One way only*.; Ian Mikardo, *Back-Bencher* (London: Weidenfeld and Nicolson, 1988), 120-21.

[86] Newman, *John Strachey*, 121-30.

[87] See footnote 27. Commenting on this episode, the *Manchester Evening News* reminded its readers of this episode. In the context of the resignation row, the leader writer criticised Bevan's behaviour the previous autumn when he denied having derided the rearmament programme during lunch with American journalists; see "Double Talk," *Manchester Evening News*, 24 April 1951.

[88] A few days after Bevan's resignation, Gaitskell conceded that the economic situation had deteriorated slightly since the budget had been drawn up in a speech to the Scottish Labour Party; see "'We can rearm without losing economic independence'," *Manchester Guardian*, 30 April 1951. Despite some hostile questioning, the audience seemed to accept the Chancellor's assessment; see diary entry, 11 May 1951; reprinted in Williams, ed., *Diary of Hugh Gaitskell*, 257-61.

spending announced in the budget.[89] At the same time as introducing prescription charges, the government planned to increase pension payments thus alleviating the major social inequity in postwar British society.[90] For Bevan, this shift in spending priorities masked the social injustice of the budget as inflation would immediately reduce the real spending power of industrial workers and pensioners.[91] In his reply to the PLP, the Chancellor dismissed this criticism by referring to the tax increases planned to ensure an equitable distribution of the domestic burden of the rearmament.[92] To some extent, both sides justifiably claimed to be striving for social justice.

Although they realised the seriousness of the challenge, ministers seemed at a loss as to how they should respond to what seemed to be a caustically formulated argument. On the front bench, the consensus seemed in little doubt about the true facts: rearmament was a necessity; some sacrifice would be unavoidable, and a common purpose characterised Anglo-American relations. Bevan and Wilson conceded the first two points, but strongly objected to the third statement. In his resignation speech, Wilson stated unequivocally that he "... strongly [supported] an effective defence programme."[93] Bevan even indicated support for rearmament as long as the defence programme remained consistent with the "... maintenance of the standard of living of the British people and the maintenance of the social service."[94] However, their position was not entirely consistent. As the *Manchester Guardian* pointed out, while Bevan and Wilson opposed the introduction of a ceiling on health service expenditure, both accepted implicitly the massive reduction in food subsidies which directly affected the living standards of families with low incomes.[95]

Since all participants in this acrimonious row accepted that rearmament necessitated some sacrifices, government ministers might have been better advised to stress the areas of agreement rather than defending the necessity of rearmament and the budget. For Strachey, the disagreement was about the speed rather than the necessity of rearmament. Given the potential damage to the Labour movement, the health charges amounted to an insufficient reason for resignation.[96] In this context, the Minister of War remained convinced that the Labour government's primary objective, the preservation of world peace,

---

89 Diary entry, 24 April 1951; reprinted in Benn, *Years of hope*, 149-53 (quote:151).

90 A point emphasised by C. F. Carter, "The Impact of the Rearmament on Britain," *Public Finance / Finances Publiques* 7 (1952): 46-8.

91 487 H.C. Deb. 5s. col. 38.

92 Diary entry, 24 April 1951; reprinted in Benn, *Years of hope*, 149-53.

93 487 H.C. Deb. 5s. col. 228.

94 487 H.C. Deb. 5s. col. 37.

95 "Dangerous for Constituencies," *Manchester Guardian*, 24 April 1951.

96 "Health charges," *Manchester Guardian*, 30 April 1951.; Newman, *John Strachey*, 126-7.

could only be achieved through speedy rearmament. Since the dismissal of General MacArthur, Strachey detected that the American military leadership shared the British desire to prevent an escalation of the Korean war into a global conflict. Indeed, the Minister of War reminded an audience in Keighley of the sacrifice made by American troops in Korea for this shared objective.[97] Focusing on Bevan's criticism of the budget, Gaitskell pointed out that the Attlee government remained firmly committed to achieving the rearmament programme through increasing domestic production. By curbing domestic consumption and investment, the Chancellor hoped to contain inflation, maintain living standards and free sufficient resources to finance increased defence procurement. In this respect, Gaitskell and his Treasury advisers believed in a similar economic strategy to that of the Truman administration. Since both governments tried to achieve rearmament through economic expansion, British ministers could hardly criticise the American policy approach. Moreover, if the world-wide shortages turned out worse than anticipated, the budget would have to be tightened by further expenditure cuts, rather than providing scope for increased social expenditures as Bevan seemed to think possible. Therefore, it was "... just a bit too imaginative to attack the budget as involving either a departure from Socialist principle or a frontal attack on the social services."[98] For Gaitskell, the debate would benefit from a differentiation between the impact of world-wide rearmament and the domestic consequences of the British defence programme. In the wake of the resignation crisis, government ministers decided to brave the attack and repeated the same message up and down the country: being committed to rearmament, the government would carry out the defence programme. This attitude was aptly summed up by James Callaghan in a speech in Enfield:

> [Bevan, Freeman and Wilson] have left [the government] either too late or too soon. Too late if they oppose the (rearmament) programme; too soon if they believe it will fail.[99] [(Brackets) in the original]

Despite its concerted efforts, the government failed in its attempt to quell the rebellion. The resignations revealed the degree to which the Labour Party lacked able backbenchers to fill the gaps left in the ministerial ranks.[100] With

---

[97] John Rylands University Library Manchester, Labour Party Archive JRULM LPA International Department. Box: Korean War. Documents. Correspondence. etc. 1950-51: folder Korea War. File of notes. documents. cuttings produced.: Text of Speech by John Strachey in Keighley, 19 May 1951.

[98] "'We can rearm without losing economic independence'." *Manchester Guardian*, 30 April 1951.; diary entry, 24 April 1951; reprinted in Benn, *Years of hope*, 149-53.

[99] "'We can rearm without losing economic independence'." *Manchester Guardian*, 30 April 1951.

[100] "After the shock," *Manchester Guardian*, 25 April 1951.

the government's authority further impaired, some newspaper leader writers called for an early election which now seemed more than likely.[101] To most observers, the second Attlee government seemed tired. The long years in government (including the wartime coalition government) now started to take its toll among the senior ministers some of whom had been forced to resign due to ill health. During the budget crisis, Attlee had to go into hospital to receive treatment for severe duodenal pain. In his absence, both sides in the budget dispute seemed determined to seek confrontation rather than a face-saving compromise. In the light of the events surrounding the budget, Attlee resolved to seek an early election in the autumn.[102]

A long summer in British politics (May–October 1951)

For American officials, the resignation crisis presented a dilemma. In their reports to Washington, they remained convinced that the British government should expand its defence effort beyond the £4,700 million ceiling. American officials seemed to assume in their assessments that the British economy could bear a further increase of military production. As a consequence, American officials were unimpressed with Gaitskell's budget, because of the likely inflationary impact of the budget measures. At the same time, American officials voiced concern about the potential political fall-out from the resignations of Bevan and Wilson. From their perspective, Bevan's and Wilson's views might create a problem, if their accusations undermined the Attlee government's commitment to the British defence programme. While this seemed unlikely for the moment, American officials worried that the United States would receive the blame for any deterioration in Britain's economic situation. In such an eventuality, many British observers might accept the Bevanite story and attribute domestic inflation to American raw material stockpiling and western rearmament. For the first time, American officials acknowledged that "... there may be practical political limits beyond which the British Government cannot proceed ..." with rearmament.[103]

In the wake of the resignation crisis, the publication of *Only One Way Forward* reinforced the impression that the Americans had pressured the Attlee government to rearm. A spate of newspaper articles reminded readers that the initial £3,600 million defence programme had been contingent on the receipt of substantial American military aid. These stories recounted that Gaitskell had left out a reference to the £550 million the British government requested at the

[101] "Why not June?," *Manchester Evening News*, 25 April 1951.
[102] Harris, *Attlee*, 473-88.
[103] NARA RG 59. Box 3531: 741.5-MAP/5-1051: MDAP Monthly General Report (April 1951), despatch Tuthill - Department of State, 10 May 1951.

behest of the then American ambassador, Lewis Douglas. In July, *The Economist* severely criticised the allocation of American military aid suggesting that the larger a government's defence effort, the less likely it was to receive military aid. As a consequence, the report lamented that "[t]here is at present a dangerous premium on lack of effort; the United Kingdom, for instance, is not as good a candidate for American help as Italy."[104] *The Economist* attributed this unfair allocation to the absence of criteria for determining which country contributed its fair share and which were free riders. Perturbed by these comments, American officials approached *The Economist*'s editor, Geoffrey Crowther, to discuss the article. While the article might have overstated its case, Crowther insisted that it accurately reflected the feeling among Treasury officials that the United States had broken its word over military aid.[105]

To some extent, the article reflected the growing irritation in Whitehall about the slow progress of the on-going NATO burden-sharing exercise. In the eyes of British officials, some governments seemed to delay the process of assessing national defence contributions through obtuse questions designed to expose the unworkability of the MTDP and to press their case for American military aid. Despite the scale of the British defence effort, British policy-makers had to acknowledge that meeting Britain's MTDP commitments would require a further £2,000 million increase in defence expenditure. Given the likely political opposition, ministers could not contemplate such an increase without an agreement on financial burden-sharing which addressed British grievances. Incensed by this questioning of the British defence effort, Shinwell commented to his officials that Britain was "...being pushed around by small countries who are unwilling to do much."[106] Gaitskell informally discussed possible ways of accelerating western European rearmament with other finance ministers and OEEC officials during a visit to Paris. Stressing the growing economic problems, Gaitskell argued that an agreement on burden-sharing demanded firm American commitments on military aid to Europe.[107] At the same time British officials became concerned that American proposals outlining further increases in western defence efforts to meet the MTDP targets would delay an agreement on burden-sharing.[108]

104 "Fair Shares in Arms," *The Economist*, 14 July 1951.

105 NARA RG 59. Box 3531: 741.5-MAP/8-251: MDAP Monthly General Report (July 1951), despatch Tuthill - Department of State, 2 August 1951.

106 PRO DEFE 7/547: "Submission to F.E.B. of Information on the Cost of our Interim Force Contribution", memorandum Dean - Shinwell, 26 June 1951.

107 Diary entry, 8 August 1951; reprinted in Williams, ed., *Diary of Hugh Gaitskell*, 265-6.

108 PRO DEFE 7/547: M.A.C. (54) 124 (Revised), "Report of the Financial and Economic Board on the Defence Burden Exercise", Brief for the Chancellor of the Exchequer, 31 August 1951.; FRUS 4i (1951), 959-61: Gifford - Secretary of State, 6 September 1951.

Despite acknowledging difficulties with its implementation, many American representatives still regarded the British defence programme as insufficient, because the projected effort would not fulfil Britain's MTDP commitments. At the same time, American officials became slightly more receptive to British concerns regarding the availability of raw materials. In April 1951, the Truman administration allocated a large amount of sulphur to Britain, which alleviated this shortage in the short term. During the coming months, British officials discussed the raw material situation and prices with Charles Wilson, the Director of Defense Mobilisation in London and Winthrop Brown, the Director of the Office of International Material Policy in Washington. However, these discussions achieved little more than a general agreement over the difficulties of regulating world raw material supplies.[109] Indeed, one American senator accused the British government of profiting from the price increases in some raw materials. American representatives in London were more aware of the political and economic problems and stressed the strategic importance of British bases for American war plans in presentations to a visiting delegation of senators. During the same briefing, Batt stated that in the ECA mission's judgement the current British defence programme represented the maximum effort which could reasonably be expected in present circumstances.[110] As Britain's economic crisis deepened, the telegrams continually took the same line arguing for some financial support for British rearmament.[111] In September 1951, matters came to a head during discussions before the scheduled North Atlantic Council (NAC) meeting in Ottawa. Gaitskell drew attention to Britain's growing economic problems and ruled out any further increase in the British defence effort.[112] Against this background, British ministers refused to back American proposals for western rearmament and demanded an equitable burden-sharing agreement. The British refusal left the Truman administration isolated within the Alliance. At Ottawa, American officials realised that the American position over western rearmament and military aid undermined the willingness of their western European partners to carry out their defence

[109] Diary entries, 6 May, 13 and 19 July 1951; reprinted in Cairncross, ed., *Robert Hall diaries*, 156-7 and 160-61.; FRUS 4i (1951), 945-6: Memorandum of Conversation, by the Director of the Office of International Materials Policy (Brown), 13 July 1951.; *ibid.*, 947-52: Memorandum by the Director of the Office of International Materials Policy (Brown), 17 July 1951.

[110] NARA RG 59. Box 3531: 741.5-MAP/7-1351: "UK MDAP Team Briefing for Senate Foreign Relations Committee meeting in London July 11, 1951", despatch Tuthill - Department of State, 13 July 1951.

[111] FRUS 4i (1951), 952-5: Holmes - Secretary of State, 17 August 1951.; *ibid.*, 955-9: Holmes - Secretary of State, 27 August 1951.

[112] FRUS 4i (1951), 966-70: Memorandum of Conversation, by the Assistant Secretary of State for Economic Affairs (Thorp), 6 September 1951.

programmes.[113] In order to avoid the impending crisis in the Alliance, Acheson, Schuman and the new British Foreign Secretary, Herbert Morrison agreed that a renewed examination of western defence efforts be conducted by a small group of experts under the aegis of a Temporary Council Committee (TCC).[114] The TCC exercise led to American acceptance of the British claims that the rearmament programme represented an excessive burden for the domestic economy. As a result, Britain now received considerable American military aid to assist with its economic problems. In this sense, the report belatedly vindicated the Attlee government's attempts to secure American financial aid to finance rearmament.[115]

Emplotting the antagonistic nature of the Anglo-American relationship

During the first year of the Korean war, Anglo-American relations were marred by constant tensions. While both governments presented a united front in opposing communist aggression in Korea as well as in western Europe, British and American policy-makers faced different political pressures at home and abroad. The overarching objective of American foreign policy remained the preservation of American preponderance. An essential element in the American cold war strategy remained the defence of western Europe in order to deny its economic resources to the Soviet Union. At the same time, the bipartisan consensus on foreign policy collapsed with a number of Republican senators openly criticising Acheson's foreign policy as being responsible for communist advances in Asia. Against this background, Truman and his senior foreign policy-makers felt under pressure to be seen as in control of events. As a consequence, the administration engaged in a certain amount of posturing over Korea. For example, Truman's blunder over the use of nuclear weapons in December 1950 has to be seen as an attempt to silence the administration's domestic critics.[116]

On the other side of the Atlantic, the Attlee government faced similar domestic constraints. Its small parliamentary majority made the government vulnerable to pressure from opposition in its own ranks. Moreover, Churchill

[113] The development of American military aid policy is discussed in Till Geiger and Lorenza Sebesta, "National Defense Policies and the Failure of Military Integration in NATO: American Military Assistance and Western European Rearmament, 1949-54," in *The United States and the Integration of Europe: Legacies for the postwar era*, eds. Francis H. Heller and John R. Gillingham (New York: St. Martin's Press, 1996), 258-63.

[114] Acheson, *Present at the creation*, 559-60.

[115] Diary entry, 11 December 1951; reprinted in Cairncross, ed., *Robert Hall diaries*, 187-8.

[116] On this point, see Roger Dingman, "Atomic Diplomacy during the Korean War," *International Security* 13 (1988): 60-69.

harried the government by talking up the Soviet threat and criticising their inadequate response. Many British policy-makers shared American threat perceptions and regarded western rearmament as the top priority. After the outbreak of the Korean war, Treasury advisers accepted the necessity of increasing the British defence effort, but attempted to balance the needs of economic recovery and rearmament. To maintain the support of its MPs, ministers stressed that the defence programme did not place an undue burden on the economy and was conditional on the receipt of substantial American military aid. These ministerial statements were designed to reassure the left-wing that the increase in defence expenditure would not lead to a reduction in the welfare budget. At the same time, the Attlee government assured American foreign policy-makers that Britain fully supported their foreign policy. By endorsing American proposals for western European rearmament, British foreign policy-makers hoped to be treated as partners rather than supplicants by their American counterparts. However, American policy-makers rebuffed British advances for a special relationship interpreting the Attlee government's attempts to maintain domestic support for rearmament as its failure to contribute fully to the western defence effort. While both governments faced similar domestic constraints, policy-makers on both sides of the Atlantic seemed insufficiently aware of the potential conflict of interests faced by their counterparts. Confronted with domestic criticism, both governments concentrated on addressing the concerns of their detractors at home. For example, Attlee travelled to Washington in December 1950 predominantly to calm nerves at home.

In this sense, the behaviour of both governments closely resembled that of the Janus-faced actor described by Robert Putnam in his seminal study on diplomacy and domestic politics. Putnam argues that foreign policy-makers participate in a two-level game. In the domestic arena, politicians try to maximise political support for their foreign policy by balancing the interests of different constituencies. At the conference table, negotiators try to obtain the most favourable agreement keeping its impact to a minimum or achieving maximal concessions. To be successful, policy-makers have to balance maintaining domestic support and negotiating hard for the best deal.[117]

Following the logic of Putnam's two-level games, the Attlee government's commitment to the expanded £4,700 defence programme precipitated its demise, because senior ministers failed to maintain party support for their foreign policy. However, the fragility of the cabinet consensus for rearmament had been evident since the announcement of the £3,600 million defence programme in September 1950. Behind the scenes, Bevan and his supporters

[117] Robert D. Putnam, "Diplomacy and domestic politics: the logic of two-level games," *International Organization* 42 (1988): 427-60, particularly 433-5.

continued to warn that they regarded any reduction in social welfare expenditure as a result of increased defence expenditure as unacceptable. Nevertheless, British ministers and officials neglected to bring home to their American counterparts the extent to which domestic political constraints limited the scope for further increases in the British defence expenditure. At the same time, British policy-makers failed to realise that American officials regarded the unwillingness of the Labour government to reduce welfare expenditure as an indicator that the British economy could withstand a further expansion of the rearmament effort. As a consequence, they pressed their case for military aid on the basis of the contemplated size of the British defence programme rather than stressing that support for rearmament within the government might dissipate if Britain did not receive substantial aid. Until summer 1951, British Labour ministers believed that support for American policies on western rearmament would ensure a degree of influence over American foreign policy and conduct of the Korean war.

As Driberg pointed out, the resignation crisis brought home to American foreign policy-makers the political difficulties faced by the Attlee government at home harried by the opposition for not doing enough and by its own left wing. As an immediate consequence of the ensuing political crisis, American aid officials became sympathetic to British aid requests providing a substantial shipment of sulphur to aid the British defence programme. This sudden change of heart revealed the profound impact of the resignation crisis on Anglo-American relations allowing other government ministers such as Morrison and Gaitskell to take a harder line against continued American demands for further increases in Britain's defence effort.[118] As Britain's economic crisis deepened during the summer of 1951, British ministers started to demand a reappraisal of the British defence effort within the framework of a wider NATO review at the NAC meeting in Ottawa.[119] This British rebellion led by Gaitskell against American policy prepared ground which allowed the incoming Conservative government under Winston Churchill to scale down the British defence effort shortly after its election victory in October 1951 without damaging the Anglo-American relationship. Given his belated fierce resistance to American demands, some criticisms of Gaitskell by the Bevanites were unduly harsh. Moreover, the fact that the TCC report in February 1952 recommended a reduction of the British defence burden vindicated Gaitskell's insistence in a document to the PLP in November 1951 that multilateral negotiations would prove the only sensible way forward for Britain.[120]

---

[118] Diary entry, 23 April 1953; reprinted in Driberg, *Best of both worlds*, 14-16.

[119] Diary entries, 9 and 16 November; reprinted in Williams, ed., *Diary of Hugh Gaitskell*, 274-93.

[120] Document 8: "Dollar Aid and Defence", Memorandum by Hugh Gaitskell, 23 November 1951; reprinted in Williams, ed., *Diary of Hugh Gaitskell*, 293-9.

Historians have tended to overlook Gaitskell's success in standing up to the Truman administration, because the election defeat allowed the critics of the government's rearmament policy to claim that they had correctly predicted the deepening economic crisis. However, this analysis emphasised the centrality of the Anglo-American relationship in the developments leading to the political and economic upheavals of 1951. In their resignation speeches, Bevan and Wilson instrumentally linked America's behaviour to Britain's economic plight. As Harold Wilson reminded parliamentarians in his resignation speech, ministers had

> ... embarked on this re-armament programme as part of a joint effort by the members of the Atlantic community and of the Commonwealth. We embarked on the basis that our partners would make available our rightful share of the materials available. We have not had our rightful share; I hope we may still get it. But today British industry stands disorganised and threatened by partial paralysis. The American Government and people have got to choose between their partners' defence programme on the one hand, and their own stockpiles and the level of their own restrictive civilian consumption on the other. Until the right choice is made our defence programme remains an illusion.[121]

For Bevan and Wilson, this unneighbourly conduct threatened to undermine Britain's third way between Communism and "... the harshness and brutalities of free enterprise."[122] Through their massive spending power, American capitalists denied British producers the resources to co-operate with the excessive American demands for western rearmament. Effectively, American capitalism rather than Communism threatened to end Britain's project of democratic socialism. By resisting international allocation of raw materials, the Truman administration acted as a henchman for American capitalism preventing the equitable distribution of economic resources. In their speeches, Bevan and Wilson described the Anglo-American relationship as workable in the present crisis because of the different economic systems. Before an audience in Tredegar, Bevan denied accusations of anti-Americanism, but continued to draw attention to the problem of American size. Since American policy threatened to cause unemployment in Britain, Bevan concluded that "[i]t would be impossible to have a political alliance, if there were economic war."[123]

This line of argument did not convince most contemporary observers. The leader writer of the *Manchester Guardian* suspected that Bevan's anti-American rhetoric served a different purpose because by blaming American

---

[121] 487 H.C. Deb. 5s. col. 226-31 (quote: col. 229).

[122] 487 H.C. Deb. 5s. col. 231.

[123] "Bevan will not vote against the government," *Manchester Guardian*, 30 April 1951.

obstinacy, he could revoke his support for continued rearmament.[124] Arguably, Bevan could not resign over the proposed ceilings on social expenditure, since Gaitskell's budget struck an acceptable balance between maintaining the defence programme and curbing overall demand. Therefore, political friends urged Bevan to resign over rearmament, rather than the health charges.[125] In view of his misgivings since the previous autumn, a resignation over the defence programme seemed the better political strategy. Since his support had always been contingent on an international agreement on subordinating rearmament to economic growth and stability, Bevan could now successfully portray the Anglo-American relationship as undermining Labour's domestic project of democratic socialism or planned democracy.[126]

To a large extent, America's refusal to grant military aid to Britain precipitated the political crisis of 1951, which could otherwise have been avoided. In the absence of such aid, rearmament forced the Chancellor to contain the rising costs of the welfare state. Bevan, Wilson and many left-wingers regarded this decision as the first step towards dismantling this essential element of democratic socialism. By relying on a foreign scapegoat, Bevan and Wilson distracted attention from the domestic roots of their disagreement over the emerging contradictions of the British welfare state. Bound up in Anti-American rhetoric, rearmament offered an opportunity to fight for the future of Labour's democratic socialist project. Given their belief in the common purpose of British and American governments, government ministers did not even address, much less answer convincingly, this central element in Bevan and Wilson's argument: "Are we perhaps being too subservient to the United States?"[127] By not answering this question, the government validated Bevan's claim that American pressure over rearmament had led to the cuts in social expenditure.[128] The failure to refute the accusation of subservience reflected the conviction of ministers that they were pursuing an independent foreign policy restraining American aggression. For ministers, British influence over American policy was contingent on the determination to carry out the defence programme with or without American aid. Nevertheless, ministers failed to convince the Bevanites that their influence on Washington was not just a delusion. In the months following the resignations, economic developments added to the credence of Bevan's story. After the Labour Party lost the 1951 election, the internal debate over rearmament continued. In

---

[124] "Swan Song," *Manchester Guardian*, 24 April 1951.

[125] Harris, *Attlee*, 474.

[126] This analysis draws on Laclau's observation that an antagonistic relationship (e.g. worker and employer) is not necessarily contradictory (incompatible), but contingent on reference to outside factors which produce the conflict; see Ernesto Laclau, *New Reflections on the Revolution of Our Time* (London: Verso, 1990), 5-18.

[127] "Closing the ranks," *Manchester Guardian*, 26 April 1951.

[128] "The split," *Manchester Evening News*, 23 April 1951.

response to a resolution from Michael Foot and Richard Crossman, Gaitskell attempted to answer the government's critics.[129] This belated attempt failed, not least because the newly elected Conservative government decided to cut the defence programme significantly in response to Britain's growing balance of payments crisis. When announcing these defence cuts, Churchill agreed that Bevan had accurately criticised the expanded defence programme as unworkable the previous spring.[130] The internal feud over Korean war rearmament continued unabated, because the two conflicting versions of events reflected the differences between both factions over almost every aspect of Party policy. Arguably, this prolonged internal debate distracted the Labour Party from offering solutions to Britain's long-term economic problems.[131] Simultaneously, this line of argument evolved into the assertion that Britain's slow economic growth was attributable to Korean war rearmament and the resulting excessive defence burden. By the mid-1950s, this explanation had become an integral part of the growing discourse of declinism.[132]

This analysis begs the question whether the Attlee government should have resisted American demands for further increases in the rearmament programme earlier. The idea of the Anglo-American partnership prevented British policy-makers from realising the extent to which domestic opposition shaped the decisions of the American foreign policy community. If they had realised this, British officials would have been aware that, given the strained relationship between the Truman administration and Congress, Britain was unlikely to receive any aid as long as the Labour government supported American policies for western rearmament within NATO. While American pressure arguably precipitated the political crisis, it was the deepening economic crisis which persuaded the supporters of British rearmament to adopt a harder line towards the United States over rearmament. Despite being regarded as a stooge of American imperialism by the Bevanites, Gaitskell created the political context in which the new Conservative government could reduce defence expenditures and press the case for military aid. However, American policy-makers only acquiesced to this cut in the British rearmament drive by the incoming Conservative government because they had come to realise that continued pressure for further increases in western European defence efforts threatened to undermine the western alliance. Therefore, it must remain questionable whether a different policy on rearmament might have prevented the resignation crisis or the subsequent battle for the soul of the Labour movement.

---

[129] Document 8: "Dollar Aid and Defence", Memorandum by Hugh Gaitskell, 23 November 1951; reprinted in Williams, ed., *Diary of Hugh Gaitskell*, 293-9.

[130] 494 H.C. Deb. 5s. col. 2601-2.

[131] C. A. R. Crosland, *Britain's Economic Problem* (London: Jonathan Cape, 1953), 211-12.

[132] For example, see Andrew Shonfield, *British Economic Policy since the War* (Harmondsworth: Penguin, 1958), 91-5.

Part II

British defence production policy

Chapter 4

'The next war is bound to come': Defence production policy, supply departments and defence contractors in Britain, 1945–57

The experience of the Second World War underlined the importance of a healthy economy in the age of mechanised warfare. The revolution in warfare brought a greater reliance on large scale mechanisation of the military, and a strong armaments industry and engineering sector had become one of the pillars of military power. The ability of the allies to outproduce their enemies was seen as instrumental in their victory over Germany and Japan.[1] Immediately after the Second World War, however, the Labour government had been determined to restrict severely the resources going to defence in order to facilitate the restoration of a balanced peace economy as soon as possible.

> Defence policy must be compatible with the national need not only because of the heavy demands made on national resources - both manpower and material - by the Armed Forces, but also because a successful defence policy must find its roots in healthy social and economic conditions.[2]

Even though the Labour government intended to give priority to the civil economy in the immediate post-war period, British defence spending as a share of the GDP exceeded the share devoted to defence in all other major industrialised countries – even that of the United States – by nearly 50 per cent.[3] By 1957 – as is quite apparent from the Defence White Paper of that year

---

1 Mark Harrison, "Resource Mobilisation for World War II: the U.S.A., U.K., U.S.S.R. and Germany, 1939-1945," *Economic History Review* 41 (1988): 171.

2 Ministry of Defence, *Statement relating to Defence 1947*, Cmd. 7042 (London: His Majesty's Stationery Office, 1947), 2.

3 In 1947 the United Kingdom still spent roughly 10 per cent of GDP on defence. This was almost twice the proportion spent on defence by the United States (5.25 per cent of GDP). In 1948 the United Kingdom (7.26 per cent of GDP) spent proportionally 1.5 times more than the United States (4.78 per cent). This ratio changed radically over the next few years. At the peak of the Korean war rearmament programme, the United States (14.83 per cent of GDP) spent proportionally 1.4 times as much as the United Kingdom (10.45 per cent of

– the government was concerned that the hitherto large defence effort had been detrimental to the strength of the British economy, and sought to adopt a cheaper defence policy.[4] This statement reflected the growing appreciation of the cost of defence and realisation that Britain was no longer a major power.[5]

A real problem for the government is to decide between two priorities: a sound defence budget and an adequate national defence posture.[6] It is hard to understate the central dilemma – whether the budget or defence needs should take priority – as a constant source of conflict within the government. The element of choice made it very hard to determine how much of the nation's output should be devoted to defence. Given the increased military commitments after the war, Bevin and most of the Labour Cabinet were determined to ensure that the services received enough money to meet these commitments. During the immediate post-war period financial and economic pressures forced the government to free itself of at least some of these commitments.[7] At that time financial pressure presented defence planners with the serious problem of trying to formulate a defence policy that would overcome the mismatch between the British defence commitments and the available financial resources.[8]

Many analysts believe that the British government's inability to resolve this basic dilemma was to the detriment of Britain's post-war economic performance. For example, the failure of the British economy to achieve the investment ratio of other Western European countries is often attributed to the high level of defence expenditure and to the increased share of social investment, particularly in the housing programme. Among others, Martin Chick has argued that the Labour government curtailed productive investment because industrialists lacked political representation within the decision-

---

GDP) (my calculations, based on Organisation for European Economic Co-operation, *Statistics of National Product and Expenditure, 1938 and 1947 to 1955* (Paris: Organisation for European Economic Co-operation, 1957).)

4 Ministry of Defence, *Defence: Outline of future policy*, Cmnd. 124 (London: Her Majesty's Stationery Office, 1957), 1-2.

5 C. J. E. Harlow, *The European Armaments Base: A Survey. Part 2: National Procurement Policies* (London: Institute of Strategic Studies, 1967), 7.

6 Charles J. Hitch and R. M. McKean, *Economics of Defense in the Nuclear Age* (Cambridge: Harvard University Press, 1960), 48.

7 Michael Dockrill, *British Defence Policy since 1945* (Oxford: Basil Blackwell, 1988), 34-9.; Paul M. Kennedy, *Realities behind Diplomacy: Background influences on British external policy* (London: Fontana, 1985), 327-8.. The withdrawal from Greece is often interpreted as a clear sign that the economic strain of these additional commitments was too much for the limping British economy; see Frank K. Roberts, "Ernest Bevin as Foreign Secretary," in *The Foreign Policy of the British Labour Governments, 1945-1951*, ed. Ritchie Ovendale (Leicester: Leicester University Press, 1984), 33-4.

8 Anthony Gorst, "British military planning for post-war defence, 1943-1945," in *Britain and the First Cold War*, ed. Anne Deighton (Basingstoke: Macmillan, 1990), 91-108.

making process.[9] Britain's recurring balance of payments problems have been blamed on the relatively high overseas military expenditure.[10] Others have suggested that the poor record of British productivity growth is a direct result of the generous share of defence related research and development expenditure and a comparatively large defence industry.[11] While some empirical evidence[12] does not stand up to careful scrutiny, more qualitative evidence suggests that some industries were hard hit by increased military expenditure during the Korean war defence programme from 1950 to 1954.[13]

In contrast with most studies, this chapter tries to analyse the economic impact of British defence expenditure within a macroeconomic context. This analysis rests on the premise that defence spending influenced the economy directly through the purchase of goods and services. For example, massive expenditure on military aircraft provided a major incentive for aircraft producers to develop and build combat rather than civilian aircraft. Most of the analysis will concentrate on the defence production policy of the supply departments and the defence industry after 1945. It will look in detail at procurement of military aircraft and tanks. The study will form the basis of an assessment of the macroeconomic implications of the procurement policy of

---

[9] Martin Chick, "Economic Planning, Managerial Decision-Making and the Role of Fixed Capital Investment in the Economic Recovery of the United Kingdom, 1945-55," (Ph.D. thesis, University of London, 1986), 31-58. The figures for social investment given by Sidney Pollard (Sidney Pollard, *The Development of the British Economy, 1914-1967*, 2nd ed. (London: Edward Arnold, 1969), 407.) suggest that the share of social investment of total gross domestic capital formation rose from 10.7 per cent in 1937-38 to 15.3 per cent in 1947-48 and 14.8 per cent in 1950-51. This increase seems hardly that significant if one bears in mind that the share of GDP invested nearly doubled compared with pre-war years. Indeed, Alan Milward (Alan S. Milward, *The Reconstruction of Western Europe, 1945-51* (London: Methuen, 1984), 484-5.) argues that social investment may have created a more stable environment for private investment and thus "crowded in" investment. See also the comments of Jim Tomlinson, "Labour's management of the national economy, 1945-51: Survey and Speculations," *Economy and Society* 18 (1989): 8-9.

[10] Kennedy, *Realities behind Diplomacy: Background influences on British external policy*, 319-20.

[11] Mary Kaldor, "Technical Change in the Defence Industry," in *Technical Innovation and British Economic Performance*, ed. Keith Pavitt (Basingstoke: Macmillan, 1980), 114-19.; Chris Freeman, "Technical Innovation and British Trade Performance," in *De-industrialisation*, ed. Frank Blackaby (London: Heinemann, 1978), 66-9.

[12] There are three comprehensive surveys of the economic impact literature: Steven Chan, "The impact of defence spending on economic performance: A survey of evidence and problems," *Orbis* 29 (1985): 403-34.; Gavin Kennedy, *Defense Economics* (London: Duckworth, 1983).; and Judith Reppy, "On the economics of national security," in *Security and Arms Control, volume 1: A guide to national policymaking*, eds. E. A. Kolodziej and P. M. Morgan (New York: Greenwood Press, 1989).

[13] Joan Mitchell, *Crisis in Britain 1951* (London: Secker & Warburg, 1963), 230-45.

the supply departments. Such an appraisal should provide a more adequate explanation of the transmission mechanism of defence policy.

An industrial policy for the next war

The 1946 Defence White Paper outlined four principles that were to guide military procurement policy.[14] On the one hand, the government planned to maintain design teams in the armaments sector by concentrating its production expenditure on research and development of new weapons systems; on the other hand, the production capacity of the industry was to be kept intact through limited repair and maintenance contracts. According to the White Paper the services were to rely on stocks left over from the war rather than to be allowed to place orders for new equipment or stores. The only exceptions were to be jet aircraft and a limited number of new tanks.[15] At the same time, the defence planners hoped that the armaments industry would contribute as much as possible to the reconstruction of the British economy. Even though the Labour government intended to give priority to the civil economy, it also stated quite clearly that it intended to maintain a nucleus of capacity in the key armaments industries to be able to respond to any military threat more quickly than in the 1930s.

Post-war planning and reconstruction

In late 1943, discussions between a number of government departments started concerning the future of the aircraft industry. At the time the Treasury felt that the annual allocation of about £100 million (1943 prices) for the procurement of aircraft out of the defence budget of £500 million was realistic as long as the public would tolerate this high level of defence expenditure.[16] This meant that after the war the output in the aircraft industry had to be reduced by roughly 90 per cent of its production level in 1942. In order to achieve this reduction the Treasury suggested that some development projects should be cancelled and that most of the productive capacity be released for civilian purposes at an early stage in order to avoid large-scale scrapping of new equipment at the end of hostilities.[17] While most officials were concerned about maintaining aircraft

---

[14] Ministry of Defence, *Statement relating to Defence*, Cmd. 6743 (London: His Majesty's Stationery Office, 1946), 7.

[15] Ministry of Defence, *Statement relating to Defence 1947*, 5.

[16] Public Record Office, Treasury (hereafter: PRO T) 160/1407/F.18576: "Post-war expenditure", Gilbert - Brittain, 7 November 1943.

[17] PRO T 225/653: Gilbert - Eady and Barlow, 17 December 1943.

production after the end of the war, Keynes was anxious to avoid the wholesale destruction of aircraft which seemed to him "an extreme case of digging holes on the ground".[18] While maintaining production was one of the major concerns, officials also worried about the structure and regional distribution of the industry. Some rationalisation and concentration of development work was seen as unavoidable to meet the Treasury objective that there should be a fair measure of competition both in price and quality within the industry.[19] As early as 1946, concern grew in Whitehall about whether the dependence of the aircraft industry on government contracts was excessive and whether the industry should be rationalised even further.[20] From 1945 to 1950, the Treasury maintained, at considerable expense, 19 aircraft manufacturers through development contracts and repair work. In 1950, the size and structure of the aircraft industry was reviewed and the suggestion raised to concentrate production further by reducing the number of manufacturers eligible for government contracts to 13.[21] In approving the rationalisation plans in July 1950, the Defence Committee stressed the vital importance of maintaining the war potential of the industry for the future defence of Britain.[22] In the end, the Korean war delayed restructuring of the industry until the late 1950s, when the government decided to encourage mergers within the aircraft industry.[23]

In 1944, the Ministry of Supply tried to develop a post-war tank production policy. The original plans drawn up in 1944 envisaged that besides the Royal Ordnance Factory (ROF) at Leeds and Vickers-Armstrong, two further private firms should be encouraged to maintain a tank production capability. The original plans stated quite clearly that the Ministry intended to attract the interest of the potential contractors (Leyland, Vauxhall, Nuffield Mechanisation, English Electric) through sufficient orders. Vauxhall was very

---

[18] PRO T 225/653: Keynes - Eady, 17 December 1943.; Eady - Barlow, 18 December 1943.; Gilbert - Eady, 23 December 1943.; Keynes-Gilbert, 3 January 1944. Keynes suggested in his *General Theory of Employment, Interest, and Money* that the Treasury could increase employment in an economy with large-scale unemployment by burying money in the ground and allowing private firms to dig it out again; see John Maynard Keynes, *The General Theory of Employment, Interest and Money*, ed. Royal Economic Society (London: Macmillan, 1974), 129-30.

[19] PRO T 225/653: Eady - Barlow, 18 December 1943.

[20] PRO T 225/653: Japp - Blunt, 3 June 1946.

[21] PRO T 225/369: draft memorandum "Size and shape of the aircraft industry: need for planning to preserve war potential"., Musgrave - Humphrey-Davies, 18 February 1950.; Humphrey-Davies - Pitblado, 29 March 1950.; Minute of a meeting to consider draft paper, 20 April 1950.

[22] PRO CAB 131/8: minutes of a meeting of the Defence Committee, DO 11(50)2, 11 July 1950.

[23] G. D. H. Henderson, "Government and Industry," in *The British economy in the nineteen-fifties*, eds. G. D. N. Worswick and P. H. Ady (Oxford: Clarendon Press, 1962), 360-39.

reluctant to take on further defence work.[24] When Leyland was offered a contract for a tank design team the directors refused, believing that the post-war reconstruction boom would offer them far more lucrative opportunities than the design contract offered to them by the Ministry.[25] Interestingly enough, English Electric at the time made several approaches to the Ministry in an attempt to obtain a tank production contract. As a tank manufacturer, English Electric was very much a second best solution for the Ministry, which argued that this company lacked the expertise to build tanks. Despite the wishes of the Ministry of Supply to keep four independent tank design teams after the war, the War Office lacked the funds to order a large number of new tanks. As a consequence, English Electric decided in 1949 to give up its small tank production and transferred its work to Vickers.[26] Another problem arising from the limited tank production after 1945 was that both Vickers and ROF Leeds had great difficulty in obtaining certain components, particularly large castings for tank turrets. The small scale of orders for such components made the sub-contractors less interested in continuing to supply the parts in sufficient numbers and in time to allow for continuous production in the tank factories.[27]

The rather negative attitude of Leyland to the advances of the supply departments was shared by other industries. For example, the radio industry showed little or no interest in Ministry of Supply contracts for the development of a communications system for aircraft. The small volume of defence work available did little to lure firms that were hoping to exploit the potential mass-market for radio and television sets. At the same time, research and development in the communications field was cut by 30 per cent and some of the scientists were transferred to other more important development programmes (e.g. Atomic Energy, and guided weapons).[28]

In October 1945, the government decided that 23 Royal Ordnance Factories were to be kept under government control. The decision about which factories were to be kept was based on several considerations. Most importantly the Ministry of Supply wished to retain at least one production facility for each weapon type. Consideration was also given to location and the local labour

[24] PRO WO 185/232: Gibb - Duncan, 30 October 1944.; Micklem - Hancock, 14 September, 1944.; "Post-war organisation for design and production of tanks", memorandum by Hancock, 19 October 1944.

[25] PRO WO 185/232: Note of a meeting with Leyland directors, 5 July 1945.

[26] Cambridge University Library (hereafter: CUL) Vickers J99: letter Nelson - Micklem, 5 December 1949.; letter Micklem - Nelson, 7 December 1949.

[27] CUL Vickers J99: Micklem - Muirhead, 13 January 1950.; Muirhead - Micklem, 17 January 1950.; Muirhead - Micklem; 27 March 1950.; Pickworth - Micklem, 20 March 1950. See also PRO WO 185/162: minutes of a meeting of the ROF Central Production Committee, 17 October 1949.

[28] PRO AIR 20/6937: Croyton - Robb, 19 March 1948.

situation. In order to preserve a nucleus of essential labour, employment at the ROFs was fixed at about 40,000. As the service requirements in the first post-war years were insubstantial, due to adequate weapons and ammunition stocks left over from the war, capacity utilisation in the ROFs during this period remained very low. It was decided that this idle capacity should be used to meet the urgent demands of government departments or industry and to contribute either directly or indirectly to the export drive. A report of the Select Committee on Estimates, however, revealed that the possibilities of using the ROFs' capacities economically were very limited.[29] The disappointing capacity utilisation of the ROFs led the committee to conclude that some of the factories should be run down even further as long as there were no new orders forthcoming. This experience was shared by private ammunitions manufacturers such as Vickers. The degree of under-utilisation of capacity caused so much concern among the directors of Vickers that in 1948 the board decided to hold an inquiry into its causes and implications. The inquiry found that while most factories could be used for civilian production, this could only be achieved at the cost of a loss of efficiency. As some of the Vickers factories worked at only 50 per cent of their capacity and most of the work carried out was civilian orders, the report was rather pessimistic about the future prospects of most plants unless new government contracts could be obtained.[30]

This analysis reveals the essence of the supply departments' industrial policy. The salient features of the policy were maintenance of key production and design facilities for a future large-scale war economy, ensuring the health of the defence contractors through repair contracts or spreading of research contracts across the firms and sustaining a fair degree of competition among the defence contractors. In the early post-war years, when there was hardly any procurement of new weapons, the maintenance of this additional capacity in an economic environment characterised by shortages and still severely restrained by controls must have exacerbated the problem of excess demand.

Matters improved after the government started to place larger defence production contracts in the summer of 1948, but the defence industry was really saved by the Korean war defence programmes. The industrial policy tended to subsidise the final stage of armaments production (i.e. assembly plants) rather than to encourage the formation of integrated defence contractors which would produce most of the specific weapons systems. This policy rested on the notion that in the event of major rearmament most of the economy

---

[29] House of Commons, *Seventh Report from the Select Committee on Estimates, Session 1947-48: Royal Ordnance Factories*, vol. 288, House of Commons Papers 200 (London: His Majesty's Stationery Office, 1948).

[30] CUL Vickers 725: Final Report of the Committee on Reserve Capacity for Armaments Production, 10 May 1948.

would have to be converted to a war footing. This approach seems to have ignored the possibility of a more capital-intensive defence posture based on the constant procurement of highly sophisticated weapons systems that was to become typical for the military-industrial complex of the nuclear age.[31] In other words, the supply departments' industrial policy can best be described as an industrial policy for all-out war rather than for the age of economic deterrence. Thus the desire to maintain the greatest possible number of armaments producers rested on the basic assumption of the likelihood of a future global war of attrition. The idea of fostering competition among the individual armaments played only a minor role in the deliberations of the supply departments.[32] Indeed, competition and the rate of technical innovation may well have been higher had fewer larger firms competed for the limited number of defence projects for which the supply departments could invite tenders.[33]

---

[31] Michael Geyer, *Deutsche Rüstungspolitik, 1860-1980* (Frankfurt/Main: Suhrkamp, 1984), 173-5.; Mary Kaldor, *The Baroque Arsenal* (London: Abacus, 1983), 47-54. The reorientation towards an increasingly capital-intensive defence posture slowly evolved out of the military containment doctrine. Military containment was the response to the perception among politicians that the Cold War had escalated to a state of permanent crisis; see Warner R. Schilling, "The Politics of National Defense: Fiscal 1950," in *Strategy, Politics and Defense Budgets*, eds. Warner R. Schilling, Paul Y. Hammond, and Glenn H. Snyder (New York: Columbia University Press, 1962), 8-10.; John Lewis Gaddis, *Strategies of Containment: A critical appraisal of post-war American national security policy* (New York: Oxford University Press, 1982), 90-92. Consequently, many politicians in the United States and Britain called for a substantial increase in defence outlays in the late 1940s. As an integral part of this strategy the United States committed itself to frontline defence and the stationing of troops in Europe and the Far East. The economic implications of massive rearmament led to increased reliance on highly sophisticated weapons systems and the threat of massive retaliation; see Gaddis, *Strategies of containment*, 133-6 and 142-52. European countries started to adopt capital-intensive defence postures in the late 1950s; see Geyer, *Deutsche Rüstungspolitik*, 200-217. In Britain the publication of the 1957 Defence White Paper marked the end of the transition towards a capital-intensive strategy; see Ministry of Defence, *Defence: outline*.

[32] Peck and Scherer have argued convincingly that there can be no truly competitive market for weapons; see Merton J. Peck and Frederic M. Scherer, *The Weapons Acquisition Process: An Economic Analysis* (Boston: Graduate School of Business Administration, Harvard University, 1962), 57-60. In the British case, the desire of the supply department to maintain the semblance of competition between weapons manufacturers reflected a risk aversion strategy. By awarding several development contracts for a weapons project (e.g. jet fighters, V-bombers), weapon procurement agencies tried to ensure that at least one system would be available in the event of war; compare also Peck and Scherer, *Weapons acquisition process*, 488-92. In other words, the objective was to ensure technical competition between defence contractors rather than the existence of a competitive market; see PRO CAB 131/9: DO (50) 47, "Size and shape of the aircraft industry: need for planning to preserve war potential", 28 June 1950.

[33] This conjecture draws on the theoretical work of Schumpeter who argued that monopolistic competition could be justified on the grounds that larger firms innovate more rapidly than smaller firms. The profit accrued due to the competitive advantage gained through technical advance should be seen as positive rather than negative as it leads to continued growth of the economy; see Morton I. Kamien and Nancy L. Schwartz, *Market Structure and*

The plans of the proponents of this industrial policy were opposed by a small group of Keynesian officials who believed that in the prevailing economic circumstances defence expenditure and particularly equipment expenditure should be reduced rather than increased.[34] They believed that defence expenditure represented a potential policy tool to combat unemployment. In the crisis of 1947 they argued that the resources devoted to defence production should be reduced even further.[35] In the discussions on the autumn budget, Bevin and Alexander were able to prevent such cuts in the size of the defence industry.[36] When the supply departments in 1948 asked for an increase in defence production to prepare for rearmament in the early 1950s (in order to achieve a state of Defence preparedness by 1957 under the informal ten-year rule), one official of the Central Economic Planning Staff condemned such an expansion as a folly that might endanger the progress of the British

---

Innovation (Cambridge: Cambridge University Press, 1982), 7-13 and 22-48. Empirical studies do not necessarily support these hypotheses. Indeed, most studies found that quite the reverse was true for most large firms; see Kamien and Schwartz, *Market structure*, 49-104. Some analysts have argued that this is particularly true for the defence sector as it tends to be far more concentrated than the rest of the economy; see Kaldor, *Baroque arsenal*, 65-72.; Kennedy, *Defense economics*, 155-61. Given the high degree of technical uncertainty and considerable amount of time needed to develop a new weapons system, the high degree of concentration within the defence industry can be regarded almost inevitable; see Kennedy, *Defense economics*, 164-9. Indeed, Galbraith has argued that the willingness of the government to underwrite large scale research projects is an intrinsic characteristic of the new industrial state, which emerged in post-war America; see John Kenneth Galbraith, *The New Industrial State*, 2nd. ed. (Harmondsworth: Penguin, 1972), 336. In this light the supply departments' industrial policy must be seen as delaying the move towards a higher degree of concentration among defence contractors. By the mid-1950s, critics urged the government to encourage such a concentration of research, development and production, particularly in the aircraft industry; see Ely Devons, "The Aircraft Industry," in *The Structure of British Industry: A Symposium*, ed. Duncan Burn (Cambridge: Cambridge University Press, 1958), 62-5. The contention here is that if the government had encouraged mergers in the defence sector earlier, this would have been beneficial in two ways. First, the need to subsidise smaller inefficient firms would have been greatly reduced. Secondly, through the concentration of design teams and production facilities as well as available financial resources on fewer development projects more contracts might have been completed; compare also Harlow, *National procurement policies*, 10-14.

[34] PRO T 247/71: "Sir W. Eady's note on the cost of defence in relation to the budget and our foreign exchange reserves", Keynes - Bridges, 23 March 1945.; PRO T 225/653: Keynes - Gilbert, 3 January 1944.

[35] PRO T 171/392: note by Trend of a meeting of Dalton on details of the budget with Bridges, Hopkins, Eady, and Gilbert, 30 September 1947.

[36] George C. Peden, "Economic Aspects of British Perceptions of Power on the Eve of the Cold War," in *Power in Europe? Great Britain, France, Italy and Germany in a Postwar World, 1945-1950*, eds. Josef Becker and Franz Knipping (Berlin: Walter de Gruyter, 1986), 249-50.

economy towards a full recovery from the war.[37] Such qualms were not shared by the hawkish majority in the Defence Committee and the start of phased rearmament was approved in summer 1984.[38]

The evidence seems to suggest that while very little was actually spent on the production of new equipment and stores between 1946 and 1949, the contribution of the defence contractors to the reconstruction of the British economy and the export drive was very limited. At the same time, the defence sector enjoyed a favourable access to labour and raw materials. Thus, there can be little doubt that the retention of a nucleus of a war economy contributed to the excess demand in the economy and should be treated as an additional opportunity cost of Britain's defence posture.[39] In other words, between 1945 and 1950 the supply departments subsidised the under-utilisation of capacity in certain sectors of the economy which otherwise might have shifted away from defence work into civilian markets and contributed towards easing the general excess demand.

The defence programme

When in the wake of the North Korean invasion an increased defence programme of £3,600 million was conceived, the British government planned to repair Britain's military deficiencies as quickly as possible in order to deter the Soviets from starting a new global war. The original intention was to use existing capacity,[40] but by the time Attlee made his statement on the defence programme to the House of Commons in January 1951, not only had the programme been increased to £4,700 million but several projects to enlarge capacity in some armaments industries had been approved.[41]

The production account of the key metals, engineering and vehicles sectors reveal that defence production rose slowly through 1950, gathered momentum in 1951 and levelled off after 1953. Table 4.1 also shows that there was hardly

---

[37] PRO T 229/704: Hitchman - Plowden. 22 October 1948.; see also: Gilbert - Brook, 24 July 1948.; Plowden Brittain, 19 August 1948.; Helmore - Graswell, 20 August 1948.

[38] PRO CAB 131/5: DO 17(48)1, minutes of a meeting of the Defence Committee, 23 August 1948. At that time Robert Hall reassured the government that the economic effects of rearmament would be limited to a small deterioration in the balance of payments; PRO CAB 21/2104: "Economic impact of increased defence expenditure", Hall - Richett, 8 September 1948.; "Defence Programme", Johnston - Attlee, 8 September 1948.

[39] For example, see PRO CAB 21/2104: note by Plowden on a conversation with Finletter and Bliss, 29 September 1948.

[40] PRO T 229/850: Spicer - Pitblado, 29 December 1950.

[41] Cabinet Office, *Defence Programme: Statement made by the Prime Minister in the House of Commons on Monday, 29th January, 1951*, Cmd. 8146 (London: His Majesty's Stationery Office, 1951), 6-7.

Table 4.1

Production account of the metals, engineering and vehicles industries, 1948–57

	in £ mn 1948 factory or cif values									
	1948	1949	1950	1951	1952	1953	1954	1955	1956	1957
SUPPLY										
Production (net)	2580	2730	2950	3150	3140	3215	3520	3875	3760	3835
Imports (excl. reexport)	50	50	45	55	75	65	55	65	70	75
Total	2630	2780	2995	3205	3215	3280	3575	3940	3830	3910
DEMAND										
Consumer Expenditure	165	180	210	225	220	275	335	390	340	380
Defence	160	180	200	285	415	470	465	455	430	405
Gross Domestic Capital Formation	785	835	890	920	865	900	980	1090	1130	1210
Export	765	860	990	985	975	960	995	1105	1200	1240
Other use	755	725	705	790	740	675	800	900	730	675
Total	2630	2780	2995	3205	3215	3280	3575	3940	3830	3910

Source: Central Statistical Office. *National Income and Expenditure 1958*. (London: Her Majesty's Stationery Office, 1958), Table 17.

any reduction in the value of production for export and investment despite the increase in production for defence.[42] On the other hand, it is notable that the production in these key sectors of the economy more or less stagnated from 1951 to 1953. It is hard to assess to what extent this stagnation was caused by the defence programme or whether it reflected the deterioration in Britain's terms of trade.

If the industrial policy of the supply departments was a rather mixed blessing in the immediate post-war period, this changed dramatically with the outbreak of the Korean war. In 1950 the existence of a large armaments industry should have eased the opportunity cost of converting to large-scale production for defence. The excess capacity within the defence industry provided scope for a rapid and fairly smooth transition in the early stages of the rearmament programme.[43] Indeed, Table 4.2 shows that production for most defence equipment rose quickly. It reveals also the extent to which certain parts of the services had relied on stocks of ammunition and engineering stores from

[42] Alec Cairncross, *Years of Recovery: British Economic Policy, 1945-51* (London: Methuen, 1985), 228-32.

[43] PRO T 229/372: Strath - Jay, 11 September 1950.

Table 4.2

Defence equipment (except aircraft), 1948–52

Ministry of Supply Defence Production Index (1948 = 100)

Financial Year	Total	Ammunition	Weapons Instruments	Signals Radar Searchlights	Eng. Stores Transport	Arm. Vehicles	Clothing
1948/49	95	105	110	95	114	81	91
1949/50	159	198	225	56	520	100	78
1950/51	160	185	248	83	396	104	121
1950/51							
Q1	144	179	184	61	491	75	92
Q2	130	149	184	59	335	90	97
Q3	176	220	280	97	356	119	136
Q4	189	193	340	115	402	133	158
1951/52							
Q1	227	243	280	93	544	178	202
Q2	241	235	277	92	492	233	220
Q3	268	...	...	...	...	...	...
Q4	358	...	391	...	828	340	329
1952/53							
Q1	352	348	397	156	1005	214	390
Q2	421	428	459	89	995	380	394

Note: ... not available

Source: PRO CAB 134/263, CAB 134/264, CAB 134/265, CAB 134/266, CAB 134/267, CAB 134/884: Economic Steering Committee Minutes and Memoranda.

the war. Table 4.3 shows very clearly that the Air Ministry had kept the aircraft industry in work through large repair and maintenance contracts, which explains the relative fall in the amount of repair work done. Both tables show that the defence contractors were well able to increase production significantly during the first year of the defence programme. The electronics industry seems to have experienced great difficulty in supplying radar, radio and other communications equipment.[44] This may reflect the particular problems caused by the cut in research and development of such equipment.[45] There are other

[44] PRO CAB 130/65: GEN 344: Production of Jet Aircraft; minutes of an ad-hoc meeting of ministers in the PM's room at the House of Commons, 23 November 1950.

[45] PRO AIR 20/6937: Croyton - Robb, 19 March 1948.

Table 4.3

Aircraft production, 1948–52

Ministry of Supply Defence Production Index (1948 = 100)

Financial Year	Total	Airframe	Engine	Aircraft Repair	Propellers	Instru-ments
1948/49	111	112	107	125	121	100
1949/50	135	117	185	115	137	133
1950/51	122	105	178	49	99	154
1950/51						
Q1	104	77	176	51	94	128
Q2	119	104	168	62	76	155
Q3	134	109	182	41	119	175
Q4	131	118	184	43	108	158
1951/52						
Q1	166	158	223	55	113	164
Q2	161	145	223	48	146	190
Q3	165	...	...	...	...	...
Q4	167	166	243	45	152	291
1952/53						
Q1	199	163	273	61	153	343
Q2	171	124	247	57	108	361

Note: ... not available

Source: PRO CAB 134/263, CAB 134/264, CAB 134/265, CAB 134/266, CAB 134/267, CAB 134/884: Economic Steering Committee Minutes and Memoranda.

indications that the defence programme caused little industrial disruption in the first year. For example, employment in the small arms and munitions industry grew only in the second year of the defence programme, after the high excess demand for labour started to drop.[46] It is difficult to gain a clear picture of the extent to which cuts in defence expenditure by the Churchill government and

[46] Ministry of Labour, *Ministry of Labour Gazette* (London: Her Majesty's Stationery Office, various dates).; total employment rose from 44,500 (1951) to 72,900 (1954); Business Statistics Office, *Historical Record of the Census of Production, 1907 to 1970* (London: Her Majesty's Stationery Office, 1978), 31. Also compare Tables 4.4 and 4.5. When the increased defence programme was drawn up, experts did not expect that rearmament would lead to a significant increase in the labour force of defence contractors. At the same time, they voiced concern about the economic implications of the increased manpower levels of the Armed Forces; PRO T 229/372: "Labour-problems of additional defence production programmes", minutes of a meeting held in Strath's room, 14 August 1950.; minutes of a

Table 4.4

Performance indicators for the aircraft industry, 1949–58

	Index of output at constant 1958 prices	Numbers of employees (June)	Output per employee in £	Capital-output ratio
1949	58	183,315	1281.4	0.355
1950	57	179,465	1286.3	0.378
1951	58	193,178	1215.9	0.364
1952	73	236,420	1530.6	0.327
1953	95	261,644	1470.3	0.311
1954	107	278,998	1553.2	0.315
1955	97	294,947	1331.9	0.401
1956	97	307,632	1277.0	0.427
1957	101	311,936	1311.3	0.472
1958	100	301,419	1343.6	0.521

Source: Ministry of Aviation. *Report of the Committee of Inquiry into the Aircraft Industry.* Vol. Cmnd. 2853. (London: Her Majesty's Stationery Office, 1965), Appendix C Table 1, Appendix E Table 1, and Appendix H Table 1.

the super-priority scheme[47] affected defence production, because in late 1952 the Economic Steering Committee gave way to pressure from the Ministry of Supply that for security reasons the Defence Production Index should no longer be circulated to the committee.[48]

The experience of the aircraft industry provides a good illustration of these general remarks. Aircraft production did not really expand until 1952 – two years into the defence programme. The number of workers started to increase immediately after the outbreak of the war in Korea but grew faster between

meeting held in the Financial Secretary's room to discuss labour problems likely to arise out of expanded defence production programmes, 17 August 1950.

[47] Throughout 1951, there were signs that raw material shortages impeded the defence programme. When the Churchill government revised the defence programme, ministers decided that priority should be given to the production of a small number of weapons systems (e.g. jet fighters, tanks). The super-priority scheme allowed contractors and subcontractors first priority in the purchase of steel and other basic materials. On the super-priority scheme, see PRO CAB 128/24: Cabinet Conclusions 30 (52), 13 March 1952. See also CUL Vickers J99: Sandys - Micklem, 26 March 1952.

[48] PRO CAB 134/811(1: Economic Steering Committee, ES(53)5, minutes, 17 July 1953. Sec also PRO T 229/851: "Scope of super-priority", Jenkins - Turnbull, 16 February 1953. For the original cabinet decision see PRO CAB 128/24: Cabinet Conclusions 30(52), 13 March 1952. The Minister of Supply submitted two reports to the Cabinet, which describe the procedure of the scheme in general terms. They are less than helpful; see PRO CAB 129/52, Cabinet Paper (52) 120, 15 April 1952.; and PRO CAB 129/52, Cabinet Paper (52)187, 10 June 1952. After the report in June, the Ministry ignored the original request of the Cabinet.

June 1951 and June 1952 than during the first twelve months of the defence programme, when excess demand for labour had already eased. The extent of surplus capacity in the aircraft industry is indicated by a significant rise in productivity during the period. As table 4.4 shows, both output per worker increased and the capital-output ratio of the industry improved in the period 1951 until 1954, when output in the aircraft industry reached the peak production level envisaged in the defence programme. The cuts of the 1954 Sandys' defence review meant that expenditure for new aircraft and other new equipment was spread over a longer period, which led to a drop in labour productivity as well as a deterioration of the capital-output ratio, although this may reflect the fact that aircraft production had become increasingly capital intensive.

The slow improvement in the productivity figures at the start of the defence programme indicates that at the beginning the aircraft industry had major problems in adjusting to the new large government orders. When the Ministry of Supply and the Treasury reviewed the size of the aircraft industry in early 1950, the prospects and under-utilisation of capacity varied substantially among firms. While firms producing jet fighters had full order books, the producers of transport planes and flying boats faced serious problems and depended heavily on government subsidies (e.g. Handley Page, Bristol Aeroplane Company).[49] As the production of jet fighters was expanded, it became obvious that existing capacity for the production of jet engines was insufficient to meet increased demand. It was then decided, well in advance of the adoption of an overall defence production programme, to expand the capacity for the production of jet engines.[50] At the time, the approval of the expansion of capacity was seen as an exceptional deviation from the basic principle of a defence programme on the basis of existing capacity.[51] This episode shows that the industrial policy of the supply departments had preserved the industry's capacity rather than attempted to adjust its structure to the changing technological environment.[52]

Another area where the supply departments sought an expansion of the existing capacity was in the production of the tanks. This is an even more bizarre case, for it was apparent from the beginning that such an expansion

---

[49] PRO CAB 131/11: minutes of the Defence Committee, DO 3 (50) 4, 31 January 1951.; PRO T 225/369: DO (50) 47: "Size and shape of the aircraft industry", Humphrey-Davies - Cripps, 4 July 1950.

[50] PRO CAB 1311/65: GEN 344: Production of jet aircraft: minutes of an ad-hoc meeting of ministers in the PM's room at the House of Commons, 23 November 1950.

[51] PRO T 229/850: Spicer - Plowden, 13 January 1951.

[52] In a minute in 1944, Keynes warned that this might be the consequence of the supply department's industrial policy towards the aircraft industry; see PRO T 225/653: Keynes - Gilbert, 3 January 1944.

would represent a clear departure from the principle underlying the original defence programme. As even the supply departments admitted, any new capacity (conversion of ROF Dalmuir, new tank factory in Leyland) created under an expansion scheme was unlikely to make any substantial contribution to filling the current deficiency of tanks as part of the defence programme. In other words, under the auspices of the defence programme the supply departments tried to complete their original post-war plans to have at least three independent tank manufacturers.[53] Not only would the existing capacity have sufficed to produce most of the additional tanks the War Office needed, but the supply departments exaggerated the extent of the British deficiency in tanks.[54] When the scheme was first floated by the Ministry of Supply, the Treasury opposed the project because it entailed the expansion of capacity contrary to the original intention of the defence programme. In early January 1951, the Treasury opposition started to fade despite serious misgivings about the way the whole project had been pushed through.[55] Under pressure from Shinwell, Gaitskell finally approved the construction of a new tank factory to be operated by Leyland on the understanding that the Treasury would not be asked to approve any further expansion of production capacity.[56] It soon became obvious that the War Office would not be able to buy the additional tanks it had on order, so the government started to look around for foreign buyers of the superfluous tanks rather than phasing tank production over a longer period.[57] As a consequence, foreign buyers were able to profit indirectly from the government's super-priority scheme which deprived other export industries of much needed basic materials (e.g. steel).[58] By mid-1952 it was quite clear that the expanded capacity at Vickers and the ROF Leeds was

[53] PRO T 229/850: Preliminary report, Combat Vehicle Task Force, 12 October 1950.; Turnbull - Spicer, 20 October 1951.; Spicer - Turnbull, 26 October 1950.; Hutchinson - Wheeler, 31 October 1950.; Spicer - Pitblado and Turnbull, 7 November 1950.

[54] PRO T 229/850: Spicer - Pitblado, 5 January 1951.

[55] PRO T 229/850: Jones - Pitblado, 5 January 1951.; "Increase of capacity for production of tanks", Spicer - Plowden, 13 January 1951.; Plowden - Armstrong, 15 January 1951.

[56] PRO T 229/850: Shinwell - Gaitskell, 18 January 1951.; Compton - Plowden, 18 January 1951.; Gaitskell - Shinwell, 19 January 1951.

[57] PRO T 229/850: Alexander - Cherwell, 18 January 1952.; Shaw - Jenkins, 25 July 1952.; Jenkins - Shilitto, 25 July 1952.; memorandum D(52)42 by Sandys, 25 October 1952.; PRO T 229/851: Macpherson - Shaw, 9 February 1953.; CUL Vickers J99: Muirhead - Dumphie, 1 July 1952.

[58] PRO T 229/851: "Scope of super-priority", Jenkins - Turnbull, 16 February 1953.

already too large to be sustained by demand, even without the addition of Leyland and Dalmuir.[59]

The expansion of capacity within the aircraft industry as well as tank production represented large shares of the investment in aircraft and vehicle industries.[60] In the aircraft industry, almost half of all investment in those years was financed by borrowing. An unusually high proportion of borrowed funds was obtained from banks in the form of bank advances. This suggests that under government pressure the banks did give preference to defence contractors while they were forced to restrict severely their lending to other industries.[61] The regional aspect of these investments seems even more important. Most of the new expansion took place in pockets of high excess demand for labour: Preston/Blackburn,[62] Coventry,[63] Bristol[64] and Greater London.[65] Even outside the immediate vicinity of these industrial centres, the ROFs encountered problems in attracting enough skilled craftsmen for their factories in Leeds and Woolwich.[66] Most expansion projects entailed building new factories rather than converting existing Ministry of Supply reserve shadow factories. This in turn placed extra pressure on the overloaded building sector.[67] The increased demand for steel created extra pressures within the vehicle and aircraft industries. While most of the defence contractors had serious problems in obtaining components,[68] private companies had to reduce

---

[59] CUL Vickers J99: Dumphie - Muirhead, 22 July 1952.; Muirhead - Dumphie, 24 July 1952. The ROF Leeds and Dalmuir started to reduce working hours in 1953; see PRO WO 185/162: minutes of a meeting of the ROF Central Production Committee, 18 May 1953.

[60] PRO T 229/850: Jones - Pitblado, 5 January 1951.

[61] Ministry of Aviation, *Report of the Committee of Inquiry into the Aircraft Industry*, Cmnd. 2853 (London: Her Majesty's Stationery Office, 1965), 21 and Appendix H Table 4.; and Till Geiger and Duncan M. Ross, "Banks, institutional constraints and the limits of central banking: Monetary policy in Britain and West Germany, 1950-52," *Business History* 33 (1991): 138-56.

[62] PRO T 229/850: "EPC(51)26: Tank production: Leyland agency factory", paper by Bretherton, 19 March 1951.; EPC(51)26: note by Jenkins, 21 March 1951;. PRO T 229/372: Shawcross - Gaitskell, 8 May 1951.

[63] PRO T 229/373: "Labour situation in the Coventry area in relation to the defence programme", draft paper, 9 November 1951.

[64] John Lovering, "Defence expenditure and the regions: The case of Bristol," in *Defence Expenditure and Regional Development*, ed. M. Breheny (London: Mansell, 1988), 127-9.

[65] Susan Willet, "The impact of defence procurement on the electronics sector: a London case study," in *Defence Expenditure and Regional Development*, ed. M. Breheny (London: Mansell, 1988), 142-3.

[66] PRO WO 185/162: minutes of a meeting of the ROF Central Production Committee, 30 April 1951, 30 July 1951, 29 October 1951.

[67] PRO T 229/850: Jones - Pitblado, 5 January 1951.

[68] CUL Vickers J99: memorandum "Centurion tank production", 10 January 1951.; Muirhead - Micklem, 31 January 1951.; Crawford - Micklem, 21 February 1951.; PRO WO

production and to some extent replace sheet and alloy steel with carbon steel or even in some cases with timber.[69]

Military procurement: incentives and negative side-effects

The preceding sections examined the effects of the industrial policy of the supply departments. This policy seems to have exacerbated the overall excess demand in the economy first by subsidising inefficient production and then by expanding the defence sector unduly during the Korean war defence programme. This raises two important issues. On the one hand, why were defence contractors better placed than civilian firms in obtaining scarce labour and raw materials? What were the incentives for a defence contractor to maintain excess capacity at a time of almost inexhaustible demand? On the other hand, did defence production policy adversely affect overall economic performance? If so, how? And to what extent?

The analysis of the relationship between the supply departments and defence contractors revealed the high degree of continuity of procurement policy throughout the period. At the time when the post-war production plans were drawn up, war production was at its peak. The planners in the supply departments were still in virtual control of the economy. Moreover, they had access to vital information for any post-war planning. For example, using preliminary public expenditure plans, the planners had a rough idea of the likely demand for military hardware in the immediate post-war years. Within these parameters they were able to evolve a compromise between the desirable and the feasible. More importantly the policy-makers had at their disposal the power to direct resources, particularly labour and steel. This allowed them to control the scaling-down of war production and release of labour. In this process the supply departments had a tremendous advantage by virtue of their privileged access to information, their influence over the running-down of the war economy and their familiarity with the allocation process.[70]

185/162: minute of a meeting of the ROF Central Production Committee, 30 October 1950.; PRO T 229/850: Spicer - Butler, 30 January 1952.

[69] Modern Record Centre MSS 226/ST/1/5/1: Standard Motor Co. Ltd., minutes of the executive directors' meeting, 5 February 1951, 10 January 1952, 14 March 1952. (I am grateful to Tim Whisler for letting me use his notes.)

[70] The important role of strategic planning, information and knowledge within a war economy is stressed by W. Peter Howlett, "Towards a model of the central decision-making process in a war economy," in *Discussion Paper in Economics*, ed. University of Stirling Department of Economics (1989). Peck and Scherer argue that the uncertainty intrinsic to the weapons acquisition process may lead to the overcommitment of resources; see Peck and Scherer, *Weapons acquisition process*, 500-501.

The dominant position of the supply departments within the war economy as compared with civilian production gave them advantages both in defining strategic objectives and pushing them through. Civilian producers were curtailed by their dependence on steel allocations and their ability to obtain labour. Another factor which inhibited their freedom was the necessity of increasing British exports quickly after the war. To achieve this objective the government gave preferential treatment in the allocation of steel to exporters. The privileged position of the defence contractors in the immediate post-war period is borne out by the fact that despite being more expensive, some Royal Ordnance Factories secured work from civilian producers because they had the manpower resources.[71] In the environment of the post-war shortages such preferential treatment placed defence contractors in a strong position to compete for civilian contracts. This enabled them to retain inefficient capacity and created a disincentive to change.

The privileged position of the defence contractors depended on their close relationship with the supply departments. Several defence contractors loaned managers and technical experts to the Ministry of Supply and the Ministry of Aircraft Production during the war. This created strong ties that were to last into the post-war period. To cite one particular case, the post-war tank production programme was drawn up while Robert Micklem (on loan from Vickers) was chairman of the Tank Board and the Armoured Vehicle Division of the Ministry of Supply. After the war, Micklem returned to Vickers to become one of the directors.[72] It was hardly surprising that he was given responsibility for tank production at Vickers. His ties with the Ministry of Supply remained close. The evidence suggests that the personal involvement of many of these managers made them more reluctant to abandon production facilities that were part of their own post-war production plans.

Such factors should not be exaggerated, because to some extent defence contractors were caught in a trap. Originally, planners intended to maintain reserve capacity by repair contracts. At no time was it envisaged that defence production would reach a level sufficient to utilise this capacity fully. The planners' aim had been to provide for the possibility of full-scale rearmament in the future.[73] As post-war production plans had been exceedingly optimistic

[71] House of Commons, *Royal Ordnance Factories (1948)*, vii-viii.

[72] *Who's Who*, (London: Adam and Charles Black, 1952), 1969.

[73] The defence planners' assessment of the likelihood of global war may seem unduly pessimistic with hindsight. Post-war leaders as well as the general public felt strongly that they should not appease the Soviet Union. These sentiments might be best described as a reaction to the catastrophic consequences of Appeasement; see Mass-Observation, *Peace and the Public* (London: Longmans, Green & Co., 1947), 21-2.; Donald C. Watt, "Britain, the United States and the opening of the cold war," in *The Foreign Policy of the British Labour Governments, 1945-1951*, ed. Ritchie Ovendale (Leicester: Leicester University Press, 1984),

in their financial assumptions, actual production levels fell short of the expectations. There were several reasons for this. Less money was available for defence in the post-war budgets than had been expected during the war.[74] As a consequence of the increased British military commitments all over the world, a lower proportion of the defence budget itself went towards defence production.[75] The planners underestimated the increase in development and production cost of modern weapons systems.[76] The low level of arms production meant a significant loss of economies of scale compared with wartime.

This unplanned shortfall in demand led to an increase in excess capacity among defence contractors, and the financial problems facing the government gave rise to growing uncertainty about the future military procurement budgets. The combination of these two factors resulted in defence contractors being left in a different position. The precariousness of their financial situation precluded them from investing in new equipment to reduce their dependency on the government. While most weapons contractors were able to adapt some of their specialised machinery to civilian production, they found it increasingly hard to compete with the lower production costs of their civilian rivals.[77] If defence contractors had tried to develop civilian production at the expense of their military production capacity, the government might have excluded them from tendering for future arms contracts. This was a risk a defence contractor could not afford. Even approaches to the government for a subsidy to keep the surplus capacity in being were regarded as inherently risky.[78] To escape this predicament, defence contractors would have had to invest in new products and machinery for which they lacked the financial resources and which might have destroyed their relationship with the government on which their survival depended. Even if the firms had the financial resources they found it hard to

---

54-9.; and Wilfried Loth, *Die Teilung der Welt: Die Geschichte des Kalten Kriegs, 1941-1955*, 7th rev. ed. (München: Deutscher Taschenbuch Verlag, 1989), 130-31.

[74] PRO T 160/1407/F. 18876: "Post-war expenditure", Gilbert - Bridges, 7 November 1942 assumed that three years after the end of the war £550 million (in 1942 prices) would be spent on defence. In 1948 prices this would have been almost £850 million (my calculation; this estimate makes some allowance for the loss of economies of scale in the production of new equipment). Actual expenditure was £770 million.

[75] PRO T 160/1407/F. 18876: "Post-war expenditure", Gilbert - Bridges, 7 November 1942; expected that £220 million (in 1942 prices) or £369 (in 1948 prices, my calculation) would be spent on new equipment. The 1948 Defence White Paper set aside £188 million for expenditure on production and research. This heading includes the acquisition of new weapons.

[76] Kaldor, "Technical change," 105-12.

[77] House of Commons, *Royal Ordnance Factories (1948)*.

[78] CUL Vickers 652: Report on capital expenditure 1947/48, Committee on Capital Expenditure and Commitments, 19 June 1947.

obtain the necessary machinery or skilled labour. It seems unlikely that any new investment would have yielded immediately high returns. Such factors lowered the expectations of management and made the defence contractors even more wary.[79]

At the same time, their civilian counterparts were doing rather better. In almost all sectors most firms had over-full order books and were making record profits.[80] Despite excess liquidity, firms found it difficult to expand or launch new products because shortages reduced the availability of key materials or labour. Large investment projects involving building work were held up by the government by the denial of building licences or by the general shortage of materials and labour.[81] All this is typical of supply-constrained economies.[82] It is hard to estimate how much disruption these constraints caused but there can be little doubt that the surplus capacity and preferential access to raw materials and labour of the defence contractors exacerbated the supply position. A rough estimate suggests that the loss in production in the defence field from 1947 to 1950 may have been as much as 2 to 3 per cent of manufacturing output or 0.5 to 1 per cent of GDP per annum.[83] This suggests that the supply departments industrial policy inhibited the government's effort to reduce the excess demand within the economy in the immediate post-war period.

The 1949 devaluation reveals the extent to which the economy was subject to supply constraints. Firms found it hard to expand output sufficiently quickly to profit from the increased competitiveness of British exports. Many industries including the textile industry were working overtime until late 1951.[84] As already explained above, firms were either unwilling or unable to expand their productive capacity, though this would have been the only successful way of overcoming the excess demand at home. A rough indication of the extent of excess demand for labour is provided by the unemployment rates in industry.[85]

---

79 J. C. R. Dow, *The Management of the British Economy, 1945-60* (Cambridge: Cambridge University Press, 1964), 162 and 286-9.

80 Tomlinson, "Labour's management."

81 Dow, *Management of the British economy*, 149-53, 162 and 341-3.

82 János Kornai, *Growth, Shortage and Efficiency* (Oxford: Basil Blackwell, 1982), 48-50.

83 My calculations based on Table 4.1, the 1958 GDP estimates from the Central Statistical Office (Central Statistical Office, *National Income and Expenditure 1958* (London: Her Majesty's Stationery Office, 1958).) and the ratio of defence equipment expenditure (official NATO Figures, B. Cros, "Statistical information - Les donnés d'équipement dans le total des dépenses de défense et le pourcentage des forces armées dans la population active, 1949-1987," (NATO Communication, Ref.: SAS(87)151, 1987).)

84 Ministry of Labour, *Ministry of Labour Gazette*, various issues. For example, the report on the labour situation in Coventry emphasised the high proportion of overtime work at Courtaulds in Coventry; PRO T 229/373: "Labour situation in the Coventry area in relation to the defence programme", draft paper, 9 November 1951.

85 Dow, *Management of the British economy*, 335-43.

Table 4.5

Unemployment rate in selected industries, 1949–54

	May 1949	May 1950	May 1951	May 1952	May 1953	May 1954
			in per cent			
Vehicles	1.0	0.9	0.5	0.7	0.8	0.5
Aircraft production and repair	1.1	1.0	0.5	0.4	0.5	0.4
Engineering, Shipbuilding, Electrical Goods	1.8	1.6	1.0	1.3	1.5	1.2
Shipbuilding	5.5	5.8	3.7	3.4	4.3	3.7
Engineering	1.4	1.1	0.7	1.0	1.2	0.9
Ordnance and small arms	2.5	2.6	1.6	1.3	1.0	0.9
Metal Industry	1.2	1.1	0.8	1.1	2.5	1.3
Textiles	0.7	0.6	0.5	15.6	1.4	1.0

Note: The employment figures are taken from the published figures for the end of April, while the unemployment figures are taken for early May from the published figures in the same issue of the *Ministry of Labour Gazette*.

Source: Ministry of Labour. *Ministry of Labour Gazette*. (London: Her Majesty's Stationery Office), various dates.

As a rule of thumb, the lower the unemployment rate, the higher the possibility of excess demand for labour in the specific industry. Table 4.5 shows that at the beginning of the defence programme there was considerable unemployment both in the shipbuilding and the small arms and ordnance industries. The figures in Table 4.5 reveal an interesting pattern. In some of the defence industrial categories (i.e. aircraft, ordnance and small arms but excluding shipbuilding), the unemployment rates continue to fall until 1954, in all other industries unemployment drops until May 1951, only to rise again. As most industrial categories display this pattern, the dislocation caused by the increased manpower requirement of the forces, adverse shifts in the terms of trade and the raw material shortages probably led to more dislocation than the defence programme itself.[86] This seems particularly true for the textile industry which suffered severely from the dramatically changed market conditions caused by the shift in raw materials prices.[87] One of the consequences of the collapse of international demand in 1952 was that the textile industry could not

[86] Mitchell, *Crisis in Britain*, 56-85 and 230-45.; Cairncross, *Years of recovery*, 228-32.

[87] John Singleton, "Lancashire's last stand: Declining employment in the British cotton industry, 1950-1970," *Economic History Review* 39 (1986): 102-3.

export as much as the government had originally hoped. This shortfall increased the pressure on the balance of payments. Rearmament inhibited the continued growth of engineering exports. This forced the government to tighten import controls, which prolonged the "disequilibrium system".[88] Through the displacement caused by the Korean war, roughly 3 per cent of output growth was lost in the period 1951 to 1955.

The preceding analysis suggests that the defence production policy of supply departments contributed significantly to the excess demand within the British economy in the period 1945 to 1955. Although it is currently impossible precisely to measure the loss of output to the British economy, it is clear that to understand the effects of this industrial policy in the period from 1945 to 1955 requires a detailed analysis of the supply and the constraints. Only then will it become clear just how far Britain's large defence effort contributed to the relatively poor performance of the British economy.

---

[88] Dow, *Management of the British economy*, 162.

Chapter 5

The wasting of high technological potential?: The British warfare state, the aircraft industry and technological nationalism, 1950–58

By 1955, most observers agreed that something had gone wrong with the British aircraft industry. A string of disasters such as Comet crashes in 1954 had led to the growing recognition that the domestic industry was falling behind its American, French and Russian rivals. As pointed questions started to be asked, the government had to admit in a white paper to serious problems in the procurement of military aircraft. Several of Britain's latest military aircraft suffered from a number of serious problems affecting their performance.[1] These reports dashed the bright hopes most observers had had for the industry's future a decade earlier at the end of the Second World War. At the time, most observers had been convinced that British aeronautical engineering led the world in jet engine technology. Over the next ten years, some of the pioneering efforts of British aircraft firms maintained this image of world leadership in aircraft technology. However, despite some remarkable successes in this period, the reputation of the industry had become decidedly tarnished by 1955.

This development sparked a heated debate about the reasons for this demise of technological prowess. While some critics attributed the problems to the industry itself, other observers firmly blamed the government. In a sense, this debate challenged a treasured assumption about the industry's contribution to saving the country from invasion during the Battle of Britain.[2] For some observers, the victory of air power confirmed the ingenuity of British aircraft designers, if not their superiority.[3] Such interpretations often singled out the

---

[1] Ministry of Defence, *The Supply of Military Aircraft*, Cmd. 9388 (London: Her Majesty's Stationery Office, 1955).

[2] A myth partly created by films like *The First of the Few*, dir. Leslie Howard, with Leslie Howard, David Niven, and Rosamund John, 1942). On this point, see also *The Myth of the Few*, Secret History, prod. Scottish Television Productions, (Channel 4, 25 July 2000).; and Richard J. Overy, *The Air War, 1939-1945* (New York: Stein and Day, 1981), 264-7.

[3] This impression arose from the higher bomb-load of the Lancaster bomber compared to that of the B-17 (see Martin Middlebrook, *The Battle of Hamburg: The Firestorm*

initiative shown by private entrepreneurs in developing advanced fighter aircraft with little government support before the Second World War. Writing in the *Sunday Express* in July 1955, Max Aitken, for example, dismissed accusations that the industry was failing invoking the historical contribution to the country in its darkest hour.

> I say [the finger] is being pointed at the wrong people. There is nothing wrong with the [aircraft] manufacturers. We owe our very existence to them.
>
> The Spitfire, Mosquito, Hurricane, and Lancaster were designed and produced by these men. In their time, these aircraft led the world and made the Royal Air Force the most advanced air force of all the nations.
>
> Have these men suddenly lost their skill? Men like Dobson of A.V.Roe, Spriggs of Hawkers, Verdon-Smith of Bristols, men like de Haviland and Handley-Page? Of course they have not. They are still the supreme aircraft builders.

Since the glorious record of these men was above reproach, Aitken continued to name the five 'guilty men' for the demise of the British aircraft industry: a government scientist, Ben Lockspeiser, and the four Ministers of Supply, George Strauss, John Wilmot, Duncan Sandys and Selwyn Lloyd. He blamed this group for splitting up the close working relationship between the Royal Air Force (RAF), the Ministry of Aircraft Production and the industry after the end of the war by creating a new separate Ministry of Supply. The new Ministry hemmed the industry in by dictating its research and development work rather than permitting manufacturers to develop their own aircraft. Moreover, he identified a number of decisions that delayed the development of a super-sonic aircraft by several years. According to Aitken, these ill-advised government decisions permitted the American, Russian and French aircraft industries to overtake the domestic aircraft firms.[4]

While Aitken's views represented one extreme, this historical dissonance between perceived technological potential and the reality of a tarnished record has continued to plague the debate about the post-war development of the British aircraft industry. Confronted with the perplexing picture of the British aircraft industry in the crucial decade after the Second World War, declinist authors have focused on certain aspects of this story in order to offer an explanation for the industry's demise. For example, Andrew Shonfield criticised the technological nationalism underlying government policy as a consequence of which ministers persisted in procuring every type of aircraft

---

Raid (Harmondsworth: Penguin Books, 1984), 287-8.) or the fact that American bombers relied on British navigational and blind bombing equipment in the later stages of the war (see Max Hastings, *Bomber Command* (London: Pan Books, 1999), 189.)

[4] Max Aitken, "I blame five men for our setback in the air," *Sunday Express*, 10 July 1955.

domestically whatever the economic cost.[5] Having lambasted the aircraft industry's wartime record in the *Audit of War*, Correlli Barnett directed his scorn in the sequel to this book *The Lost Victory* at the Brabazon programme as a misguided and ultimately failed attempt to develop the next generation of civilian aircraft after 1945.[6] However, as contemporary analysts, historians have failed to reach a consensus on the perceived failure of the British aircraft industry to live up to its technological potential in the immediate post-war period.

In order to decipher the effects of the various actions undertaken by both the government and the industry, this chapter closely analyses the discursive strategies the key actors employed to shape British aircraft production in the first decade after the Second World War. To some extent, these discursive strategies reflected and justified the practices and actions of both policy-makers and aircraft manufacturers. In line with Roger Chartier's argument, these discursive strategies will be regarded then as attempts to negotiate between the interests of an actor and the institutions and practices of the wider society.[7] For this reason, contemporary newspaper reports provide a very valuable picture of the relative persuasiveness of these discursive strategies and how they determined the scope of government intervention in the workings of the aircraft industry. As the following analysis will show, newspaper reports praised British technological leadership in the late 1940s, while they also worried over plant closures and the impact of cuts in defence expenditure. After the outbreak of the Korean war, such concerns gave way to the problems of meeting the ambitious targets of the rearmament programme. At the same time, the likely impact of the western military alliance on the British aircraft industry became a recurrent theme for the aeronautical correspondents of the British press. By the mid-1950s, the growing problems associated with both military and civilian aircraft projects started to dominate newspaper columns. These reports fostered the impression that domestic aircraft manufacturers seemed to be falling behind their American competitors. Based on this analysis, the concluding section will place the issues emerging from contemporary discussions into their wider context in a search to understand the industry's development in the first post-war decade.[8]

---

5 Andrew Shonfield, *British Economic Policy since the War* (Harmondsworth: Penguin, 1958), passim, particularly 89-97.

6 Correlli Barnett, *The Audit of War: The illusion and reality of Britain as a great nation* (Basingstoke: Macmillan, 1986), 124-58.; Correlli Barnett, *The Lost Victory: British dreams, British realities, 1945-1950* (Basingstoke: Macmillan, 1995), 228-46.

7 Roger Chartier, *On the Edge of the Cliff: History, language, and practices* (Baltimore: Johns Hopkins University Press, 1997), 19-20.

8 This analysis is based on the newspaper clipping files of the Labour Party Research Department held at the John Rylands University Library Manchester. The references here follow the attribution of articles to individual newspapers by the archivist.

Technological potential of the British aircraft industry

At the end of the Second World War, many British observers forecast a bright future for the British aircraft industry, because of its technological excellence, the ingenuity of its aircraft designers and its skilled work force. At the same time, industry representatives reiterated the need for government support in order for the industry to develop its full technological and commercial potential. In their statements, they enlisted the contribution of air power to the Allied victory to justify such subsidies. For example, the controller of Rotol, R. H. Coverley, told a luncheon gathering in February 1945 that

> technically we were at least abreast of our allies, and that, with the proper support, the British industry could retain this position, if not attain technical superiority. [...] The country and the Empire owed it to the industry that everything possible should be done to help it to maintain the high position in peace that it had so magnificently won in war.[9]

In the same talk, the speaker predicted that it would be another 15 to 20 years before jet propulsion would replace the conventional propeller engines. Despite such scepticism, other commentators emphasised the British technological leadership in the design of jet engines. In 1945, a Meteor fighter equipped with the newest jet engine demonstrated the feasibility of supersonic flight, while a converted British bomber became the world's first jet-powered civil aircraft. These developments led the President of the British Society of Aircraft Constructors, Verdon Smith, to declare at the Radlett air show in September 1946 that:

> the technical superiority [of British aircraft manufacturing] which carried us through the war has not been lost. [... Indeed, we] may be reasonably confident that the first plane to travel over the international speed course at 1,000 kilometres (621 miles) an hour will be British.[10]

The aircraft industry's outstanding technological potential remained a recurring theme of newspaper reports. This favourable assessment led many observers to call for unquestioning government support for the industry.

Despite these achievements, the transition from wartime to peacetime production proved less than smooth. In February 1945, the *Daily Worker* reported the protests of workers against the imminent closure of some wartime aircraft factories in London, Manchester and Coventry. According to these

---

[9] Our Aeronautical Correspondent, "Future of British Air Industry: Technically Abreast of U.S.A.," *The Times*, 9 February 1945.

[10] L. G. S. Payne, "Britain stages greatest show of Aircraft," *The Daily Telegraph*, 13 September 1946. The British Society of Aircraft Constructors organised its annual air shows in Radlett near St. Albans until 1948, when the event was moved to Farnborough.

reports, workers particularly objected to government plans to disperse the industry away from large urban centres, because of the vulnerability to air attacks in a future war. The protests revealed considerable unease among aircraft workers about their employment prospects at the end of the war. At the same time, the ensuing wrangle revealed profound disagreements over post-war transition between government departments. While the Board of Trade favoured an early return to peacetime production, the Ministry of Aircraft Production insisted that the future of individual factories had yet to be decided.[11] In order to smooth the transition to peacetime production, many aircraft factories converted to the production of a variety of urgently needed civilian goods such as prefabricated houses in the immediate post-war period.

In its White Paper on Civil Aviation published in late 1945, the Attlee government announced the development of a new generation of civilian aircraft in order to enable the domestic aircraft industry to catch up with their American rivals. The government announcement attributed the loss of competitiveness of British civil aircraft to the wartime agreement that Britain should abstain from developing transport aircraft for the duration of war. However, the government plans to equip new nationalised British airlines with British-built planes soon ran into severe problems. While the use of converted bomber aircraft proved uneconomic, the delivery of newly developed aircraft such as Avro Tudor I was delayed by technical problems, demands for changes from the airlines and insufficient performance. As a consequence of these delays, British Overseas Airways Corporation (BOAC) with the support of the Ministry of Civil Aviation sought permission to purchase tried and tested American aircraft, such as the Lockheed Constellation and the Boeing Stratocruiser for its Atlantic routes in preference to the Tudor. Despite the BOAC's reluctance to purchase the Tudor, the Ministry of Supply continued its financial support for the plane, which British South American Airways operated successfully on its own routes. From mid-1946, the potential purchase of American planes led to widespread criticism of government policy, because of the potential harm to the British civil aircraft industry arising from the failure to buy the Tudor.[12] *The Daily Telegraph*'s aeronautical correspondent, L. G. S. Payne, went even further in his criticism stating that British government policy ignored the demands of the world market and led to the development of aircraft which proved uncompetitive in price, performance and economy of operation. Due to the de facto nationalisation of the industry, he blamed the planners in the Ministry of Supply for this failure since

---

11 "Govt. War Plants May be Closed Next June," *Daily Worker*, 8 February 1945.; Ben Francis, "Factory to Close - Would Be in Danger Zone in Next War," *Daily Worker*, 22 February 1945.

12 Ronald Walker, "Our Air Prestige," *News Chronicle*, 22 July 1949.

> it should have occurred to [them] that the continued production of non-competitive British civil aircraft, which are unwanted at home and unsaleable abroad, has become a waste of time, money, manpower and material. This country cannot afford and the Government should no longer encourage it.[13]

Therefore, he argued, the government should pursue the development of jet-powered aircraft rather than continue building interim types such as the Tudor.[14] In this debate, a Labour MP, Frank Beswick, similarly questioned the wisdom of a "Buy British" policy at any price, but castigated aircraft manufacturers for failing to build economical aircraft despite large amounts of government subsidy.[15]

Even after the Tudor fiasco, most commentators continued to regard the future prospects of the industry as excellent. Such statements reflected the firm belief that the world would choose to fly the technologically superior British aircraft when they became available in the early 1950s. Therefore, all commentators called for continued government support for the Brabazon aircraft programme despite the rising costs of many projects. To some extent, such optimism seemed justified, because the American leadership in the field of large civilian aircraft arose from wartime designs powered by reciprocating propeller engines.[16] However, generous government support allowed British aircraft manufacturers to steal the march on their American rivals in developing civilian aircraft using turbo-prop or jet engines. Following the Tudor debacle, the press celebrated the maiden flights of the world's first turbo-prop airliner, the Vickers Viscount, the jet-powered de Havilland Comet and the Bristol Brabazon in the late 1940s, claiming they confirmed the far-sightedness of the government's civil aviation programme.[17] At the same time, the American government showed considerable interest in the Canberra

---

[13] L. G. S. Payne, "Our Planes to the World: Are We Doing All We Can to Make Flying Cheaper?," *The Daily Telegraph*, 3 July 1947.

[14] L. G. S. Payne, "Britain's Long-term Policy for Transocean Airliners: The Industry Should Concentrate On New Gas-Turbine Types Now," *The Daily Telegraph*, 5 February 1948.

[15] Frank Beswick, "Battle of the Airliners," *Reynold's News*, 18 July 1948. Frank Beswick served in Transport Command during the war, was elected as Member of Parliament for Uxbridge in 1945 and became Parliamentary Secretary in the Ministry of Civil Aviation during the second Labour government, 1950-51.

[16] Our Aviation Correspondent, "The British Aircraft Industry-I: Comparison with the U.S.," *The Times*, 23 November 1946.; Our Aviation Correspondent, "The British Aircraft Industry-II: Jet Power Prospects Bright," *The Times*, 25 November 1946.

[17] Our Aviation Correspondent, "New Machines for British Civil Aviation: First Flights of the Comet and Brabazon," *Financial Times*, 27 July 1949.; Frank Beswick, "Who Said We Couldn't Build Planes?," *Reynold's News*, 31 July 1949.; Courtenay Edwards, "Jet Airliner Triumph: First Tests Stagger Experts," *Daily Mail*, 11 August 1949.; and "U.S. Interest in U.K. Aircraft: New Types May Change Competitive Position," *Financial Times*, 19 September 1949.

bomber and many western European governments were equipping their air forces with British built jet fighters.[18] These developments seemed to confirm British technological leadership particularly in aero-engine development.

Despite the success of the Canberra, delays in the development of British heavy bombers prompted the British government to consider accepting the American offer of a number of obsolete B-29 bombers. This offer was first mooted by an announcement by American defence officials. According to press reports, the Air Ministry was initially less than thrilled about the offer of surplus wartime bombers, which the United States Air Force was replacing with a new generation of planes. British officials were reportedly concerned about the costs involved in training pilots to fly and crews to maintain these planes, which would merely serve as a stop-gap until the new British-built jet bombers entered service. After some consideration, the British government decided to accept the American bombers, as they would provide RAF pilots with valuable experience in high altitude flying which would ease the transition to the new jet bombers when they finally entered service.[19] Nevertheless, it is intriguing that this story attracted relatively little attention at the time as it would have cast a negative light on the industry.

This story soon disappeared as a renewed crisis engulfed the British aircraft industry in early 1950, after the government announced large cuts in defence expenditure as part of its austerity measures following the devaluation of sterling in September 1949. In a letter to the Prime Minister, Clement Attlee, the industry warned that the defence cuts would lead to large job losses, the breaking up of design teams, and dislocation in the industry. Industry spokesmen insisted that the cuts would undermine the industry's war potential and appealed to the government to reverse its decision.[20] As a consequence of the defence cuts, the Hawker Aircraft Company decided against opening a new production line for jet fighters in a disused wartime shadow factory in Blackpool. The local Conservative candidate tried to use this decision for political point scoring in the ongoing general election campaign criticising the government for not knowing how many fighter aircraft the RAF required. He suspected that the government would soon announce the purchase of American planes, because ministers lacked faith in the British aircraft industry.[21]

---

[18] "U.S. Interest in British Jet Bomber," *The Times*, 30 January 1951.

[19] L. G. S. Payne, "R.A.F. May Re-equip with Superforts: U.S. Offer would be Accepted: Jet Bombers Delayed," *The Daily Telegraph*, 12 November 1949.

[20] Our Aeronautical Correspondent, "Cut in Aircraft Orders: Several Companies May Be Affected," *The Times*, 2 February 1950.; Our Aeronautical Correspondent, "Cut in Aircraft Programme: Firms Ask For Review," *The Times*, 7 February 1950.; Our Air Correspondent, "Aircraft Firms' Warning: Serious Effects of Reduced Orders," *Financial Times*, 13 March 1950.

[21] "Squires Gate Bombshell is No. 1 Talking Point," *West Lancashire Evening Gazette*, 11 February 1950.

In the debate over the defence cuts, the press sided with the industry giving ample space to its case against the government. The nature of the cuts in defence expenditure gave rise to an added concern as the proposed savings disproportionately affected the procurement of transport aircraft. This cut fuelled speculations that the Atlantic alliance had reached an agreement regarding the supply of military aircraft. As part of this agreement, the rumours suggested that the Attlee government had agreed to leave the production of heavy bombers and transport aircraft to the United States in return for supplying fighter aircraft to other European member states of the North Atlantic Treaty Organisation (NATO).[22] These speculations prompted the *Daily Worker* to claim in a headline that the American government was directly responsible for the laying off of 400 British aircraft workers.[23] Writing in the same paper a couple of days later, George Sinfield criticised "the Government [for] allowing the Americans to dominate the British aircraft industry."[24] In this context, six A. V. Roe shop stewards protested about the arrival of American B-29 Superfortress bombers at a time when "thousands of aircraft workers are losing their jobs [and] the aircraft industry has no work to cover the period while jet bombers are developed".[25] As this analysis shows, the slant of press reporting strongly suggested that Labour ministers seemed ready to sell out British industrial interests.

Over the coming months, the government failed to make its case effectively in this debate. Neither the parliamentary election nor a statement by the Minister of Supply, George Strauss, at the end of May ended the speculations about the potential implications of western defence co-operation for the industry. Commenting on this statement, the *Financial Times* called in an editorial on the government to clarify its plans for the future of the sector. The editors took up the industry's concerns warning ministers that the country would be deprived of a vital component of its defence production base, if the government agreed that the British aircraft manufacturers should specialise in the production of fighter aircraft. The editorial went on to remind the government that the experience of the last war showed the importance of an industrial nucleus, which allowed the wartime expansion of production. Indeed, the industry felt that sacrificing the continued development of heavy bombers would waste their considerable technological know-how and would undermine Britain's leadership in jet-powered civilian aircraft. In this context, the editorial writer reminded readers that any such decisions would have implications for

---

22 Our Air Correspondent, "Reduced Orders for the Aircraft Industry: Likelihood of continued decline in demand at home and overseas," *Financial Times*, 18 February 1950.

23 "Uncle Sam orders sack for 400," *Daily Worker*, 21 February 1950.

24 George Sinfield, "Dollarcraft and sackings in our factories," *Daily Worker*, 3 March 1950.

25 "Protest over Superforts," *Daily Express*, 29 March 1950.

the balance of payments. While buying American heavy bombers would cost valuable dollars, the loss of the potential export earnings from the future sale of British jetliners might prove even more costly. On this point, the writer again referred to the wartime experience in order to remind readers that specialisation of aircraft production during the Second World War had given the American industry a competitive advantage in the post-war market for commercial passenger aircraft.

> The purely economic argument cannot be overlooked here. Exports of British aircraft are substantial earners of foreign exchange. It would be hard to compensate this country for the loss that would result if the asset represented by the ingenuity of our designers were not exploited to the full, because they were not allowed to specialise on the more saleable types of aircraft. The experience of the war, when America owing to her concentration on transport aircraft, gained a big start in the commercial field, has not been forgotten.[26]

In an accompanying article, the paper's air correspondent commented that it might be more advantageous if NATO countries continued to produce the full range of arms domestically. Indeed, the journalist pointed out that it was far from certain that American aircraft manufacturers would be able to produce better bombers than their British counterparts. Therefore, he argued it would be better if Britain maintained its own defence procurement policy and weapons production in concert with its NATO allies.[27]

As this analysis shows, press reporting in the late 1940s portrayed the British aircraft industry as being at the forefront of the technological development. While praising the ingenuity of British aircraft designers, commentators singled out government policy for criticism. The constant references to the "glorious" wartime record of the industry isolated the sector from any critical scrutiny prior to the outbreak of the Korean War.

The Korean War defence programme and aircraft industry

At first, the unexpected outbreak of the Korean War on 25 June 1950 heightened rather than removed the uncertainty hanging over the future of the industry. The fighting in Korea raised the spectre of an global conflict in the foreseeable future and prompted the Attlee government to step up its defence preparations. As a first measure, the Minister of Defence announced an increase of £100 million in the defence budget at the end of July. Almost a

---

26 "Joint Defence," *Financial Times*, 31 May 1950.

27 Our Air Correspondent, "U.K. Industry and Atlantic Pact: Concern Over Uncertain Prospects: Need for Clearer Policy," *Financial Times*, 31 May 1950.

third of the additional expenditure would be spent on procuring additional latest versions of Vampire and Meteor jet fighters for the RAF. Moreover, the minister stressed that this additional procurement programme would be a small fraction of the likely overall rearmament programme without, however, giving any indication of its likely shape. Given the concerns over the recent cuts in military aircraft procurement, one would have expected the industry and observers to welcome this announcement unreservedly. The air correspondent of the *Financial Times*, for example, saw the statement as a sign of the emergence of a clear policy for the aircraft industry, particularly as this announcement came on the back of a recent House of Lords debate during which a government spokesman confirmed that the creation of collective NATO forces would not entail abandoning a balanced air force and aircraft industry. However, the article also noted the potential problems arising from the additional aircraft orders. The additional work would primarily benefit De Havilland, Rolls-Royce and Gloster Aircraft whose existing production lines were fully occupied with current work. As a consequence, the two airframe firms considered moving production to other factories, De Havilland to its new factory in Chester and Gloster Aircraft to other aircraft firms within the Hawker-Siddeley group. Indeed, a spokesman for Hawker Siddeley pointed out that potential for switching production work between firms of the same group proved to be a major advantage. The real problem, however, would be to increase jet engine production sufficiently to meet the increased demand. At the same time, the article warned that the additional military aircraft orders might reduce the export of civilian aircraft and affect other industries such as the radio industry.[28] With the announcement of rearmament, the emphasis of reporting shifted from being primarily concerned with technological achievement and employment levels to devoting considerable column space to the likely problems of a renewed military build-up.

The scale of the government's rearmament programme emerged in mid-August. However, the press could only speculate how ministers intended to spend the planned £3,400 million over the next three years. Therefore, reporters could only speculate about the likely impact of an accelerated production programme on the aircraft industry. The crucial question raised in one report was how the additional orders would be distributed across the industry without damaging its export orders. Some of the additional work could absorb the idle capacity at some aircraft firms currently engaged in the development of the planned jet-powered strategic bombers. However, a *Financial Times* report noted that the biggest problem would be to recruit the

---

[28] Our Air Correspondent, "More Aircraft Needed: New orders for jet fighters," *Financial Times*, 28 July 1950.

additional 100,000 workers needed for the aircraft industry in order to fulfil the rearmament programme given the high levels of employment in other sectors.[29]

A month later, Payne criticised the government for providing an insufficient lead to the industry. In contrast to other voices, he rejected the argument that all exports of aircraft benefited the country. While attention normally focused on the development of civilian airliners, Payne pointed out that since 1945 Britain had primarily exported the latest type of military aircraft and engines all over the world including Eastern bloc countries. Ministers had justified such exports with the argument that they helped to maintain the industry's war potential which could be expanded in the case of another military threat emerging. He proceeded to cast doubt on the logic of this policy, because it depended on the ability to expand capacity and production after the outbreak of hostility. However, Payne pointed out that the time for a build-up of production no longer existed in the age of nuclear warfare. Given the lengthy development time of new aircraft, he urged the government to place production orders for the latest available types. Ministers should prioritise rearmament over exports and abandon the development of civilian airliners with limited commercial prospects such as the Brabazon and Saunders Roe flying boats. However, Payne went further suggesting that the British aircraft firms should collaborate closely with their American and French counterparts and consider relocating its production to Canada or the United States beyond the range of Soviet bombers. In his view, the severity of threat demanded that rearmament should take priority over all other public expenditure plans, because any half-hearted effort would undermine the country's military security.

> Our approach to the problems of rearmament must be realistic. If we think that we can rearm without interfering with plans for public expenditure in other directions we are likely to fall between two stools. Military security has to be the sine qua non which must take precedence over the realisation of all our hopes.[30]

As might be expected, other papers were less sanguine about the prospect of surrendering Britain's "hard-won lead" in the development of civilian airliners. Under the headline "can we still lead in civil aircraft?", the *Financial Times*' aviation correspondent lamented the continued uncertainty about the industry's prospects. The article points out that the level of increased work required as part of the rearmament remained uncertain as long as it was unclear whether or not the United States would support the additional British defence effort financially. At the same time, the problem of finding additional workers might

---

29 Our Aviation Correspondent, "Aircraft and Defence," *Financial Times*, 18 August 1950.

30 L. G. S. Payne, "Rearmament means a New Deal for Our Aircraft Industry," *The Daily Telegraph*, 11 September 1950.

undermine the expansion of the industry's production in the coming months. In this context, the writer commented that while the aircraft industry struggled to find more employees, other sectors persisted in using outmoded production methods in order to maintain high levels of employment. As a result, the industry now faced the question of whether it would have to sacrifice its export potential in order to meet the needs of the rearmament programme. The article concluded by criticising the government for having done little to remove the uncertainty about the aircraft industry's future despite the radically changed circumstances.[31]

This view clearly reflected the growing concerns of the aircraft industry. An article published in late November renewed this criticism of government policy. However, the emphasis of the criticism shifted away from the potential difficulty of finding additional workers for the industry. Instead, the article bemoaned the fact that the government had yet to give the industry any detailed information about the distribution of rearmament orders. In this context, the report noted that the decision to place the recent Canberra order with several aircraft firms indicated an intention to spread rearmament orders between firms with idle capacity. However, the *Financial Times* correspondent focused on the industry's concerns that the current orders remained insufficient to fill much of the industry's idle capacity. In the absence of firm orders being placed, the government's assurances did little to counter the growing anxieties of aircraft manufacturers that rearmament orders might be reduced if no American dollar aid was forthcoming. Therefore, the writer urged the supply departments to involve the industry more fully in the current planning of the defence programme.[32]

With the placement of large production orders for the Canberra in November 1950 and for the Venom the following month, the defence programme was finally gathering pace at the end of the year.[33] In early January 1951, the Hawker-Siddeley group decided to shift production of its A. W. Hawksley factory from prefabricated houses to the latest type of Armstrong-Siddeley Sapphire jet engines. In order to increase production, the firm started

---

[31] Our Aviation Correspondent, "Can we still lead in civil aircraft?," *Financial Times*, 7 October 1950.

[32] Our Air Correspondent, "Aircraft Industry and Government Policy: Concern over lack of information: First orders getting under way: Contracts placed for jet fighters and bombers," *Financial Times*, 25 November 1950. A major beneficiary of the Canberra order was Handley Page which had lost a government order for Hastings transport planes in the cuts the previous spring. Besides the main contractor English Electric, two other aircraft firms, A.V. Roe and Shorts received production orders for the Canberra medium bomber; see Our Air Correspondent, "Handley Page New Contract: Canberra jet bomber," *Financial Times*, 23 November 1950.

[33] On the Venom order, see "Manufacture of Venom Aircraft," *The Times*, 30 December 1950.

recruiting 4,000 additional workers and building houses in nearby towns.[34] However, the growing order books prompted renewed concerns that labour shortages might affect the expansion of output. The chairman of the Hawker-Siddeley group, Thomas Sopwith, told a shareholders' meeting that the government should take steps to direct labour in order to ensure that the aircraft industry could recruit the additional workers required to produce the aircraft urgently needed for Britain's air defence. In his address, he referred to the considerable time it had taken during the last war to expand production. While crediting him with the best of intentions, the leader writers of the *Manchester Guardian* doubted whether company directors should call on the government to impose restrictions on the movement of labour, because such interventions were likely to cause undue alarm among the population. In contrast to Sopwith, the editorial pointed out that the RAF had prevailed in 1940 due its qualitative advantage over its opponent. Therefore, the government had quite rightly been delaying the decision to place large scale production orders in order to ensure that the RAF would be equipped with the most advanced aircraft at the start of another global conflict. At the same time, the editors thought the government had delayed for too long in spelling out its defence programme to the country and urged the Prime Minister, Clement Attlee, to use his speech the following day to remove this uncertainty.[35]

However, such a clarification of the government's plans had to wait until Attlee's statement on the expanded £4,700 million defence programme on 29 January 1951.[36] In the meantime, the government announced its decision not to order any more Brabazon aircraft beyond the two prototypes currently under construction, because it now believed that the aircraft would be uneconomic as a commercial airliner. The plane's main contractor, Bristol Airplane Company, defended the project as being a valuable experiment in aircraft design. Not convinced by the company's statement, *The Times* reporter commented that many observers would see the price of pushing back the frontiers of aircraft technology as excessive in this case.[37] To sweeten the loss of a production

---

34 Ronald Walker, "Jets oust prefabs," *News Chronicle*, 8 January 1951.

35 [, 1951 #94]"Warning," *Manchester Guardian*, 5 January 1951.[, 1951 #94;, 1951 #94;, 1951 #94;, 1951 #94]

36 Cabinet Office, *Defence Programme: Statement made by the Prime Minister in the House of Commons on Monday, 29th January, 1951*, Cmd. 8146 (London: His Majesty's Stationery Office, 1951).

37 Our Aeronautical Correspondent, "Future of Brabazon: No orders for production: Government decision," *The Times*, 12 January 1951.; Ronald Walker, "Cabinet writes off another £12 million," *News Chronicle*, 11 January 1951. After the one prototype built had completed 400 hours of flight trials, the then Minister of Supply, Duncan Sandys, ordered the dismantling of the aircraft along with another partially completed second prototype; see "Brabazon Project Abandoned: £12 millions spent: Planes to be dismantled: Valuable lessons," *Manchester Guardian*, 21 July 1953.; Our Air Correspondent, "Brabazon Airliner to Be Scrapped," *Financial Times*, 21 July 1953.

contract for the Brabazon, the company had already received a production order for the Venom fighter aircraft designed by de Havilland.[38] Given concerns over the rearmament programme, the discontinuation of the Brabazon project created rather fewer ripples than might otherwise have been expected. At the same time, the press celebrated the deal to build the new Armstrong-Siddeley Sapphire jet engine under licence in the United States. The initial tests confirmed that the British engine would significantly improve the performance of the latest type of F-84 jet fighter. This prompted one reporter to argue that

> [t]hus technical history is repeating itself, for during the war the north American Mustang fighter was given a large improvement by the substitution of a British Rolls-Royce engine for the original United States power unit. It was with the British engine that the Mustang achieved its successes. Today the use by the Americans of British engines would be facilitated by the licence agreements that have been entered into between British and American manufacturers.[39]

The press put a similar gloss on American interest in building the Canberra medium bomber under licence in the United States for the American air force. The prototype sent to America for an evaluation set a new speed record on its flight across the Atlantic. The feat was celebrated by the British press, but led to speculation about the engines of the aircraft, a more powerful version of the Rolls-Royce Avon jet engine. One report commented on the reluctance of the supply department to release any technical information about these new jet engines.[40] These stories reflected as well as reinforced the wide-spread perception that the British aircraft industry led the world at least in the development of jet propulsion technology.

These orders assured the industry work for the next two years, but they did not provide a long-term blueprint for the industry's future. As one press report noted, government had yet to take several big decisions about the next generation of supersonic jet fighters and heavy bombers. The biggest question mark related to whether or not these decisions would have to be taken in consultation with Britain's NATO allies.[41] The Prime Minister's statement on the defence programme ended such speculations announcing that the government would soon place large-scale production orders for supersonic fighters and heavy bombers currently under development. Despite the inherent risk of ordering aircraft off the drawing board, the press celebrated this

---

[38] "Manufacture of Venom Aircraft."

[39] Student of the Air, "British jet engine for U.S. fighter," *Manchester Guardian*, 11 January 1951.

[40] Student of the Air, "The Canberra's Engines," *Manchester Guardian*, 23 February 1951.

[41] Our Air Correspondent, "Defence Orders for Aircraft: New pattern of work taking shape," *Financial Times*, 23 January 1951.

decision as a vote of confidence in the technical ability of the British aircraft industry.

> "This is no gamble," I was told yesterday by a representative of the aircraft industry. "The RAF know what they want and the plans for this new bomber have shown them that it will do what they want." The bomber is being built by a famous aircraft firm which built bombers during the last war.
>
> The RAF is satisfied that in its class it will beat anything in the world.
>
> The first of the new planes is expected to fly shortly—much sooner than usual.[42]

In contrast to the fanfares for this order, the announcement by the Secretary for Air, Henderson, that the government was considering procuring American F-84 jet fighters, received little attention. While noting the plans, *The Daily Telegraph*'s correspondent, Payne, dwelled on the fact that many squadrons of the Royal Auxiliary Air Force remained equipped with Spitfires and were under strength. Moreover, the article pointed out it would be several years before all British fighter squadrons would be equipped with the faster jet fighters still under development. As a footnote, he added the statements of Wing Commander J. E. Johnson about the impressive performance of Russian MIG-15 jet fighters in Korea, which were able to give the best western fighter, the F-84, a "good run for its money".[43] At the same time, neither Payne nor his colleagues commented on the underlying contradiction between the blind faith of the Air Staff in the British aircraft industry's ability to produce world-beating bombers and the unspoken fact that the latest British jet fighter aircraft were outclassed by both American and Russian planes.

As production started to build up in late spring 1951, the press reports began focusing on mounting problems faced by the industry in expanding output. The reports continue to highlight the potential knock-on effect if the industry failed to recruit sufficient skilled workers and engineers. To some extent, the industry's difficulties were attributed to government cuts in the procurement budget which had forced firms to reduce their workforce during the lean years following the end of the Second World War. While the adoption of the

---

[42] G. Leslie Carter, "RAF order untried bomber," *Daily Herald*, 1 February 1951. See also Our Aviation Correspondent, "Aircraft Orders to be Spread: Sub-contracting by other industries," *Financial Times*, 1 February 1951.

[43] L. G. S. Payne, "Faster RAF Jets 'As Soon As Possible': Orders placed for secret aircraft," *The Daily Telegraph*, 8 February 1951. In this article, Payne suggests that the government might not place production orders for the Hawker P`1081 (later code-named Hunter) and the Vickers 535 (Swift), because it was currently developing even faster jet fighters. However, his description of the aircraft and their likely performance makes it clear that the minister was referring to these two aircraft as the advanced types with which the government planned to reequip the RAF. The confusion here suggests that the government preferred to shroud its plans in secrecy.

Canberra by the United States proved the technical ability of the industry, a *Financial Times* report pointed out that the Canberra was unlikely to enter service before the middle of 1952 despite four firms being engaged in the plane's production. In this context, jet engine production gave cause for concern because increasing output required the massive expansion of production capacity. As part of the rearmament drive, the report noted that the government planned to build a new factory in East Kilbride for Rolls Royce and a shadow factory to be managed by Standard Motors. However, little progress had been made on either project. While the report headlined the shortage of machine tools affecting the expansion of aircraft production, the text did not expand on the problems experienced by the industry. At the same time, the report noted that the industry did not suffer from any significant shortage of raw materials "since it heads the list of priorities". Moreover, the industry remained confident that it would be able to acquire the needed materials through its established supply network.[44]

Commemorating the first successful flight of the first British jet-powered aircraft on 15 May 1941, the *Financial Times* ran a series of articles by two pioneers of jet engine design, Frank Halford[45] and Frank Whittle in May 1951. Halford started the series with a broad analysis of the recent developments and the impact of jet engines on military and civilian aviation. In his first article, Halford claimed that Britain stole the march on its allies in the development of jet engines, because military requirements largely dominated aeronautical engineering during the war and the immediate post-war period. Rather than developing jet engines, American aircraft firms had been preoccupied with improving the performance of propeller engines for their new civilian airliners launched at the end of the war. In contrast, British producers concentrated on extending their lead in jet engine design in order to enhance the performance of fighter aircraft. At the same time, Halford pointed out that foreign competitors were threatening Britain's technological lead in jet propulsion. Indeed, he admitted that British firms had been slow in adopting after-burners and water injection to assist thrust during take-off and combat.[46] While development efforts centred initially on jet engines with centrifugal compressors, designers realised at an early stage the advantages of axial compressors in terms of fuel efficiency and higher thrust. However, this improvement had to be set against "the inherent complication, fragility and cost of the axial compressor with its

[44] Our Air Correspondent, "Standards to Make Aero Engines?: New plant needed for "Avon" jet," *Financial Times*, 27 April 1951. On the adoption of the Canberra by the United States Air Force, see also "U.S. Switch To Our Jet: American bomber dropped in favour of Canberras: Thousands may be built under licence," *Evening News*, 14 April 1951.

[45] Halford directed the development and mass production of the Goblin and Ghost jet engines at de Havilland. At the time, he was also the president of the Royal Aeronautical Society.

[46] Frank B. Halford, "The Jet Age in Aviation-II," *Financial Times*, 16 May 1951.

thousands of small rotating and fixed blades."[47] Given the scope for further improvements of both engines designs, Halford argued that the debate over the relative merits of compressor types would continue for some time to come. However, the tenor of his analysis suggested that he thought that centrifugal compressors would be preferred by airlines because of their greater simplicity and reliability.[48] In his two articles, Whittle concentrated on the wartime development of the first jet engine speculating that the pure jet engine would eventually displace turbo-prop engines even over short distances. In his concluding paragraph, he warned that the English Channel no longer represented a real obstacle for modern jet bombers. Therefore, he stressed that government should urgently address the problems of air defence in the jet age by developing faster fighter aircraft.[49]

Over the next few months, the press highlighted the challenges faced by British aero-engine producers to increase jet engine production. Attention focused on the problems of expanding the output of the blades for the new high performance jet engines using an axial compressor. *The Economist* first raised the alarm by predicting that existing capacity could not produce the 200,000 fan blades required for a monthly output of 100 axial compressor jet engines. Not only did axial compressor engines require more fan blades, but they also needed to be manufactured to higher specifications of precision and durability. Unless this bottleneck could be overcome, the government's decision to build several new production lines would do little to increase the output of axial compressor engines. Given the potential knock-on effect for the rearmament programme, the writer of the article echoed suggestions from some circles in the industry that it would be better to continue building jet engines with centrifugal compressor jet engines until the industry mastered producing large quantities of fan blades. The article accused the Ministry of Supply and the Air Ministry of failing to appreciate the severity of this potential problem. Given the foreseeable shortage of fan blades, the writer concluded that the supply departments were wrong to abandon the further development of centrifugal engines and should work closely with the industry to overcome this potential bottleneck.[50]

Several newspapers used the 1951 Farnborough air show as an occasion to reflect on the achievements of the aircraft industry and the problems of the defence build-up. Most articles celebrated the new fighter aircraft such as the Hawker P 1067 and Vickers Swift with their swept wings or the four jet Vickers Valiant heavy bombers. While noting the industry's design prowess,

---

47 Frank B. Halford, "The Jet Age in Aviation-I," *Financial Times*, 15 May 1951.

48 Halford, "The Jet Age in Aviation-II."

49 Frank Whittle, "The Past, Present and Future of Jets-I," *Financial Times*, 17 May 1951.; Frank Whittle, "The Past, Present and Future of Jets-II," *Financial Times*, 18 May 1951.

50 "Aero Engines," *The Economist*, 28 July 1951.

the reports also noted the industry's continued problems in recruiting skilled workers and the growing material and component shortages affecting production. In an article in the *Daily Mail*, Courtenay Edwards summarised:

> [t]he lesson of Farnborough is that while the men in Britain's aircraft drawing offices have skilfully sketched the outline of the air force needed to keep the peace, there are not enough men, materials, and tools in the adjoining workshops to turn our paper squadrons into warplanes with teeth.

Moreover, he noted that British manufacturers had yet to produce a long-range all-weather fighter and rocket-propelled interceptors, which should form part of a balanced air force in the jet age.[51] Similarly praising the achievements of the "native British school of design", *The Economist* noted that the industry did not require additional floor space beyond the planned construction of jet engine production lines and fan blade production capacity. However, the writer wondered how the industry's future could be secured when the orders from the rearmament programme would dry up at the end of 1954. While it was important to develop the export market for the new generation of jetliners, civilian demand would prove insufficient to sustain the industry without continued military orders.

> This fact is cold comfort for the bulk of the aircraft industry unless military customers can be found. It is not a wholly encouraging picture in this time of bright optimism. The Farnborough show has proved clearly that the British aircraft industry has the designing ability of a calibre not surpassed in the world. It would be disappointing, indeed, if the industry's commercial ability was not equal to the task of finding a world market for its product.[52]

The Times Washington correspondent reported that the American press largely agreed with British analysts about the superiority of British planes, but that the *Wall Street Journal* criticised the industry's poor production record quoting one observer as saying: "They are good designers, but not producers. Above all, they are super salesmen."[53] However, the *Manchester Guardian* noted that American aircraft firms were experiencing similar problems to their British counterparts in expanding production.[54]

On balance, the press continued to sing the industry's praises during the first year of the rearmament programme. With the display of the next generation of

---

51 Courtenay Edwards, "Our Blue-print Squadrons," *Daily Mail*, 11 September 1951.

52 "The New Aircraft," *The Economist*, 15 September 1951.

53 Our Own Correspondent, "U.S. Praise for British Jet Aircraft," *The Times*, 25 September 1951.

54 "How To Make More Planes," *Manchester Guardian*, 27 September 1951.

military aircraft at Farnborough, the outline of a new jet powered Royal Air Force emerged, even though the growing production problems meant that these new types would not enter service for at least another 2 years. Many press reports continued to blame the supply departments for causing the problems by running down the industry in the months prior to the outbreak of the Korean War and for not having foreseen the problems caused by the decision to order primarily axial compressor jet engines.

The aircraft industry under new stewardship

On the eve of the general election in October 1951, sources from the aircraft industry predicted according to a *Financial Times* article that the growing shortages particularly of turbine blades could delay the production of the military aircraft by at least six months if not several years. The report referred to a recent statement by the Society of British Aircraft Constructors (SBAC), which implicitly criticised the supply departments for not taking the necessary remedial action.

> "The evil consequences of these omissions," the society warned, "cannot now be avoided. It still remains to be seen whether action will be taken to stop the drift into even greater difficulties."[55]

Two days later, the Conservatives gained a narrow parliamentary majority and it fell to the new government to assume stewardship of the rearmament programme and the aircraft industry.

After taking office, the new Prime Minister, Winston Churchill, added to the industry's worries by announcing a thorough review of the rearmament programme in his speech during the Defence Debate in early December. A month after his announcement, the air correspondent of the *Financial Times* urged the government to take urgent steps to prevent further slippages in the defence effort. The article blamed the previous government for forcing the industry to downsize just before the outbreak of the Korean War and for spreading production orders between firms without proper thought being given to the availability of skilled labour and materials. Contrary to the expectations of the last administration, the writer noted that the aircraft industry had not been able to recruit additional workers set free by the reduced production of consumer goods. Due to the failure to expand production, the article warned that Britain's hard-won technological lead would be lost to other countries. In

55 Our Air Correspondent, "Aircraft Output Hampered: Serious problems developing: Shortages may soon be fully apparent: Turbine blades hold-up to engine production," *Financial Times*, 23 October 1951.

order to capitalise on the industry's success in developing a number of outstanding planes, the government should take urgent steps to fulfil the Prime Minister's promise "to give priority in materials to the requirements of the air force."[56] This message was reinforced by Sopwith at the annual meeting of the Hawker-Siddeley group in the middle of January 1952. In his speech, he noted that besides continued problems of recruiting skilled workers, most aircraft firms faced serious delays in obtaining vital materials. In many cases, it took longer to receive supplies of steel, alloys and other metals than during the Second World War. Reporting on his speech, the *Manchester Guardian*'s financial editor also pointed out that the American aircraft industry faced similar production problems due to the growing complexity of modern military aircraft.[57]

At the same time, the first prototype of the Vickers Valiant crashed when one of its engines caught fire after it had just completed its basic flight testing. Despite the crash, the Air Ministry confirmed its production order for the first of Britain's new heavy bombers which were to carry the country's nuclear weapons.[58] A month later, the *Financial Times*' air correspondent reported two other blows to the British aircraft industry. First, he reported that Frank Whittle was thinking about taking up the offer of an American aero-engine producer, because he was disappointed about "the way development of jet engine is going on in this country." However, he devoted most of his article to the second setback for the industry, the government's announcement that the Royal Air Force would be equipped with Canadian-built F-86 Sabre fighters, because the designs of the advanced British fighters had not been completed yet. The report agreed that the government was right to order these American planes as a stop-gap in order to modernise the RAF's air defence capability. As the Hawker P 1067 was unlikely to enter production soon, the American and Australian governments decided to cancel their plans to build the plane under licence for their air forces. To make matters worse, the Australian government considered building Sabre jet fighters instead. Rather intriguingly, the report noted that

> "[t]he inability of the British aircraft industry to get its prototypes into large-scale production, in spite of the superiority of those prototypes, is

[56] Our Air Correspondent, "Air Rearmament Delays: Industry's concern at slow progress: Expansion checked as shortages persist: Hope of new measures this year," *Financial Times*, 2 January 1952.

[57] Our Financial Editor, "Air Defence Delays: Materials and Labour short," *Manchester Guardian*, 17 January 1952.

[58] "Fire in Valiant 'Accidental': Production to go on," *Manchester Guardian*, 14 January 1952.; "Production of Atom Bomber: No change in plans following crash," *Financial Times*, 14 January 1952.; "Vickers Valiant Crash: No change in plans for production," *The Times*, 14 January 1952.

> not confined to fighters. Production of the English Electric Canberra jet bomber is lagging behind the re-equipment needs of the R.A.F."

This failure might lead to the embarrassing situation whereby the Americans might supply American-built Canberras to other western European NATO member states rather than finance their production in Britain through an offshore procurement contract. Despite these "danger signals in the air", the article did not blame the government, but implicitly the industry for this poor production record.[59] In announcing measures to speed up production, Churchill, however, attributed the failure to the delays in placing sizeable production orders by the previous administration. As the *Economist* noted, even if substantial orders had been placed earlier, the decision to adopt axial compressor engines would have held up production of the new generation of planes for the RAF.[60]

Over the next months, this debate rumbled on. Extending one of Whittle's jet engine patents, the judge in the case castigated the industry for not taking up the idea of a by-pass engine and sympathised with Whittle's frustration about the fact that his ideas had been ignored by established aero-engine producers.[61] An article in *The Economist* expressed similar incredulity that the government had neglected to develop by-pass engines based on the more reliable centrifugal compressor. According to the report, Power Jets Research and Development Ltd. was prevented from pursuing Whittle's ideas, when this publicly owned firm was transformed into a patent holding company and its research and development work was taken over by the National Gas Turbine Establishment. The article concluded with a stinging critique of government procurement policy for jet engines:

> Security makes it difficult to obtain all the facts necessary to form a balanced opinion of jet engine development in this country, but this at least seems clear. Remarkable engines have been designed, but apparently without much consideration about putting them into production. Blades, for example, might have been designed from the start in a way that made it possible to produce them by less extravagant methods. Moreover, the development of other, possibly more important, engines appears to have been needlessly delayed. Nor has it ever been explained satisfactorily why the man who was responsible for developing the jet engine has held no post connected with engines since he resigned from a post in the Ministry of Supply in 1948. Much of the value of his original work lay in designing a jet engine that could be put into

[59] Our Air Correspondent, "Danger Signals in the Air," *Financial Times*, 20 February 1952.

[60] "Rearmament and Engines," *The Economist*, 3 March 1952.

[61] "Unexploited Jet Invention: Patent Extended," *Manchester Guardian*, 26 February 1952.

> production several years ahead of any others then being developed. Such an advantage would be immensely valuable today.[62]

As this quote shows, the press reports about the patent case reflected a new theme in the debate about the aircraft industry's record: the brilliant genius whose ideas were being ignored by government, and in this case also by industry.

In March 1952, the government announced measures to speed up aircraft production by awarding 'super priority' to five aircraft and Avon jet engines now in production. The tenor of the press reports reflected that the supply situation was generally easing even in the availability of skilled labour and machine tools. The government announced that it would provide additional housing for workers in the industry as well as giving firms preferential access to steel and materials.[63] At the same time, a *Financial Times* report published just before the government's announcement reiterated claims that while shortages did affect production, the delays were caused by problems with the air frame rather than as feared with the engine.[64] Nevertheless, the Hawker-Siddeley group decided to set up two new production lines for the Hawker Hunter at its Hawker Aircraft factory in Kingston-upon-Thames and at its Gloster Aircraft subsidiary in Gloucestershire. To ease its space problems, the firm leased the Warner Brothers film studio close to its Kingston plant for additional storage.[65]

While one press report praised the industry's modern assembly line production methods, another reported that the Ministry of Civil Aviation imposed a limit of 10,000 flying hours on Viking aircraft, because inspections found cracks caused by metal fatigue in the plane's main wing spar.[66] Over the coming months, newspaper columns reflected by now familiar themes: reports on the successful development of a new jet engine and the problems caused by continued shortages of skilled workers, machine tools and materials. While the industry at least maintained its export commitments to civilian customers

62 "Rearmament and Engines."

63 Our Aeronautical Correspondent, "More fighters for R.A.F.: 'Super-priority' plans," *The Times*, 10 March 1952.; Our Air Correspondent, "Aircraft instead of sinks and washing machines," *The Sunday Times*, 9 March 1952.; Our Air Correspondent, "Priority for Aircraft: Industry's better feeling: Extension of Programme eases problems: Speedy measures looked for shortages," *Financial Times*, 17 March 1952.

64 A *Financial Times* Correspondent, "The New Interceptor Fighters," *Financial Times*, 7 March 1952.

65 Our Air Correspondent, "Gloster's New Contract To Build Hunter Jet Fighter," *Financial Times*, 7 May 1952.; Our Air Correspondent, "Hawker's Lease on Studio: More Space for Jet Fighters," *Financial Times*, 5 April 1952.; L. G. S. Payne, "Two Firms to Make R.A.F. Jet: Hawker Hunter on 'Super-Priority' list," *The Daily Telegraph*, 9 May 1952.

66 "Limit for Vikings Ordered: Main wing spar replacements - 'Fatigue'," *Daily Mail*, 4 April 1952.; Our Air Correspondent, "Building the Comet," *Financial Times*, 9 March 1952.

abroad, the tool shortage threatened to delay the production of the Hawker Hunter despite the Hawker-Siddeley's decision to build two further production lines at its factories in Blackpool and Baginton near Coventry.[67] At the same time, one report noted that Britain might lose its technological leadership in the development of jet engines, because the National Gas Turbine Establishment lacked vital equipment for altitude testing of new engines. Instead, British aero-engine firms relied on installing engines in aircraft in order to test them, but this method proved rather unreliable and not always feasible. While several American companies had their own altitude chamber or could test their new engines in the facilities of the National Advisory Committee for Aeronautics, none of the British firms could afford to build an altitude chamber. Indeed, several British firms had benefited from having their engines tested in the altitude chambers of American companies producing them under licence. The report noted that hitherto British companies had tended to share equipment in the past, but wondered whether this would be sufficient in the future. More intriguingly, the reporter concluded by saying that

> [i]n the opinion of many British development engineers only a small portion of the test equipment available in America is needed here. But the need for certain items is becoming pressing.[68]

This quote reflects either supreme confidence in their own technical ability or a degree of arrogance by British aircraft engineers.

During its ten months in office, the Conservative government sought to ease the pressure of the defence programme on the economy and the defence sector. After its review of the defence programme, the government extended the time period of the rearmament effort, but also adopted measures to accelerate the production of new aircraft for the RAF through the super-priority scheme. Conservative politicians blamed the previous Labour government for the delay in getting the defence programme off the ground. By summer 1952, the press reports show that the supply constraints affecting aircraft production had largely been overcome. While celebrating the industry's achievements, the press started on occasion to critically examine its record. Nevertheless, the press continued largely to promote the industry's agenda.

---

[67] Our Air Correspondent, "Air Rearmament Progress: Skilled labour still short: Sub-contracting now more widespread: Industry maintaining exports," *Financial Times*, 10 June 1952.; Our Air Correspondent, "Bristol Olympus Jet's Record Power," *Financial Times*, 30 June 1952.; Our Special Correspondent, "Developing New Jet Engine: Fuel saving with greater power," *The Times*, 30 June 1952.; L. G. S. Payne, "Tool Shortage Threat to Priority Jet," *The Daily Telegraph*, 4 July 1952.

[68] *Daily Telegraph* reporter, "British Jet Lead in Peril: Equipment Lag: Test altitude chamber needed: Cost too high for most firms," *The Daily Telegraph*, 7 August 1952.

The debate on the aircraft industry starts

Just as the supply constraint hampering aircraft production disappeared, a major change in government strategic thinking threatened to bring about a another shift in government policy toward the industry. These speculations were prompted by Churchill's speech during the defence debate before the summer recess suggesting that the government regarded a major war in Europe as increasingly unlikely in the foreseeable future while accepting the reality of a long cold war. As *The Economist* pointed out in a feature-length survey of the industry in September 1952, this change in the government's strategic assumptions meant that defence procurement would be less geared towards a massive build-up of the armed forces in anticipation of a global conflict, but would be directed towards the steady updating of military hardware in order to maintain military capabilities and deter a potential military threat. As a consequence, the government intended to reduce the numbers of military aircraft to be procured as part of the defence programme and instead concentrate resources on developing the next generation of military aircraft and missiles. However, the reduction in defence procurement prompted renewed questions about the overall size of the industry. This change in defence procurement policy potentially spelled trouble for those aircraft firms which had relied on obtaining sub-contracts in order to stay afloat. In future, the government might not continue its practice of dividing production orders between several firms as it had during the initial phase of rearmament, but rather place the order with the prime contractor.

Such a shift in policy, however, raised the question whether the government could continue to support the current number of aircraft firms through development contracts. Indeed, *The Economist*'s survey highlighted marked differences in the workload of individual companies. For example, de Havilland and Vickers found it difficult to juggle the combined demands of large military production orders and launching new civil airliners. At the same time, a firm like A. V. Roe had survived with a minor order for a long-range anti-submarine aircraft, the Shackleton, based on the Lancaster bomber and the development contract for one of the new generation of heavy bombers which flew a few days earlier at the Farnborough air show. Therefore, some analysts argued for concentrating the available work with a smaller number of firms, but most observers regarded maintaining of the largest possible number of design teams as preferable, because competition between designers clearly encouraged innovation and technological excellence. *The Economist* article stressed that British aircraft firms would have to excel at actually producing aircraft as well as develop them. As far the future was concerned, the article highlighted the competing demands on the industry in terms of improving aircraft performance. In order to achieve these improvements, new planes had to carry more equipment and fuel adding to their overall weight. While airframe design had kept pace with these developments, the article highlighted the fact that the industry relied on foreign canons for fighter aircraft, faced shortcomings in the supply of electronic component and equipment from domestic sources, and still relied on manual rather than power-assisted controls for its aircraft. As the industry relied to a large extent on military orders, *The Economist* asked whether or not the change in defence policy would affect the future shape of the RAF.[69]

A close reading of the Prime Minister's speech suggested that while the possibility of an imminent major war had diminished, the increased risk of total annihilation meant that the country had become more vulnerable than it had been after Dunkirk. To some extent, the formation of the Atlantic alliance and western rearmament redressed Britain's strategic weakness in the cold war. Given this changed situation, the government faced difficult strategic decisions as to whether British air power should be subjugated to the requirements of NATO or whether its general air power capabilities should be maintained for the cold war as well as small local (colonial) wars. *The Economist* praised Churchill for taking "the vital decision that chiefs of staff find it so hard to recommend", but asked whether or not the country could afford to sustain an RAF with balanced air power capabilities.[70] If British defence planners continued to insist on a balanced air force of fighters, bombers, transport and reconnaissance aircraft, they at least had to prove the case for procuring the needed aircraft from domestic production. The authors advocated a public debate on the integration of military aircraft production within the alliance in order to reduce the cost of balanced air power.

> On the face of it an agreement within Nato, which would allow nations to specialise in what they do best and rely on allies for the rest, would seem to offer to this country a way of making the best of its productive resources without a crippling effort to do everything. Air strategy must not be allowed to crash between too many tempting stools.[71]

In the end, the writers of this authoritative survey reserved their judgement on this question given the limited information available to outsiders. Despite the government's secrecy about defence policy and weapons development, it was rather ironic that the British public learned of the existence of a new Rolls Royce bypass jet engine from the American specialist press a month later.[72]

---

69 "Aircraft and Airpower," *The Economist*, 5 September 1952, 592-6.

70 "Aircraft and Airpower," 596-8 (quote: 596).

71 "Aircraft and Airpower," 598.

72 Our Air Correspondent, "New British Aero Engine: Rolls Royce develops first 'by-pass' jet," *Financial Times*, 23 October 1952.; L. G. S. Payne, "Jet Taken off Secret List," *The Daily Telegraph*, 23 October 1952.

As the coming months showed, the debate called for by *The Economist* never really got off the ground, but was overtaken by events. Before the government revealed the impact of its defence review, the American government announced a large offshore procurement (OSP) order for British fighter aircraft for the RAF. However, this order depended on the industry's ability to modify the planes in accordance with American demands. As a consequence, the Swift had been given preference over the Hunter, because its large-scale production had already commenced and therefore it was almost certain that the planes could be delivered before 30 June 1955 as stipulated by the contract.[73] Moreover, several firms secured substantial export orders which promised to employ the capacity freed by cutbacks in the defence programme. While Vickers managed to sell 15 Viscount aircraft to Canada, Hawker-Siddeley signed a contract with the Brazilian government for 70 Meteor jet fighters.[74] However, other firms such as Shorts in Belfast relying on subcontracts demanded additional work to keep its production lines going.[75] In the meantime, the aero-engine designer, Roy Fedden, used the first R. K. Pierson Memorial Lecture organised by the Royal Aeronautical Society to call for strengthening existing British design teams rather than dissipating them.[76]

At the beginning of December, the Minister of Supply, Duncan Sandys, finally revealed the outcome of the defence review. While the government decided to reduce the number of aircraft it intended to order, Sandys stressed that the output of military aircraft would continue to expand over the next few years. Given their limited nature, observers expected that the impact of the planned cutbacks would be relatively minor. The ending of the Meteor production badly hit the Gloster Aircraft Company which had to make about 3,000 workers redundant. However, most of the affected workers found employment almost immediately with other aircraft firms in the area. At the same time, ministers hoped that the planned reduction in military aircraft

---

[73] Our Air Correspondent, "Foreign Inquiry For Vickers Swift," *Financial Times*, 10 January 1953.; Our Air Correspondent, "Production Prospects in Britain," *Financial Times*, 13 October 1952.; Our Own Correspondent, "U.K. Aircraft for Europe: Value of orders may reach £25 m.: Plans for purchase of Swift fighters: Talks in London expected soon," *Financial Times*, 13 October 1952.

[74] Our Aeronautical Correspondent, "15 Jet Airliners for Canada: British firms £4m. contract: Effect on balance of payments," *The Times*, 20 November 1952.; Our Air Correspondent, "Biggest Dollar Order: Canada's 34,100,000 for Airliners," *Manchester Guardian*, 20 November 1952.; Our Correspondent, "Meteors Sold to Brazil: Contract for 70 signed," *The Times*, 20 October 1952.

[75] Our Aeronautical Correspondent, "Canberra Made in Belfast: Maiden-flight," *The Times*, 31 October 1952.; Our Air Correspondent, "Aircraft Exports May Rise: Release of more capacity likely: Outcome of defence review: Need for firm orders for production," *Financial Times*, 14 November 1952.

[76] "Maintaining Lead in Aviation: Importance of strong design teams," *The Times*, 13 November 1952.

orders would free sufficient capacity for the industry to meet its export orders and continue contributing to the balance of payments. Indeed, at a press conference called to explain the changes in the defence programme Ministry of Supply officials revealed that the government contemplated extending the super-priority scheme to include a number of other military aircraft projects as well as potentially civilian airliners.[77] On balance, the press welcomed the extension of super-priority to the Viscount, Comet and the Bristol Britannia in order to further their export chances. However, some observer voiced concerns that by extending the scheme, it would lose its effectiveness in speeding up aircraft production and that producers might exploit their privileged status to stockpile materials.[78]

While the press was encouraged by the imminent resumption of military aircraft exports, editorials castigated the American Civil Aeronautics Administration (CAA) for not accepting the British airworthiness certificates for the Comet and the Viscount. In the eyes of British officials, the American procrastination amounted in the words of *The Times* leader writer to nothing less than a "technical barrier to trade".[79] In response to British criticism, the CAA rejected claims that it had refused to validate British airworthiness certificates, but stressed that its officials were still engaged in negotiations with their British counterparts. Since the British Air Registration Board had always accepted American airworthiness certificates in the past, such statements sounded like prevarication in order to deprive British jetliners of access to the lucrative American market.[80] However, the CAA insisted that it would only

---

[77] "Air Rearmament Changes: Supply Minister's assurance: Continued expansion in military output: Labour force may rise 10,000 next year," *Financial Times*, 6 December 1952.; Our Aeronautical Correspondent, "Effects of Cuts on Aircraft: Continued rise in output: Speed-up of 'Super-priority' types," *The Times*, 8 December 1952.; Our Air Correspondent, "More Details Expected To-Day," *Financial Times*, 6 December 1952.; L. G. S. Payne, "Output Switch to New Planes: 10,000 more workers for aircraft firms: Minister explains arms drive changes: World demand for British airliners still growing," *The Daily Telegraph*, 6 December 1952.

[78] Derek Dempster, "A Hustler Loses its Sting," *Daily Express*, 10 January 1953.; Our Air Correspondent, "The Super-Priority Scheme," *Financial Times*, 1 January 1953.; "Speeding Production of Aircraft for Export: Priority extended to civilian types," *The Times*, 30 December 1952.

[79] Our Aeronautical Correspondent, "British Certificates of Airworthiness: Talks in Washington," *The Times*, 24 January 1953.; Our Aeronautical Correspondent, "Export of British Military Aircraft: Available from current production lines," *The Times*, 29 January 1953.; Our Air Correspondent, "Exports of Aircraft," *Financial Times*, 20 January 1953.; "A Technical Barrier to Trade," *The Times*, 28 January 1953. Several press reports incorrectly referred to the Civil Aeronautical Administration by its original name Civil Aeronautical Authority, which it held from its formation in 1938 until its reorganisation in 1940; see T. A. Heppenheimer, *Turbulent Skies: The history of commercial aviation* (New York: John Wiley and Sons, 1995), 123-4.

[80] "Certificates for Jet Airliners: Lord Brabazon on U.S. refusal," *The Times*, 25 April 1953.; Our Air Correspondent, "U.S. Attitudes on Jets: Lord Brabazon comments,"

grant an airworthiness certificate after a thorough investigation of the Comet, because of its revolutionary new design.[81] While this investigation was still dragging on, the American government demanded in October 1953 that any sale or operation of plane should be subject to prior approval by Anglo-American security authorities. This request reflected American concerns that the Russians might be able to obtain an Avon engine from an overseas operator. Other voices objected to the Comet using London and New York airports, because of the higher noise level of its engines.[82] In the meantime, the crash of a Comet in May 1953 did not undermine the export prospects, because rumours about the aircraft's safety were quickly squashed by attributing the accident to the prevailing weather conditions.[83] At the same time, the announcement of cuts in the American aircraft programme dented the potential for exports of military aircraft.[84]

Since all exports depended on the British aircraft industry delivering planes of high quality and on time, press reports repeatedly examined how British aircraft production could be speeded up. The industry itself took the issue of its production record seriously. In December 1952, production engineers from the aircraft industry met at the University of Southampton to discuss problems of aircraft production. According to an article in *The Times*, the chief designer of Bristol Aeroplane Company, A. E. Russell, urged the industry to "use 'aggressive but enlightened' principles in producing aircraft which would challenge the American export position."[85] In his contribution to the conference, the works director of de Havilland Aircraft, H. Povey, told the assembled audience that his firm had taken considerable risks in building a production line for the Comet before completing the first prototype. Unless the firm had taken this decision, it would not have been able to capitalise on Britian's technological lead and launch the jetliner well before its American rivals. In summing up, the Deputy Controller of Supplies (Air) at the Ministry

---

Financial Times, 25 April 1953.; Our Own Correspondent, "Certification of U.K. Jets: U.S. statement on issue," *Financial Times*, 30 April 1953.

[81] "Certification of Jet Aircraft: Lord Brabazon on talks with U.S.," *The Times*, 19 June 1953.; Our Own Correspondent, "Jet Aircraft Licences: U.S. requirements defined," *The Times*, 7 May 1953.

[82] Our Air Correspondent, "More Realistic Air Targets Urged," *Financial Times*, 18 September 1953.; Student of the Air, "Comet II: Another U.S. objection: Keeping Avon secret," *Manchester Guardian*, 8 October 1953.

[83] Student of the Air, "Need to Scotch Rumours: Comet disaster," *Manchester Guardian*, 4 May 1953.

[84] Our Air Correspondent, "Aircraft Export Prospects Good: All-time record of £5m. in March: Revival of military sales to Europe: Deliveries of turbine airliners under way," *Financial Times*, 7 May 1953.

[85] Our Air Correspondent, "U.K. Aircraft Production: 'Use aggressive methods'," *The Times*, 20 December 1952.; Our Correspondent, "Aircraft Industry's Needs: More research urged," *The Times*, 22 December 1952.

of Supply, W. C. Puckey, highlighted the considerable cost of modifications to aircraft design after firms had started to tool up for production. Therefore, firms should enhance the role of production engineering in all stages of aircraft development. To improve the industry's production record, he called for more research into production processes and the use of new materials.

The growing concern about the delays in British aircraft production was also reflected in a Select Committee of Estimates' report on the rearmament programme published in June 1953. In his coverage of the report, the *Evening Standard* correspondent took up the suggestion of the committee chairman, Ralph Glyn that the production rate could be speeded up by ordering military aircraft off the drawing board as Ministry of Aircraft Production had done during the war. In his reply, Air Marshal John Boothman stressed that the aircraft rushed into production during the war had been improved models of planes already in production in contrast to the latest types just entering production. Nevertheless, Boothman could not provide a satisfactory answer as to why it took almost twice as long for new British aircraft to enter active service compared to Russian and American planes.[86] In its coverage of the report, *The Times* highlighted that the committee criticised the wasteful nature of dividing aircraft orders between several producers. The committee noted that this practice resulted in orders of fairly small numbers of aircraft for each firm. Given their small scale, such orders did not justify the considerable investment needed to build several new production lines. Therefore, the committee recommended that this practice should be abandoned in order to benefit from the economies of scale associated with longer production runs. Indeed, the report went further and urged the government to explore the possibility that greater co-operation in arms production between NATO states could further lower the cost of military aircraft.[87] While stressing the potential for reducing the cost of military aircraft, the committee voiced its concern about the dependence of aircraft firms on the supply of foreign machine tools and called on the government to correct this strategic weakness.[88]

The theme of the rising cost of military aircraft also featured at the second two-day conference on aircraft production problems again held at the University of Southampton and organised by the Southern Section of the Institution of Production Engineers. On the first day of the conference, the chief designer of Shorts, D. Keith-Lucas called for a simplification of aircraft design in order to reduce not only the weight and price of modern jet fighters

---

[86] Evening Standard Political Correspondent, "How Beaverbrook Speeded the Planes," *Evening Standard*, 9 June 1953.

[87] "Economy in Air Defence: Cooperation urged between allies," *The Times*, 10 June 1953.

[88] Our Industrial Correspondent, "Cost of Military Aircraft: Call for economies in production," *Financial Times*, 10 June 1953.

but also the number of complicated electronic systems. While this gadgetry might be indispensable, he voiced concerns that due to the increased costs the government would be unable to procure fighters in sufficient numbers to secure Britain's air defence. This intervention highlighted the growing conflict between quantity and quality affecting peacetime defence procurement. Another speaker, the superintendent of Vickers-Armstrong's Supermarine factory S. P. Woodley, argued that production costs could be reduced by using heavy forging presses in order to machine the skin panels more cheaply and accurately. In his view, the development of ever larger forging presses would revolutionise aircraft production and therefore, British aircraft firms would fall behind their American rivals unless they invested in such machinery despite its high cost.[89]

On the second day of the conference, the Chief Engineer of British European Airways (BEA), Beverley Shenstone, sparked off a heated public debate by criticising the standard of workmanship in the British aircraft industry. In his intervention, he bluntly stated that

> in the United Kingdom, the average finish given to an aircraft is far inferior to that given to the average American aircraft. Parts and assemblies are not treated well in the shops and in one wing factory the impression was that after manufacture they dragged the wings along the shop floor.

As a result, even brand-new British planes looked like they had been in service for years creating an unfavourable impression with the travelling public. He went on to lament the poor standard of electrical wiring of British planes forcing airlines to renew it within the first couple months of operation. Moreover, he pointed out that British aircraft had a much shorter operational life span than similar American planes, because they suffered more from fatigue.[90] His intervention drew a prompt and furious response from the SBAC who attacked his comments as the unsubstantiated wholesale condemnation of British aircraft "calculated to appeal less to the trained technical mind than

---

[89] "Make Planes Simpler, Urges Designer: New shapes for faster speeds: Aircraft of future may be like guided missiles," *Recorder*, 19 December 1953.; Our Aeronautical Correspondent, "Aircraft of the Future: Experiments with new shapes," *The Times*, 19 December 1953.; Our Air Correspondent, "Simpler Aircraft to Cut Cost: Need for large forging presses urged," *Financial Times*, 19 December 1953.

[90] The quote and the summary is based on "Importance of Good Finish on Civil Aircraft: Criticism of British workmanship," *Manchester Guardian*, 21 December 1953. For other reports of Shenstone's intervention, see Arthur Brenard, "Britain's new planes are criticised," *Sunday Express*, 20 December 1953.; "British Aircraft Finish 'Inferior': B.E.A. expert's comparison with American methods: Company 'plagued' by adjustments," *The Observer*, 20 December 1953.; Our Aeronautical Correspondent, "British Aircraft Standards: Finish 'inferior' to American: Engineer's criticism," *The Times*, 21 December 1953.

to the emotions of the general public."[91] The Society particularly objected that any criticism was being aired in public rather than through its internal technical committee system.[92] Indeed, the SBAC criticised the conference organisers for providing a platform for these damaging remarks when the industry had supported their efforts in the hope that the conference would be "of positive technical benefit to British aviation."[93] In a letter to the editor of *The Times*, Geoffrey de Havilland accused Shenstone of undermining the industry's export prospects by besmirching its reputation for quality.[94] Speaking at a prize-giving ceremony for apprentices, the managing director of A. V. Roe, Sir Roy Dobson, dismissed Shenstone's criticism by pointing to the achievements of recipients as evidence of the high standards of British workmanship. The press seized on his remark that the irresponsible comments by one individual in a private capacity "should not be taken too seriously" in an attempt to end the furore.[95] Trade unionists joined the chorus of outrage accusing Shenstone of denigrating the industry without supporting his claims by evidence.[96] Under the concerted pressure of the industry, BEA partly disowned the remarks of its chief engineer.[97] However, another pioneering aircraft designer, Sir Frederick Handley-Page inadvertently added credence to Shenstone's claim that British aircraft components were not interchangeable, by saying that "spares should be ordered at the same time as the aircraft, not a later date."[98] While press reports focused on Stenstone's remarks, a second speaker at the conference, Air Marshall Owen Jones, similarly criticised the poor quality of riveting and lack of interchangeability of spare parts.[99] The *Manchester Guardian*'s Student of Air pointed out that BEA had played an instrumental role in developing the

---

[91] "British Plane Makers Reply to Critic: Plea was to 'public emotions'," *The Daily Telegraph*, 21 December 1953.; "British Planes Defended: Criticisms 'that come strangely'," *Manchester Guardian*, 21 December 1953.

[92] Our Air Correspondent, "Criticism of U.K. Aircraft: Industry asks for Full Details," *Financial Times*, 22 December 1953.

[93] "British Planes Defended: Criticisms 'that come strangely'."

[94] Geoffrey de Havilland, "Production of Aircraft: British standards upheld: To the Editor of the Times," *The Times*, 22 December 1953.

[95] "Criticism of British Aircraft: 'Not to be taken too seriously'," *The Times*, 23 December 1953.; Our Air Correspondent, "Reply to Criticism of U.K. Aircraft," *Financial Times*, 23 December 1953.

[96] Daily Worker reporters, "Aircraft Slur Refuted: BOAC and union chief back protests," *Daily Worker*, 21 December 1953.; "Stop This Mischief, Say Plane Men," *Daily Herald*, 23 December 1953.

[97] "Criticism of British Aircraft: 'Not to be taken too seriously'."

[98] Our Aeronautical Correspondent, "British Aircraft Standards: Finish 'inferior' to American: Engineer's criticism." *The Times*, 21 December 1953.

[99] "Problems of Aircraft Production: A Report on the Second Conference by the Southern Section of the Institution of Production Engineers and held at the University of Southampton on December 18 and 19, 1953," *Aircraft Engineering* 26 (1954): 49-50.

current generation of British civilian aircraft. Therefore, if those aircraft were now deemed deficient then BEA would have to share the blame.[100]

The furore prompted one reader of the *Manchester Guardian*, W. Page, to write to the editor asking, why everyone seemed to be rounding on BEA and its chief engineer when aircraft firms failed to deliver the fantastic planes they had been promising for years. Far from being reassured by the statements of the industry, he asked "where are the 'bread and butter' planes" justifying these claims.[101] Indeed, the paper's aviation expert agreed with the sentiments claiming in an article that Britain was falling "far behind in fighter aircraft development." The article noted that American firms were testing research aircraft capable of flying over 500 miles per hour faster than British planes while no similar development of rocket-powered aircraft seemed to be undertaken in Britain. The Student of Air called on the government to explain what future it saw for manned interceptors in air defence in the age of anti-aircraft missiles rather than hiding behind the Official Secrets Act. From the available information, he assumed that the government had quietly surrendered to the United States not only the development of long-range bombers, but also its traditional field of fighter aircraft. Bluntly put the government had to answer two questions:

> If manned fighters are required why are we not developing them? If guided missiles can take over the responsibility for defence why are we still concentrating so much effort on manned fighters.[102]

Responding to the letter to the editor by Page, the SBAC deputy director, M. Ionides, highlighted the resource constraints on aircraft development in Britain. While the press had focused on the criticisms of quality, the conference had highlighted the challenges faced by the industry arising from the discovery of new alloy metals and development of new machine tools. In this context, he pointed out that "no budget foreseeable, short of a major war, is enough to meet the cost of what is technically possible and militarily desirable." The industry reacted strongly to the suggestions of poor workmanship, because it depended on its reputation in export markets in order to maintain its position as an economically and strategically vital industry.[103]

---

[100] Student of the Air, "Criticism of British Aircraft A 'Condemnation of B.E.A.': Corporation has power to reject bad work," *Manchester Guardian*, 22 December 1953.

[101] W. A. Page, "British Aircraft: Letter to the Editor," *Manchester Guardian*, 24 December 1953.

[102] Student of the Air, "Britain Far Behind in Fighter Development: Best U.S. planes 500 m.p.h. faster," *Manchester Guardian*, 23 December 1953.

[103] M. G. Ionides, "British Aircraft: Letter to the Editor," *Manchester Guardian*, 1 January 1954.

Where are the aircraft?

Over the coming months, the government's technological choices became a favourite target of its critics. For example, critics recalled the government's decision to cancel the Miles M.52 supersonic plane after an American rocket-powered plane showed that the United States was taking the lead in the development of supersonic aircraft in December 1953.[104] This sentiment was echoed by Sir Thomas Sopwith in his address to the annual meeting of the Hawker Siddeley group. The company published his critical remarks on government procurement policy under the title of "Private Enterprise in Action" as a full page advertisement in *The Times* on the same day as the meeting.[105] The publication of the speech prompted an angry response from the Labour MP, Frank Beswick, who asked why Hawker-Siddeley seemed to be unprepared to spend more on research and development out of its own resources preferring instead to rely on public funds.[106] The BEA chairman, Lord Douglas of Kirtleside, agreed with Beswick that the aircraft industry should not always criticise the government when things went wrong, while claiming the credit for any successes. However, he endorsed Sopwith's call for more money to be spent on research and development. Unless additional resources were forthcoming, the British aircraft industry would fall further behind its American rival with its unlimited resources.[107]

At the same time, other voices argued that the Air Ministry's insistence on maximum performance was misguided. For example, the Managing Director of Folland Aircraft, William Petter, pointed out that western air forces would no longer be able to afford to procure adequate numbers of fighter aircraft for air defence because of the increased cost of standard fighters such as the F-86 or the Hunter.[108] In order to meet the need for larger numbers of fighter aircraft, Folland Aircraft designed a light fighter code-named *Gnat* as a private venture and promoted the aircraft for use by NATO.[109] However, the government rejected these proposals in its reply to the suggestion by the Select Committee on Estimates that the government should investigate lowering the production cost of the latest fighter aircraft by selling them to other NATO countries. The

---

104 Ronald Walker, "Britain Losing Jet Power Lead," *News Chronicle*, 7 January 1954.

105 "Private Entreprise in Action: Sir Thomas Sopwith, C.B.E., reviews British air power, calls for bold research policy, warns against complaceny: Annual Report and Statement of the Chairman ... Hawker Siddeley Group," *The Times*, 7 January 1954.

106 Frank Beswick, "Aircraft Development: To the editor of the Times," *The Times*, 21 January 1954.

107 Douglas of Kirtleside, "Development of Aircraft: Retaining Britain's lead: To the editor of the Times," *The Times*, 22 January 1954.

108 William E. W. Petter, "The Cost of Fighter Aircraft," *Financial Times*, 5 January 1954.

109 "The Case for a Light Fighter," *Financial Times*, 10 March 1954.

government argued that additional orders of British-built fighters depended on foreign governments and the availability of American military aid. Therefore, the scope for increasing British aircraft production by obtaining export orders was limited.[110] Undeterred by these reports, Folland launched the prototype for the *Gnat* at the Farnborough air show in September 1954. However, the future of this project depended on whether it could defeat rival British, French and Italian projects for a light fighter bomber.[111]

Despite the Comet crashes in the first months of 1954, the press continued to celebrate the industry's ongoing successes such as the test flight of the first supersonic English Electric P-1 fighter and mounting orders for the Viscount airliner.[112] Nevertheless, the *News Chronicle* air correspondent, Ronald Walker, asked pointedly "where are the planes?" on the eve of the Farnborough air show in September. Indeed, he suggested that the government should discontinue funding the industry unless it could finally produce the promised planes such as the Hunter, the Swift and the V-bombers. He noted that all these planes had yet to enter RAF service despite having been shown off as prototypes at Farnborough for several years.[113] Three months later, the RAF received the first Hawker Hunters built under American offshore procurement contracts.[114] At the same time, *The Observer* portrayed the bleak picture of the industry's position following American criticisms of British aircraft including the latest military types. According to the paper, many American observers believed that British firms lagged behind in "basic aerodynamic knowledge" and failed to deliver on innovative designs. Its correspondent argued that the industry had reached the end of the road after a string of disasters including the crashes of the Comet and several military prototypes earlier in the year. As a consequence, the government would have to re-examine the industry's position "in the national technical and industrial structure". The article noted that this bleak picture contrasted with the prevailing perception only a year ago that the industry was ahead of its rivals in terms of aircraft technology and innovative design. However, the writer had no explanation for the unexpected reversal of fortune for "this mercurial mixture of individuality, science and technology",

---

110 Our Political Correspondent, "Planes for Western Allies: Ministry's report," *Manchester Guardian*, 21 May 1954.

111 D. M. Desoutter, "Advantages of a Lighter Fighter," *Manchester Guardian*, 6 September 1954.; L. G. S. Payne, "N.A.T.O. Experts See Chief of Light Jet Firm: Fighter's future," *The Daily Telegraph*, 10 September 1954.

112 A Financial Times Correspondent, "Jets After Ten Years," *Financial Times*, 10 July 1954.; L. G. S. Payne, "Supersonic Fighter's 'Perfect' Test Flight: British plane can beat speed of sound on level," *The Daily Telegraph*, 5 August 1954.

113 Ronald Walker, "Tell These Firms - No Plane, No Cash," *News Chronicle*, 7 September 1954.; Ronald Walker, "Where Are the Planes?," *News Chronicle*, 6 September 1954.

114 Our Aeronautical Correspondent, "New Aircraft for R.A.F.: 350 machines by next June: Results of U.S. aid," *The Times*, 4 December 1954.

but blamed its downfall on the service departments and the state-owned airlines.[115] A few days later, Churchill admitted to the House of Commons that the government was considering the creation of a new department similar to the wartime Ministry of Aircraft Production to overcome the serious problems affecting aircraft production. The press seized on the Prime Minister's claim that the delays in delivering new military aircraft were partly due to the decision to build only a small number of pre-production prototypes. As a consequence, the loss of a prototype might seriously hold up production of a new aircraft. Therefore, the government decided to follow the American practice of ordering more prototypes in future.[116]

After the government admitted the problems in the procurement of military aircraft, press reports attributed the industry's poor record to inadequate levels of pay to attract skilled labour and insufficient training of shop-floor workers and managers.[117] In February 1955, the government published a white paper on the supply of military aircraft blaming the delay in developing a supersonic fighter on the Labour government's decision to cancel a project for such a plane in 1946.[118] Given the undeniable evidence of failure, commentators started searching for a magic solution to overcome these problems. For example, the Air correspondent of *The Daily Telegraph* argued that British aircraft manufacturers should concentrate on the production of smaller planes as suggested by William Petter.[119] Roy Fedden proposed that the industry should capitalise on its strength in developing innovative designs in co-operation with the American aircraft manufacturers.[120] Within a short few months, the tenor of press reporting changed from the almost unquestioning celebration of the industry's achievements whether real or imagined to the

---

[115] A Special Correspondent, "British Aircraft Troubles," *The Observer*, 19 December 1954.

[116] *Daily Telegraph* reporter, "Basic Faults in 2 Types: Design and weapons," *The Daily Telegraph*, 22 December 1954.; Our Parliamentary Correspondent, "Speeding Aircraft Production: Sir Winston considering special ministry," *Financial Times*, 22 December 1954.; Ronald Walker, "R.A.F. Gamble Lost Us Jet Lead," *Daily Herald*, 22 December 1954.

[117] For example, *The Daily Telegraph* commissioned a series of articles from Roy Fedden on the problems of the industry: Roy Fedden, "The Price of Mediocrity: More engineers needed: Better value research: Supply Ministry weakness," *The Daily Telegraph*, 2 February 1955.; Roy Fedden, "What is Wrong with British Aircraft Production?," *The Daily Telegraph*, 1 February 1955. A similar series of articles was published in the *Daily Herald*: Alan Hodgson, "Cut the firms who can't do the job," *Daily Herald*, 28 February 1955.; Alan Hodgson, "We've got the brains, but pay is too low," *Daily Herald*, 1 March 1955.; and Alan Hodgson, "Inefficiency must be scrapped NOW," *Daily Herald*, 2 March 1955.

[118] Our Political Correspondent, "Delays in Equipping the Air Force: White Paper puts blame on the Labour government: Strong night defence," *Manchester Guardian*, 17 February 1955.

[119] Student of the Air, "Case for concentrating on smaller aircraft: Britain's production troubles," *Manchester Guardian*, 10 March 1955.

[120] Roy Fedden, "Soothing Syrup about Aircraft," *The Daily Telegraph*, 6 May 1955.

search for what had gone wrong with industry. In many ways, Max Aitken's article in July 1955 accusing the men at helm of the Ministry of Supply of causing the industry's downfall reflected the deep disillusionment about the waning dream of the industry's technological potential.

Conclusions

If historians are obsessed with finding the origins of a story in the archives, this is particularly true for those seeking to retrace the causes of decline.[121] However, the danger is that the visit to the archive will become a search for the decisive documents which will allow the historian to tell the story he or she already knows with the benefit of hindsight. In order to escape this dilemma, this chapter has relied exclusively on an unorthodox archival source: the newspaper clipping files of the Labour Party Research Department. The analysis focused not only on the development of the aircraft industry, but also on how the press reported on the sector. By relying on the contemporaneous accounts of outside observers, this analysis revealed the picture presented to the British public by the newspapers. Of course, the image created by the press accounts was itself flawed and incomplete. Nevertheless, newspaper reports reflect the discursive constructions of the relationship between government and the aircraft industry, which define the political scope for government intervention. Therefore through a close reading of the archival evidence, this concluding section examines this political space further.

This source is not unproblematic, because the Labour Party Research Department maintained its newspaper clipping archive in order to advise the party on policy matters. In the case of the aircraft industry, the department repeatedly analysed the question of whether or not the sector should be nationalised. After consulting with senior Labour politicians familiar with the industry, its researchers briefed the National Executive on whether or not the sector should be nationalised both in 1948 and 1953. As David Edgerton has shown, the party shelved the idea of nationalising the industry in 1948, because its advisers felt that public ownership would not strengthen the government's control over the industry since the state as the largest buyer of aircraft already effectively exercised substantial power over its development. He attributes this decision to Labour politicians no longer regarding the nationalisation of the arms industry as a moral imperative as many had in the early 1930s.[122]

[121] On the obsession of western historians with the origins of developments, see Carolyn Steedman, *Dust* (Manchester: Manchester University Press, 2001), 66-7.

[122] David Edgerton, "Public ownership and the British arms industry, 1920-50," in *The Political Economy of Nationalisation in Britain, 1920-50*, eds. Robert Millward and John Singleton (Cambridge: Cambridge University Press, 1995), 173.

The analysis of this chapter shows that nationalisation did not figure largely in the public discussion. Indeed, the press coverage remained highly critical of government policy towards the industry until 1953, when the press started to ask probing questions about the industry's production record. As the doubts about its performance grew, the industry started to emphasise the importance of private initiative in order to maintain Britain's lead in the air.[123] *The Times* attacked the Labour Party's proposals to nationalise the industry in similar fashion in April 1953.[124] However, this direct attack was not only remarkable because of its exceptional nature, but also because an internal Labour Party working party had just recommended abandoning any plans for nationalisation of the aircraft industry unless firms were failing to deliver in terms of aircraft development and export performance. The brief argued that the industry depended on its design teams for its success, but that the generation of pioneering designers still dominating the industry would undoubtedly oppose nationalisation. On balance, the brief argued that little had changed since the National Executive decided against nationalisation in 1948, because it felt that the aircraft industry remained ahead of other industries in terms of productivity and technology. Given the general impression that the industry was doing well, it would be difficult to persuade the electorate of the need to nationalise the aircraft industry.

> The general success of the industry makes any project for further state interference difficult because of the twin objections – fear of disturbing the smooth running of the industry and the difficulty in putting it across to the electorate at large. For these reasons the NEC are advised to oppose this particular resolution while drawing attention to the fact that their proposal will be vigorously implemented should the need arise.[125]

This quote confirms the findings from the close reading of the press coverage on the industry. Prior to *The Economist* survey article published in September 1952, the industry could hardly do anything wrong as far as the general press was concerned while it continued criticising government policy. Arguably, this perception changed when the industry was seen as failing to deliver the aircraft which press reports had continually celebrated as major advances. Even if the supply departments were partly to blame for the delays in aircraft production,

---

[123] For example, see the discussion of Povey's remarks at the conference on aircraft production problems held at Southampton University in December 1952; Our Air Correspondent, "U.K. aircraft production."

[124] "Aircraft and the State," *The Times*, 13 April 1953.

[125] John Rylands University Library Manchester, Labour Party Archive, (hereafter: JRULM LPA): JRULM LPA Research Department. folder: Aircraft Industry.: Plan for Engineering, February 1953. A similar case is put forward by Frank Beswick in a Fabian Society pamphlet published in October 1955: Frank Beswick, *Plan for the Aircraft Industry*, Fabian Research Series No. 176 (London: Fabian Society, 1955), 17-18.

the industry was no longer perceived as faultless. However, the change in the public mood prompted the industry to extol the virtues of private enterprise and initiative in aircraft development in large advertisements in the daily press.[126] Given the changed climate, these ads were seen as touting for business and therefore as offensively strengthening the moral case for nationalisation.[127] Arguably, this change in public perception created a change in political climate which allowed the Conservative government to reorganise the industry and to merge existing firms into larger airframe and aero-engine companies in the late 1950s.[128] As this discussion shows, the discursive construction of the industry's achievements reflected only certain aspects of industrial policy. Apart from nationalisation, newspapers rarely reported on how wartime mobilisation had changed Britain's industrial landscape as a result of which the North West of England emerged as a major centre of aircraft and arms production.[129] These hidden biases in press reporting highlight the problem of different agendas preoccupying the press, policy-makers and historians as reflected in their reports, official documents and historical analyses respectively.

There are a number of obvious limitations of exclusively using newspaper clippings to analyse government policy towards the aircraft industry. Journalists repeatedly pointed out that the secrecy surrounding many aircraft projects made it difficult to properly assess government policy decisions.[130] Firms similarly starved journalists of details because of their supposed commercial sensitivity.[131] Nevertheless, contemporary press reporting reveals the existence of a dominant discourse which celebrated the development of new aircraft and aero-engines as a sign of technological excellence. These claims of technological leadership rested on a narrative which portrayed the industry as having played a crucial role in securing the Allied victory in the

---

126 For example, see "Private enterprise in action." *The Times*, 7 January 1954.

127 Beswick, *Plan*, 2-3.

128 On this point, see also G. D. H. Henderson, "Government and Industry," in *The British economy in the nineteen-fifties*, eds. G. D. N. Worswick and P. H. Ady (Oxford: Clarendon Press, 1962), 361-2.

129 On this point, see Edgerton, "Public ownership," 183. Regional and local developments rarely found their way in the columns of the national press. A rare exception is: Our own Reporter, "Aircraft Engineering A New Staple Industry: Housing one difficulty in development," *Manchester Guardian*, 7 September 1953. It is probably symptomatic that this article appeared in the one national paper not based in London. The impact of the aircraft industry on the economic development of the Manchester industrial district is further explored in: Till Geiger, "A false dawn? Military procurement and Manchester industrial district, 1935-1960," in *Clusters and Networks in English Industrial Districts, 1750-1970*, eds. Andrew Popp and John F. Wilson (Aldershot: Ashgate, 2003), 251-70.

130 On this point, see "Aircraft and Airpower," 598.

131 For example, the designers and test pilot of the Comet at de Havillands were highly secretive in their dealings with the press; see Peter King, *Knights of the Air: The life and times of the extraordinary pioneers who first built British aeroplanes* (London: Constable, 1989), 397-400.

Second World War. This discursive link predisposed observers to side with the industry in the immediate post-war period. As the analysis of press reporting shows, the industry used the political capital created by this aura effectively to limit the state intervention in their day-to-day operations and perpetuate this narrative through its annual Farnborough air show.

The fact that the government became the main target of press criticism, suggests that the supply departments were unsuccessful in establishing a counter-narrative to the dominant discourse that the industry had played a crucial role in saving the country from invasion and in winning the air war. Indeed, the Ministry of Aircraft Production tried to promote an alternative interpretation by publishing its own popular account of wartime aircraft production, entitled *The Aircraft Builders*, written by the author, Nigel Balchin, for a wider audience in 1947. This booklet attributed the successful wartime production effort to the symbiotic relationship between Air Ministry doctrine and British engineering tradition.

> Quality before quantity has always been a tradition of British workmanship. On a less sentimental note and more practical grounds, our engineering industry is more accustomed to high-quality production on a moderate scale than to low-quality mass production. Further, we are a comparatively small nation with limited man-power, and to send pilots into battle in anything but machines of the very highest class would be to invite heavier losses in personnel than we could afford.[132]

This official account of the wartime production effort reflected the convictions of policy-makers and shaped the discussions about aircraft procurement for civilian and military aircraft in the immediate post-war period. The Air Ministry remained committed to obtaining the best available aircraft for the Royal Air Force after 1945. At the same time, the British aircraft industry returned to its traditional production system of flexible specialisation, which many observers believed had produced the successful wartime aircraft types. However, the acrimonious public debate about aircraft procurement reflected in contemporary press reports strongly suggests that the close knit relationship between the Air Ministry and the aircraft manufacturers had broken down with the end of the war.

Arguably, this discursive frame distracted attention from the fact that the considerable achievements of British air power in the Second World War had required a disproportionate share of the country's war effort. In order to mount its independent strategic air offensive, Britain diverted resources to producing heavy bombers at the expense of re-equipping the Army with tanks and other military equipment, which as a consequence had to be obtained from the

---

[132] Ministry of Aircraft Production, *The Aircraft Builders: An Account of British Aircraft Production, 1935-1945* (London: His Majesty's Stationery Office, 1947), 7.

United States. Far from being a war-winning strategy as British air strategists had hoped, the emphasis on the strategic air offensive led to an unbalanced war production effort. Indeed, Max Hastings has suggested that a light bomber force using Mosquito bombers might have made a larger contribution to allied military victory while absorbing less resources.[133] Judging by the press reports, contemporary analysts rarely asked the question whether or not the country could support the balanced air force the Air Staff desired before the review of the rearmament programme by the Conservative government in 1952. To some extent, the severe criticism of the planned cuts in the defence budget prior to the election in February 1950 shows that the government failed to persuade the general public of the resource constraints restricting its ability to sustain its war potential policy and the pursuit of quality over quantity in the development and procurement of military aircraft. Arguably, the authoritative *Economist* survey of British airpower in September 1952 put this issue on the agenda asking awkward questions about the need to maintain a balanced air force equipped with British built military aircraft within the context of the western alliance.

Prior to 1952, press criticism of government policy claimed ministers did not support the aircraft industry adequately. In this context, the government's war potential policy became only rarely and even then only indirectly a target of the critics. On whole, the press did not realise that the war potential policy had become financially unsustainable by the end of the 1940s, because the government was spreading its development and procurement budget over too many projects and producers. As the analysis presented here shows, most observers agreed with the government about maintaining the largest possible number of aircraft design teams and achieving technological excellence in all fields of aircraft design by deliberately pushing back the technological frontiers. While the critics lambasted the government for the shortages of turbine blades in the early stages of the rearmament programme, most observers failed to associate this failure with the neglect of aircraft production and the modernisation of aircraft factories prior to the outbreak of the Korean war. On the one hand, this analysis exonerates ministers from some of the criticisms about the war potential policy advanced in the previous chapter.[134] On the other hand, the occasional press report reflected at least some awareness of the problems underlying defence procurement policy in the late 1940s. For example, one report published in December 1948 highlighted the production problems faced by the jet engine manufacturers in producing sufficient numbers of blades in order to meet the demand for British jet engines.[135]

---

[133] Hastings, *Bomber Command*, passim, particularly 346-52. See also George Raudzens, "War-Winning Weapons: The Measurement of Technological Determinism in Military History," *Journal of Military History* 54 (1990): 426-31.

[134] See chapter 4.

[135] "Production Problems in Jet Engines," *Financial Times*, 16 December 1948.

Table 5.1

British Aircraft Production as measured by sales to final buyers, 1949–60 in £ million at constant 1958 prices

Year	Government: Research and Development	Government: Procurement	Home Civil	Export	Total	Ratio of Government R&D to Procurement
1949	40	147	14	35	235	27%
1950	48	126	23	34	231	38%
1951	50	140	13	32	235	36%
1952	49	201	14	32	296	24%
1953	58	244	19	64	385	24%
1954	74	297	12	50	433	25%
1955	76	248	14	56	393	31%
1956	91	194	27	81	393	47%
1957	97	174	41	97	409	56%
1958	85	140	50	130	405	61%
1959	88	149	35	120	397*	59%
1960	79	178	30	111	405*	44%

Note: * including Assistance to Transport Aircraft

Source: Ministry of Aviation. *Report of the Committee of Inquiry into the Aircraft Industr Cmnd. 2853*. (London: Her Majesty's Stationery Office, 1965), 119, Appendix I Table 1.

According to another report, the government admitted in March 1949 that the shadow factories retained under the war potential policy would require not only massive investment in new machinery but also the training of new workers before they could resume production in a rearmament drive.[136] These isolated reports show that the problems faced by the aircraft industry during the Korean war were arguably predictable, but these discordant statements were drowned out by the dominant discourse supporting the industry in the late 1940s. The same was true for the lone voices warning that government policy was ignoring the future requirements of the military and the airlines.

As the industry started to be perceived as failing to deliver the long hyped up new generation of jet aircraft, observers became more sympathetic towards the dilemmas faced by government policy-makers. As the 1952 *Economist* survey of the industry shows, the Ministry of Supply sanctioned the

[136] Our Air Correspondent, "Concern Over Shadow Factories," *The Sunday Times*, 6 March 1949.

development and commissioned prototypes of aircraft in order to preserve a large number of design teams, but these were unlikely to be procured in large enough numbers to justify the development costs. In the early stages of the Korean war, the government often divided production contracts between several firms in order to retain their production capacity as war potential. However, this practice meant that the design firm often could not recoup their own substantial expenditure in developing the aircraft.[137]

It is less obvious from contemporary press reporting that the changes in military strategy embraced by the Defence Staff in June 1951 and announced by Churchill a year later triggered a rethinking of defence procurement policy which culminated in the 1957 Defence White paper.[138] These changes occurred rather slowly, because the war potential policy remained deeply institutionalised within the supply departments. As Table 5.1 shows, the government continued to increase the research and development budget for new aircraft, while reducing aircraft production after the end of the Korean war. In this context, it is important to remember that American military aid for the RAF helped to prop up production levels at British aircraft firms in the mid-1950s (see Table 5.2). Due to American support, many British defence contractors such as Vickers remained fully employed throughout the 1950s.[139] At first, the press was highly critical of the government decision accepting the American offer of 70 decommissioned B-29 Superfortress bombers in 1950.[140] While the press welcomed the prospect of substantial OSP orders when they were first mooted in 1952, it resented American criticism of British planes a few years later.[141] American financial support enabled the Air Staff to adhere to its plans for a balanced air force including its own independent strategic bomber force equipped with the best available aircraft. At the same time, the RAF's quality doctrine contributed to the production problems, which arose due to the constant changes in the design of fighter aircraft during the early 1950s. Using the Soviet threat, the service departments sustained their ambitious plans pleading over-riding defence needs in a political climate marked by an overarching concern with national security.[142]

---

137 "Aircraft and Airpower."

138 H. J. Yasamee and K. H. Hamil, eds., *Documents on British Policy Overseas, series 2, volume 4: Korea, June 1950 - April 1951* (London: Her Majesty's Stationery Office, 1991), 432-4.: "Defence Policy and Global Strategy - Revision of D.O.(50)45", Memorandum by the Chiefs of Staff, D.O.(51)64 (CAB 131/11), 7 June 1951.; "Aircraft and Airpower."

139 J. D. Scott, *Vickers: A History* (London: Weidenfeld and Nicolson, 1962), 358.

140 Payne, "R.A.F. May Re-equip with Superforts: U.S. Offer would be Accepted: Jet Bombers Delayed."; "Protest over Superforts."; Sinfield, "Dollarcraft and sackings in our factories."

141 "The Price of Charity," *Daily Express*, 26 August 1955.

142 For a similar observation about military technology in the United States during the cold war, see Merritt Roe Smith, "Introduction," in *Military Enterprise and Technological*

Table 5.2

Military Aircraft Production Budget and American Military Aid, 1949–60

Financial Year	Military Aircraft Procurement Budget	Air Production Budget (gross)	US Military Aid for RAF	US Military Aid as % of Aircraft Procurement
	Estimated expenditure in £ millions			
1949/50	51	83		
1950/51	55	96		
1951/52	81	151		
1952/53	111	216	30	27%
1953/54	140	266	50	36%
1954/55	156	267	45	29%
1955/56	186	292	27	14%
1956/57	165	263	38	23%
1957/58	158	247	10	6%
1958/59	130	230		
1959/60	124	239		

Source: Air Estimates, Parliamentary Papers. London: Her Majesty's Stationary Office, various years.

Similarly ambivalent was the relationship of the press with the North Atlantic alliance. At first, many observers feared that in the name of military integration the British government would have to agree to concentrate on the development and production of fighter aircraft and thereby would undermine the British aircraft industry. These concerns emanated from a sense that the American aircraft industry had benefited from the British government's agreeing to abandon building transport aircraft during the Second World War. At the same time, most observers seemed to labour under the assumption that the development of heavy bombers rather than military transport aircraft would have a direct spin-off for the development of civilian airliners. This impression was created by the conversion of wartime bomber into airliners after 1945, but reinforced by British aircraft firms such as A. V. Roe proposing to build a civilian airliner based on the Vulcan strategic bomber.[143] However, *The Economist* pointed out in its 1952 survey that if Britain specialised in mass-producing fighter aircraft and civilian airliners, it could not only reduce the

Change: Perspectives on the American Experience, ed. Merritt Roe Smith (Cambridge: MIT Press, 1985), 9-10.

[143] "Plans for Delta Wing Transport: AVRO 'Atlantic' to cruise at 600 M.P.H.," *Financial Times*, 12 June 1953.

considerable cost of maintaining a balanced air force, but also free up production capacity for building civilian aircraft for export. In this context, the writer asked whether or not Britain should maintain its own independent strategic bomber force rather than relying on the American nuclear umbrella.[144] Other voices such as the aircraft designer, William Petter, argued that the government should shift its resources from procuring the best fighter to encouraging NATO to buy larger numbers of light fighters to counter the Soviet threat in the air.[145] These critical voices began to question the Air Staff's adherence to its traditional quality doctrine emphasising maximum performance over economy in military procurement. Writing in 1957, Andrew Shonfield took this critique further by arguing that the decision to develop and procure strategic bombers had absorbed a disproportionate amount of Britain's limited resources without significantly improving its own or western military security.[146] The development of an independent strategic bomber force arguably exposed another weakness of the British system of defence procurement. Given the considerable uncertainty about aircraft technology, the supply departments placed development contracts for three bombers with different wing designs in order to ensure that one of these V-bombers would be available before the outbreak of another global war. This strategy of sponsoring several development projects is rational in a situation of high technological uncertainty, but only cost-effective if the supply department only proceeded with one winning design after a certain point in the development process.[147] In the case of the V-bombers, all three designs succeeded leaving the supply department with the awkward choice of which of the three to procure in significant numbers. However, the cancellation of any of the three projects would potentially have undermined the economic viability of the designing aircraft firm. Faced with this dilemma, the British government decided to procure all three bombers despite the increased cost and associated wasting of resources due to duplication of types.

As this concluding section underlines, contemporary discourse surrounding the aircraft industry and technology selectively emphasised certain facets as well as obscuring other important aspects of the sector's development in the immediate post-war period. The hype of its technological achievements protected the industry from any probing criticism until the early 1950s. Prior to the Korean war, policy-makers contemplated changing their industrial policy

---

[144] "Aircraft and Airpower."

[145] Petter, "The Cost of Fighter Aircraft."; "The Case for a Light Fighter."

[146] Shonfield, *British economic policy*, 96.; see also Malcolm W. Hoag, "What Interdependence for NATO?," *World Politics* 12 (1960): 370-71.

[147] On this point, see Richard R. Nelson, "Uncertainty, learning and the economics of parallel research and development efforts," *Review of Economics and Statistics* 43 (November, 1961): 351-64. I am grateful to Jonathan Zeitlin for drawing my attention to this article.

towards the sector or attempting to restructure the industry at their peril. As a consequence, aircraft development and procurement policy remained wedded to a strategy conceived during the Second World War. Under this policy, policy-makers accepted the wasting of resources and inefficiency in order to sustain the largest possible number of aircraft design teams in the immediate post-war period.[148] However, chapter 4 showed that this policy not only proved financially unsustainable, but it also prevented the modernisation of aircraft production in line with the advances in aircraft technology. At the same time, this development was not foreseeable. A major change in British defence strategy in summer 1951 prompted a policy shift from preparing for another global war to a more long-term procurement strategy in order to maintain the readiness of the British armed forces. Revelations about the poor production record of the industry during the Korean war led to a pronounced shift in public discourse in autumn 1953 with the hype about technological prowess being replaced by a mixture of feelings ranging from anxiety about potential failure to deepest gloom. This perceived radical change in fortunes continues to shape the discourse of the industry's decline when it reflects the disappointment of inflated expectations which ignored Britain's smaller resources and technological base.

---

[148] Edgerton, "Public ownership," 173.

Chapter 6

Maintaining the war potential: Rearmament and productivity in the British ammunition industry in the 1950s

In the military competition of the cold war, many western analysts perceived the West as being at a disadvantage against the command economies of the Soviet bloc. In contrast to the central planners in eastern Europe, western governments could not redirect economic resources to military purposes and investment. According to this analysis, the western democracies might be defeated in the cold war, because of their inability to match the higher proportion of national income devoted to defence and capital formation by the state socialist countries. To keep up with the Soviet bloc, western European nations would have to increase productivity to afford rearmament as well as investment to expand their economies. Such arguments became a recurring theme in contemporary studies of the future development of the international political economy in the cold war. One such study was *The Economics of Freedom*, an analysis of the progress of western European recovery sponsored by the Council of Foreign Relations.[1] As a close reading of NSC-68 reveals, this line of argument also informed American foreign policy response to the Soviet threat in the cold war.[2] In his book on the Marshall Plan, Michael Hogan notes that similar views gained importance in the months prior to the outbreak of the Korean war.[3] According to Jacqueline MacGlade, liberal Marshall Plan officials tried to defend their productivity drive in Europe against hard-liners in the United States by emphasising its vital contribution in the politico-economic struggle against the Soviet Union. To some extent, the emerging discursive construction of the political economy of the cold war presented a compromise

---

1 Howard S. Ellis, *The Economics of Freedom: The Progress and Future of Aid to Europe* (New York: Harper & Brothers, 1950), 17-41.

2 John Lewis Gaddis, *Strategies of Containment: A critical appraisal of post-war American national security policy* (New York: Oxford University Press, 1982), 104-5.; and Till Geiger, "Economic Growth and National Security: National income analysis, western rearmament, and cold war strategy, 1950-1952," *International History Review* (2004 forthcoming).

3 Michael J. Hogan, *The Marshall Plan: America, Britain, and the reconstruction of Western Europe* (Cambridge: Cambridge University Press, 1987), 340-44.

between the two camps among American policy-makers balancing the need for western rearmament and economic recovery.[4]

For the most part, the British policy-making community shared the American political economic analysis of the cold war.[5] Like their American counterparts, many British policy-makers perceived western rearmament and the productivity drive as intrinsically linked. For example, Graham Hutton argued in his summing-up of the British productivity mission reports that higher productivity levels would allow Britain to shoulder "... an even larger defence burden" as well as improve its economic position and the living standards of the population.[6] After the outbreak of the Korean war, British economic policy-makers initially assumed that continued rapid productivity growth would ease the burden of rearmament on the economy.[7] This policy statement acknowledged that renewed rearmament presented a particular challenge to the British government. Since 1945, the British economy had experienced severe labour and skill shortages particularly in the engineering industry. In the absence of unemployment, an expansion of defence production could only be achieved by diverting resources from peace to military production or through improvements in productivity. As a consequence, the Attlee government redoubled its efforts to emphasise the necessity of further productivity growth in order to meet the challenges presented by the intensification of the cold war.

The existing literature on the Anglo-American Council on Productivity (AACP) argues that the British state supported the concept of productivity missions to the United States, but was frustrated by the complacency of industry.[8] Given the monosponistic power which the government exercised over the defence sector, one might have expected the defence industry to lead the way in the adoption of modern (American) production techniques. Taking this argument further, David Edgerton suggests that military procurement contributed to modernising the economy through the state's commitment to

---

4 Jacqueline McGlade, "The US Technical Assistance Program: From revolutionary vision to productivity drive," in *Catching up with America: Productivity missions and the diffusion of American economic and technological influence after the second world war*, ed. Dominique Barjot (Paris: Presses de l'Université de Paris-Sarbonne, 2002), 67-86.

5 Donald McLachlan et al., *Defence in the Cold War: The Task for the Free World* (London: Royal Institute of International Affairs, 1950), 94.

6 Graham Hutton, *We Too Can Prosper: The promise of productivity* (London: George Allen and Unwin, 1953), 18.

7 Treasury, *Economic Survey for 1951* (London: His Majesty's Stationery Office, 1951).

8 Jim Tomlinson, "The Failure of the Anglo-American Council on Productivity," *Business History* 33 (1991): 82-92.

maintaining technological excellence in the defence sector.[9] In contrast to this controversial interpretation, most historians maintain that the high priority accorded to defence procurement distracted attention from the need for industrial restructuring of the civil economy.[10] Nevertheless, John Lovering argues that the defence industry implemented Fordist industrial relations far more readily than other industries.[11] At the same time, the two previous chapters have shown that government-industry relations influenced the overall performance of the military factories due to their dependence on defence procurement contracts.

Despite being more susceptible to government pressure, there was only one AACP sponsored productivity mission in this sector and that involved the ammunition industry.[12] In this sector, the state-owned Royal Ordnance Factories (hereafter: ROF(s)) accounted for a large proportion of the existing ammunition production capacity in Britain. The officials in charge of the ROFs saw their factories as performing an important role in demonstrating good management practice particularly in the field of labour relations. This philosophy of management regarded the Joint Production Committees as central to managing the change from war to peace production.[13] Private defence contractors also adopted Joint Production Committees in response to gentle persuasion from the government. This raises the question why the government did not succeed in convincing other defence industries to improve productivity by adopting American production technology. As previous chapters show, the supply departments had only limited leverage over defence contractors after the outbreak of the Korean war because they needed the co-operation of often reluctant potential contractors. Besides the ammunition productivity mission, British aircraft manufacturers sent an industry team to study American aircraft production. However, senior managers in the aircraft industry regarded the team's findings as irrelevant, because of the differences in the scale of production in both countries.[14] The lukewarm reception of its report suggests that the industry may have initiated its mission in order to

---

[9] David Edgerton, *England and the Aeroplane: An Essay on a Militant and Technological Nation* (Basingstoke: Macmillan, 1991), 83-5.

[10] Andrew Gamble, *Britain in Decline: Economic policy, political strategy and the British state* (Basingstoke: Macmillan, 1994), 215-16.

[11] John Lovering, "Military expenditure and the restructuring of capitalism: the military industry in Britain," *Cambridge Journal of Economics* 14 (1990): 457.

[12] Anglo-American Council on Productivity, *Final Report of the Anglo-American Council on Productivity* (London: Anglo-American Council on Productivity, 1952), 9-10.

[13] Ian Hay, *R.O.F: The Story of the Royal Ordnance Factories, 1939-1948* (London: His Majesty's Stationery Office, 1949), 94-6.

[14] House of Commons, *Tenth Report from the Select Committee on Estimates, Session 1951-52: Rearmament*, vol. 288, House of Commons Papers (London: Her Majesty's Stationery Office, 1952), 13, question 254.

forestall government pressure. This discussion highlights the conflicting interests of governments, defence contractors and the wider economy in fighting the cold war.

Before analysing these issues in greater depth in the concluding section, the following three sections will examine the origins, the organisation and the report of the Ammunition Productivity Team's visit to the United States. This analysis is followed by an examination of the productivity mission's impact on labour productivity in the British ammunition industry. The conclusions then assess the war potential policy based on the findings of this case study and in the light of the previous chapters.

The origin of the mission

Given the historical context of Korean war rearmament, it is tempting to assume that the ammunition productivity mission arose directly from the accelerated British defence effort after the outbreak of the Korean war. However, this productivity mission was set up in the summer of 1951 almost a year into the rearmament programme. Therefore, the timing of it suggests that the growing economic crisis in Britain due to the rearmament drive and the slower than expected expansion of arms production led to this late addition to the AACP list of industry teams.

As chapter 4 shows, the economic crisis arose in part because the economic planners wrongly assumed when drawing up the British expanded rearmament programme that defence production could easily be expanded for rearmament, because of considerable idle capacity throughout the defence industry. The under-employment in the defence sector arose from the deliberate government policy to maintain the nucleus of military production capability referred to as a "war potential" which could easily be expanded in a future global war. As a consequence, there existed considerable scope for productivity improvements through better utilisation of underemployed defence production capacity. At the outset of Korean war rearmament, economic and defence policy-makers attempted to allocate defence work in such a way as to minimise the impact of rearmament on the remainder of the economy and overall productivity growth. The minutes of a discussion of the likely labour problem arising from additional defence work noted that "[d]islocation of industry must be minimised if the annual increase in productivity were to remain unaffected."[15]

[15] Public Record Office, Kew (hereafter: PRO), Treasury (hereafter: T) PRO T 229/372: "Labour Problems of the Additional Defence Production Programme", minutes of a meeting in Strath's room at the Treasury, 14 August 1951.

Therefore, British economic policy-makers initially perceived little need for productivity missions in the defence sector.

In order to preserve the war potential of its plants, the Royal Ordnance Factories accepted private production contracts for civilian goods in the immediate post-war period. For example, the Royal Arsenal at Woolwich experimented in producing oil-drilling equipment. Other ROFs were engaged in producing prefabricated houses or building blocs in order to alleviate the impact of the severe timber shortage on the building industry. While ROF Chorley and Swynerton took up the manufacture of clothing, other ROFs started producing everything from electric cookers to milk bottle stoppers.[16] However, such work proved in most cases unprofitable and had to be subsidised by the taxpayer. In its reports, the House of Commons Select Committee on Estimates found that these production contracts did little to preserve the production capacity or to maintain the skills of the workforce.[17] Despite such reservations, the same group commended the war potential policy in 1952 with the benefit of hindsight by arguing "... that if the labour had not been retained the [Royal Ordnance] Factories would have found themselves in the most serious plight when large-scale production was resumed in 1950."[18] To some extent, the considerable idle capacity allowed for a rapid increase in productivity without significant additional investment and inputs. However, unsuitable factories, outmoded machinery, and an aging workforce soon limited the potential for such improvements in productivity. Many of the ROF ammunition and filling plants had been built in a rush during rearmament in the 1930s. Most of their machines dated from the early stages of the Second World War and required excessive maintenance which disrupted the production process. The majority of their skilled workers had been recruited during the Second World War. As a consequence, old age and ill health contributed to a relatively high rate of absenteeism in most munitions plants in the late 1940s. These structural problems only became apparent as the rearmament drive gathered pace in spring 1951. At the same time, growing shortages of labour, coal, steel and essential raw materials started to hamper the rapid build-up of defence production affecting ammunition production in several regions.[19] While economic policy-makers continued to argue that the rearmament

---

16 Hay, *ROF*, 69-75.

17 House of Commons, *Seventh Report from the Select Committee on Estimates, Session 1947-48: Royal Ordnance Factories*, vol. 288, House of Commons Papers 200 (London: His Majesty's Stationery Office, 1948).

18 House of Commons, *Twelfth Report from the Select Committee on Estimates, Session 1951-52: Royal Ordnance Factories*, vol. 288, House of Commons Papers 327 (London: His Majesty's Stationery Office, 1952), xi.

19 PRO WO 185/162: minutes of a meeting of the ROF Central Production Committee, 30 April 1951, 30 July 1951, 29 October 1951.

programme contributed only marginally to the overload of the economy,[20] these shortages also slowed production in civilian sectors of the economy. As a consequence, the impending economic crisis caught the supply departments and the economic policy-making community by surprise pushing the issue of productivity firmly back to the top of the policy agenda.

To summarise, the Attlee government aimed to accomplish rearmament through continued economic expansion. Given considerable idle capacity in the defence sector, economic planners did not expect armaments manufacturers to experience any productivity problems. Therefore, the government seemed primarily concerned with increasing productivity throughout the economy, rather than specifically in defence production during the initial phase of rearmament. Given the imperative of the rearmament, increased productivity in the defence industry remained a secondary issue. When increasing shortages threatened to undermine this strategy, the AACP and the supply departments became suddenly interested in improving productivity levels in the defence industry.

Organisation of the ammunition team

In contrast to other British productivity missions, the Ministry of Supply (MoS) rather than the AACP co-ordinated the selection of the members of the Ammunition industry team.[21] As Table 6.1 shows, four of the fourteen team members came from the MoS including the team leader and secretary. Of the remaining ten members, half worked in ROFs and for private defence contractors such as Ferranti, I.C.I., and two smaller firms. Therefore, the public sector representatives outnumbered members from private industry by almost 2 to 1. The MoS appointed as team leader the Chief Inspector of Armaments, Brigadier E. Merill Ransford, and as secretary the Military Assistant to Deputy Controller of Supplies (Munitions Production), Colonel W. Paget Careless (*sic*). In contrast to the other team members, both men were military officers seconded to the Ministry and represented to some extent the military end-user. The other civil servants occupied senior positions in the MoS as Assistant Director of Ammunition Production and Assistant Director of Royal Ordnance Factories. All representatives from private industry were senior technical engineers or works managers. To redress the predominance of managers and senior staff, the contingent from the ROFs included one foreman and three

[20] PRO CAB 134/333: E.S.(51)36: Report on Rearmament; note by Central Statistical Office, 22 May 1951.; see also chapter 4.

[21] British Productivity Council, *Ammunition: Report of a British Productivity Team on Ammunition which visited the United States in 1952* (London: British Productivity Council, 1953), 1.

Table 6.1

Members of the Ammunition Industry Team, January/February 1952

Brigadier E. Merrill Ranford *Team Leader*	Chief Inspector of Armaments, Ministry of Supply
Colonel W. Paget Careless *Team Secretary*	Military Assistant to Deputy Controller of Supplies (Munition Production), Ministry of Supply
James S. Ashbey	Deputy Chief Tool and Plant Engineer, Ferranti Ltd.
Reginald A. Bellamy	Assistant Production Manager (Ammunition Department), I.C.I. Ltd.
William C. Brooks	Machine Operator, ROF Woolwich
William F. Houghton	Foreman, Controlled Inspection, ROF Birtley
George Kershaw	Technical Manager, Greenwood & Batley Ltd.
Harry Latham	Works Manager (Fuze Factory), Ferranti Ltd.
Jonas H. Leese	Millwright, ROF Radway Green
Sampson Meigh	Process Worker, ROF Swynnerton
Richard A. P. Morgan	Superintendant, ROF Birtley
Frederick S. Poulton	Assistant Director of Ammunition Production, Ministry of Supply
Victor E. Smith	Senior Armament Engineer, Proctectile & Engineering Co. Ltd.
Stephen E. Van Ryssen	Assistant Director of Royal Ordnance Factories, Ministry of Supply

Source: British Productivity Council. *Ammunition: Report of a British Productivity Team on Ammunition which visited the United States in 1952*. London: British Productivity Council, 1953, x.

shop-floor workers, but also the superintendant of one factory.[22] Among the workers at least one, Sampson Meigh, was a shop steward for the Transport and General Workers' Union and head of the Joint Production Committee at ROF Swynnerton.[23] Therefore, the team divided into three broad groups: senior decision-makers from the MoS, the engineers/works managers from private industry and workers from the Royal Ordnance Factories. Due to this curious composition, certain fields of expertise predominated: public procurement of ammunition, production management and tooling, and inspection or quality control. In contrast to other productivity teams, this mission included a large

[22] British Productivity Council, *Ammunition*, x.

[23] House of Commons, *Royal Ordnance Factories (1952)*, 149.

number of civil servants reflecting the instrumental role of government in defence procurement.[24]

After the initial discussions in the summer of 1951, the AACP secretariats tried to arrange the team's visit at the earliest possible time. During the autumn of 1951, the team prepared for its mission to the United States by touring a number of munitions factories in London and north-west England. While the team's preparations proceeded to plan, the mission's visit was thrown into jeopardy by the difficulties obtaining the necessary security clearances.[25] Due to the delay, the team only received the itinerary for their visit a day before sailing to the United States. Therefore, the team had no opportunity to influence the programme of their visit and to request the inclusion of a visit to a small munitions plant. In the United States, the team toured fifteen different defence plants. On balance, the selection of government arsenals and contractor-operated factories gave a representative picture of the ammunition procurement process in the United States. During their plant visits, team members endeavoured to study all stages of the production process. However, several visits were rushed due to the tight schedule preventing a thorough investigation of the production process and technology. Moreover, the team's schedule included visits to several unfinished factories which had not yet commenced full-scale production. With the exception of the government arsenals, the team saw only large plants geared to the mass production of ammunition and fuses. In its report, the team criticised the emphasis on mass production, which failed to take into account the smaller scale of British ammunition plants and production.

At the outset, the team intended to study all aspects of American ammunition procurement. Prior to its arrival in the United States, the team decided to concentrate on increasing the output of British munitions factories in the short term. To some extent, this decision reflected the urgent need to increase output without massive investment in new production facilities. Therefore, the team hoped to find ways to improve productivity in British ammunition factories where cramped conditions prevented the introduction of American mass-production technology.[26]

---

[24] Hervé Joly noted that a similarly large contingent of civil servants participated in the French aircraft industry mission; see Hervé Joly, "Sociology of the members of the French productivity missions to the USA, 1949-1954," in *Catching up with America: Productivity missions and the diffusion of American economic and technological influence after the second world war*, ed. Dominique Barjot (Paris: Presses de l'Université de Paris-Sarbonne, 2002), 187.

[25] Security clearances were normally granted for AACP industry teams within a month of application; see Anglo-American Council on Productivity, *Final Report*, 22-4.

[26] British Productivity Council, *Ammunition*.

Contents of the report

A close reading of the mission's final report suggests that the team failed to identify any specific productivity problems in British ammunition factories. Throughout its eighty pages, the report conveys the conviction that the quality of British ammunition compared favourably with American shells, bullets and fuses. Indeed, the report is obsessed with the quality of the end product. This emphasis is not surprising given that the team leader was responsible for ensuring the quality of armaments in the MoS. The implicit claim about the high standard of British arms production amounted to a veiled criticism that American producers aimed to maximise quantity at the expense of quality and safety standards.

Besides the obligatory reference to the productivity-minded American work-force, the main recommendations of the report can be summarised under the following six headings.

1. *Production Engineering*: The team admired the careful planning of factory floor space which allowed the extensive use of conveyor belts and ensured a continuous flow of production. As a result, the degree of automation reduced the physical strain on machine operators also therefore reducing fatigue. On balance, the team found that the working environment in the American ammunition factories compared favourably with the conditions in British plants in terms of lighting, cleanliness, and constant temperature on the shop floor. However, the team expressed doubts whether the smaller scale of British production contracts could justify the initial investment needed for building ammunition factories along American lines.
2. *Production management*: Impressed by the contribution of American workshop managers, the team recommended that British foremen should be given more training and management responsibility.
3. *Procurement procedures*: Nearly a fifth of the team's report concerned the overall organisation of ammunition procurement in the United States. In its summary, the team singled out the close co-operation between the government and industry in design, development, production and inspection of ammunition. It was suggested that such an active partnership between government and industry might provide the key for improved productivity in the British munitions factories.
4. *Scientific management*: The team attributed the excellent industrial relations in American munition plants to the predominance of time-work remuneration rather than piece-rates. Therefore, the team concluded that labour disputes could be avoided through the use of time and motion studies to fix basic rates in British munition factories.

5. *Quality assurance*: While critical of American quality standards, the team argued that considerable productivity gains could be made in the inspection of small arms ammunition through introducing American water-trap equipment to test fire bullets.

6. *Local management of government arsenals*: Persuaded by the American example, the team recommended that the managers of British government factories be given a greater degree of independence in managing their factories.

While commenting favourably on some aspects of American ammunition production, the report repeatedly emphasised the different scale of American and British production contracts and existing facilities. This emphasis reflected the experience of wartime production when productivity rose significantly as production increased in both countries. Indeed, the productivity estimates published by Raymond Goldsmith immediately after the end of the war suggest that Britain slightly narrowed the productivity gap between British and American military production from 0.36 in the late 1930s to 0.41 in 1944.[27] In his seminal comparative study of productivity levels in Britain and the United States, Rostas implicitly accepts this finding by stating that the productivity of British munitions factories remained well below that of American plants. However, his study does not provide any estimate of the productivity differential.[28] A later comparative study of Anglo-American productivity levels carried out for the OEEC explicitly excluded ordnance from its comparison of productivity in the metal goods sector.[29] The team itself voiced doubts about the accuracy of such statistics by quoting an American expert as saying that "Statistics are like a Bikini bathing suit. What they reveal is suggestive, but what they conceal vital."[30] In the eyes of the Ammunition industry team,

---

27 Raymond W. Goldsmith, "The Power of Victory: Munitions Output in World War II," *Military Affairs* 10 (1946): 79, Table 3. However, it should be noted that Goldsmith's estimates are problematic, because they are based on aggregate output per person-hour figures and compare pre-war output figures in all manufacturing industries (1935-38) with those in munitions production in 1944. His comparison does not take into account the different economic conditions which prevailed in the various belligerent countries he compares. Nevertheless, these estimates provide a rough indication of the productivity gains through the mass production of weapons during the Second World War.

28 L. Rostas, *Comparative Productivity in British and American Industry* (Cambridge: Cambridge University Press, 1948), 43-5.

29 However, the authors of this study claimed that the productivity level for other metal goods production closely corresponded to that of the sector as a whole. This would suggest that output per head in the American ammunition industry was almost 3 times as high as in British factories; see Deborah Paige and Gottfried Bombach, *A Comparison of National Output and Productivity of the United Kingdom and the United States* (Paris: Organisation for European Economic Co-operation, 1959), 171-4.

30 British Productivity Council, *Ammunition*, 2.

statistics obscured the different scale of production orders permitting American producers to benefit from the economies of scale offered by mass production. At the same time, the team seemed satisfied that British ammunition production compared favourably with American producers given the smaller scale of existing plants in terms of quality and efficiency.

A follow-up study to the ammunition productivity report published in 1956 attributed the considerable improvements in working practices and production management directly to the wide-spread use of such investigations. This second report noted that as a result of these work studies the ROFs would be able to expand production more rapidly in response to a sudden upsurge in demand than in previous crises. Due to improved productivity, prices for most types of ammunition remained stable or fell despite increased labour and material costs. The follow-up study attributed the improvements in productivity to the introduction of some of the measures outlined in the original report of the productivity mission such as improved production planning, productivity-related pay for production workers, wider use of mechanical handling devices, and systematic training of all staff including the managers.[31]

The productivity drive and the British ammunition industry

The self-satisfied tenor of the report and the positive appraisal in the follow-up review suggest that the productivity problem in the British defence industry had been grossly overstated. In contrast to the ammunition productivity team, the available statistics strongly suggest that productivity improved mainly due to the increase in production following the outbreak of the Korean war, but only slightly after the end of the rearmament drive. The positive assessment by the AACP reports flew in the face of criticisms by American military aid officials and British parliamentarians who argued that the shortcomings in the defence procurement process and the management of the ROFs lowered the efficiency of British ammunition production.

Given the claims of the AACP follow-up report regarding productivity improvements, it is important to examine the available figures from the census of production closely. However, it should be noted that the existing statistics are rather limited and problematic in several respects. For example, the *Historical Record of the Census of Production, 1907 to 1970* only gives figures for four years and for the small arms and ordnance industry of which the ammunition industry would have been a sub-group. Fortunately, the four years for which figures are reported 1948, 1951, 1954 and 1958 reflect the key

---

[31] "Greater Efficiency in Arms Factories: Prices Kept Down," *The Times*, 1 October 1956.

Table 6.2

Output, employment and productivity in the British Small Arms and Ordnance industry, 1948–58

	Net Output at 1958 prices	Total employment	Net Output per person employed at 1958 prices	Wages and salaries as percentage of net output
	£ million	Thousands	£	
1948	17.0	27.4	621	82.0
1951	29.4	44.5	661	83.5
1954	64.2	72.9	880	66.9
1958	37.4	41.4	902	69.6

Source: Business Statistics Office. *Historical Record of the Census of Production, 1907 to 1970*. (London: Her Majesty's Stationery Office, 1978), 30-31, Table 1.; my calculations (see footnote 35).

turning-points of the industry's development in the immediate post-war period. As Table 6.2 shows, wage costs accounted for more than 80 per cent of the industry's net output in 1948 and 1951 suggesting that the industry's capacity remained under-employed until well into the Korean war defence programme.[32] While figures for 1954 marked the peak of the Korean war rearmament drive, figures for 1958 reflected the industry's contraction in response to the 1954 cuts in the defence budget. Therefore, these figures shed considerable light on the industry's development despite their limitations. In order to allow productivity comparisons, the output figures need to be adjusted to real prices which is itself problematic. The figures for net output and net output per employee given in Table 6.2 are calculated by deflating the actual figures with the price index for all finished goods and services on the home market used in the national accounts for this period.[33] Based on these figures, labour productivity as measured by net output per employee rose by 6.6 per cent between 1948 and 1951, and by 33.1 between 1951 and 1954, but only by 2.6 per cent between 1954 and 1958.[34] On balance, this finding strongly

[32] The Ministry of Supply Defence Production Index suggests that ammunition production rose from 100 in 1948 to 198 in financial year 1949/50, remained at that level (185) in 1950/51 and rose to 224 in the first nine months of 1951. After the third quarter of 1951, ammunition production nearly doubled bringing to 404 in the first half of financial year 1952/53 (1 April-30 September 1952); see also chapter 4, 132, Table 4.2.

[33] Central Statistical Office, *National Income and Expenditure 1968* (London: Her Majesty's Stationery Office, 1968), 20, Table 16. The advantage of using this price index is that the index is based on 1958.

[34] These calculations depend on the choice of price index used as deflator for the actual figures given in Business Statistics Office, *Historical Record of the Census of Production, 1907 to 1970* (London: Her Majesty's Stationery Office, 1978), 30-31, Table 1.

suggests that the major improvement in labour productivity occurred due to increased demand for ammunition and small arms from when rearmament gathered pace after 1951 until the defence review of 1954 led to renewed reductions in the production of these items. Contrary to the claims of the follow-up study to the ammunition productivity report, net output per employee increased at a much lower rate than in the previous two periods despite all the steps taken to improve productivity following the original AACP report. Clearly, this analysis cast considerable doubts on the veracity of claims regarding the productivity improvements reported in the British Productivity Council's follow-up study.

In his dissertation, Philip Winston cites the production figures for the sector as evidence that due to the country's relative economic decline British industry had become incapable of responding flexibly to a sudden shift in demand due to a military crisis such as the Korean war.[35] This criticism seems slightly unfair as the industry expanded its output rapidly despite severe supply constraints whilst improving its efficiency in using the additional inputs. Nevertheless, the increase in small arms and ammunition production was largely achieved through additional inputs by expanding the workforce. During the rearmament programme (1951-54), additional workers increased net output by a factor of 1.86 compared to a factor of 1.17 in the period 1948 to 1951.[36] The reduction in the workforce following the defence programme was not accompanied by a similar loss in efficiency. Net output fell only by a factor 0.92 reflecting continued slight improvements in overall productivity, but also a degree of renewed labour hoarding within the industry. In this sense, the case of the small arms and ordnance industry provides further evidence that the

---

However, the use of different price indices does not materially change the interpretation of the figures presented below. The increase in labour productivity for the period 1954 to 1958 varies from -5.3 per cent (based on price index for goods and services purchased by the public sector) to 3.9 per cent (based on price index for total final output) using the indices calculated by Charles H. Feinstein, *National Income, Expenditure and Output of the United Kingdom, 1855-1965* (Cambridge: Cambridge University Press, 1972), T132-3, Table 61. Both figures are considerably lowered than the productivity improvements in the two other periods: 3 and 4.5 per cent respectively for the period 1948 to 1951 and 27.9 and 35.2 per cent respectively for 1951 to 1954. Using the price index for explosives produced by the private sector yields a slightly higher increase in labour productivity of 6.3 percent for the period 1954 to 1958, which would amount to an annual rate of less then 1.6 per cent. Unfortunately, this index is only available for this third period; see Central Statistical Office, *Annual Abstract of Statistics*, vol. 96 (London: Her Majesty's Stationery Office, 1959), 295, Table 343.

[35] Philip Alastair Winston, "The British Government and Defence Production, 1943-50," (Ph.D., University of Cambridge, 1982), 316-17. However, Winston uses the actual figures for net output given in *Historical Record of the Census of Production* which distort the relative importance of the additional inputs.

[36] The figures in the text refer to the ratio of the change in net output to the change in employment in the industry.

Table 6.3

Capital Expenditure in the Small Arms and Ordnance Industry, 1948–58

	New Building Work	Plant and machinery		Total (acquisitions less disposals)	Capital Expenditure as percentage of net output
		Acquisitions	Disposals		
	£ million				
1948	0.1	0.5	0.1	0.6	5.3
1951	0.4	1.9	0.1	2.3	10.0
1954	0.8	4.5	1.2	4.3	7.9
1958	0.7	5.1	2.7	2.2	5.9

Source: Business Statistics Office. *Historical Record of the Census of Production, 1907 to 1970*. London: Her Majesty's Stationery Office, 1978., 140-41, Table 4 and 30-31, Table 1.

British government's war potential policy stultified capacity in the defence industry rather than preserving a modern arms industry which could adapt to renewed expansion without massive additional inputs.

At the same time, the rearmament drive led to a massive increase in investment expenditure at the outset of the defence programme in order to modernise the industry resulting in improvements in labour productivity. As Table 6.3 shows, the investment rate after 1954 returned to its pre-Korean war level in line with the contraction of demand. However, the increased building of new factories reflects the limited potential for improving existing facilities constructed during the Second World War. The ratio of new building to net investment in plant and machinery rose from 22 per cent in 1951 and 24 per cent in 1954 to 29 per cent in 1958. For example, ROF Chorley in Lancashire had been built during 1939 and 1940 on the principle of separating filling workshops from one another as provided for by 1873 Production Act in order to limit the impact of any explosion. As a consequence, the 1,000 acre site contained over 1,500 separate buildings creating major problems of moving materials and semi-finished products between workshops. Even though the ordnance factory had been built to form part of the war potential after the end of hostilities, the layout of the site now restricted the potential for modernising its facilities by introducing conveyors and other mechanical handling devices used in the new ordnance factories in the United States.[37] Similarly, its layout

[37] On ROF Chorley, see Hay, *ROF*, 56-7.

would have made an alternative use difficult.[38] Given the advances in the manufacture and handling of explosives, efficient production mattered more in the prolonged cold war context than limiting the potential impact of an explosion because of the lower risk of such an event occurring.

The critical observations which American military aid officials in western Europe made at the time lend additional weight to these statistical findings. Following the outbreak of the Korean war, the American government procured large amounts of ammunition from western European producers both for its own forces in Europe and for the armed forces of its allies in order to improve the readiness of NATO troops in the European theatre. The American government purchased these large quantities of locally produced ammunition through offshore procurement (OSP) contracts which exempted the sale of these items from taxation or export restrictions while providing much needed dollars for western European economies.[39] Accounting for the lion's share of OSP orders awarded to NATO countries, this large-scale American procurement of ammunition in western Europe exposed the extent of the productivity gap between American, British and other western European munitions factories. Few western European producers could cover their production costs at the American target price which had been fixed at 110 per cent of the American procurement cost for the same shell. Therefore, most western European governments subsidised OSP orders to reduce bid prices to the American target price. Citing the rules governing British public expenditure, the MoS refused to subsidise the ROFs' tenders for OSP contracts which disadvantaged them compared to continental producers receiving subsidies. However, American military assistance officials attributed the lower productivity level of British plants to the MoS's policy of dividing OSP contracts between a number of different plants to spread the employment effects as widely as possible. In their eyes, this practice disregarded the potential for making economic efficiency gains from mass producing a particular item.[40]

The British policy of spreading ammunitions contracts over a number of ROFs reflected the heightened concern among British policy-makers about the vulnerability of many factories to air attacks. For example, after 1945 the ROF

---

[38] Michael F. Fogarty, *Prospects of the Industrial Areas of Great Britain* (London: Methuen, 1945), 224-5.

[39] For a general discussion of American OSP policy and its impact on western European defence industries, see Till Geiger and Lorenza Sebesta, "A Self-Defeating Policy: American Offshore Procurement and Integration of Western European Defence Production, 1952-56," *Journal of European Integration History* 4 (1998): 55-73.

[40] National Archive and Record Administration, Washington, Record Group 469, Defence Production, box 2, folder Ammunition-2: memorandum for the Under Secretary of the Army and the Assistant Secretary of the Army (Material), "Report and recommendations concerning MDA-OSP Program" by van Cleve and Saltonstall, 1 June 1953.

Board shifted work increasingly away from the Royal Arsenal at Woolwich to more remote factories outside London. Nevertheless, policy-makers decided to retain the site in the immediate post-war period despite the acute shortage of work rather than relocating all munitions production away from the capital. This decision reflected concerns about the retention of a skilled workforce and the accumulated expertise at what had been the primary centre for ammunition production in the past. With the renewed expansion of munitions production under the Korean war rearmament drive, policy-makers allocated work to ROFs outside London because of growing concerns about the vulnerability of the Woolwich site thus throwing the future of the largest ROF into serious doubt. As a consequence of this policy, officials directed new machinery to other ROFs. While modernised production facility for small arms ammunition outside London worked well below capacity, the outmoded workshops at Woolwich also produced small arms ammunition in order to keep them employed. The 1952 report on the Royal Ordnance Factories by the House of Commons Select Committee on Estimates criticised this uneconomic allocation of work and suggested that all the production of .303 rifle ammunition should have been concentrated at the most modern plant.[41] Prior to a renewed global conflict, this policy deprived the armed forces of urgently needed ammunition, while deploying existing production facilities uneconomically. As the insistent questioning by the House of Commons Select Committee on Estimates in 1952 revealed the MoS largely disregarded cost control in order to maintain the war potential of the Woolwich arsenal and the other ROFs.[42]

Nevertheless, the Select Committee on Estimates report concluded that the ROFs were efficiently managed while identifying a number of problems arising from the relationship between the MoS and the ROFs. Until 1952, the ROFs had been "... operated as a part of the Ministry of Supply." As a consequence, the ROF board could not sanction any expenditure or employ staff without the prior approval of the ministry's chief accounting officer. This close institutional link restricted the ability of individual factory managers to improve productivity on the shop floor, because they lacked the budget to experiment with different production processes or offer additional incentives to their workforce.[43] In March 1952, the new Conservative Minister of Supply, Duncan Sandys announced a number of changes to the management structure of the ROFs. As part of these changes, the ROF received their own separate budget like a government department or nationalised industry. At the same

[41] House of Commons, *Royal Ordnance Factories (1952)*, xii–xv.

[42] House of Commons, *Royal Ordnance Factories (1952)*, 81-2, questions 1815-21.

[43] All ROF superintendents at this time were male. Despite accounting for a considerable proportion of the workforce, women tended to be underrepresented on joint production committees, because they tended to be classified as unskilled workers; see House of Commons, *Royal Ordnance Factories (1952)*, 136, question 2600.

time, the government established a new Board of Management to advise on future strategy for the ROFs. However, these changes did not alter the close institutional relationship with the MoS. The Controller of Supplies (Munitions) remained responsible for the ROFs. While granting more autonomy to the ROFs, the extent of central control still curtailed the managerial prerogatives of ROF superintendents who continued to exercise less decision-making power than the heads of American government arsenals. These reforms of the existing management structures significantly stopped short of reviewing the defence procurement procedures as the Ammunition Team report had suggested.

Contrary to the impression created by the original ammunition industry productivity report, the ROF ammunition factories paid workers on a time-work basis prior to the AACP mission's visit to the United States. As an unofficial history of the ROFs' contribution to the British war effort noted, time and motion studies were widely used in ROFs in order to determine the piece-rates for certain types of work in the filling factories.[44] Despite the long use of such labour management techniques, these systems gave rise to a degree of tension between management and workers. The shortage of qualified staff trained in work study caused a certain amount of grievances over the wage rates. Bonuses presented a particular problem due to the reluctance of ROF management to extend bonus payments to auxiliary staff and elected worker representatives attending committee meetings.[45] Work study and performance-related pay led to a widening gap between the earnings of production and inspection staff. In the same week as the publication of the glowing follow-up productivity review on the industry in 1956, the inspectors at ROF Maltby went on strike demanding that their wages be brought in line with those of production workers.[46] The only article on productivity published in the staff magazine *ROF News* satirised the process of work study. The anonymous piece strongly suggested that far from encouraging the workforce, attempts to improve productivity were actually counter-productive. Penned by an "ROF Checker", the article reflects the grievances of the ROF inspection staff over the fact that the earnings of production workers normally exceeded their own.[47] Despite the long-standing tensions over the pay differential, ROF managers could not persuade workers to fully accept American labour management techniques in the British ammunition industry.

To some extent, the development of the British ammunition industry during the Korean war rearmament programme revealed the shortcomings of the original AACP report. The productivity mission had focused on short-term

[44] Hay, *ROF*, 93-4.

[45] House of Commons, *Royal Ordnance Factories (1952)*.

[46] "Arms inspectors on strike over ten year old pay claim: 'Getting less than men under us'," *Manchester Guardian*, 4 October 1956.

[47] An ROF Checker, "Productivity," *ROF News*, November 1957.

improvements in labour productivity, which could be easily accomplished with additional inputs of labour and materials. As a consequence, the report underestimated the massive investment in new facilities and machinery needed in order to modernise the industry for the cold war. While the retention of a war potential allowed a fairly smooth expansion of ammunition production, the existence of under-employed capacity did not remove the need for new investment in munitions factories. However, the modernisation of the industry diverted machine tools and other scarce resources from other sectors of the economy at a time of economic crisis. As this discussion shows, the new investment resulted in only limited improvements in productivity, because of the renewed retrenchment of defence production after the end of the Korean war. The curtailment of defence procurement led again to a certain degree of labour hoarding by munitions factories. To some extent, OSP contracts for ammunition helped to maintain employment in British ammunition plants for a number of years following the defence cuts in the 1954 budget.[48] When American military aid petered out in the late 1950s, the British government eventually decided to reorganise the ROFs and closed excess capacity.[49] In this sense, the government stuck to its policy of modernising the war potential of the munitions industry until it became obvious that this policy could no longer be sustained.

Conclusion

This discussion of ammunition production highlights weaknesses in the management of defence procurement in Britain due to the contradictory nature of the war potential policy. As the government's procurement agency, the Ministry of Supply attempted to balance several conflicting policy objectives. Among these, the maintenance of the production capacity for military equipment and supplies tended to override all economic considerations. Besides this overriding objective of maintaining the war potential, officials regarded strategic considerations such as the location of munitions production as more important than efficient production. In the absence of clear pressures to contain costs, economic considerations rarely entered into the decision-making process. By ignoring the economic performance of the arms manufacturers, government policy contributed to the failure of the defence sector becoming a modernising example for British industry in general. As previous chapters have shown, the failure to resolve this conflict over the

48 Geiger and Sebesta, "Self-defeating policy," 60-61.

49 Stewart Mitchell, "A Christmas Message," *ROF News*, December 1957.

priorities of British defence procurement policy reduced the overall effectiveness of the British warfare state.

However, this assessment privileges economic efficiency but underestimates Britain's strategic and economic vulnerability. Taking into account these factors, the war potential policy addressed several potential weaknesses impairing the country's ability to mobilise for renewed global conflict.[50] The large domestic defence industry allowed the rapid expansion of production in the early stages of Korean war rearmament. The existence of a skilled workforce facilitated the transition to a cold war economy in an over-employed economy with severe labour shortages. The war potential compensated to some extent for the fact that Britain had a relatively small heavy industry and capital-goods sector compared to the other major powers except France in this period. This situation became a crucial factor during Korean war rearmament, because as the example of the ammunition industry shows a large proportion of defence factories required modernisation. During the first year of the defence programme, the Attlee government placed large orders for machine tools, which the domestic machine tool industry could not meet despite its wartime expansion thus forcing the government to purchase mainly specialised machine tools abroad.[51] This massive investment in the modernisation of defence factories marked the turning point in British defence procurement strategy to a permanent cold war economy based on a more constant and predictable acquisition of military supplies. As the case of the ammunition industry indicates, this development led to significant improvements in labour productivity despite renewed labour hoarding by the late 1950s. Over the next few years, Britain adopted a similar defence procurement strategy to that of the United States less due to the assimilation of American technology and management techniques than to the changed nature of warfare in the nuclear age. The increased reliance on firepower in the Second World War and the Korean war led to the growing awareness among British defence planners of the importance of building up ammunition stocks in order to ensure the readiness of the British armed forces for renewed armed conflict. As the Secretary of State for War, Anthony Head, acknowledged in March 1953, this "very considerable problem" of military supplies placed a considerable strain on the MoS. In this context, he stressed the need for increased economies in military procurement in general.[52]

---

[50] The following analysis builds on theoretical considerations of the war potential concept by Klaus Knorr, *The War Potential of Nations* (Princeton: Princeton University Press, 1956), passim, particularly 183-98.

[51] Knorr, *War Potential*, 192-3. This point will be developed further in chapter 9.

[52] House of Commons, *Official Report*, vol. 512, Parliamentary Debates (Hansard), Fifth Series (London: Her Majesty's Stationery Office, 1953), (hereafter: 512 H.C. Deb. 5s.), col. 865.

This change towards a more capital-intensive defence posture gave rise to much more stable long-term arrangements between the government and the domestic defence industry in most western European countries. While national governments attached greater importance to economic efficiency, the provision of military supplies remained the domain of national producers as supply departments preferred to buy from domestic producers. This preference undermined American proposals for the integration of western European defence production.[53] American policy-makers argued from the inception of NATO that by integrating defence procurement member states would benefit from the economies of scale involved in large-scale production of arms and military supplies. As western Europe's largest arms producer, British defence industry stood to gain from such proposals. Therefore, British policy-makers strongly supported efforts to integrate western European defence production during the discussion of the NATO Medium Term Defence Plan in early 1950. At a meeting of the Military Committee, the British defence minister, Emmanuel Shinwell, indicated that Britain would be willing to surrender part of its industrial sovereignty for western rearmament.[54] However, before NATO could discuss the integration of western defence production, the outbreak of the Korean war led to a massive increase in the Alliance's defence efforts taking up the spare capacity in British defence plans mainly with domestic weapons orders. As subsequent developments show, British policy-makers remained remarkably reluctant to subjugate domestic defence production to the demands for integrated procurement of weapons systems in the Alliance.[55] This reluctance is surprising, because the British politicians shared the same perspective on the need for western rearmament and accelerated productivity as their American colleagues.

Similar problems arose over the standardisation of weapons and military supplies within the Alliance. When NATO decided to adopt the .300 rifle as the standard infantry weapon, the Churchill government decided to adopt the Belgian .300 FN automatic rifle in order to promote standardisation of weapons among NATO forces.[56] Dismayed by the government's action, British politicians protested that this decision would deprive the British army of a superior British rifle with a slightly smaller calibre, which had just been developed at great expense. The government's critics again suspected

[53] Cees Wiebes and Bert Zeeman, "Eine Lehrstunde in Machtpolitik: Die Vereinigten Staaten und ihre Partner am Vorabend der NATO-Gründung," *Vierteljahrshefte für Zeitgeschichte* 40 (1992): 421.

[54] Escott Reid, *Time of Fear and Hope: The making of the North Atlantic Treaty, 1947-1949* (Toronto: McClelland and Stewart, 1977), 238.

[55] Geiger and Sebesta, "Self-defeating policy," 69-73.

[56] Parliamentary Correspondent, "Belgian rifle fired by Sir W. Churchill; Visit to range on way to Downing Street," *The Times*, 26 January 1954.

American pressure behind the Churchill government's decision to adopt.[57] Despite the suspicions of the government's detractors, the American government also adopted the Belgian rifle. Given the scale of demand for the new rifle, this meant that several countries including Britain and the United States started producing it under licence for their armed forces.[58] At the same time, this episode raises questions as to why Shinwell authorised the continued development of a .280 rifle prior to a NATO agreement on the calibre of the new standard rifle.[59] Nevertheless, the adoption of the Belgian FN automatic rifle became the "most successful example of standardisation in the Alliance."[60] This success story not withstanding national procurement policies militated against the integration of defence production within the alliance and not just against the Americanisation of western European defence factories.[61]

Despite the considerable inefficiencies in the British ammunition industry, the decision to preserve Britain's war potential proved a rational strategy in a period marked by rapid technological change and a highly uncertain strategic situation. As the military requirements for the nuclear age became more certain, British defence planners brought the military budget and the defence industrial capacity into line with reasonable mobilisation for the cold war. When strategic considerations are balanced against economic factors, it is hard to see how this learning process could have been accelerated. However, the case of the ammunition industry yet again highlights the fact that British defence planners spread resources too widely in allocating available production orders rather than concentrating work at the most efficient or reliable producer in the private or public sector. As a result, the British warfare state under-performed in the period of the first cold war.

---

[57] According to its supporters, the advantage of the British .280 mm rifle lay in its reduced weight and visible flash making it more difficult for an opponent to pinpoint the direction of fire on the battlefield; see Woodrow Wyatt, "How the Yanks scotched our rifle," *Reynolds News*, 24 January 1954. As the debate on the Army Vote in the House of Commons showed Wyatt's views were shared by the Labour front-bench which tried to use this episode for political point scoring; see for example Strachey's and Wyatt's speeches; see 512 H.C. Deb. 5s., col. 870-71 and 1020-22.

[58] George Thayer, *The War Business: The International Trade in Armaments* (London: Weidenfeld and Nicolson, 1969), 279-80.

[59] "Rival Rifles," *Manchester Guardian*, 3 February 1954.

[60] C. J. E. Harlow, *The European Armaments Base: A Survey. Part 2: National Procurement Policies* (London: Institute of Strategic Studies, 1967), 4.

[61] Geiger and Sebesta, "Self-defeating policy."

Part III

The economic impact of British defence expenditure

Chapter 7

The British defence effort and investment during the transition from war to peace, 1945–55

A major problem for economic historians analysing the impact of military expenditure on the normal working of the economy in the immediate post-war period is the fact that liberal economic theory has largely ignored the economic impact of war on economic development.[1] This theoretical deficit reflects the fact that mobilisation for modern industrial warfare can only be achieved through suspending the normal operation of the economic system. While accepting the necessity to plan the wartime economy, most British economists believed that after the end of hostilities the allocation of goods and services should again largely be left to the market mechanism. Within this general consensus, liberal economists disagreed about the extent to which the state should provide vital public services and intervene to modify market allocation to ensure greater economic justice.[2] In line with these views, liberal economic thought regards war as inimical to the common good, because it undermines international free trade and the efficient allocation of goods. Despite the devastating impact of the two world wars, liberal economists largely treated wars and post-war reconstruction as exogenous shocks.[3] To the present day, the majority of defence economists remain primarily interested in studying the economic impact of a nation's defence effort on normal economic development.[4] This emphasis reflects the general preoccupation of economic theory with finding stable economic relationships in order to forecast economic development accurately.

---

[1] On this point, see Alan S. Milward, *War, Economy and Society, 1939-1945* (Harmondsworth: Penguin, 1977), 1-2. An exception is the recent volume on the economic impact of the Second World War: Mark Harrison, ed., *The Economics of World War II: Six great powers in international comparison* (Cambridge: Cambridge University Press, 1998).

[2] For example, see the contrasting views of two economic advisers to the wartime government, Lionel Robbins and James Meade: Lionel Robbins, *The Economic Problem in Peace and War* (London: Macmillan, 1947).; and James Edward Meade, *Planning and the Price Mechanism: The liberal-socialist solution* (London: George Allen and Unwin, 1948).

[3] Walter Adolf Jöhr, *Theoretischen Grundlagen der Wirtschaftspolitik: Die Konjunkturschwankungen* (Tübingen: J.C.B. Mohr (Paul Siebeck), 1952), 51-3.

[4] On the objectives of defence economics, see Todd Sandler and Keith Hartley, *The Economics of Defense* (Cambridge: Cambridge University Press, 1995), 1-15.

The relative lack of research on the economic impact of wars also reflects the victory of Anglo-Saxon liberal economic theory over rival schools of economic thought which treat wars as an integral part of capitalist economic development. Alongside many Marxist economists, exponents of the German historical school, such as Werner Sombart, maintained that wars in early modern Europe contributed to the rise of western capitalism since the Renaissance. According to Sombart, the state played a crucial role in expanding capitalist activity through increased military demand leading to the emergence of large enterprises and engendering key technological advances in metallurgy, machinery and industrial production methods.[5] Possibly due to Sombart's support for the Nazi movement, British economic historians and economists rejected his theories of capitalist development in the 1940s as an essentially teleological explanation rather than a historical interpretation of events.[6] Writing at the height of the Second World War, John Nef argued that far from contributing to economic development, "prolonged warfare [...] was undoubtedly a serious handicap to economic prosperity in early modern times." Extrapolating from his findings on the early modern period, Nef concluded that

> the length and character of wars, and the nature of a country's participation in them, determine the extent to which they interfere with material progress, and with the growth of private initiative and large-scale enterprise. In general, the longer the war, the greater its intensity, the more it draws the people and resources of a nation away from peaceful pursuits, the more it is fought on the nation's own territory, the more disastrous the terms of peace, the greater the damage that it causes to the nation's economic well-being.[7]

Arguably, this conclusion amounts to a rather poignant and remarkably accurate assessment of the likely impact of the Second World War on the British economy. In this sense, Nef's argument reflected a different *Zeitgeist* from that underlying the Sombart thesis. Rather than treating capitalism as an unstoppable force dominating all human action, it emphasised the importance of private initiative and human agency in economic development. This interpretation effectively rejected the inherent pessimism of teleological explanations, which had contributed to the defeatism of the inter-war period and the rise of fascism. Therefore, T. S. Ashton implored fellow economists and economic historians in his inaugural lecture at the London School of

---

[5] Werner Sombart, *Krieg und Kapitalismus* (München: Duncker und Humblot, 1913), 1-15.

[6] J. M. Winter, "Introduction: The economic and social history of war," in *War and Economic Development: Essays in the memory of David Joslin*, ed. J. M. Winter (Cambridge: Cambridge University Press, 1975), 4-6.

[7] John U. Nef, "War and Economic progress, 1540-1640," *Economic History Review* 12 (1943): 37.

Economics in February 1946 to "cast out the devil of Teutonic mysticism from the house" and concentrate instead on studying how individual entrepreneurs and firms overcame adversity and thrived.[8] Given the profound impact of the Second World War on the British economy, it is understandable that Nef and Ashton perceived war as a disruptive influence potentially contributing to economic decline. The general acceptance of their views at the time arguably meant that economic historians as well as historians of technology have remained biased against the study of the inter-relationship between war, military enterprise and long-term economic and technological development.[9]

If historians have neglected the study of the inter-relationship of war and economic development, they have also ignored the potential adverse impact of the conversion process from war to peace production on long-term economic development after 1945. In their recent survey of the economic impact of the Second World War, Mark Harrison and his collaborators focus on the major belligerents on the long-term impact which wartime mobilisation had on economic development but they discount the impact of the conversion process in the immediate post-war period.[10] Despite the lack of a detailed examination of the conversion process in Britain after 1945, most analysts hold the view that the transition was remarkably smooth given the massive shift of resources involved.[11] In contrast to this general consensus in the literature, Nick Crafts has suggested that the growing literature on the current economic reform process in Central and Eastern Europe might improve our understanding of Britain's post-war transition from war to peace. His analysis suggests that the Attlee government adopted a flawed economic strategy in light of the experience of economic transition in the former state socialist countries. In contrast to current wisdom favouring radical liberalisation, British economic policy opted for the gradual removal of economic controls. Crafts contends that the delayed liberalisation reduced the potential for economic growth and improvements in productivity. As he acknowledges, the policy choices of the Attlee governments "... were, however, heavily constrained by political circumstances."[12]

---

[8] Thomas S. Ashton, "The Relation of Economic History to Economic Theory," *Economica* 13 (May, 1946): 94-6.

[9] Winter, "Introduction," 4-6.; Merritt Roe Smith, "Introduction," in *Military Enterprise and Technological Change: Perspectives on the American Experience*, ed. Merritt Roe Smith (Cambridge: MIT Press, 1985), 29-32.

[10] Harrison, ed., *Economics of World War II*, 1-2.

[11] Alec Cairncross, *Years of Recovery: British Economic Policy, 1945-51* (London: Methuen, 1985), 499-509.; Peter Southwood, *Disarming Military Industries: Turning an outbreak of peace into an enduring legacy* (Basingstoke: Macmillan, 1991), 9-14.; and Sandler and Hartley, *Economics of defense*, 285-6.

[12] N. F. R. Crafts, "Adjusting from War to Peace in 1940s Britain," *Economic and Social Review* 25 (1993): 1-20 (quote: 20).

As part of the conversion process from a war to a peace economy, British policy-makers faced crucial decisions about scaling down Britain's defence effort in line with its diminished economic and military power in the post-war world.[13] Putting forward the consensus view, Alec Cairncross accepts that Britain's defence effort may have been excessive, but maintains that "[t]he real problem for Britain was that the role she was asked to play was one beyond her strength."[14] However, other historians criticise ministers for not facing up to the fact that the country could ill afford its global military commitments.[15] But did excessive military expenditure contribute to lower investment in the immediate post-war period and subsequently to slower economic growth? At first glance, this problem resembles the question frequently asked by defence economists, as to whether or not short-term changes in defence expenditures have a long-term adverse impact on economic growth.[16] While defence economists analyse relatively small changes in the defence budget, analysts of post-war conversion are trying to assess the impact of a massive reduction. Given the totally different magnitude of change, the crucial questions are whether Britain's defence effort was scaled down enough at the end of the war and whether the continued high levels of defence expenditures adversely affected economic recovery. In particular, the question must be did the defence effort divert resources from much needed reconstruction investment in the normal productive process as opposed to war production? As previous chapters have shown, Britain's post-war defence procurement strategy probably exacerbated the excess demand in the economy thus necessitating a continuation of economic controls and thereby potentially delaying a more rapid transition to a peace economy. Therefore, an analysis of the likely effect of defence expenditures in this period has to be placed within the context of post-war recovery.

This chapter examines the relationship between the British defence effort and investment in the immediate post-war period starting with an assessment of the economic impact of the Second World War on post-war recovery and particularly investment rates. This discussion will be followed by an analysis of the implications for investment of the post-war transition from a war to a peace economy. Based on this analysis, the two following sections will examine whether Britain's relatively high defence effort crowded out investment in the immediate post-war period.

---

13 Edward Hallett Carr, *Conditions of Peace* (New York: Macmillan, 1944), 175-80.

14 Cairncross, *Years of recovery*, 508.

15 Correlli Barnett, *The Lost Victory: British dreams, British realities, 1945-1950* (Basingstoke: Macmillan, 1995), 46-102.

16 Ron Smith, "Military Expenditure and Investment in OECD Countries, 1954-1973," *Journal of Comparative Economics* 4 (1980): 20-21.

Post-war recovery and the economic legacy of the Second World War

In 1945, the British government published a report to Parliament which estimated that the country lost roughly 25 per cent (£7,300 million) of its estimated pre-war wealth (£30,000 million). Within this overall figure, British experts assumed that the internal disinvestment in non-essential industries amounted to £885 million largely due to the inability of firms to replace worn-out machinery or outmoded factories. The internal disinvestment was dwarfed by the external disinvestment in the form of selling British overseas investments in order to pay for essential imports during the war (£4,200 million) and the destruction of buildings, capital goods and shipping due to war damage (£2,200 million). In their calculations, Treasury officials discounted the considerable government-funded investment in new factories and machine tools for the war production effort.[17] In their contribution to the Harrison volume, Broadberry and Howlett show that the official 1945 report over-estimated the reduction in the nation's capital stock by almost 25 per cent or nearly 6 per cent of pre-war national wealth. However, subsequent studies showed that the economy substantially benefited from government-financed wartime investment after the end of the war. Therefore, they argue that the figure for destruction (£1,240 million at constant 1938 prices) and internal disinvestment (£612 million at constant 1938 prices) has to be reduced by the amount of government investment (£513 million at constant 1938 prices) during the war. Compared to the net losses in terms of war damage and internal disinvestment, the British losses of human capital (£144 million at 1938 prices) remained rather limited.[18] Given the limited losses of human capital, this chapter will focus primarily on the inter-relationship between the defence effort and capital formation in the immediate post-war period.

Due to the rise of Keynesian economic theory, contemporary economists devoted considerable attention to the emerging trends in capital formation and investment behaviour in the immediate post-war period. Their analyses of the economic conversion process and policy advice predominantly focused on the need to compensate for net losses in the domestic capital stock. For example, John Hicks in his inaugural lecture at the University of Oxford in 1947 argued that after prolonged starvation of new capital during the war effort, the *normal productive process* would require substantial new investment to recover fully and achieve pre-war productivity levels. During the initial period of

---

[17] Treasury, *Statistical Material Presented During the Washington Negotiations*, Cmd. 6707 (London: His Majesty's Stationery Office, 1945), 13-14. All figures in the 1945 report seem to be either at 1945 replacement costs or in current prices.

[18] Steven Broadberry and Peter Howlett, "The United Kingdom: 'Victory at all costs'," in *The Economics of World War II: Six great powers in international comparison*, ed. Mark Harrison (Cambridge: Cambridge University Press, 1998), 68-71.

reconstruction, industry would experience a shortage of capital as well as labour until the conversion to peacetime production was completed. In his analysis, Hicks refers to peace production as the normal productive process and argues in line with liberal economic thinking that after the cessation of hostilities military production should no longer be regarded as productive and contributing to the national income.[19] Taking this line of argument further, his analysis implies that continued high levels of military expenditure would divert resources from the normal productive process and reduce productive investment. As a consequence, industry may be unable to exploit existing opportunities to modernise its production facilities. In the long term, Britain's defence effort would be paid for in terms of slower economic growth and productivity gains.

As the analysis of earlier chapters has demonstrated, the continued high military demand after 1945 preserved to some extent the changes in the industrial structure brought about by the war effort. Peter Howlett has demonstrated that wartime mobilisation engendered more pronounced changes in Britain's industrial structure than the inter-war period. These changes then endured post-war conversion and recovery.[20] In their study of British economic growth, Matthews, Feinstein and Odling-Smee suggest that the forced wartime expansion of agricultural and manufacturing production brought these sectors up against diminishing returns. Despite higher total factor inputs, these sectors experienced slower growth in the total factor productivity than in the inter-war period (1924-37) or in the period of the Great Boom (1951-73).[21] An example of this effect is the British machine tool industry. Wartime mobilisation resulted in the massive expansion of production, but its peacetime production remained significantly below the wartime peak during the immediate post-war period.[22] The extreme cyclical nature of the demand for machine tools discouraged investment in the industry, particularly in research and development. As the examples of the aircraft and ammunition industries show, substantial over-capacity in defence-related industries adversely influenced productivity levels throughout the sector prior to the outbreak of the Korean war.[23] Arguably, the significant reduction in demand for particular products dampened investment activity in some industries. Moreover, political pressure for nationalisation of some industries added to the degree of economic uncertainty about the long-term prospects of many industries in the immediate

---

[19] John R. Hicks, "World Recovery After War: A theoretical analysis," *Economic Journal* 57 (1947): 151-64.

[20] Broadberry and Howlett, "Victory at all costs," 63-4.

[21] R. C. O. Matthews, Charles H. Feinstein, and J. C. Odling-Smee, *British Economic Growth, 1856-1973* (Oxford: Oxford University Press, 1982), 235 and 228-9, Table 8.3.

[22] R. C. Tress, "The Armed Economy," *London and Cambridge Economic Service* 29 (1951): 4. See also the detailed discussion in chapter 9.

[23] See chapters 4, 5 and 6.

post-war period. The potential impact of this heightened economic uncertainty about economic demand and property rights is difficult to quantify, but it may have had a substantial negative impact on post-war investment rates.[24] For this reason, this sceptical interpretation emerging from recent economic historical writing is highly critical of contemporary economic policy advice for a phased lifting of economic controls at the end of the war in order to minimise the economic disturbances arising from the conversion process.[25] Indeed, earlier studies of the transition process from war to peace economy stressed that the policy commitment of governments to maintain economic demand contributed to a relatively smooth transition after 1945 in contrast to conversion after the end of the First World War.[26]

A key concern of contemporary economists was the potential psychological impact on business confidence and investment behaviour of a sudden collapse of demand as a consequence of immediate decontrol of the economy at the end of the war production effort. This line of thought partly emanated from Keynesian economic analysis and the experience of the inter-war economic crisis. As Keynes pointed out in *General Theory of Employment, Interest and Money*, economic actors discount extraneous events like wars in normal economic calculation.[27] However, exogenous shocks like war or transition periods induce major and largely unpredictable changes in the nature of economic relationships particularly if they are accompanied with changes in the economic system.[28] During such periods of dislocation, economic agents find it difficult to predict future economic development due to the constantly changing economic signals and relationships. Lacking reliable information from historical precedents, it seems reasonable to assume that economic agents privilege their perceptions of current economic conditions. For example, a severe economic depression will plunge economic agents into deep pessimism about the likelihood of economic recovery. In this case, perceptions are shaped by the rapid fall of demand, rising unemployment, and downward pressure on prices and profits. Therefore, state intervention might restore business confidence and thereby induce an economic up-turn.[29] At the end of economic

---

24 On this point, see Broadberry and Howlett, "Victory at all costs," 63-4.; and Jöhr, *Konjunkturschwankungen*, 188.

25 Martin Chick, *Industrial Policy in Britain, 1945-51: economic planning, nationalisation and the Labour governments* (Cambridge: Cambridge University Press, 1998), 1-2. As an example of such policy advice, see Richard H. Tawney, "The Abolition of Economic Controls, 1918-1921," *Economic History Review* 8 (1943): 1-30.

26 Sandler and Hartley, *Economics of defense*, 285-6.

27 John Maynard Keynes, *The General Theory of Employment, Interest and Money*, ed. Royal Economic Society (London: Macmillan, 1974), 143.

28 Jöhr, *Konjunkturschwankungen*, 187-9.

29 Keynes, *General Theory*, 315-16.; see also G. L. S. Shackle, *The Years of High Theory: Invention and Tradition in Economic Thought, 1926-1939*, 1983 ed. (Cambridge: Cambridge University Press, 1967), 129-34.

mobilisation for the Second World War, economic agents in Britain expected a lifting of state control of all economic activity accompanied by a general improvement in economic conditions. However, many policy-makers feared that an uncontrolled liberalisation of the economy would lead to increased uncertainty about future economic growth and political instability.[30] While the conversion process freed resources engaged in war production, other factors potentially threatened to undermine a smooth economic transition to a peace economy. After the suspension of American Lend-Lease aid, the emerging balance of payment constraint forced British policy-makers to adopt measures to increase exports in order to pay for essential imports. However, these measures prevented the early reduction of the considerable excess demand in the British economy. As a result, economic policy-makers faced considerable discontent among the population expecting rapid improvements in their living standards after the deprivations of the war effort. The economic situation was further complicated by the uncertainty about the future structure of the international economy and the settlement of the country's considerable international debt. In the light of these problems, economic policy-makers remained reluctant to dismantle existing economic controls fearing that liberalisation would lead to a repeat of the scramble for resources after the end of the First World War.[31]

This preference for a gradual economic transition from a war to a peace economy reflected a widespread belief that market allocation of goods in short supply would inevitably lead to social inequities and potentially to political instability. However, if the state allocates goods in short supply on the basis of the changed pattern of industrial use in wartime, such an allocation may hinder the recovery of industries producing primarily peace goods and not involved in war production. As previous chapters show, British defence procurement policy maintained a significant degree of over-capacity in defence-related industries thereby contributing to the high level of excess demand. Being able to retain workers and to secure scarce materials, defence contractors arguably benefited from the continued economic controls. Therefore, the key question is whether economic controls curbed post-war investment and hindered post-war economic development.

British post-war conversion and investment

This analysis has highlighted post-war conversion as the crucial nexus between wartime and post-war economic development by suggesting that the process

---

30 This policy is outlined in Ministry of Reconstruction, *Employment Policy*, Cmd. 8195 (London: His Majesty's Stationery Office, 1944), 6-10.

31 Chick, *Industrial Policy*, 1-15.

did not go far enough or was not accomplished fast enough and therefore preserved the detrimental wartime changes in the British industrial structure. In order to examine this process, this section examines the changes in British investment behaviour in the immediate post-war period.

Given the scale of wartime mobilisation, a return to peacetime production was inevitably accompanied by considerable displacement of resources. In the short term, new and returning workers had to be re-acclimatised to the production process. Machine tools required refitting for normal production. As a consequence, one would expect labour productivity to drop in the initial phase of conversion. Depending on the general economic outlook, firms will seek to replace the machinery worn out or damaged during the war in the medium term. This large investment demand will then compete with the pent-up consumer demand in the initial post-war period. Due to lower productivity, the high levels of demand for consumer as well as capital goods will add to the inflationary pressure or excess demand in the economy. In the absence of economic controls, economic theory suggests that most firms will try to capitalise on this surge in demand by increasing prices. In turn, rising prices will lead to increased wage demands by trade unions. Such demand-pull inflation would occur despite potentially substantial un(der)employment due to the transition to normal peace production. Therefore, excess demand will inevitably occur during the transition from war to peace economy, even if industrial capacity has grown during the war.[32] Despite the considerable disinvestment reported by Broadberry and Howlett, contemporary estimates of the United Nations Economic Commission for Europe show that the number of machine tools in British factories increased substantially during the Second World War.[33] However, these machine tools had been installed in munitions factories throughout the whole of Britain. Immediately after the war, some of these factories stood idle as no buyers could be found for the new factories or their machine tools.[34] In this sense, the damaged capital stock did not initially represent a major bottleneck impeding a speedy transition to peace production, but limited investment might prejudice sustained recovery and ultimately economic growth.

Since economists expected an increasing supply of consumer goods to mop up the excess demand in the medium term, they argued that investment projects

---

32 Hicks, "World recovery," 153-6.; Joan Robinson, *The Generalisation of the General Theory and other Essays*, 2nd ed. (Basingstoke: Macmillan, 1979), 12.

33 United Nations. Economic Commission for Europe. Research and Planning Division, *Economic Survey of Europe since the War: A Reappraisal of Problems and Prospects* (Geneva: United Nations. Department of Economic Affairs, 1953), 2-3, Table 2.

34 Indicative of such conversion problems is the fate of the munitions factory on the Tullos Estate in Aberdeen; see Till Geiger, "Opposition in the Shadows of an Emerging Conflict: The Aberdeen Trades Council, government policy and voicing dissent in the cold war, 1945-1955," *Northern Scotland* 13 (1993): 107-8.

increasing consumer goods production should be given priority. Indeed, Hicks noted that "[a] policy which concentrates on long-period investment thus tends to prolong the strain in what may be a very dangerous way." However, investment with a long gestation period might well yield higher productivity growth. Demand management would have to strike the difficult balance between containing excess demand and encouraging continued recovery. For example, higher interest rates would favour investments with quick returns and consumer goods production more generally. At the same time, higher interest rates may damage business confidence and lead to lower investment. In order to avoid this trap, the government could adopt direct controls and fiscal measures to contain the excess demand. In the final analysis, monetary policy might have a role in reducing excess demand. Therefore, economic policy-makers should not rule out raising interest rates.[35] Taking into account expectations, Joan Robinson argued that "... a rise in the interest rate which is expected to be reversed is a greater deterrent to investment than one which is regarded as permanent."[36] In the immediate post-war period, the British government's cheap money policy led to the expectation of an imminent increase in interest rates. As the interest rate had fallen below the full employment level, the constant expectation of an interest rate rise discouraged some investment. Higher interest rates would have made saving an attractive alternative to spending during a period of excess demand. Moreover, higher rates would have encouraged investment with high short-term returns. However, the Attlee government's cheap money policy under Dalton reflected the need to finance nationalisation rather than a deliberate Keynesian policy of lowering interest rates to encourage long-term investment and help maintain full employment.[37] Indeed, many British economic policy-makers believed that the issue of higher interest rates lacked efficacy as an economic policy tool given continued shortages of vital materials and labour.[38]

Most British economic policy-makers regarded reducing the excess demand as the most pressing problem in the transition from war to peace economy.[39] While there was limited room for changes to be made in public spending from year to year, the government could reduce overall demand by cutting defence expenditures radically. In deciding the appropriate level of defence expenditures, the government's former chief economic adviser, James Meade, pointed out that "due regard must be paid to the fact that in the immediate future there is a prospective strain on total resources for other purposes."

---

[35] Hicks, "World recovery," 156-64 (quote:158).

[36] Robinson, *Generalisation*, 54-5 (quote: 55).

[37] Susan Howson, *British Monetary Policy, 1945-51* (Oxford: Clarendon Press, 1993), passim.

[38] Chick, *Industrial Policy*, 4-6.

[39] Neil Rollings, "British budgetary policy, 1945-54: a Keynesian revolution?," *Economic History Review* 41 (1988): 283-98.

However, he suggested that by adjusting public investment plans economic policy-makers could most effectively curb overall demand in the economy.[40] Another eminent economist, Roy Harrod, similarly argued that the excess demand in the economy arose directly from excessive public sector investment crowding out private investment plans.[41] The liberalisation of investment in 1946 added to the excess demand within the economy forcing the government to curb overall demand through tightening of its fiscal policy. By holding back private consumption, the government continued to allocate a large proportion of the annual increase in national output towards increasing investment. Many economists albeit reluctantly agreed with the government's policy of regulating overall investment given the severe supply constraints in the economy.[42] Against this background, it would be wrong to interpret the initial economic policy choices as reflecting a deliberate decision to finance a continued global military presence at the expense of productive investment. This interpretation rejects the criticism of a number of historians who argue with the benefit of hindsight that the Attlee governments pursued the wrong priorities in its economic policy in the initial post-war period. For example, Correlli Barnett suggests that the combined burden of the defence effort and the post-war social investment in improved welfare provision and housing undermined the country's long-term economic development. In this view, these politically motivated choices about investment priorities reflected a general complacency among British politicians about the true financial and economic state of the country. While Barnett argues that British management remained similarly complacent about its competitiveness, he nevertheless maintains that Britain's relative economic decline could have been averted if the government and business had devoted more resources to productive investment.[43] This line of argument presupposes the existence of a trade-off between on the one hand defence and/or social welfare expenditure and on the other productive investment. However, the analysis presented here shows that policy-makers are rarely faced by a clear choice between certain expenditure and therefore the existence of such choices was more illusory than real.[44] For example, the political crisis over the 1951 budget arose from a decision involving relatively small amounts in terms of the defence and social welfare budgets.[45] As this

40 Meade, *Planning*, 21-2.

41 Roy Harrod, *Are these Hardships Necessary?* (London: Rupert Hart-Davis, 1947), 28-43.

42 Jim Tomlinson, "Marshall Aid and the 'Shortage Economy' in Britain in the 1940s," *Contemporary European History* 9 (2000): 149-51.

43 Barnett, *Lost victory*, passim, particularly chapter 13.

44 On this point, see William K. Domke, Richard C. Eichenberg, and Catherine M. Kelleher, "The Illusion of Choice: Defense and Welfare in Advanced Democracies, 1948-1978," *American Political Science Review* 77 (1983): 19-35.

45 See chapter 3.

analysis shows, economic policy-makers in the late 1940s saw allocation decisions on investment, defence and social expenditure primarily in the context of post-war transition from a war to a peace economy rather than choosing to spend the country's resources on defence and social investment at the expense of productive investment.

Did the defence effort crowd out productive investment?

While it is difficult to sustain the notion that ministers deliberately chose to maintain the country's global military presence at the expense of productive investment, the defence effort may have crowded out investment. For example, Martin Chick highlights the fact that Britain's level of gross domestic capital formation as well as net investment remained well below that of other Western European countries in the immediate post-war period. While Chick agrees that economic policy-makers attempted to free resources for productive investment, he nevertheless criticises the government's allocation of resources for gross domestic capital formation. He argues that the government devoted excessive resources to the housing programme and to other social investments given its election promises. At the same time, ministers deemed it impossible to cut private consumption further given the already austere rations and imprudent to leave the Soviet threat around the world unopposed. Chick emphasises the problems faced by post-war chancellors in pushing through further cuts in defence expenditure, which meant Britain spent more on defence as a proportion of GNP than other western countries in the immediate post-war period. In this sense, the Korean war defence programme added to existing demand pressures thereby further reducing the available resources for productive investment. However, Chick notes that in 1951 gross domestic capital formation in British manufacturing industry exceeded that in West German industry. Nevertheless, he maintains that despite the support of economic policy-makers within government, productive investment suffered in this process of industrial policy-making as it lacked strong political representation at ministerial level.[46] In contrast to Barnett's suggestion of a trade-off between public consumption and productive investment, Chick argues that deficiencies in economic planning led to a slow completion of many projects reducing the efficacy of investment throughout the economy. For example, the government's housing programme continued to be plagued by shortages of skilled labour and materials. In turn, these shortages not only held up completion of other building projects, for example in industry, but also directly contributed to the high levels of excess demand in the economy. As

---

46 Chick, *Industrial Policy*, 1-40.

previous chapters of this book show, the continued high levels of excess demand in the economy contributed to the low rate of overall investment and slow economic growth in this period. In this sense, this analysis suggests a vicious economic cycle whereby the investment programme contributed to excess demand necessitating government intervention to contain inflationary pressures leading to further cuts in investment.

A closer look at the figures for social investment, however, also supports a radically different interpretation. For example, Sidney Pollard argues that the share of social investment of total gross domestic capital formation rose from 10.7 per cent in 1937/38 to 15.3 per cent in 1947-48 and 14.8 per cent in 1950-51.[47] This increase hardly seems significant if one keeps in mind that the share of GDP nearly doubled compared with pre-war years. While Chick suggests that social investment absorbed a larger proportion of gross domestic capital formation than Pollard claims, he acknowledges that post-war productive investment significantly exceeded its pre-war level in absolute terms.[48] Such evidence nevertheless supports Alan Milward's claim that social investment created a more stable environment for private investment and thus "crowded in" investment.[49] If one accepts this line of argument, the higher levels of defence and public expenditures stabilised demand preventing a repetition of the boom and bust experience, which followed the First World War. Contemporary Marxist economists maintained that capitalist economies relied on military expenditure to maintain demand and to appropriate a larger share of the surplus value of production for the ruling elites. In this sense, the arms race served the interest of capitalists as military expenditure became an independent source of demand controlled by capitalists and financed by taxation of the working class.[50] This analysis resembles Rosa Luxemburg's analysis of the pre-First World War arms race, which suggested that the arms build-up had been financed out of indirect taxation.[51] However, direct taxation assumed far greater importance by the end of the Second World War with a top rate of income tax reaching up to 97.5 per cent and arguably reducing the incentive to invest.[52] In this sense, the state taxed capital rather than labour to fund this pre-

---

47 Sidney Pollard, *The Development of the British Economy, 1914-1967*, 2nd ed. (London: Edward Arnold, 1969), 407.

48 Chick, *Industrial Policy*, 19-23.

49 Alan S. Milward, *The Reconstruction of Western Europe, 1945-51* (London: Methuen, 1984), 484.

50 John Eaton, *Economics of Peace and War: An analysis of Britain's Economic Problems* (London: Lawrence & Wishart, 1952), 34-45.

51 Rosa Luxemburg, *Die Akkumulation des Kapitals: Ein Beitrag zur ökonomischen Erklärung des Imperialismus* (originally published in 1923), (Frankfurt am Main: Verlag Neue Kritik, 1970), 367-80.

52 Crafts, "Adjusting from war to peace," 8-10.

condition of capitalist production in the immediate post-war period.[53] While high income taxes may have deterred some investors, higher defence expenditure after 1945 might have nevertheless crowded in investment through the stabilisation of total demand.[54]

The first of these two rival interpretations that military expenditure crowded out investment, rests on the assumption that the division of national expenditure between investment, defence expenditures, and non-military public and private consumption remains fairly stable over time. Taking this argument further, some economists and political scientists argue that consumers regard public expenditure for social and public services as part of their private income. Therefore, voters resist any reduction in public services.[55] During the lifetime of the post-war Labour governments, ministers found it next to impossible to curtail social welfare reforms in order to increase defence expenditure given the expectations of the electorate for comprehensive welfare reforms and improvement of housing conditions.[56] This line of argument implies that an increase in the defence outlay will mean a cut in overall investment. If as some contemporary economic growth models suggest the investment rate partly determines the economic growth rate then an excessive defence effort may lead to a sub-optimal investment rate for long-term economic development. In this case, the initial choice concerning the division of national expenditures between defence expenditures and investment largely determined the rate of economic growth.

In contrast to the proposition of crowding out, the thesis of the crowding-in effect suggests that military expenditure led to an increasing propensity to invest in the economy. Proponents of this thesis argue that continued expansion counteracted fears that the initial restocking boom after the end of the war would be followed by a slump as in the inter-war period. In this sense, the cold war arms race contributed to economic expansion and thereby created conditions favourable to long-term economic growth. However, expansionary forces merely added to the (excess) demand in the economy which was already fully employed and lacked substantial reserves of unemployed resources. In these circumstances, rearmament may well lead to hyper-inflation unless the expansionary forces are checked by deflationary measures.[57]

---

[53] The suggestion that the defence effort (except in time of war) should be treated as a precondition of production rather than a final output is shared by some liberal economists; see Simon Kuznets, "National Income: A New Version," *Review of Economics and Statistics* 30 (1948): 156.

[54] Milward, *Reconstruction*, 490.

[55] Smith, "Military Expenditure," 21.

[56] Steve Fielding, "What did 'The People' want? The meaning of the 1945 General Election," *Historical Journal* 35 (1992): 623-39. See also chapter 3.

[57] Robinson, *Generalisation*, 69-70.

Table 7.1

Military Expenditure and Investment as a Share of GDP, 1948–57

	Defence Expenditure as percentage of GDP	Gross Domestic Capital Formation as percentage of GDP	Percentage Share of Investment and Defence Expenditure
1948	7.3	14.3	21.6
1949	7.2	14.7	21.9
1950	7.5	15.3	22.8
1951	9.2	15.2	24.4
1952	11.2	15.4	26.6
1953	11.0	16.2	27.2
1954	10.3	16.5	26.8
1955	9.4	17.1	26.5
1956	9.3	17.4	26.7
1957	8.4	17.8	26.2

Source: Defence expenditure including current expenditure plus defence-related gross domestic capital formation (trading and non-trading) excluding sale of surplus war stocks and strategic stocks (at current prices); gross domestic capital formation: Central Statistical Office, *National Income and Expenditure 1958* (London: Her Majesty's Stationery Office, 1958), Tables 1, 44 and 45.

Based on the first proposition, one would expect that the overall proportion available for either investment or military expenditure was somewhere in the region of 26.5 per cent of output based on the figures for the early 1950s. However, a closer look at Table 7.1 reveals that in the late 1940s the proportion spent on defence or invested fell far short of this level. Indeed, investment and defence expenditure exceeded 26 per cent of GDP for the first time in 1952 thus supporting the "crowding in" proposition. Therefore, defence expenditures contributed to higher investment levels prior to the outbreak of the Korean war. However, the share of total output invested stagnated for the only time in the period 1950-52 remaining at roughly 15.3 (1950) per cent, 15.2 (1951) and 15.4 (1952). At the same time, military expenditure rose from 7.5 per cent in 1950 to 9.2 per cent in 1951 and 11.2 per cent in 1952. This would suggest a break in the previously existing favourable upward trend in investment accompanied by a slightly increasing defence effort. At least, in the immediate post-war period, the crowding in effect seemed to predominate. The Korean war defence programme ended this virtuous cycle interrupting the constant increase in the proportion of GDP invested. After the Korean war rearmament drive, yet another effect emerged. While the proportion of GDP invested rose, the share spent on defence fell rapidly leading to the paradoxical situation whereby the overall proportion of GDP spent on investment and the defence effort declined slightly by the mid-1950s. In a sense, this observed trend could best be described as the "crowding-out effect in reverse". The relationship between military expenditure and investment seems have characterised three different trends in the immediate post-war period: first a crowding-in effect, then a Korean war or displacement effect, followed by a reversed crowding-out effect. Therefore, the empirical evidence reveals a rather more complex relationship between investment and military expenditure than suggested by the economic studies reviewed above.[58] Moreover, this analysis provides further support for the proposition that high defence expenditure does not necessarily reduce the propensity to invest.

Proponents of the crowding-out effect might challenge this interpretation by suggesting that the observed crowding-in effect arose from the relaxation of the restrictive economic policy relating to investment in the late 1940s. This line of argument implies that state intervention prevented a higher productive investment rate, which would have led to faster economic growth. Therefore, the low investment rate resulted from the government's attempts to keep demand in line with available supply through fiscal policy measures.[59] In order to curb total expenditure, the government restricted productive investment. Indeed, on several occasions private productive investment was cut to allow for continued social, particularly housing, investment.[60] This notion linking slow economic growth to low rates of productive investment had become widely accepted in public discourse about British economic development by the mid-1950s.[61] Some observers linked the low productive investment to the relatively high defence expenditure.[62] These explanations treat the growth of the net capital stock as the decisive factor for economic growth. However, the aggregate investment ratio is nothing but an imperfect proxy for the contribution of business investment to growth, since it can be influenced by factors such as relative price differences between countries, the composition of output, the availability of raw materials, the type of capital good installed, the ownership of industry, and the infrastructure of an economy.[63] Indeed, the incremental

---

58 The existence of these rather different effects is also born out by the empirical results of simple regression models for a slightly longer period; see Till Geiger, "Studies in the political economy and economic impact of British defence expenditure and American military aid to Britain, 1945-1955," (Ph. D. Dissertation, University of Aberdeen, 1998), 133-42.

59 Rollings, "British budgetary policy," 283-98.

60 Cairncross, *Years of recovery*, 446-62.

61 Terence W. Hutchison, *Economics and Economic Policy in Britain, 1946-1966: Some aspects of their inter-relations* (London: George Allen and Unwin, 1968), 125-30.

62 Andrew Shonfield, *British Economic Policy since the War* (Harmondsworth: Penguin, 1958), 35-6.; Public Record Office, Treasury [hereafter PRO T] 234/248: "Comparison of Defence Outlays in Western Europe", note by Mr. Scammell, attached to a note from Spicer - Vinter., 1 July 1957.

63 Andrea Boltho, "Growth," in *European Economy: Growth and Crisis*, ed. Andrea Boltho (Oxford: Oxford University Press, 1982), 33.

capital-output ratios reported for the European manufacturing industries suggest that investment in Britain proved less effective than for example in West Germany throughout the 1950s and 1960s. A comparative Organisation for Economic Co-operation and Development study undertaken in the early 1960s showed that British entrepreneurs tended to be more risk averse than their continental counterparts suggesting that British investment was for the most part defensive.[64] The reports of the Anglo-American Productivity Council voiced similar criticisms in the early 1950s. American observers particularly criticised the attitude prevalent among British participants that British practice is best suited to British conditions. British managers, however, continued to believe that the differences in the general level of productivity between the United States and Britain were explained by the high investment ratio in the United States in the inter-war years even though the capital-output ratio had fallen in the United States since the 1920s.[65] Among British manufacturers, the widespread feeling was that the highly skilled British labour force would give the manufacturing industry a competitive advantage over other countries in producing specialised quality equipment made in small quantities to meet the customers' special demands in the world market. The imperative to increase exports and to keep down investment meant that industrialists and government officials became primarily interested in short-term improvements in productivity rather than in addressing the deficits in British management practices exposed by the reports of the Anglo-American Council on Productivity.[66]

The question remains whether higher investment in the immediate post-war period would have induced faster economic growth. In their authoritative study of British economic growth, Matthews, Feinstein and Odling-Smee suggest that productive investment yielded higher returns in the immediate post-war period supporting the claims for a crowding-in effect. However, the authors are reluctant to conclude that higher rates of productive investment would lead automatically to higher levels of economic growth.[67] Nevertheless, newer endogenous growth models conclude that the Attlee government's policy regarding productive investment contributed to slower economic growth.[68] As

---

[64] Bruce R. Williams, *International Report on Factors in Investment Behaviour* (Paris: Organisation for Economic Co-operation and Development, 1962), v.12-13 and x.11-12.

[65] Jim Tomlinson, "The Failure of the Anglo-American Council on Productivity," *Business History* 33 (1991): 85-8.

[66] Tomlinson, "Failure," 89-91.; Jonathan Zeitlin, "Americanizing British Engineering?: Strategic debate, selective adaptation and hybrid innovation in post-war reconstruction, 1945-1960," in *Americanization and its Limits: Reworking US technology and management in post-war Europe and Japan*, eds. Jonathan Zeitlin and Gary Herrigel (Oxford: Oxford University Press, 2000), 145-7.

[67] Matthews, Feinstein, and Odling-Smee, *British economic growth*, 393.

[68] Crafts, "Adjusting from war to peace," 10-16.

this analysis shows, there is little consensus among economists and historians on this point. If one accepts a crowding-in effect for the immediate post-war period, lower defence expenditure might not have resulted in higher investment. While it may be impossible to resolve this debate definitively, these issues can be explored further with the help of some counterfactual experiments.

Counterfactual economic growth without the defence burden

Since many analysts attribute Britain's relatively poor economic growth record to its low investment rate, it is important to examine this question as part of international comparison. Most available comparable international series of national income statistics start in 1950 in order to exclude any distortions caused by the transition from war to peace in the late 1940s. Indeed, many western European countries experienced extremely high economic growth as their economies returned to pre-war output levels.[69] However, this analysis has shown that the late 1940s and the Korean war period are very important in the British context. Therefore, the following counterfactual experiments are based on the constant price gross national product (GNP) estimates published by the Organisation for European Economic Co-operation in 1957, because they include figures for the late 1940s.[70] These statistics are not unproblematic, but they allow limited comparisons. Since their national output never fell below their pre-war levels, the inclusion of Britain, the United States and Sweden in this comparison is fairly straightforward. The same is true for the Netherlands and Belgium, which recovered sufficiently by 1947 and 1948 respectively. Since the West German economy only reached its pre-war output level in 1951, it has been excluded from the following analysis. France and Italy attained their pre-war GNP levels in 1949 and 1950 respectively.[71] While both countries have been included in the following counterfactuals, their high growth rates in the late 1940s distort to some extent their incremental capital-output ratios.[72]

[69] Nicholas Crafts and Gianni Toniolo, "Postwar Growth: an overview," in *Economic growth in Europe since 1945*, eds. Nicholas Crafts and Gianni Toniolo (Cambridge: Cambridge University Press, 1996), 3 and Table 1.2.

[70] All figures are estimates at constant 1954 prices and 1954 exchange rates. Organisation for European Economic Co-operation, *Statistics of National Product and Expenditure, 1938 and 1947 to 1955* (Paris: Organisation for European Economic Co-operation, 1957), 103 and part 3, 175-204.

[71] Crafts and Toniolo, "Postwar growth," Table 1.2.

[72] The incremental capital-output ratio has been calculated by dividing the average growth rate by the GDP percentage share of gross domestic capital formation at constant prices as suggested by Williams, *Investment behaviour*, iii.1-4.

Table 7.2

Counterfactual Economic Performance, 1948-50

	Incremental Capital-Output Ratio	Average Investment-Income Ratio	Counterfactual Investment-Income Ratio	Average Annual Growth Rate	Average Annual Counterfactual Growth Rate
United Kingdom	4.14	14.1	21.5	3.3	5.1
United States	3.80	16.8	21.5	5.7	7.9
Sweden	5.79	19.6	24.0	3.4	4.1
Netherlands	5.31	22.4	27.4	4.2	5.1
Belgium	4.12	15.9	19.0	3.8	4.6
France	2.40	20.6	26.8	8.5	11.6
Italy	2.65	19.6	24.5	7.4	9.3

Source: My calculations are based on the estimates in Organisation for European Economic Co-operation, *Statistics of National Product and Expenditure, 1938 and 1947 to 1955*, (Paris: Organisation for European Economic Co-operation, 1957), 103, 186, 188-9 and 198.

Nevertheless, both countries should be included, because they were the largest western European NATO member states after Britain.

In the context of this discussion, the obvious counterfactual question is what would Britain's economic growth rate have been if every penny spent on the defence effort in the late 1940s had been invested instead. As Table 7.2 suggests, the British economy would have grown at over 5 per cent per annum in the period 1948-50 assuming that the incremental capital-output ratio remained unchanged. The extent to which a country's economic performance would improve depends on the size of its defence effort and its incremental capital–output ratio: the larger its defence effort and the lower its incremental capital–output ratio are, the larger the improvement in its growth rate. Given its relatively large defence effort compared with other countries, Britain's gross domestic capital formation would have increased by over 50 per cent. The effect of the increase in investment is illustrated by a comparison with Belgium, which has a similar incremental capital-output ratio to Britain but devoted a much smaller share of GNP to defence. At the same time, Britain would not have gained as much as some other countries from the additional investment because of its relatively high incremental capital-output ratio. For example, with the same counterfactual gross domestic capital formation rate the United States achieved a substantially higher economic growth rate. While the Netherlands just matched Britain's counterfactual economic growth rate,

Table 7.3

Actual and counterfactual GNP per capita, 1950 and 1955
GDP per capita in US $ at 1954 prices and exchange rates

	1950	1955 actual	1955 counter-factual I	1955 counter-factual II
United Kingdom	801	907	1,058	1,015
United States	1,930	2,163	2,784	2,689
Sweden	949	1,064	1,147	1,297
Netherlands	518	619	639	739
Belgium	853	967	1,074	1,187
France	771	917	1,091	1,015
Italy	292	384	462	444

Source: My calculations are based on the estimates in Organisation for European Economic Co-Operation, *Statistics of National Product and Expenditure, 1938 and 1947 to 1955*, (Paris: Organisation for European Economic Co-Operation, 1957), 18, 103, 186, 188-9 and 198.

Sweden would have achieved a lower growth rate than Britain despite both having much higher counterfactual investment-income ratios. Despite devoting a smaller proportion of GNP to defence, the French and Italian counterfactual economic growth rates would have increased more in absolute terms than the British rate, because of their low incremental capital-output ratios.

The other interesting question is to assess the hypothetical impact on living standards of the western countries, if the resources mobilised for Korean war rearmament had instead been invested in the economy. The counterfactual reported in Table 7.3 assumes that the resources spent on defence in the period 1950-55 would have been invested in addition to normal investment and that the national incremental capital-output ratios would have remained at their late 1940s level.[73] In order to illustrate the magnitude of the likely change, two different counterfactual living standards have been calculated. Counterfactual I is based on gross domestic capital formation (GDCF) plus defence expenditure. In counterfactual II, GDCF is replaced with non-residential GDCF in order to focus on productive investment and the per capita output figure is calculated on the basis of the incremental capital-output ratio for non-residential GDCF in 1949 and 1950. Table 7.3 shows that British living standards would have increased massively if the resources devoted to fighting the cold war had been invested instead. However, the improvement would not have been sufficient to

[73] In the period 1950-55, the incremental capital-output ratios rose for all countries except the Netherlands where the ratios fell considerably suggesting that rearmament contributed to improving the productivity of investment.

affect Britain's standing in terms of output per head relative to the other countries in this comparison. While the European countries slightly narrowed the productivity gap between themselves and the United States in the first half of the 1950s, both counterfactuals suggest that the gap would have widened significantly in the same period, if the United States had invested its massive defence effort in its economy. Another interesting feature of Table 7.3 is that the counterfactual GNP per capita figures calculated on the basis of non-residential GDCF reflect a steep increase in house construction in most countries except in the Netherlands and Belgium where the increase was less marked.

On balance, these experiments show that under the extreme assumptions of these counterfactuals, Britain would have benefited substantially from the higher investment, but that its standing in the GNP per capita league table would have remained unchanged relative to the other western European countries, but deteriorated relative to the United States. If Britain had continued to invest the same proportion of GNP as in 1950, its GNP per capita would have risen to $947 in 1955 assuming that its incremental capital-output ratio had remained unchanged. If one assumes that GDCF had risen at the same rate as between 1948 and 1949, Britain's GNP per capita would have risen to $949 in 1955. The minor increase in GNP per capita of about $40 over the actual figures suggests that slower economic growth was largely due to the rise of the incremental capital-output ratio rather than due to the displacement effect noted in the investment rate due to the Korean war. This finding suggests that the observation by Matthew, Feinstein and Odling-Smee about the higher returns of investment in the immediate post-war period may be nearer to the truth than the claims of the declinist literature about the effect of rearmament on the investment rate.

Concluding observations

This examination of the impact of the post-war defence effort on the investment rate is necessarily inconclusive. On the one hand, this analysis found that defence expenditure seems to have stabilised overall economic demand and investment engendered in the immediate post-war period. On the other hand, some economic historians such as Sidney Pollard have claimed that restrictive government policy in the late 1940s and during Korean war rearmament reduced productive investment thus setting Britain on a lower growth path. As a consequence, he argues that

> Once set on a lower growth path, it proved harder to accelerate [the growth rate] than in countries where recovery from a very low point had forced a high rate of investment and a basic flexibility straight away.[74]

However, the observed crowding-in effect for the immediate post-war period arguably undermines this interpretation. Paradoxically, the combined share of output set aside for the defence effort and investment increased substantially due to the massive increase of defence expenditure during the Korean war. By the mid-1950s, the proportion of GNP devoted to defence expenditure and GDCF reached a plateau of just over 26 per cent. The fact that the share remained fairly unchanged after the Korean war suggests that most British consumers accepted that the cold war confrontation between the East and the West required a permanent increase in economic mobilisation (i.e. increased defence expenditure and investment) and adjusted their consumption plans accordingly. If this was indeed the case, then economic growth theory would suggest that the increased economic mobilisation for the cold war should not have adversely affected Britain's long-term economic development.[75]

In line with the literature on this topic, the analysis of this chapter finds that defence expenditure contributed to economic stability, but it suggests negative long-term effects of high defence expenditure.[76] However, it calls into question the claims that high defence expenditure crowded out investment in the immediate post-war period. This finding confirms the analysis of previous chapters highlighting the fact that the defence effort contributed to excess demand in the economy in the immediate post-war period and after the outbreak of the Korean war. This observation suggests that high defence expenditure influenced economic development indirectly by adding to overall demand rather than directly by crowding out investment in this period. This alternative explanation would suggest that the excess demand caused by Korean war rearmament rather than excessive defence expenditure per se disrupted the emergence of a rapidly growing peace economy in Britain in the early 1950s. This thesis will be examined in more detail in the next two chapters.

---

[74] Sidney Pollard, "Economic Policies and Traditions," in *Government and economies in the postwar World: Economic policies and comparative performance, 1945-85*, eds. Andrew Graham and Anthony Seldon (London: Routledge, 1990), 296-7 (quote:297).; see also Sidney Pollard, *Wasting of the British Economy: British economic policy, 1945 to the Present*, 2nd ed. (London: Croom Helm, 1984), 31-43.

[75] David Romer, *Advanced Macroeconomics*, 2nd ed. (Boston: McGraw-Hill, 2001), 68-74.

[76] Roger Middleton, *Government versus the Market: Growth of the public sector, economic management and British economic performance* (Cheltenham: Edward Elgar, 1996), 614-17.

Chapter 8

Britain and the economic impact of the Korean war

In the mid-1950s, British policy-makers became more growth-conscious as comparative economic growth-rates suggested that British productivity levels continued to trail those in the United States. While some British politicians and economists started to call for a doubling of national income within a generation, other economists and observers started to analyse why Britain was lagging behind other countries.[1] An early contribution to this debate, Andrew Shonfield's 1958 book *British Economic Policy since the War*, linked Britain's low investment rate to its excessive defence effort. In his analysis of this relationship, Shonfield singled out Korean war rearmament as the crucial period in which government policy on investment undermined the country's long-term economic prospects. While siding with the government's critics over the scale of rearmament, he bemoaned the fact that the political dispute between Hugh Gaitskell and Aneurin Bevan over the rearmament programme distracted from the Labour government's assault on productive investment through the economic policies introduced in Gaitskell's 1951 budget.[2] With respect to Britain's defence effort, Shonfield criticised successive British governments for preferring to procure military hardware domestically rather than taking up the offers of American military aid. If they had asked for more American military aid in the form of end-items, British policy-makers could have reduced the economic burden imposed by the Korean war defence programme. Instead, the British government wasted valuable resources on developing three strategic bombers. For their part, American policy-makers supported the British defence industry, because it could serve as a convenient arsenal close to the potential European battlefield. Therefore, Shonfield suggested that this relationship amounted to "... a happy marriage between British national pride and American military convenience."[3] While Shonfield also highlighted other detrimental effects of the British defence effort such as

---

[1] On this point, see Terence W. Hutchison, *Economics and Economic Policy in Britain, 1946-1966: Some aspects of their inter-relations* (London: George Allen and Unwin, 1968), 125-30.; and Jim Tomlinson, "Inventing 'decline': the falling behind of the British economy in the postwar years," *Economic History Review* 49 (1996): 753-4.

[2] See chapter 3.

[3] Andrew Shonfield, *British Economic Policy since the War* (Harmondsworth: Penguin, 1958), 89-97 (quote: 95).

Table 8.1

Gross Fixed Investment by Type of Asset, 1949–54
£ million at 1953 market prices

	1949	1950	1951	1952	1953	1954
Vehicles, ships and aircraft	353	338	300	267	323	359
Plant and machinery	730	796	840	801	833	853
New housing	410	397	401	489	619	631
Other new building and works	502	559	529	524	549	606
Total	1,995	2,090	2,070	2,081	2,324	2,449

Source: Treasury, *Economic Survey 1955* (London: Her Majesty's Stationery Office, 1955), 23, Table 12.

the impact of overseas bases on the balance of payments, this chapter will concentrate on his analysis of the economic impact of the Korean war rearmament programme on postwar British economic development.

Shonfield mainly attributed the downturn in investment in the early 1950s to the government's economic policies adopted in the pursuit of an excessive defence effort, but particularly to the cut in initial allowances in the 1951 budget. As Table 7.1 shows, the share of GDP devoted to gross domestic capital formation stagnated thus breaking the steady upward trend of the postwar period.[4] In his analysis, Shonfield conflates two issues: first, whether this period of stagnating investment remained a temporary dislocation or had long-term effects in terms of a lower economic growth rate; and second, whether government policies contributed to the stagnating investment rate.

A detailed examination of gross domestic capital formation reveals several interesting trends (see Table 8.1). Investment in vehicles, ships and aircraft fell significantly in the first three years of the rearmament programme (1950-52) and did not recover fully to its 1949 level until 1954. Initially, the investment in plant and machinery absorbed some of the fall in the overall investment. Indeed, investment accelerated, but fell considerably in 1952 and recovered only slowly to its 1950 level in 1954. From the beginning of the Korean war rearmament, the shift to armaments production hit investment in new works even more severely. Construction of new housing remained remarkably stable and unaffected by the expansion of armaments production. Even in current price terms, investment in the manufacturing industry stagnated in 1952 and 1953. As the Economic Survey for 1955 acknowledged, aggregate figures obscured the shifts in investment. At the height of the Korean war defence

4 See chapter 7, 229, Table 7.1.

programme, government-financed investment accounted for a significant share of total investment.[5] Unfortunately, no precise disaggregated figures were compiled by the government's statisticians.[6] In 1954, private investment again increased significantly thus compensating for the fall in government-financed expansion in line with the reduction of defence production.[7]

Undoubtedly, the defence programme influenced the direction of investment in the early 1950s. However, the question remains whether the redirection of investment had lasting effects for British economic development. Given the lack of sufficient disaggregated data, economic policy-makers (and historians since) had to conjecture about the economic impact of defence expenditures on investment. In the first few months of the Korean war, the government's economic adviser argued that the existing slack in the defence industry should absorb the planned increased armaments production. Therefore, economic advice downplayed the possibility that rearmament would severely disrupt economic development.[8] In contrast to the Attlee government's contemporaneous analysis, Cairncross has suggested that the defence programme meant a massive reorientation of production in a narrow sector of industry. Therefore, the massive increase in defence production "was bound to have severe repercussions on exports and fixed investments".[9] This explanation implies that the short-term massive increase in defence expenditure had long-term implications which acutely affected the resources available and the output of a few key sectors such as the engineering, electronics and aircraft industries. However, many firms in these key sectors were working near capacity level with notable exceptions such as the machine tool industry. Therefore, the additional demand for weapons and military supplies added to the existing excess demand for the output from these key sectors. As defence contractors competed with other producers for basic materials (e.g. steel, coal, metals) and skilled labour, the rapid expansion of military procurement affected the production costs particularly in engineering industries. On the one hand, the

---

5 Treasury, *Economic Survey 1955* (London: Her Majesty's Stationery Office, 1955), 23-4, Table 13.

6 The only statistics published relate to the impact of defence expenditure on production in the metal-using industry; see Treasury, *Economic Survey for 1952*, Cmd. 8509 (London: Her Majesty's Stationery Office, 1952), 20, Table 7.; Alec Cairncross, *Years of Recovery: British Economic Policy, 1945-51* (London: Methuen, 1985), 222-4, Table 8.2.; and chapter 4, 131, Table 4.1. On the lack of sufficiently disaggregated data on an industry level and the limitations of investment data, see also A. Ghosh, *Experiments with Input-Output Models: An application to the economy of the United Kingdom, 1948-55* (Cambridge: Cambridge University Press, 1964), 98.

7 Treasury, *Economic Survey 1954* (London: Her Majesty's Stationery Office, 1954), 22-3, Table 13.; Treasury, *Economic Survey 1955*, 23-4, Table 13.

8 For the fairly optimistic assessment of the economic advisers, see Treasury, *Economic Survey for 1951* (London: His Majesty's Stationery Office, 1951), 5-9.

9 Cairncross, *Years of recovery*, 222-4 (quote: 222).

expansion of defence production increased the demand for machine tools and other capital goods. On the other hand, price increases and hold-ups in production due to the disruption in basic supplies led to delays in deliveries of machinery, postponement or abandonment of investment projects and the cancellation of export orders.[10]

If rearmament induced a massive shift in economic activity and demand, then a combination of factors, rather than just certain government policies, caused the temporary or long-term reduction in the investment rate. The economic policy response by the Attlee government rested on the implicit assumption that the initial impact of rearmament was small due to the considerable underemployment in the defence sector and auxiliary industries such as the machine tool industry. However, earlier chapters showed that material and labour shortages seriously affected the rearmament programme in its first twelve months. Bottlenecks in the economy prevented a smooth transition from peace to a cold war economy. In this context, investment in new defence production capacity created large-scale excess demand for machine tools. This redirection of investment to the defence sector led to a dislocation of the economic accumulation process thereby potentially shifting the British economy onto a lower growth path. Given the dislocation due to increased defence expenditure and the uncertainty about the future, industrialists invested less in other areas of manufacturing industry. Therefore, the cut of the initial allowance is unlikely to have caused the lower investment rate of the British economy.

This cursory critique of Shonfield's analysis supports a more sceptical view such as that offered by Joan Mitchell's book on the economic crisis of 1951 which questions the widely-held belief that the Labour government's economic policies contributed to the severity of the economic downturn. In contrast to Shonfield, Mitchell stressed that the government's assessment of the economic impact of rearmament rested on rather optimistic working assumptions about raw materials and the growth of output, but accepted that the government officials and adviser could not have foreseen the rapid deterioration in the raw material situation in the first half of 1951. The world-wide scramble for raw materials following the outbreak of the Korean war led to significant price increases raising the cost of British imports. Difficulties in obtaining vital raw materials furthermore contributed to the reversal in Britain's balance of payments. At the same time, shortages of skilled labour slowed the conversion to defence production further adding to the inflationary pressure in the economy. Given their rather optimistic assumptions, economic policy-makers

---

[10] Treasury, *Economic Survey for 1952*, 31-3.; Treasury, *Economic Survey for 1953*, Cmd. 8800 (London: Her Majesty's Stationery Office, 1953), 33-4.; Treasury, *Economic Survey 1954*, 49-51.

arguably failed to take early action to reduce the excess demand.[11] While the standard economic policy advice would be to reduce consumer expenditure and investment in order to balance overall demand, the rearmament boom arguably unbalanced the economy by expanding the output in a narrow segment of the economy. Therefore, measures to reduce peace demand may not have restored the economy to its optimal non-inflationary growth path in line with the labour supply and technical progress.[12] At the same time, a discussion about the appropriateness of Gaitskell's economic policies has to take account of the various domestic and international political pressures which constrained government action in the first fifteen months of the rearmament programme. After all, the Bevanite critics of Gaitskell's budget argued primarily against American foreign policy and its impact on the Labour project. This wider criticism informed their worries that the shortages of raw material impaired the rearmament programme and therefore should be scaled down.[13] In retrospect, their claim that the rearmament programme would over-stretch Britain's economic resources seemed to be confirmed by the onset of the economic crisis in summer 1951. However, most economic analysts revised this view by arguing that this episode proved to be a temporary balance of payments crisis due to adverse international circumstances beyond the government's control.[14]

The first three sections of this chapter will re-examine the impact of raw material price increases on the balance of payments and the impact of labour shortages on the wider economy before reviewing the government's economic policy approach. After examining these crucial aspects of the economic crisis in summer 1951, the next sections will address Shonfield's claim that the Labour government contributed to Britain's economic blight by not taking up the generous offers of American military aid. In the light of the findings of the previous sections, the conclusions will assess the overall impact of Korean war rearmament on the investment rate.

---

[11] Joan Mitchell, *Crisis in Britain 1951* (London: Secker & Warburg, 1963). For the government's economic assessment, see Treasury, *Economic Survey for 1951*.

[12] Ota Šik, *Der dritte Weg: Die Marxistisch-leninistische Theorie und die moderne Industriegesellschaft* (Hamburg: Hoffmann und Campe, 1972), 300-301.

[13] See chapter 3.

[14] J. C. R. Dow, *The Management of the British Economy, 1945-60* (Cambridge: Cambridge University Press, 1964), 64-5.; and Mitchell, *Crisis in Britain*, 144-5. In his analysis of economists' advice on government economic policy in the first twenty years after the war, Terence Hutchinson documented the extent to which economists critical of the government revised their views during and after the economic crisis of 1951; see Hutchison, *Economics and Economic Policy*, 75-82.

Raw materials and the balance of payments

In April 1951, the economy started to deteriorate thus calling into question the rather optimistic assumptions underlying the budget regarding economic growth and the balance of payments. While production failed to expand as quickly as the government predicted, Korean war rearmament contributed to a larger than anticipated demand for goods and services. Across the board, raw material shortages started to affect industrial production. Due to a rapid deterioration in Britain's terms of trade, the British current account deficit doubled in the first quarter of 1951. A larger than expected increase in world raw material prices added to the economic cost of replenishing the stocks of British industry.[15] Several factors contributed to Britain's balance of payments deficit threatening to spiral out of control after April 1951. Three months earlier in December 1950, the Labour government acceded to an American request to terminate Marshall aid to Britain a year early, because of the growing balance of payments surplus of the Sterling Area in the second half of 1950. Therefore, the country no longer received American financial assistance to cover a potential balance of payments deficit throughout 1951. At the same time, it became obvious that the balance of payments surplus of 1950 partly resulted from significant speculative inflows of capital due to rumours of impending revaluation of sterling. A reversal in these payments and capital flows contributed to the growing balance of payments deficit in the first months of 1951. Moreover, the government's delayed decision to build up a strategic stockpile of raw materials further inflated the country's import bill contributing to the current account deficit (see Table 8.2).[16]

From the beginning of the Korean war, the supply of raw materials was a matter of concern to British economic policy-makers.[17] While the economic advisers recommended building up strategic stocks of vital raw materials,

---

[15] P. D. Henderson, D. G. Holland, and Dudley Seers, "The Crisis of 1951," *Bulletin of the Institute of Statistics Oxford* 13 (1951): 305-38.; W. M. Scammell, "Rearmament: The First Year," *Westminister Bank Review* (1951): 1-8.; and Guiseppe Mayer, "Le Conseguenze Economiche e Finanziarie dovute al Programma di Riarmo del Regno Unito," (unpublished manuscript, 1952). On the balance of payments, see also the remarks of John Jewkes and Roy Harrod at a conference organised by the University of Chicago Law School for American policy-makers in White Sulphur Springs (West Virginia) in April 1951; see Roy Harrod and John Jewkes, "The Impact of rearmament on the British economy," in *Defense, Controls, and Inflation*, ed. Aaron Director (Chicago: Chicago University Press, 1952), 254-84.

[16] Leo Pliatzky, *Getting and Spending: Public expenditure, employment and inflation* (Oxford: Basil Blackwell, 1982), 13-14.

[17] For example, see Gaitskell's speeches during the defence debates in September 1950 and February 1951; see House of Commons, *Official Report*, vol. 478, Parliamentary Debates (Hansard), Fifth Series (London: His Majesty's Stationery Office, 1950), (hereafter: 478 H.C. Deb. 5s.) col. 1139-40 and 484 H.C. Deb. 5s. col. 653-7 respectively.

Table 8.2

Investment in Strategic Stockpiles and Sale of Surplus War Stocks, 1948–57

all figures in £ million at current prices

	Sale of Surplus War Stocks	Strategic Stockpiling
1948	-60	-
1949	-32	-
1950	-27	-
1951	-23	127
1952	-7	49
1953	-	42
1954	-	44
1955	-	3
1956	-	-19
1957	-	-39

Source: Central Statistical Office, National Income and Expenditure 1958 (London: Her Majesty's Stationery Office, 1958), 42, Table 45.

ministers dissuaded British industry from panic purchases.[18] When he announced the £3,600 million defence programme, Attlee asked industrial buyers "... not to increase their stocks beyond their actual needs", because otherwise the government might be forced to re-introduce (import) controls.[19] Following government advice, British producers delayed their purchases of raw materials in the early stages of the Korean war. In the meantime, government ministers sought to persuade the American government to give Britain preferential access to raw materials and other vital equipment needed for its rearmament programme in an attempt to bypass international co-ordination through NATO and OEEC.[20] After this attempt failed, British industrialists and government were forced to purchase raw materials at inflated prices in the first half of 1951.[21] When Bevan and Wilson in their resignation statements blamed the United States for this failure, the *Manchester Evening News* asked the awkward question whether or not the British government unduly restrained the

[18] Diary entry, 11 July 1950, reprinted in: Alec Cairncross, ed., *The Robert Hall Diaries, 1947-53* (London: Unwin Hyman, 1989), 122-3.

[19] 478 H.C. Deb. 5s. col. 966.

[20] Diary entry, 12 September 1950, reprinted in: Cairncross, ed., *Robert Hall diaries*, 127.

[21] Till Geiger and Duncan M. Ross, "Banks, institutional constraints and the limits of central banking: Monetary policy in Britain and West Germany, 1950-52," *Business History* 33 (1991): 143-5 and 148-9.

import of raw materials in the autumn of 1950. However, the editorial writers continued that

> ... of course, Mr. Wilson may feel that a shortsighted policy of conserving dollars has caused the running down of our raw material stocks. If this is the case, however, he should have said so.[22]

If British industrialists had defied the government and increased their raw material imports, the balance of payments would have worsened rapidly in the autumn of 1950. As a consequence, Britain would have remained eligible for American economic aid. However, the Attlee government continued to adhere to its original economic strategy during the first year of the rearmament drive and desisted from tightening import controls despite the rapid deterioration in the balance of payments.[23] In order to examine whether a different raw material policy would have been more advantageous in the economic circumstances, the following counterfactual analysis will compare the actual trade balance with two hypothetical scenarios. Scenario 1 assumes that import and export prices would have remained at the same level as in the 2nd quarter of 1950 (upper line in Graph 8.1). In contrast, the second counterfactual scenario assumes that despite the price changes exports, and imports would have continued to grow in line with the trend in the first half of 1950 (lower line in Graph 8.1).

In scenario 1 (no price increases), Britain's trade deficit would have been much smaller showing the extent to which this deterioration was due to the change in the terms of trade. However, if imports and exports had continued to increase as in scenario 2, the balance of foreign trade would have deteriorated significantly already in autumn 1950. Taking into account invisible earnings, net capital inflows and changes in the sterling balances, Britain's current account balance during the first year of rearmament (July 1950-June 1951) would have shown a deficit of £380 million rather than the surplus of £552 million.[24] The initial improvement in Britain's actual balance of trade visible in Graph 8.1 reflects the fact that the government retained effective control over

---

22 "Why not June?," *Manchester Evening News*, 25 April 1951.

23 Economists disagreed about the advisability of the government's strategy of riding out the crisis. While William Corden thinks that import controls proved rather ineffective in 1952, Ian Little, however, is critical of the government's strategy; see W. M. Corden, "The Control of Imports: A Case Study," *Manchester School of Economic and Social Studies* 26 (1958): 181-221.; I. M. D. Little, "Fiscal Policy," in *The British economy in the nineteen-fifties*, eds. G. D. N. Worswick and P. H. Ady (Oxford: Clarendon Press, 1962), 258-9.

24 My calculation is based on Till Geiger, "Studies in the political economy and economic impact of British defence expenditure and American military aid to Britain, 1945-1955," (Ph. D. Dissertation, University of Aberdeen, 1998), 270, Table A9:3. and M. F. G. Scott, "The Balance of Payments Crises," in *The British Economy in the Nineteen-Fifties*, eds. G. D. N. Worswick and P. H. Ady (Oxford: Clarendon Press, 1962), 205-30.

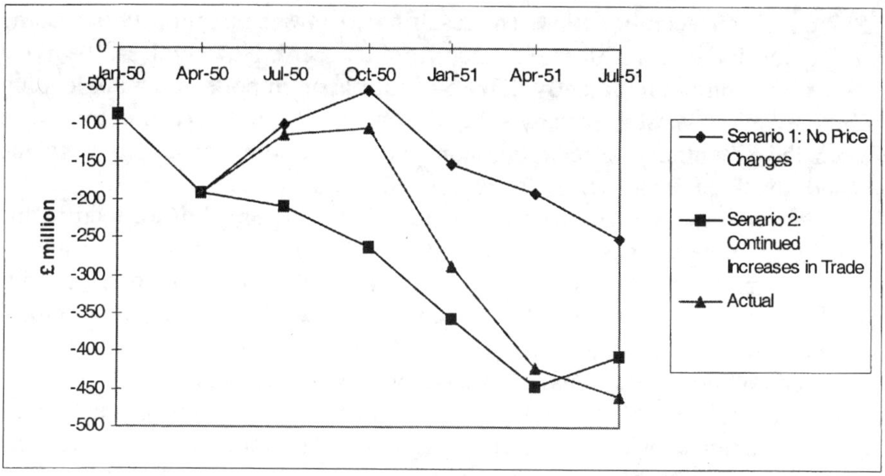

Graph 8.1: Actual and Counterfactual Trade Balance, 1950–51

Source: My calculations based on actual volume and price indices from United Nations. Economic Commission for Europe. Research and Planning Division, *Economic Survey of Europe in 1951* (Geneva: United Nations. Department of Economic Affairs, 1952), 193-4, Tables xxi and xxii.

imports even without resorting to its further administrative measures.[25] On the one hand, government purchases still accounted for roughly half of all British imports. On the other, British industrialists refrained from increasing their imports in order to avoid state intervention. Indeed, many industrialists assumed that rationing would ensure lower prices while guaranteeing an equitable distribution and entered informal industry-controlled distribution agreements.[26]

As this analysis shows, the changes in the terms of trade and payments largely explain the deterioration in the British balance of payments in the first half of 1951. However, the government policy inadvertently exacerbated the adverse changes in the international economy. This raises the question whether an alternative import policy would have allowed Britain to avert an economic crisis. A cursory comparison with other western European countries suggests that a more liberal import policy would inevitably lead to a balance of payments crisis several months earlier. For example, the West German government took no steps to curtail the panic purchases of imports in autumn 1950, which resulted in the country exhausting its European Payments Union

[25] Dow, *Management of the British economy*, 153-8.

[26] University of Warwick, Modern Record Centre (hereafter MRC), CBI Predecessor Archives MSS 200/F/3/T3/31/9, Minutes of Meeting of Panel B of the Defence Programme Committee, 24 October 1950, 27 October 1950.; Minutes of Meeting of Panel B of the Defence Programme Committee, 31 October 1950, 6 November 1950.

(EPU) quota in December 1950. The resulting crisis was temporarily overcome by the extension of a $120 million loan from the EPU. Nevertheless, the West German government reluctantly imposed controls on imports and bank lending in March 1951. West Germany's rapid recovery from this economic crisis created the potentially false impression that its economy benefited from the demand shock of increased defence expenditure in other countries.[27] As the West German case shows, increased defence expenditure did not lead to the raw material price increases. Only co-ordinated action by western governments might have prevented the scramble for raw materials and the associated price rises.[28] In this sense, the Attlee government's search for an international agreement on the allocation of raw materials can hardly be described as misguided. While international co-ordination might have been the best solution to this economic problem, the British preference for an arrangement under Anglo-American control undermined the potential support of other western European governments for such an agreement. Moreover, British policy-makers over-estimated the interest of the American government in such an arrangement and therefore persisted with this policy even when an international accord had become unlikely. In the absence of an international agreement, the second best solution would have been to stockpile raw materials at an earlier stage. However, it is important to remember that while the increased raw material prices led to the collapse of consumer demand for textiles and other consumer goods, raw material shortages and the increased prices hardly affected the rearmament programme in the first twelve months.[29]

Labour shortages and rearmament

Aside from the deterioration in Britain's international position, rigidities in the economic structure and labour mobility impeded the rapid progress of the defence programme. In the first twelve months, the supply departments were still primarily engaged in acquiring machine tools for the expansion of defence production and placing procurement orders. By the end of January 1951, the supply departments had placed production orders worth £450 million out of £750 million authorised by the Treasury. In August, orders for nearly £1,000 million had been placed amounting to half of the planned production

[27] On this point, see the different interpretations of Peter Temin, "The 'Koreaboom' in West Germany: fact or fiction," *Economic History Review* 48 (1995): 737-53.; and Werner Abelshauser, *Wirtschaftsgeschichte der Bundesrepublik Deutschland, 1945-1980* (Frankfurt am Main: Suhrkamp, 1983), 67-8.

[28] Organisation for European Economic Co-operation, *Financial Stability and the Fight against Inflation* (Paris: Organisation for European Economic Co-operation, 1951), 16-17.

[29] Treasury, *Economic Survey for 1952*, 19-21.

expenditure of £2,000 for the whole three-year programme. During the second half of 1951, the supply departments increased the proportion of placed orders to roughly 65 per cent of the planned production expenditure. These figures support the conclusion of the Central Statistical Office that "the impact of rearmament upon the civilian economy [was] not yet very marked" in May 1951.[30] In the second quarter of 1951, industrial production was 6 per cent higher than in the previous year. Only a third of this increase could be attributed to increased defence production, except in the metal-using industry. At the time, economic policy-makers seemed unaware of the extent to which the conflicting economic demands of rearmament and private consumption caused an over-heating of the economy. Due to the regional concentration of the British engineering industry, the massive defence orders started to lead to severe labour shortages for skilled workers particularly in the Midlands.[31] However, the economic impact of raw material or labour/skill shortages is notoriously difficult to measure and forecast.[32] Nevertheless, the British economy experienced over-full employment in the immediate postwar period.[33] Throughout this period, the number of unfilled vacancies often outnumbered the number of registered unemployed. To measure this excess demand for labour, the economists J. C. R. Dow and L. A. Dicks-Mireaux developed an index which relates unemployment and unfilled vacancies to actual employment (see Equation 8.1).

In their original study, Dow and Dicks-Mireaux compared the excess demand for labour between various industries. Due to the special characteristics applying to each industrial sector, Dow and Dicks-Mireaux argued that the indices for each industry are not strictly comparable. Surprisingly, Dow and Dicks-Mireaux found that the metal-working sector suffered less from excess demand for labour than other industries before the Korean war.[34] A comparison between the movements of the quarterly

---

30 Public Record Office, Kew (hereafter: PRO), Cabinet Office (hereafter: CAB): PRO CAB 134/333: E.S. (51) 36: Report on Rearmament; Note by Central Statistical Office, 22 May 1951. On the proportion of orders placed by the beginning, middle and end of 1951, see PRO CAB 134/333: E.S. (51) 8: Report on Rearmament, February 1951.; PRO CAB 134/333: E.S. (51) 52: Quarterly Report on Rearmament, 22 August 1951.; Treasury, *Economic Survey for 1952*, 19.

31 Given its large concentration of engineering industry, even major firms in Coventry could no longer recruit skilled workers, thus undermining their viability; see Nick Tiratsoo, *Reconstruction, Affluence and Labour Politics: Coventry, 1945-60* (London: Routledge, 1990), 26-7.

32 Dow, *Management of the British economy*, 130 and 333-43.

33 In 1951, the Attlee government accepted an unemployment rate of 3 per cent of the workforce as constituting full employment; see Jim Tomlinson, *Employment Policy: The Crucial Years, 1939-1955* (Oxford: Clarendon Press, 1987), 122-30. The unemployment rate was 1.2 per cent in May 1951; see Dow, *Management of the British economy*, 39, Table 2.2.

34 J. C. R. Dow and L. A. Dicks-Mireaux, "Excess Demand for Labour: A Study of Conditions in Great Britain, 1946-56," *Oxford Economic Papers* 10 (1958): 1-33.

Equation 8.1

Dow and Dicks-Mireaux Excess Demand Index for Labour

In calculating their index, Dow and Dicks-Mireaux assume that the proportion of both the irreducible number of reported unfilled vacancies and of registered unemployed is 0.5 per cent. This assumption is incorporated in the following equations.

If the excess demand for labour is positive, Dow and Dicks-Mireaux calculate the excess demand as *true vacancies less maladjustment*.[35]

$$\text{if} \quad \frac{\frac{unemployment}{employment}}{0.5} \leq \frac{\frac{vacancies}{employment}}{0.5}$$

$$\text{then} \quad Excess\ Demand = \frac{\frac{vacancies}{employment}}{0.5} - \sqrt{\frac{\frac{vacancies}{employment}}{0.5} * \frac{\frac{unemployment}{employment}}{0.5}}$$

If excess demand for labour is negative, they calculate it as *maladjustment less true unemployment*:

$$\text{or if} \quad \frac{\frac{unemployment}{employment}}{0.5} \geq \frac{\frac{vacancies}{employment}}{0.5}$$

$$\text{then} \quad Excess\ Demand = \sqrt{\frac{\frac{vacancies}{employment}}{0.5} * \frac{\frac{unemployment}{employment}}{0.5}} - \frac{\frac{unemployment}{employment}}{0.5}$$

Source: J. C. R. Dow, *The Management of the British Economy, 1945-60* (Cambridge: Cambridge University Press, 1964), 340, footnote 3.

seasonally adjusted index for the metal-working sector and for all industries reveals that rearmament had a disproportional impact on the metal-working industry (see Graph 8.2). While the demand for labour collapsed in most sectors of the economy in the fourth quarter of 1951, pronounced excess demand for labour persisted in the metal-working industries until the middle of 1952. By the end of 1953, the labour market for the metals, engineering and vehicles industries returned to reflecting the conditions on the national labour market.

[35] The authors define maladjustment "... as the amount of unemployment at the point where vacancies equal unemployment."; see Dow, *Management of the British economy*, 340, footnote 3.

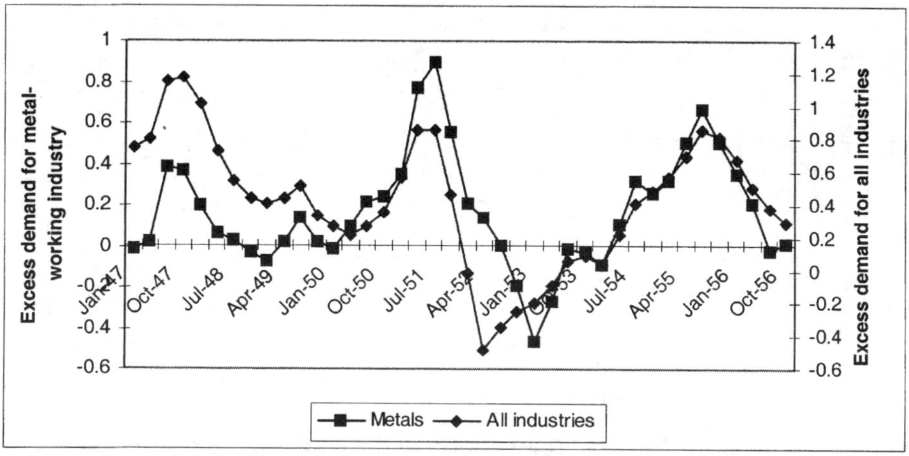

Graph 8.2: Excess Demand for Labour in Industry, 1947–56

Source: J. C. R. Dow and L. A. Dicks-Mireaux, "Excess Demand for Labour: A Study of Conditions in Great Britain, 1946-56," *Oxford Economic Papers* 10, no. 1 (1958): 31–3, Table A3.

Equally interesting is the economic impact of rearmament on regional labour markets. In the early 1950s, regional employment estimates were published once a year for May. Due to the limited availability of statistics, a comparable Dow and Dicks-Mireaux Excess Demand Index can only be calculated on an annual basis for May. Therefore, Graph 8.3 gives only a very limited picture of the shifts in the excess demand for labour. Nevertheless, two important points emerge from Graph 8.3. Against the national trend, the excess demand for labour in the Midlands rose significantly between May 1949 and May 1950, because of the increased export demand for engineering goods after the devaluation of the pound in September 1949. Therefore, the relative scarcity of skilled labour already constrained the expansion of engineering production prior to the rearmament programme.[36] Rearmament increased the excess demand for labour throughout Britain. Nevertheless, the excess demand remained below the level in the Midlands prior to the rearmament. In the Midlands, the additional demand for labour arising from the defence programme, however, rose to record levels in May 1951. This analysis underlines the regional differences in the economic impact of the defence

[36] Due to the internal constraints, "[t]he United Kingdom, however, experienced difficulties in making full use of the sales possibilities opened up by the devaluation, and its exports rose less conspicuously than those of other devaluing countries."; see United Nations. Economic Commission for Europe. Research and Planning Division, *Economic Survey of Europe in 1951* (Geneva: United Nations. Department of Economic Affairs, 1952), 69.

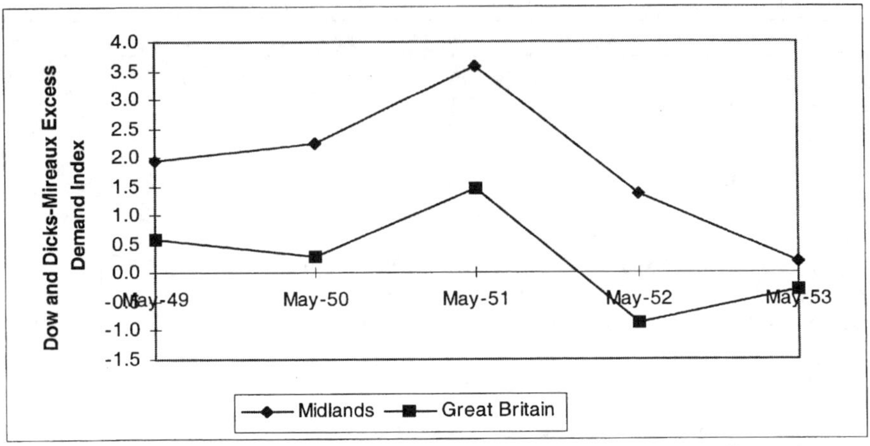

Graph 8.3: Excess Demand for Labour in the Midlands and Great Britain, 1949–53

Source: Ministry of Labour, *Ministry of Labour Gazette* (London: Her Majesty's Stationery Office, various dates).; Central Statistical Office, *Monthly Digest of Statistics* (London: Her Majesty's Stationery Office, various dates).

Equation 8.2

Alternative Excess Demand for Labour Index

$$Excess\ Demand = \frac{vacancies - unemployment}{placements}$$

programme. Regions with high concentrations of engineering industries suffered comparatively more from acute labour shortages.

Given the limited availability of regional employment data, an alternative index of excess demand for labour has to be found to analyse the changes in the demand for labour over time (see Equation 8.2). This index provides a crude measure of the *unsatisfied demand for labour* (vacancies *minus* unemployment) as a proportion of the *realisable supply of labour* (placements). As unemployment and vacancies are inversely related, this proxy for the demand of labour attempts to capture the strain on the labour market. Despite its different construction, this index approximates the movements of the Dow and Dicks-Mireaux Index and sheds more light on the movements of excess demand of labour in the summer of 1951. As Graph 8.4 confirms, regional labour shortages seriously constrained the expansion of industrial production. In the Midlands, unfilled vacancies outnumbered those registered unemployed by nearly nine to one in July 1951. During the summer months of 1951, the number of placements fell to a record low of 11,479 per month compared with

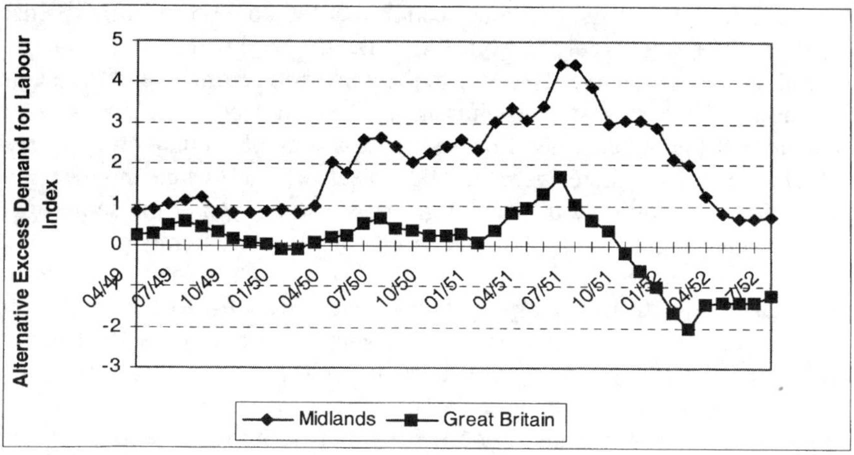

Graph 8.4: Excess Demand for Labour in the Midlands and Great Britain, 1949-52

Source: Ministry of Labour, *Ministry of Labour Gazette* (London: Her Majesty's Stationery Office, various dates).; Central Statistical Office, *Monthly Digest of Statistics* (London: Her Majesty's Stationery Office, various dates).

an average of 13,568 per month for the whole year. By March 1952, increased unemployment in other industries eased the pressure on the regional labour market and placements recovered to an average of 24,863 per month in 1952.

Nevertheless, fewer people in the Midlands continued to find new employment every month for the remaining duration of the defence programme than in the twelve months before the outbreak of the Korean war.[37] However, Graph 8.4 also shows that the alternative excess demand index for labour for the Midlands doubled in April 1950 three months prior to the beginning of the Korean war and nearly 6 months before the announcement of the £3,600 million defence programme in September 1950. Over the next ten months, the index hovered around 2.3 before rising to above 3 in February 1951. Except for the three exceptional summer months of June, July, and August, the index fluctuated between 3 and 3.4 for most of the year. The alternative excess demand index for labour for Britain shows that the increase in the excess demand for labour in early 1950 predated rearmament and was primarily due to the increased export demand following the devaluation in September 1949. The defence programme only began to exacerbate the excess demand for labour in the spring and summer of 1951. When the demand for many consumer durables collapsed due to their increased prices in summer 1951, the demand for labour eased dramatically particularly in regions with heavy concentrations of textile production. Therefore, this analysis

---

[37] My calculations based on figures from Ministry of Labour, *Ministry of Labour Gazette* (London: Her Majesty's Stationery Office, various dates).

confirms the findings of the previous section that the down-turn in the British economy in 1951 was largely attributable to the major shift in Britain's terms of trade and payments, and only partly to the conversion from a peace to a cold war economy. Nevertheless, the shortage of skilled labour clearly affected many sectors of the industry and limited the expansion of production in several sectors. For example, there were 35,600 vacancies for skilled engineers in August 1951, while only 2,000 were registered unemployed at the same time. Over the coming months, this shortage eased slightly, but aircraft firms would continue to complain about their inability to find enough trained engineers to fill all vacancies.[38] As this analysis shows, defence contractors were able to absorb a larger share of the available labour supply after summer 1951 due to the collapsing demand for many consumer durable goods. At the same time, the defence programme hampered the prospects for a speedy recovery by diverting production from capital goods for export to military hardware in the engineering sector.

While most western European countries experienced a similar deterioration to Britain in their international trading position, most countries did not face a similar severe supply constraint affecting their ability to increase domestic defence production.[39] As the United Nations Economic Commission for Europe (UNECE) pointed out in their *Economic Survey of Europe in 1951*, the British economy would have had to expand more rapidly than any other western European economy to absorb the increased defence effort without reductions in investment or consumption. Due to the economic downturn in 1951, the British economy grew insufficiently to absorb the additional demand due to the defence programme. As a consequence, Britain suffered a marked reduction in terms of non-military output as Table 8.3 shows. In contrast to Britain, the other western European economies except Denmark and possibly the Netherlands expanded sufficiently in 1951 to absorb the increased demand from rearmament.[40] Over-full employment of resources restricted the expansion of industrial production in Britain in marked contrast to other western European economies with substantial under-employment such as France, Italy and West Germany.[41] While Britain's conversion problem was arguably more severe than in other countries, they also experienced similar problems of rigidities in their economic structure and labour mobility. For example, some economists argued that western rearmament would contribute to overcoming the structural unemployment problem in some countries such as Italy and West Germany. However, other analysts rejected such suggestions

[38] Mitchell, *Crisis in Britain*, 260-61.

[39] Organisation for European Economic Co-operation, *Financial stability*, 20-23.

[40] United Nations. Economic Commission for Europe. Research and Planning Division, *Economic Survey of Europe in 1951*, 106-7.

[41] Organisation for European Economic Co-operation, *Financial stability*, 20-21.

Table 8.3

Proportionate increases in Gross National Product needed to absorb increased defence efforts

	Required in 1951 if consumption and investment at home and abroad were to be kept stable	Actually achieved 1951	1950
		(Percentages)	
United Kingdom	5	2 – 2.5	5
Denmark	4	1	8
Netherlands	3	3	8
France	3	6	2
Western Germany	3	11	13
Italy	0 – -1	6 – 7	...
Belgium	- 0.5	6	...
Norway	- 2.5	3	5
Sweden	- 4	3	5

Source: Economic Commission for Europe. Research and Planning Division, *Economic Survey of Europe in 1951* (Geneva: United Nations. Department of Economic Affairs, 1952), 106.

arguing that neither economy had recovered sufficiently to sustain the financial burden of rearmament and that increased arms production would not reduce unemployment because of the conditions prevailing on the domestic labour market.[42] While the West German economy continued to grow rapidly, the Italian economy stagnated during the years of the Korean war confirming that the increased arms demand contributed little to economic development in both countries.[43] This comparison adds weight to the interpretation put forward by Alan Milward that the negative supply shock resulting from the spiralling raw material prices disrupted the recovery of western European economies and of

[42] Ettore Cambi, "Les Rėpercussions du Rėarmement sur l'Italie," *Public Finance / Finances Publiques* 7 (1952): 83-94.; E. S. Simpson, "Inflation, Deflation and Employment in Italy," *Review of Economic Studies* 17 (1950): 203-25.; Gustav Schmölders, "The Impact of Rearmament on Western Germany," *Public Finance / Finances Publiques* 7 (1952): 100-12.

[43] On this point, for West Germany see Temin, "Koreaboom""and for Italy see Till Geiger and Lorenza Sebesta, "A Self-Defeating Policy: American Offshore Procurement and Integration of Western European Defence Production, 1952-56," *Journal of European Integration History* 4 (1998): 71-2.

intra-European trade only temporarily.[44] The question is to what extent British economic policies and rearmament prevented the country from participating in the emerging virtuous cycle of economic growth among the continental western European countries.

The economic problem and the British economic policy response

Over-full employment presented British economic policy-makers with a particularly difficult economic problem, because the existing supply constraints restricted the possibility of absorbing the additional demand due to rearmament through economic growth.[45] For this reason, British economic policy-makers remained sceptical about American suggestions that the British economy could sustain further increases in defence expenditures beyond the £3,600 million defence programme without substantial economic assistance. Unless such aid was forthcoming, they feared that the additional demand would disrupt the harmonious working of the economy. Nevertheless, the economic planners assumed that the British economy would continue to grow at its 1950 rate, which if achieved would have been sufficient to absorb the additional demand of the defence programme in 1951. In order to contain the inflationary pressure from the increased demand, economists suggested that the British government should take measures to reduce non-military public expenditures, private consumption, and investment as well as increase taxation to finance the additional defence expenditure. Moreover, the government would be well advised to take into account that the re-allocation of resources and production might lead to bottle-neck inflation. Depending on the economic circumstances, the success of government policies hinges on the response of the various economic actors. For example, it is hard to predict how the business community will react to financing rearmament by increasing taxation or public borrowing. While increased public borrowing may be seen as inflationary, deficit finance of a defence effort, which is perceived as necessary, tends to be more acceptable to entrepreneurs than using it for social welfare programmes.[46] Similarly, conventional economic theory suggests that consumers are likely to resist any reduction in their total consumption whether private or public in

---

44 Alan S. Milward, *The Reconstruction of Western Europe, 1945-51* (London: Methuen, 1984), 489.

45 Mayer, "Conseguenze economiche," (unpublished manuscript). The following analysis draws also on the theoretical analysis of the economic impact of Korean war rearmament by André Piatier, "The Economics of the Rearmament and its Effects on the Western Economics: A theoretical synthesis," *Public Finance / Finances Publiques* 7 (1952): 176-92.

46 Michal Kalecki, "Political Aspects of Full Employment," *Political Quarterly* 14 (1943): 322-31.

peacetime. Therefore, governments will be reluctant to finance increased defence expenditure through increased taxation or to mobilise the needed resources by cutting public expenditures, social investment or by restricting consumer expenditure.[47] In many ways, the British policy response to Korean war rearmament demonstrates the difficulties of adopting decisive economic measures in the face of significant political opposition. For this reason, Gaitskell's 1951 budget avoided taking extreme measures to placate popular sentiments, but failed to prevent the resignation of two senior members of the cabinet, Aneurin Bevan and Harold Wilson, over the government's policy on prescription charges. As a consequence, the Chancellor relied on inflation to reduce private consumption in real terms.[48] According to Shonfield, this timid policy approach meant that the burden of increased military expenditure fell on productive investment by default and led to slower economic growth.[49]

In his resignation speech, Bevan criticised the apparent lack of economic planning by claiming that the Treasury economists believed "... they move men about when they move pieces of paper about."[50] To some extent, the limited degree of state intervention reflected the ministers' refusal to accord priority to the defence programme.[51] Indeed, ministers reaffirmed this principle, when the cabinet approved the enlarged defence programme in January 1951.[52] In his speech during the defence debate, Gaitskell defended this approach as claiming it caused less distortion in the economic process.

> [W]e do not favour giving an overriding priority for defence. But of course there must be no doubt in the minds of all those engaged on defence production that it is essential that they should fulfil as rapidly as possible the contracts placed with them. But a simple overriding priority, as experience in the last war showed – I do not think there is any disagreement on this point – is of little benefit to defence production and does immense damage to the rest of the economy. It is in any case extremely difficult to apply in practice.[53]

On the surface, the government relied on its purchasing power and the market to allocate resources between the defence programme and other economic demands. If a conflict between the two arose, Gaitskell urged industrialists to

---

[47] Ron Smith, "Military Expenditure and Investment in OECD Countries, 1954-1973," *Journal of Comparative Economics* 4 (1980): 20-21.

[48] Dow, *Management of the British economy*, 60-62.

[49] Shonfield, *British economic policy*, 55.

[50] 487 H.C. Deb. 5s. col. 39.

[51] See Attlee's (478 H.C. Deb. 5s. col. 962-3) and Gaitskell's statements (478 H.C. Deb. 5s. col. 1137-42), when announcing the £3,600 million defence programme in September 1950.

[52] PRO CAB 21/2104: memorandum Brook - Attlee, "Cabinet discussion of Defence Programme," 24 January 1951.

[53] 484 H.C. Deb. 5s. col. 648-9.

consult the Board of Trade or Ministry of Supply, but if in doubt to prioritise defence orders. Therefore, the government relied on a "soft intervention" approach to implement the defence programme. Soft government intervention refers to situations where direct intervention is not necessary to influence the behaviour of a producer or is not needed as an effective behavioural constraint.[54] At the time, industry saw co-operation with the Ministry of Supply as a strategy for avoiding the imposition of controls and state administered rationing.[55] In line with this policy, the Labour administration reversed almost none of its earlier liberalisation measures, imposed few new restrictions, or tightened existing economic controls.[56] For example, employers did not have to notify the Employment Service of unfilled vacancies throughout the early stages of Korean war rearmament.[57] To curb non-military demand, Gaitskell opted for fiscal demand management. As Bevan's criticism of the Treasury suggested, the government's economic policy approach presumed that the resources for rearmament could be mobilised through prudent economic management.[58] The question is whether this criticism was justified.

The economic historian, Sidney Pollard, has criticised these attempts at fiscal demand management because they reduced investment demand rather than curbing consumption. He argues that organised business failed to lobby for increased productive investment, because of the corporatistic inclinations of the Federation of British Industry (FBI).[59] This criticism seems misplaced as private investment started to fall due to the growing shortages of physical resources before Gaitskell reduced the tax allowances for investment. At the same time, ministers, however, delayed urgently needed public investment such as the construction of additional electricity generation capacity in order to free resources for the defence programme.[60] Indeed, American aid officials

---

[54] The concept of 'soft' government intervention is inspired by the phenomenon of "soft budget constraint" in state socialist planned economies; see János Kornai, *Economics of Shortage* (Amsterdam: North-Holland, 1980), 306-9.

[55] MRC MSS 200/F/3/T3/31/9: D.5835: Note for Meeting of Defence Programme Committee to be held on 24 July 1951, "Distribution of Iran & Steel and of certain non-ferrous Metals," 19 July 1951.

[56] Dow, *Management of the British economy*, 158-60.

[57] No such requirement existed between 13 March 1950 and 25 February 1952; see Central Statistical Office, *Monthly Digest of Statistics* (London: Her Majesty's Stationery Office, 1952), no. 87 (December 1952) 20, Table 27, note 2.

[58] Some economic observers have agreed with Bevan's assessment; see Samuel Brittan, *Steering the Economy: The Role of the Treasury* (Harmondsworth: Penguin, 1971), 184-5.

[59] Sidney Pollard, *The Development of the British Economy, 1914-1967*, 2nd ed. (London: Edward Arnold, 1969), 470-74.; Sidney Pollard, *Wasting of the British Economy: British economic policy, 1945 to the Present*, 2nd ed. (London: Croom Helm, 1984), 36-8.

[60] PRO CAB 134/265: E.S. (51) 12th, minutes of the 12th meeting of the Economic Steering Committee, 12 April 1951. On the importance of such infrastructure investment, see also Henderson, Holland, and Seers, "The Crisis of 1951," 20.

argued that the creation of additional electricity generation capacity would assist the British defence effort more than economic aid.[61] Despite the acute shortage of building labour, the Attlee government maintained the house building programme under pressure from the Bevanites as well as the Conservative opposition.[62] As investment competed with demand arising from the defence programme, Gaitskell argued that reducing investment, rather than consumption, would prevent an over-loading of the economy.

> Without doubt it would be far better for our economy that, so far as we are able, we should meet the greater part by reducing consumption, meeting it now, and thus protect our future. But with the best will in the world, there is a limit to the extent to which we can put this principle into practice, because of the way in which the direct impact of defence production will affect our economy, for it is bound to be concentrated very narrowly on certain sectors.[63]

A few months later, this policy response already seemed woefully inadequate as a means of addressing the emerging domestic economic constraints. In line with his policy approach, Gaitskell kept the restrictive measures to a minimum in the budget and preferred voluntary credit restrictions to the tightening of monetary policy.[64] As a consequence, increased raw material costs translated into higher prices in the high street. This policy of "disinflation through rising prices" proved unpopular with many consumers, trade unionists and economists.[65] While Bevan criticised this policy as lowering living standards, economists faulted the budget for not being stringent enough.[66]

---

[61] National Archives and Record Administration, Washington (hereafter: NARA) NARA RG 59. Box 3528: 741.5/4-651: telegram, Batt - Foster, Bissell and Wood, 5 April 1951.

[62] On Bevan's position, see 487 H.C. Deb. 5s. col. 43. In October 1950, the Conservative opposition committed itself to constructing at least 300,000 new houses. Adopted in a haphazard fashion, this commitment aimed to increase house construction by 100,000 above the rate achieved by the Attlee government; see Michael Pinto-Duschinsky, "Bread and Circuses? The Conservatives in Office, 1951-1964," in *The Age of Affluence, 1951-1964*, eds. Vernon Bogdanor and Robert Skidelsky (London: Macmillan, 1970), 59-62. On the difficulty of fulfilling this pledge, see Harriet Jones, "New tricks for an old dog?: The Conservatives and social policy, 1951-5," in *Contemporary British History, 1931-61: Politics and the limits of policy*, eds. Anthony Gorst, Lewis Johnman, and W. Scott Lucas (London: Pinter, 1991), 33-43.

[63] 484 H.C. Deb. 5s. col. 646.

[64] Diary entries, 21 December 1950, 8 and 16 January 1951; reprinted in Cairncross, ed., *Robert Hall diaries*, 143.; Alec Cairncross and Nita Watts, *The Economic Section: A Study in Economic Advising* (London: Routledge, 1989), 216. On British monetary policy, Geiger and Ross, "Banks," 148-51.; Susan Howson, "The problem of monetary control in Britain, 1948-51," *Journal of European Economic History* 20 (1991): 82-5.

[65] Dow, *Management of the British economy*, 54-61 (quote: 61).

[66] For contemporary criticism, see C. F. Carter, "The Impact of the Rearmament on Britain," *Public Finance / Finances Publiques* 7 (1952): 40-44.; Scammell, "Rearmament: The

Contrary to the impression created by Bevan, the government's economic advisers, Edwin Plowden and Robert Hall, proposed the central direction of domestic investment and industrial labour through economic controls in order to achieve the proposed increases in defence production in December 1950. Besides direct intervention, the economic advisers recommended cuts in domestic investment and engineering exports in order to reduce overall demand. From the perspective of long-term economic development, Plowden and Hall remained convinced that the government should minimise any expansion in the engineering sector. If implemented, these measures would allow rearmament to be accomplished without cuts in private and non-military public consumption.[67] At the time, Hall felt that ministers seemed unwilling to adopt unpopular measures such as the direction of labour or to face up to the likely economic implications of the expanded defence programme.[68]

In the absence of government intervention, the market mechanism similarly failed to resolve conflicting economic demands quickly enough.[69] The rapid expansion of defence production required not only skilled workers and raw materials, but also large numbers of additional machine tools. As a confidential Ministry of Supply memorandum in June 1951 showed, potential domestic supply of machine tools could not meet the combined demand for civilian, export and rearmament use. Therefore, the Ministry of Supply sought to divert roughly 25 per cent of domestic demand for machine tools from civilian producers to defence contractors. In the case of capstan turret lathes, the supply departments demanded the diversion of all machines produced for domestic customers. With a view to ensuring the co-operation of the British machine tool industry, the Ministry of Supply started inspecting the order books of domestic producers in order to determine the priority of the different orders.[70] At the same time, the government decided to import additional machine tools from western Europe and the United States to ease the pressure of demand.[71] Despite concerns about the extent of the diversions, the defence programme

---

First Year," 2-5. Economic historians have largely shared this assessment, see Shonfield, *British economic policy*, 94-5.; Pollard, *Development of the British Economy*, 473.

[67] PRO T 225/704: minute Plowden and Hall - Gaitskell, 18 December 1950. On the economic policy debates, see diary entries, 10, 11 and 19 December 1950; reprinted in Cairncross, ed., *Robert Hall diaries*, 139-42.

[68] Diary entries, 18, 19, 23, and 24 January 1951; reprinted in Cairncross, ed., *Robert Hall diaries*, 144-6.

[69] PRO CAB 134/265: E.S. (51) 7th, minutes of the 7th meeting of the Economic Steering Committee, 1 March 1951.

[70] MRC MSS 200/F/3/T3/31/9: letter, General Secretary's Dept. - Members of Panel B, with 3 Attachments, 22 June 1951. For an analysis of the economic effect of rearmament on the British machine tool industry, see chapter 9.

[71] NARA RG 59. Box 3528: 741.5/2-2351: despatch, Hutton - Department of State, "Material Expansion of United Kingdom Machine Tool Output for Defense Program", 23 February 1951.

committee of the FBI accepted that they were necessary. In turn, the invited civil servants reassured the committee that the Ministry of Supply would minimise the impact on British industry.[72] As this example showed, the supply departments preferred to opt for "soft" government intervention by seeking the co-operation of the industry in prioritising defence orders. Nevertheless, the extent of excess demand for machine tools begs the question whether the Attlee government over-expanded defence production capacity rather than production itself.[73]

This analysis has stressed the importance of the political context in explaining the economic management of the defence programme. Ministerial opposition to a return to an albeit limited war economy led to an economic policy regime combining a mixture of market forces, Keynesian demand management, and soft government intervention. Given the political constraints, Gaitskell took considerable risks in his attempts to strike a balance between the acceptable and the desirable. Arguably, a more austere budget would have split the Labour Party more deeply without necessarily curbing demand more effectively.[74] As this analysis has shown, Britain's economic difficulties cannot solely be attributed to external factors as government speakers implied. While aware of the labour shortages, Bevan did not object to the maintenance of the government's house building programme, nor the expansion of British defence production capacity nor stock-piling efforts which significantly contributed to the excess demand and inflationary pressure in the British economy. Clearly, ministers committed grave errors in implementing the defence programme by ruling out substantial cuts in public expenditure or private consumption. Therefore, Bevan's constant sniping against the defence programme did not reduce the scale of the defence effort, but rather ruled out a full discussion of its economic impact. In an effort to preserve party unity, ministers embraced a non-interventionist approach, because the potential political consequences ruled out a reduction in the government social policy. At the time of crucial decisions, ministers failed to ask probing questions about the likely economic impact of certain decisions, while ruling out a more interventionist approach.

In a sense, Shonfield correctly asserted that political considerations led to the reduction in initial tax allowances for investment. However, it needs to be remembered that in his 1951 budget, Gaitskell abolished initial investment allowances from 1 April 1952. This budget measure arguably curbed long-term investment plans, but its impact had a smaller effect than the growing uncertainty about the country's future economic development.[75] Before this

---

72 MRC MSS 200/F/3/T3/31/9: Minutes of Meeting of Panel B of Defence Programme Committee, 26 June 1951, 4 July 1951.

73 See chapters 4 and 9.

74 Little, "Fiscal Policy," 257-9.

75 Dow, *Management of the British economy*, 204-9.

change in the initial allowances adversely influenced investment, the incoming Conservative government decided to curtail investment further through a variety of measures in the autumn of 1951. In this context, the new government ministers aimed to reduce the holding of stocks by companies to free resources for increased production of capital goods.[76] In the first half of 1951, companies financed their stocks through increased bank borrowing. To reverse the growth of short-term advances, the Conservative government raised interest rates and tightened the restrictions on bank lending. As raw material prices had already started to fall, these measures proved largely ineffective and potentially exacerbated the economic down-turn in 1952.[77] Following the lead of the previous Labour administration, the Churchill government sought the voluntary co-operation of the manufacturers of capital goods in giving priority to defence-related and export orders.[78] Despite its rhetorical commitment to a market-based economic policy approach, the Conservative government introduced measures to assure the preferential supply of steel and other vital materials to defence contractors.[79] Arguably, these measures did contribute to the further significant reduction of industrial investment in 1952. In this context, it is noteworthy that investment continued to decline after the Conservative Chancellor Rab Butler restored the initial allowance in April 1953.[80] While rearmament initially boosted investment in defence-related industries, the economic crisis of 1951 led to a decline in business confidence which resulted in a lower investment rate.

The economic policies of both Labour and Conservative governments tried to contain the inflationary pressure arising from the defence programme and increased import prices. Clearly, the Labour government adopted deflationary measures rather half-heartedly as it became obvious that some tightening of economic policy was required. As part of these measures, Gaitskell and his economic policy-makers tried to reduce investment by announcing cuts in the government's investment programme and initial allowances in twelve months' time. Most economists agreed on the desirability of some reduction in investment as well as calling for cuts in consumer expenditure. As this analysis suggests, such cuts proved politically almost unacceptable. If it had remained

---

[76] PRO CAB 130/72: Minutes of the 1st Meeting of a Cabinet Committee (Gen 388), 31 October 1951.

[77] Geiger and Ross, "Banks," 148-51.

[78] Treasury, *Economic Survey for 1952*, 45.

[79] PRO CAB 128/24: Cabinet Conclusions C(52)30th, 13 March 1952. Initially, the Board of Trade and Treasury expressed concerns over the effect of the "super-priority scheme" on exports; see PRO T 225/511: memorandum Shillito - Strath, "Defence Production Priorities, Sir H. Parker's letter of 31 January 1952", 4 February 1952.; PRO T 225/511: memorandum Strath - Bridges, 22 February 1952. Despite negative experiences in the past, Churchill sided in the end with the Ministry of Supply; see PRO T 225/511: PM's Personal Minute M/79/52, 27 February 1952.; PRO T 225/511: PM's Personal Minute M/120/52, 10 March 1952.

[80] Dow, *Management of the British economy*, 204-9.

in power, the government would probably have taken steps to address the emerging balance of payments crisis in the late summer of 1951. When the Conservative government came to power, it drastically tightened economic policy in an attempt to reduce the excess demand in the economy and redress the balance of payments deficit. However, some of the measures adopted by the Conservative government contributed to the economic recession. For example, the cut in the food subsidies announced by Butler in his 1952 budget further reduced real consumer demand at a time when the additional purchase power could have assisted the recovery of textile and consumer durable production in the second half of 1952. A year earlier a similar cut in food subsidies would have had the opposite effect reducing consumer demand and restraining imports. On balance, the Labour government was unduly optimistic that increased exports of textile and consumer durables would be able to compensate for the expected reduction of engineering goods available for export overseas. As a consequence, Gaitskell and his economic planners failed to take decisive measures to reduce non-military demand sufficiently and contain the inflationary pressure of increased wage demands.[81] Arguably, British economic planners could have benefited from studying closely the different economic policy approaches of other western European governments. While the corporatist arrangements between the Labour government and trade unions broke down after the outbreak of the Korean war, the Dutch government successfully reduced consumer expenditure by cutting food subsidies and raising taxes, and brokered a moderate wage agreement between the employers and the trade unions. This economic policy provided the basis for the strong recovery of the Dutch economy and in particular its balance of payments in the second half of 1951.[82] In the British case, the severe supply constraints in terms of labour and steel, the institutional arrangements underpinning wage bargaining and the tensions within the Attlee government arguably prevented the adoption of a similar package of economic policy measures.[83] At the same time, this analysis highlights one paradoxical legacy of the Korean war rearmament programme. While the economic crisis tarnished the Labour Party record on the economy, the Conservative government reaped the kudos for overseeing the eventual recovery of the British economy in spite of adopting measures which prolonged the recession.[84] In the end, neither party's economic record is impressive having

---

[81] Mitchell, *Crisis in Britain*, 230-45.

[82] Jan Tinbergen, "The Impact of the Rearmament on the Netherlands," *Public Finance / Finances Publiques* 7 (1952): 135-44.

[83] United Nations. Economic Commission for Europe. Research and Planning Division, *Economic Survey of Europe in 1951*, 106-7.; Edwin Plowden, *An Industrialist in the Treasury: The post-war years* (London: Andre Deutsch, 1990), 114-15.

[84] Mitchell, *Crisis in Britain*, 289-90.

failed to achieve a smooth conversion to a cold war economy without disrupting the long-term development of the British economy.

The defence programme and military aid

Besides his criticism of the Attlee government's handling of the Korean war programme, Shonfield also criticised the Labour government for producing the full range of weapon systems domestically and failing to take up the offers of American military aid. Some elements of this story have already been discussed in earlier chapters, but it is nevertheless appropriate to analyse the most important findings in detail to expose the flaws in Shonfield's analysis.[85]

In order to strengthen his argument, Shonfield slightly misrepresented the origins of the British commitment to domestic defence procurement, which predated the creation of the North Atlantic Alliance and American military aid to western Europe. While this analysis concurs with Shonfield's assessment that the British defence procurement strategy spread limited financial resources over too many projects, his analysis presupposed that British policy-makers could have known in 1945 that they would receive American weapons shipments to equip the British armed forces in time for any future war. In 1945, there was no evidence to suggest that the United States would support British defence efforts prior to another global war. At the same time, British policy-makers harboured no illusions as to the amount of assistance they would need from the United States to fight such a war. In the absence of American military aid, the Attlee government decided to maintain an independent British defence industry. These considerable efforts to develop modern weapons systems would have been wasted, if the British government had accepted more American end-items in the early stages of the Korean war. Shonfield provided no evidence for his assertion that substantial American military aid would have been forthcoming had the British government asked for it. Indeed, prior to the Korean war, the British government had only been offered surplus B-36 bombers and limited assistance for domestic defence production. As chapter 2 shows, British policy-makers were reluctant to accept second-hand bombers, which the United States Air Force was replacing with a new generation of planes.

After the outbreak of the Korean war, the Truman administration offered substantial aid to its western European allies, but its offer was conditional on substantial increases in western European defence efforts. However, American policy-makers remained disappointed with the proposed increases in British defence efforts and therefore rejected repeated requests for military aid. These

---

85 See chapters 1, 2, 3 and 5.

Table 8.4

British defence production and American military aid, 1950–57[86]

Expenditure Estimates £ million

Financial Year	Defence Budget	Defence Production Budget[i]	Of which Metal-using Industries	American military aid	American military aid as % of defence production budget
1950/1951	781	250	170*		
1951/1952	1,114	(~460)**	275*		
1952/1953	1,462	652	470*	85	7.6 %
1953/1954	1,637	746	510	140	18.8 %
1954/1955	1,640	748		85	11.4 %
1955/1956	1,537	664		43	6.5 %
1956/1957	1,549	613		50	8.1 %

Source: *Defence budget, Defence Production Budgets,* and *American Military Aid*: Ministry of Defence. *Statement on Defence*. (London: Her Majesty's Stationery Office, various years).

Notes: [i] figures include expenditure for ammunition and explosives
* Actual figures
** see note [87]

[86] The figures in Table 8.4 are largely drawn from the consolidated table of the defence estimates for the coming financial year, which was published at the end of the annual defence white papers. Therefore, the figures for 1950/1951 do not take into account the increases in defence budget approved after the outbreak of the Korean war.

[87] The Attlee government did not publish a Defence White Paper in 1951, because the government's defence policy had been debated after Attlee's statement on the £4,700 defence programme in January 1951; see Cabinet Office, *Defence Programme: Statement made by the Prime Minister in the House of Commons on Monday, 29th January, 1951*, Cmd. 8146 (London: His Majesty's Stationery Office, 1951).; Ministry of Defence, *Estimates 1951-1952*, Parliamentary Papers 1950-1951, 23:111 (London: His Majesty's Stationery Office, 1951). This meant that the Ministry of Defence did not publish a consolidated table for the defence estimates for the financial year 1951/52. The Financial Statement for 1951 contained a figure for the total defence estimates for 1951/52, but not for the defence production expenditure; see Treasury, *Financial Statement*, Parliamentary Papers 1950-1951, 21:148 (London: His Majesty's Stationery Office, 1951). However, it is impossible to calculate a comparable figure for defence production expenditure from the service estimates, because neither the estimates for the Admiralty nor those for the Ministry of Supply contain figures for defence production under one identifiable heading; see *Navy Estimates 1951/1952, Cmd. 8160*, (London: His Majesty's Stationery Office, 1951).; *Revised Estimates of the Sums Required in the Year Ending 31 March 1952 for Board of Trade and Ministry of Supply Services*, Parliamentary Papers 1950-1951, 25:224 (London: His Majesty's Stationery Office, 1951). However, the Air and Army estimates for 1951/52 list a figure for defence production and research which corresponds with the consolidated table in the Defence white paper; see *Air*

refusals precipitated the political crisis over Gaitskell's budget in April 1951. As the British economy plunged into a severe balance of payments crisis in summer 1951, the Labour government resisted continued American pressure to increase its defence programme. This refusal to bow to American pressure caused a crisis in the North Atlantic alliance and led to the setting up of the Temporary Council Committee (TCC) to re-examine the politico-economic capabilities of western European member states.[88] As a result of this exercise, the British government received sufficient aid to overcome the ongoing payments crisis. As Graph 2.3 shows, the dollar receipts from military aid and American armed forces in Britain covered Britain's dollar gap over the next three years.[89] Based on this analysis, Shonfield exaggerated the willingness of American governments to support British defence efforts prior to the Lisbon North Atlantic Council (NAC) meeting in February 1952. In the wake of this meeting's endorsement of the TCC report, Britain received American offshore procurement contracts to build aircraft and tanks for its own armed forces and those of other NATO countries. As Table 8.4 shows, these contracts partly financed British defence procurement until the 1957 defence review which abandoned the previous policy of maintaining the war potential of the British defence industry.

In his account, Shonfield rightly pointed out that the Truman administration regarded a strong western European defence production base as essential in order to be able to supply NATO forces directly in a future conflict thus reducing the need to ship military supplies across the Atlantic.[90] Therefore, the Truman administration insisted that a proportion of military aid should be allocated in such a way as to strengthen western European defence industries. This aspect of military aid became more important as western rearmament gathered momentum and the stocks of American surplus weapons diminished.

Estimates 1951/1952, Cmd. 8162 (His Majesty's Stationery Office, 1951); *Army Estimates 1951/1952, Cmd. 8161* (His Majesty's Stationery Office, 1951). Together, the Army and Air Force production expenditure accounted for almost 60 per cent of the total defence production budget. To these known production expenditure figures, I have added the identifiable production expenditure in the Navy and Ministry of Supply vote to arrive at the rough estimate of £460 million included in Table 8.4. On balance, this figure should be a reliable estimate of the planned defence production budget in 1951/52.

[88] On this episode, see chapter 3; but also Charles S. Maier, "Finance and Defense: Implications of Military Integration, 1950-1952," in *NATO: The Founding of the Atlantic Alliance and the integration of Europe*, eds. Francis H. Heller and John R. Gillingham (London: Macmillan, 1992), 335-51.

[89] See chapter 2, 69, Graph 2.3.

[90] The following short summary of the evolution of American military aid policy is based on Till Geiger and Lorenza Sebesta, "National Defense Policies and the Failure of Military Integration in NATO: American Military Assistance and Western European Rearmament, 1949-54," in *The United States and the Integration of Europe: Legacies for the postwar era*, eds. Francis H. Heller and John R. Gillingham (New York: St. Martin's Press, 1996), 253-76.; Geiger and Sebesta, "Self-defeating policy," 55-73.

In autumn 1951, American policy-makers realised that their ability to demand increased defence efforts from their NATO partners depended on the availability of American end-items. At the same time, the newly elected Conservative government under Winston Churchill announced plans to phase the British defence programmes over a longer period. Churchill insisted that the ongoing economic crisis made it impossible to carry out the rearmament programme within the time plan.[91] American policy-makers worried that the British decision would lead to other countries curtailing their defence programmes. Regarding their own defence programme, the British government stressed in the run-up to the NAC meeting in Lisbon that even with the cuts already announced, the fulfilment of the TCC force targets would depend on the availability of steel and other raw materials.[92] The Lisbon NAC meeting in February 1952 accepted the TCC report clearing the way for American military aid to Britain despite the government's reduction in its defence expenditure plans. Nevertheless, British officials reminded their American counterparts at the Lisbon summit that the British balance of payments crisis might force Britain to curtail its defence programme unless it received substantial assistance.[93] However, Britain did not receive any significant amounts of military aid until the second half of 1952.

Without any clear promise on military aid, British officials searched for a solution to the continued balance of payments problem by examining the prospects of arms exports in order to reduce the trade deficit. Preliminary studies revealed that arms exports might contribute between £15 million and £30 million to closing the shortfall in the balance of payments. At the same time, some of these potential exports such as the proposed sale of Venom and Vampires to South America would reduce the British contribution to the NATO aircraft programme. Similarly, other proposals would affect the re-equipment of the Territorial Army with new Centurion tanks or the air defence command of new radar equipment. Moreover, this amount proved insufficient to affect a significant reduction in the trade deficit. Therefore, some Treasury officials argued for cuts in the defence programme to release production capacity in the metal-using industry as well as steel in an effort to increase exports.[94] After investigating the problem further, the same officials pressed for an urgent radical defence review in order to assess overall defence expenditure and the economic impact of the defence effort. In this context, they raised the question whether Britain should continue to produce all types of military

[91] Mitchell, *Crisis in Britain*, 257-60.

[92] NARA RG 330. Entry 44. Box 9. folder United Kingdom: Summary of United Kingdom's comments on TCC Report, 17 January 1952.

[93] Plowden, *Industrialist in the Treasury*, 130-33.; PRO T 225/203: Brief prepared for the Air Staff, 25 July 1952.

[94] PRO T 225/201: minute Strath - Bridges, 5 March 1952.

equipment or consider obtaining at least some of its weaponry from the United States. Moreover, discussion of any future defence expenditure plans would have to take into account Britain's overseas commitments and its position vis-à-vis Germany.[95] Therefore, the head of the Treasury's Overseas Finance Division, Otto Clarke, called for cuts in all defence expenditure, which might affect the balance of payments. For example, he argued for increased investment in export industries, while recommending cuts in building work for the military. In conclusion, he urged that the government consider reducing non-sterling military expenditure, imports of defence supplies not financed by American military aid, oil consumption, defence production in the metal-using industries and overseas military expenditure in the Sterling Area.[96] In light of these dire warnings, the Treasury put forward proposals for expenditure ceilings on the items identified by Clarke including defence building work in order to:

> determine the level of resources which could be devoted to defence after meeting export requirements necessary to a satisfactory balance of payments, and making sufficient provision for investment to prevent a deterioration in the competitive efficiency of the United Kingdom economy.[97]

This paper marked a shift in Treasury thinking about the government's priorities away from rearmament to the balance of payments and for the first time the insufficient investment in many sectors of industry. Below these two top priorities, rearmament should rank third in order of importance before improving British living standards. Besides cuts in Britain's overseas military expenditure, Treasury officials now urged major increases in industrial investment, because

> [i]nvestment in manufacturing industry has probably never been sufficiently high in the United Kingdom since 1914 to give us a sound competitive position.[98]

Given the long-term nature of this under-investment, officials were reluctant to hazard a guess as to the level of investment required to restore Britain's competitiveness. Highlighting the need for increased coal and steel production, Treasury officials argued for restricting defence production in metal-using industry to £400 million per annum compared to the projected £460 million in

---

95 PRO T 225/201: minute Strath - Plowden, 19 March 1952.

96 PRO T 225/201: letter Clarke - Strath, 20 March 1952.

97 PRO T 225/201: Treasury Paper T.768-52, "Defence and Balance of Payment: Working Assumptions" (draft), 7 April 1952.

98 PRO T 225/201: Treasury Paper T.765-52, "Defence and Balance of Payment" (draft), 5 May 1952.

1952/53 and £570 million in 1953/54 in order to assure sustainable economic development.

Confronted with the Treasury's views, the service departments mounted a successful campaign against these proposed cuts in the defence programme arguing that reducing defence production in the metal-using industry below £500 million would lead to considerable unemployment and incur substantial cancellation charges. To prevent the savage cuts desired by the Treasury, the service departments stressed the importance of maintaining Britain's war potential and emphasised the prospects of arms exports. The Treasury dismissed the suggestion that defence cuts would lead to unemployment by highlighting that most redundant workers from the defence industry would in all probability find jobs immediately manufacturing peace goods preferably for export. Moreover, Treasury officials remained sceptical about the possibility of major arms exports to other European countries unless they were paid for by American military aid.[99] In this context, they pointed out that the defence programme restricted the production of civilian aircraft such as the Viscount and Comet for which there was considerable interest abroad, because aircraft firms preferred safe government orders over selling their planes on the international market.[100] In response to another plea by Butler, the Minister of Supply, Duncan Sandys, defended the limited cuts proposed by the service departments arguing that they represented the maximum achievable in order to ease the pressure on metal-using industry. However, he stressed that some defence contracts provided valuable employment in areas of heavy unemployment such as the Canberra production at Shorts in Belfast or arms production in Lancashire. For this reason, the cancellation of these orders would not reduce the demand pressure on metal-using industry.[101] While this reply failed to convince Treasury officials, they now felt that nothing would be gained by pursuing this issue further.[102] This change of mind reflected an improvement in the terms of trade and the balance of payments partly due to the inflow of American dollar aid. Moreover, Hall pointed out that "[t]he shortage of steel has been a more important factor on exports than the shortage of labour."[103] During Churchill's visit to Washington in January 1952, the British delegation succeeded in obtaining a million tons of American steel for

---

[99] PRO T 225/202: Brief on the Working Party Report (Defence Production and the Metal-Using Industries) prepared by Shillito, 16 June 1952.

[100] PRO T 225/201: E.A.(52)69. "Expansion of Aircraft Exports," note Stevenson - Clarke, 1952.

[101] PRO T 225/203: letter Butler - Sandys, 11 August 1952.; PRO T 225/203: letter Sandys - Butler, 13 August 1952.

[102] PRO T 225/203: "Reduction of defence demands on the metal-using industries," minute by Spicer on Sandys' reply, 15 September 1952.

[103] PRO T 171/413: "The economic situation," note by Hall, 3 October 1952.

the defence programme, which contributed to easing the steel shortage by the autumn.[104]

Direct American financial aid together with OSP contracts not only helped to overcome Britain's balance of payments deficit in 1952, but also continued to finance a sizeable proportion of the British defence budget until the late 1950s.[105] Therefore, American military aid prevented the reduction of defence procurement, despite the Treasury's concerns about the long-term viability of continued defence production and the potential implications for future economic development. As the analysis of chapter 5 shows, American military aid administrators tried to use offshore procurement contracts as leverage to seek modifications to aircraft design and to sustain military aircraft production. Indeed, the Eisenhower administration stopped military aid when the British government decided to curtail its defence procurement programme in 1956. In this sense, American military aid placed the government in a double bind. They could either to continue producing weapons already on order thereby blocking any attempt to reform British defence procurement policy or they could to rationalise the defence industry. The alternative would have been to reject American aid in 1952 and cut defence production in order to regain export trade. However, this solution might have undermined NATO, while depriving the country of much needed financial assistance to overcome the balance of payments crisis in the short term.

Diverging interests and the offshore procurement of British tanks

In contrast to Shonfield's claims about the potential benefits of American military aid, this analysis highlights the potential conflicts between the interests of donor and recipient of American military aid. From the onset of Korean war rearmament, many American foreign policy-makers had urged the Truman administration to increase its offshore procurement (OSP) purchases in western Europe. From the perspective of the United States, OSP contracts offered an incentive to recipient countries to increase defence production thus improving the military preparedness of the Alliance. Such direct production orders provided American aid officials with some influence over defence procurement in other NATO member states. At the same time, OSP contracts appealed to recipient governments, because they enabled them to purchase weapons for their military produced either domestically or in another European NATO

[104] On this point, see Donald MacDougall, *Don and Mandarin: Memoirs of an Economist* (London: John Murray, 1987), 84-5.

[105] Ministry of Defence, *Statement on Defence 1952*, Cmd. 8475 (London: His Majesty's Stationery Office, 1952), 3.; Shonfield, *British economic policy*, 95 and 142-3.; C. A. R. Crosland, *Britain's Economic Problem* (London: Jonathan Cape, 1953), 131.

country. Since these weapons would be paid for in dollars, OSP contracts contributed to closing the dollar gap in the country producing the weapons. For this reason, many American foreign policy-makers regarded OSP as an ideal combination of military and economic aid, because it improved military preparedness and the balance of payments of recipient countries.[106] Therefore, the TCC report attached great importance to OSP, because of this dual contribution to the western European defence effort. However, American military leadership preferred to supply end-items to their western European partners which bolstered their case for replacing the donated weapons regardless of whether the end-items were surplus stock, refurbished or brand new. From the perspective of American defence planners, end-item aid contributed directly to the development of the American military-industrial complex through subsequent procurement orders.[107] As a consequence, the availability of American weapons often determined the decisions on OSP contracts. Like other NATO countries, the American governments remained committed to maintaining the highest level of domestic defence production and therefore reluctant to place orders abroad.

As most western European countries longed to scale down their defence efforts in autumn 1951, American policy-makers hoped that increased OSP orders might provide a renewed incentive to member governments to expand or at least adhere to their defence production plans. In the aftermath of the Lisbon NAC meeting in February 1952, OSP projects became crucial to maintaining weapons projects affected by the cut-backs rather than expanding defence production in NATO member countries. OSP increasingly financed the acquisition of weapons systems, which had already been approved by national parliaments. In some cases, military considerations prompted American military aid administrators to finance the export of weapons to another NATO member through OSP.

One such case is the export of British Centurions to Denmark and the Netherlands. NATO military planners pressed for the early creation of additional armoured formations in western Europe to counter the Soviet bloc's numerical superiority in tanks. Given the lack of surplus modern American tanks, American officials actively sought an alternative source of main battle tanks for western European armed forces. In December 1951, they approached

[106] For example, see Tracy S. Vorhees, "To Prevent a 'Korea' in Western Europe," *New York Times Magazine*, 23 July 1950, 36-7.; William Y. Elliott et al., *The Political Economy of American Foreign Policy: Its Concepts, Strategy, and Limits* (New York: Henry Holt and Company, 1955), 312-15. On the evolution of OSP policy, see Geiger and Sebesta, "Self-defeating policy," 55-9.

[107] Until 1956, the American armed forces charged the Mutual Security Agency and its successors the full cost of a modern replacement for outmoded surplus equipment; see Robert E. Asher, *Grants, Loans and Local Currencies: Their Role in Foreign Aid* (Washington: Brookings Institution, 1961), 56-8.

the British government about the possibility of procuring Centurion tanks for the Dutch and Danish armies. This American interest recognised that British tank manufacturers had developed an excellent tank in the closing days of the second world war. Moreover, British tank factories had considerable spare capacity to further increase production. After lengthy negotiations, American, British, Dutch and Danish representatives agreed the terms of an initial OSP contract for 535 Centurion tanks in December 1952.[108] At the time, this OSP contract represented the largest single order placed under the Mutual Security Program in western Europe. For Britain, the total amount of the contract, roughly $90 million, significantly exceeded the total of OSP orders for the previous financial year. Indeed, the head of the Military Assistance Advisory Group (MAAG) in London, Brigadier-General Daniel Callahan described the Centurion contract as an:

> example of American aid financing the construction of British equipment for other NATO countries [and] a perfect symbol of the truly united effort we are making for the defense of the free world.[109]

From an American perspective, the offshore procurement of British Centurions solved the immediate problem that the urgent western European demand could not be met from American tank production. In this context, an important consideration remained the substantially lower price of British tanks. Indeed, the Centurion cost only three quarters of the price of the American built M47. Britain benefited directly from the dollar earnings of the OSP order. Furthermore without the OSP order, most of the British tank production capacity would have remained underemployed.[110] Given the substantial over-

---

[108] NARA RG 469. Mission to United Kingdom. Office of Production and Supply. Defense Program files. Box 3 folder Centurion tanks and wheeled vehicles: Memorandum "Meeting with M.O.S. on Centurion Tank Procurement," 9 October 1952.; NARA RG 469. Mission to United Kingdom. Office of Production and Supply. Defense Program files. Box 3 folder Centurion tanks and wheeled vehicles: "Chronology of first US Centurion contract", undated [February 1953 ?].

[109] NARA RG 469. Mission to United Kingdom. Office of Production and Supply. Defense Program files. Box 3 folder Centurion tanks and wheeled vehicles: MSA Press Release MSA/L-33, "UK's $90 million contract to build tanks for NATO under US off-shore procurement programme", 15 December 1952.

[110] NARA RG 469. Mission to United Kingdom. Office of Production and Supply. Defense Program files. Box 3 folder Centurion tanks and wheeled vehicles: Memorandum by Sowden, "Current Production and OSP Programs of (1) Combat vehicles and (2) non-combat vehicles", 18 March 1953.; NARA RG 469. Mission to United Kingdom. Office of Production and Supply. Defense Program files. Box 3 folder Centurion tanks and wheeled vehicles: Airgram Gordon - CINCEUR Heidelberg, "Offshore Procurement Program FY.1954. Analysis of Economic and Political Effects developed by Placement of 75 contracts", 19 March 1953.; NARA RG 469. Mission to United Kingdom. Office of Production and Supply. Defense Program files. Box 3 folder Centurion tanks and wheeled vehicles: Telegram 6319, Aldrich - Secretary of State, "OSP of Centurion Tanks for German Contingents", 29 May 1953.

capacity, the British government approached the MAAG in London with a proposal to supply Centurion tanks, financed through OSP, to the new West German army. The British bid received serious consideration given the price differential between American and British built tanks. Delays in the delivery of Centurions to the Dutch army undermined the chances of British tank factories receiving further OSP orders.[111] At the same time, cuts in American defence procurement freed considerable tank production capacity in the United States. This development meant that American military aid administrators decided to supply the *Bundeswehr* with American M48 rather than British tanks.[112] In this case, American interests took precedence over maintaining the British defence production base despite the lower cost of British tanks.

In his book, Shonfield claimed that if British governments had accepted American military aid, less resources would have been wasted on producing weapons domestically. However, American military aid allowed the British government to maintain the excessive defence production capacity Shonfield criticised. Despite substantial cuts in the defence procurement budget, OSP orders sustained production at many British defence contractors such as Vickers or Ferranti throughout the 1950s.[113] Therefore, American military aid locked certain parts of British industry into the relatively secure world of defence production. As a consequence, some companies such as Ferranti saw defence work as more lucrative than their ventures into competitive consumer goods or capital goods markets.[114] When American financial support came to an end in the late 1950s, the British government decided to rationalise its defence production effort and to reorganise the domestic defence industry thus suggesting that American military aid prevented an early reform of the defence procurement strategy which Shonfield criticised.

Conclusions

The economic crisis of 1951 mainly resulted from the rapid deterioration of Britain's terms of trade and payments in the first half of 1951. While raw

---

111 NARA RG 469. Mission to United Kingdom. Office of Production and Supply. Defense Program files. Box 3 folder Centurion tanks and wheeled vehicles: letter Finlay - Gordon, "Difficulties in Delivery of Centurion Tanks", 18 July 1953.; NARA RG 469. Mission to United Kingdom. Office of Production and Supply. Defense Program files. Box 3 folder Centurion tanks and wheeled vehicles: memorandum Sowden - Gordon, "Centurion Deliveries", 24 July 1953.

112 Andrew James Birtle, *Rearming the Phoenix: U.S. Military Assistance to the Federal Republic of Germany, 1950-1960* (New York: Garland, 1991), 170-71.

113 J. D. Scott, *Vickers: A History* (London: Weidenfeld and Nicolson, 1962), 358.; John F. Wilson, *Ferranti: A History, Building a Family Business, 1882-1975* (Lancaster: Carnegie, 2000), 325-6.

114 Wilson, *Ferranti*, 287-438.

material and labour shortages hampered the expansion of defence production, the rearmament programme only marginally contributed to the collapse of consumer demand which caused massive unemployment in some sectors of the economy. Political considerations constrained economic policy-makers ruling out decisive deflationary measures to soak up the excess demand created by rearmament. While the Labour government delayed tough policies, some of the measures adopted by the incoming Conservative government deepened the economic recession in its attempt to overcome the continuing balance of payments crisis. In this context, the sudden end to Marshall aid in December 1950 and the failure to receive substantial military aid in the financial year 1951/52 contributed to the severity of the economic crisis in 1951. This finding undermines Shonfield's claim that American military aid would have been forthcoming had the British Labour government only requested such financial support. While this is not the place to pursue this point further, the findings of earlier chapters indicate that given American cold war hysteria in this period, a more restrained British government policy over rearmament would not have resulted in additional aid. Moreover, the alternative socialist foreign policy outlined by the Bevanites in July 1951 would not have met Britain's primary objective to strengthen the American commitment to western European defence.

The impact of the economic crisis on the investment rate is difficult to assess partly because it is hard to determine whether the defence programme led to a shift in investment patterns. To some extent, aggregate figures obscure the underlying developments in the economy. As this analysis has shown, the shifts in production and investment in individual industries were also significant. The excessive demand on a narrow section of the capital goods industry disrupted balanced economic growth. As some Treasury officials pointed out, persisting with the defence programme after the economic crisis of 1951 held the danger that Britain "... will be simply an enormous arms factory producing unwanted goods."[115] The possibility that Korean war rearmament led to an over-accumulation in the military-industrial complex thus threatening future economic growth will be examined in the next chapter.

[115] PRO T 225/201: minute Bancroft - Shaw and Humphrey-Davies, 28 May 1952.

Chapter 9

Too much defence, too little peace production?: The British capital-goods industry, regional development and the Korean war rearmament

A recurring theme in this analysis of the British defence effort has been the conclusion that British defence procurement policy and particularly the Korean war defence programme contributed to an excessively large defence sector in the British economy. This finding echoes repeated suggestions in the existing historical literature. However, such claims are hard to substantiate because of the lack of detailed input-output data on British industry which make the precise nature of the economic impact of defence expenditure hard to trace. In this context, economic theory provides limited guidance for understanding the economic impact of the defence effort. When asked to assess the likely impact of defence expenditure, economists normally stress that the effect on economic development largely depends on the economic circumstances, which prevail prior to embarking on a major defence programme. The economic impact will differ radically depending on whether or not all productive capacity and resources of an economy are fully employed.[1] In the British case, an analysis is complicated by the fact that despite over-full employment, there remained substantial under-utilised capacity in the defence sector prior to the outbreak of the Korean war. As a consequence, British economic advisers rightly thought that rearmament could be achieved through shifting some workers and resources to defence production causing only minimal disruption to the remainder of the economy. Nevertheless, they accepted that increased defence production would absorb at least initially most of the increase in national income leading to inflation and a reduction in living standards.[2] In this sense, the Attlee government always contemplated armament in width by inducing a shift in overall composition of industrial output and providing investment

---

1 The following analysis draws heavily on the theoretical observations of André Piatier; see André Piatier, "The Economics of the Rearmament and its Effects on the Western Economics: A theoretical synthesis," *Public Finance / Finances Publiques* 7 (1952): 181-4.

2 Public Record Office (hereafter: PRO) PRO T 171/418: National Income Forecasts Working Party NIF(W.P.) (50) 44: "Report on the Economic Impact of Defence Expenditure", note by the joint secretaries, 4 September 1950.

mainly for arms production. As Table 8.3 suggested, the British economy did not grow fast enough to achieve armament in depth not to enable increased investment and higher output levels in all sectors of industry.

In order to simplify the analysis, the following study differentiates between three sectors producing capital goods, defence (or military) goods and peace goods. Peace(ful) goods are best described as all production for non-military purposes except for investment or reproduction (capital goods). For the most part, industrial statistics do not distinguish between the end-use of industrial production. The available input-output data for this period are too aggregated to reconstruct the precise composition of the demand for defence goods. One of the problems is that the same final product (e.g. a heavy goods vehicle, a Landrover) can be classified as a capital, defence (or military) and peace good depending on its intended use.

Even though the effects of the British rearmament drive on the structure of demand cannot be traced minutely, the findings of the previous chapters suggest the following transmission mechanism of this demand shock to the economy. In the first instance, increased defence expenditures added to the existing demand from the shipbuilding, vehicle and aircraft industry. In response to the additional demand, defence contractors attempted to increase their purchases of basic materials and hire additional workers. Given the constraints of labour and basic materials in the British economy on the eve of the Korean war, rearmament increased the excess demand particularly for labour and steel in this period.[3] In addition, the creation of additional capacity in the defence production capacity added to the demand for capital goods with potential repercussions for industrial investment. Due to the persistent supply constraints, increased defence expenditures reduced domestic purchases of peace goods and exports of capital and peace goods. As a consequence, the multiplier effect of the additional demand was relatively small.

Aside from the restricted availability of resources, British defence procurement policy contributed to the overall economic impact of the rearmament drive. To some extent, its effect will depend on whether or not the government grants defence contractors preferential access to labour and basic materials. After all, the British government still controlled the allocation of coal and to a substantial degree steel in this period. Indeed, the government tightened steel controls in 1951.[4] With favoured access to basic materials, defence contractors might be able to capitalise on the relatively protected market for weapons. As a consequence, defence procurement might change the economic structure of the economy thus reinforcing the growth of a military-

[3] J. C. R. Dow, *The Management of the British Economy, 1945-60* (Cambridge: Cambridge University Press, 1964), 112-21.

[4] Dow, *Management of the British economy*, 158-62.

industrial complex within the economy.[5] This line of argument raises the crucial question, whether or not Korean war rearmament led to the creation of excessive capacity in the defence sector which had adverse consequences for the competitiveness of British industry. This chapter will examine two specific aspects of this question. The first section analyses the impact on the capital goods sector of increased investment in defence production capacity. The following section studies the impact on regional economic development of locating new armament factories in Scotland.

The impact of increased military investment on the capital goods industry

From the inception of the Korean war defence programme, government economists acknowledged that the major burden would fall on the metal-using industry and in particular the capital goods sector of the economy. The economic impact of rearmament on this sector would be crucial for several reasons. As a major exporter of manufactured goods, metal-using industries played a crucial role in the government's export strategy of achieving an external balance.[6] Within this diverse industrial grouping, the manufacturers of capital goods occupied a crucial position for the future economic development of Britain. This smaller grouping includes not only the manufacturers of machine tools and electrical machinery, but also shipbuilding, vehicle and aircraft industries. Most defence contractors are located in this latter industrial grouping (see Table 9.1).

Without precise information about the changes in the final use of industrial output for the following years, the effects of any enlargement of defence production capacity are hard to assess. Therefore, most analyses base their conclusions on output and production statistics. For example, Cairncross argues that a large part of British industry was unaffected by the rearmament programme as

> [t]he big increase in the output of armaments was heavily concentrated on a limited range of engineering industries: aircraft, electronics, shipbuilding and ordnance factories. Of these four, only electronics looks

---

5 François Perroux, *La coexistence pacifique* (Grenoble: Presses Universitaires de Grenobles, 1992), 450-51.

6 T 171/418: National Income Forecasts Working Party NIF(W.P.) (50) 44: "Report on the Economic Impact of Defence Expenditure", note by the joint secretaries. This sector accounted for almost half of all British exports in this period; see Treasury, *Economic Survey for 1952*, Cmd. 8509 (London: Her Majesty's Stationery Office, 1952), 16-19, Table 6.; Treasury, *Economic Survey 1954* (London: Her Majesty's Stationery Office, 1954), 26-5, Table 4.

Table 9.1

Total dependence of metal-using industry on different components of final demand in 1948

(Percentages of total demand)

	Defence	Fixed Assets	Exports
Iron and steel (melting, rolling and casting)	4.8	31.3	31.8
Iron and steel (tinplate and tubes)	4.4	20.9	43.2
Non-ferrous metals	5.2	30.5	32.0
Motors and cycles	5.5	27.2	35.6
Aircraft	57.5	17.2	20.0
Rail locomotives and rolling stock	5.3	32.1	23.6
Shipbuilding	13.3	31.0	21.8
Machine tools, etc.	0.9	38.8	39.1
Constructional engineering	0.7	86.1	8.4
Mechanical engineering	4.9	40.1	32.2
Electrical engineering	5.5	36.2	27.9
Radio and telecommunications	6.3	20.3	14.9
Tools, wire, etc.	6.8	19.4	30.3
Hard and hollow-ware	5.5	36.2	27.9
Instruments, etc.	4.0	12.2	23.7

Source: A. Ghosh, *Experiments with Input-Output Models: An application to the economy of the United Kingdom, 1948-55* (Cambridge: Cambridge University Press, 1964), 17, Table 3.2

in the least a plausible example of an industry that might suffer a loss of momentum and competitive power as a result of rearmament.[7]

Based on this conclusion, the loss of competitiveness of British exports reflects the end of the post-war seller's market and the re-emergence of the West German economy in the world market.[8]

---

7 Alec Cairncross, *Years of Recovery: British Economic Policy, 1945-51* (London: Methuen, 1985), 232.

8 For a comparison of the export performance of both countries, see Alan S. Milward, *The European Rescue of the Nation-State*, 1994 paperback ed. (London: Routledge, 1992), 396-424.

Other historians have drawn a sombre picture of the economic impact of rearmament implying that the producers of peace goods were starved of resources. In the absence of detailed input-output data, the difficulty lies in exposing structural shifts in the economy away from peace to defence goods production. The example of the metal-working machine tool industry illustrates this point. In 1948, the dependence of this industry on defence expenditure was less than 1 per cent (see Table 9.1). In this period, defence procurement was restricted to the limited acquisition of new weapons, research and development contracts, and repair work.[9] Rearmament led to a renewed expansion of the defence production capacity and the replacement of existing machinery in Britain. Therefore, machine tool manufacturers were indirectly affected by the increase in defence procurement. Indeed, the production statistics for certain engineering products reveal that the production of metal-working machine tools increased remarkably during the Korean war rearmament (see Table 9.2). From the available figures, this steady expansion was exceptional in the period. The positive impulse of the Korean war rearmament programme strengthened the competitiveness of British metal-working machine tool manufacturers comparing favourably with the American producers in terms of production costs. Compared to other machinery production, the metal-working machine tool industry's productivity levels were relatively high. On the world market, British producers of metal-working machinery remained competitive in this period.[10] Overall, the machine tool output expanded 30 per cent in the first year and 60 per cent over three years during the Korean war rearmament.[11] In spite of this impressive increase in machine tool production, British defence contractors imported almost £15 million worth of machine tools in 1951 and £30 million in 1952 "... from the United States and Europe for the equipment of armaments factories."[12] Indeed, Britain became the largest importer of metal-working machine tools from West Germany in 1951 and further increased its imports in 1952. The additional demand from Britain and the United States contributed to the remarkable stability of West German machinery export in this period.[13]

---

[9] See chapter 4.

[10] Deborah Paige and Gottfried Bombach, *A Comparison of National Output and Productivity of the United Kingdom and the United States* (Paris: Organisation for European Economic Co-operation, 1959), 39.

[11] Board of Trade, *The Machine Tool Industry: A Report by the Sub-Committee of the Machine Tool Advisory Council appointed to consider Professor Melman's Report to the European Productivity Agency* (London: Board of Trade, 1960), 21.

[12] Treasury, *Economic Survey for 1953*, Cmd. 8800 (London: Her Majesty's Stationery Office, 1953), 34-5, Table 24.

[13] Alan S. Milward, "The Marshall Plan and German Foreign Trade," in *The Marshall Plan and Germany*, eds. Charles S. Maier and Günter Bischof (New York: Berg Publishers, 1991), 464-76, Tables 10.6 and 10.7.

Table 9.2

Production of metal-working machine tools, 1947–55

	1947	1948	1949	1950	1951	1952	1953	1954
Numbers	44,807	44,840	44,104	44,904	53,664	*60,000**		
in £1,000					48,590	62,006	66,180	65,530

Notes: * Estimate based on the production for part of the year.

Source: Treasury, *Economic Survey for 1952* (London: Her Majesty's Stationery Office, 1958), 32, Table 32.; Treasury, *Economic Survey for 1953* (London: Her Majesty's Stationery Office, 1958), 35, Table 25.; Treasury, *Economic Survey 1954* (London: Her Majesty's Stationery Office, 1958), 51, Table 28.; Treasury, *Economic Survey 1955* (London: Her Majesty's Stationery Office, 1958), 50, Table 26.

At first glance, the metal-working machine tool industry benefited from the expansion of defence production during Korean war rearmament. However, the production figures are slightly deceptive. On the eve of the Korean war, the production of metal-working machine tools in Britain was about half the peak production levels during the Second World War. As a consequence of wartime mobilisation, the pool of metal-working machine tools had been enlarged for the purposes of military production.[14] While the *Statistical Digest of the War* records that roughly 11,300 metal-working machine tools were produced in 1943, this figure is not strictly comparable to the figures in Table 9.2 as it does not include small machinery.[15] One report estimated that the number of metal-cutting and metal-forming machine tools in Britain increased from 700,000 to 800,000 during the period of the Second World War.[16] Therefore, the production figures for metal-working machine tools reported in the *Statistical Digest of the War* are almost certainly an under-estimate, but Steven Broadberry and Peter Howlett have argued that government financed investment during the war compensated for most of the disinvestment in the economy.[17] However, most of this investment would have been in the metal-using industry rather than in consumer goods industries. At the same time, government subsidised the retention of considerable defence production capacity under its policy of maintaining the war potential of the British

[14] R. C. Tress, "The Armed Economy," *London and Cambridge Economic Service* 29 (1951): 4.

[15] Central Statistical Office, *Fighting with Figures: A Statistical Digest of the Second World War* (London: Her Majesty's Stationery Office, 1995), 179, Table 7.29.

[16] United Nations. Economic Commission for Europe. Research and Planning Division, *Economic Survey of Europe since the War: A Reappraisal of Problems and Prospects* (Geneva: United Nations. Department of Economic Affairs, 1953), 3, Table 2.

[17] Steven Broadberry and Peter Howlett, "The United Kingdom: 'Victory at all costs'," in *The Economics of World War II: Six great powers in international comparison*, ed. Mark Harrison (Cambridge: Cambridge University Press, 1998), 68-9.

economy. As a result, many of the newly installed machine tools were located at defence plants, which only made a limited contribution to the production of peace goods after the war. At the same time, the collapse of the demand for machine tools after the end of war mobilisation suggests the absence of large penned-up reconstruction demand from consumer industries.

Whatever the reasons for depressed demand for capital goods, the Korean war defence programme provided a tremendous boost to the metal-working machine tool industry. Excess demand allowed the price of metal-working machine tools to rise in this period contributing to an increase in the imports of machine tools.[18] Nevertheless, the marked increase in the value of machine tool production suggests that the increased demand for machine tools also induced a shift towards the production of highly specialised precision machinery for defence production during the Korean war. By the end of the decade, a study undertaken by Seymour Melman for the European Productivity Agency argued that Western machine tool manufacturers concentrated too much on the production of highly sophisticated machinery. The report warned that North America and Western Europe would become uncompetitive in price terms unless it redirected its production to compete with the Soviet Union and other mass-producers of machine tools. In the United States, Melman argues that this development led to a permanent increase in price levels for metal-working machine tools, thus reducing overall investment in the manufacturing industry.[19] Since the mid-1950s, the Department of Defense reinforced this trend by sponsoring the development of highly sophisticated, numerically controlled machine tools. Government development contracts put more emphasis on precision and performance than on the economic efficiency of machine tools. State sponsorship of numerically controlled machine tool technology favoured larger manufacturers and indirectly more capital-intensive production methods in industry.[20] Indeed, Anthony DiFilippo suggests that this government pump-priming contributed to the relative decline of the American machine tool industry.[21] At the same time, Frederic Scherer points out that American industry never fully exploited the potential of numerically controlled machine tools and computerised process-control technology in peace

[18] Economist Intelligence Unit, *Britain and Europe: A Study of the Effects on British Manufacturing Industry of a Free Trade Area and the Common Market* (London: Economist Intelligence Unit, 1957), 106.

[19] Seymour Melman, *The Permanent War Economy: American Capitalism in Decline*, rev. ed. (New York: Touchstone, 1985), 81-2 and 90-91. For a summary of Melman's European Productivity Agency report; see Board of Trade, *Machine Tool Industry*, 6-20.

[20] David F. Noble, "Command Performance: A Perspective on Military Enterprise and Technological Change," in *Military Enterprise and Technological Change: Prespectives on the American Experience*, ed. Merritt Roe Smith (Cambridge: MIT Press, 1985), 329-426.

[21] Anthony DiFilippo, *Military Spending and Industrial Decline: A Study of the American Machine Tool Industry* (New York: Greenwood Press, 1986).

production in the 1960s.[22] Both interpretations offer different explanations of declining economic growth rates, but disagree whether the development arose due to the failure of the machine tool industry to supply the machines demanded by consumer industries or due to the failure of industrial users to employ the new machinery to its full potential.

A similar development occurred in Britain from the mid-1950s onwards. The Melman report suggested that Western European machine tool manufacturers had been reluctant to integrate numeric control units in their products.[23] The Economist Intelligence Unit attributed this development to deep conservatism within the industry, expectations of falling demand at the end of post-war recovery, and a pronounced lack of investment in the machine tool industry during the Korean war boom.[24] This line of argument suggests that as a consequence of sudden increase in demand during Korean war rearmament, British machine tool manufacturers concentrated on supplying machines to the defence industry and neglected research and development in new technologies. At the same time, aircraft manufacturers continually complained about the difficulties in obtaining high precision machine tools from domestic producers.[25] In reply, British machine tool manufacturers defended themselves against the accusation of complacency referring to on-going experiments with the new technology. According to the industry, the lack of information about the economics of numerically controlled machine tools presented the greatest obstacle to their wide scale adoption in industry. Industry representatives highlighted the tests carried out by Royal Ordnance Factories in order to gather such data. Indeed, the industry called on the government to consider continued support of industrial trials.[26] Business historians generally agree that it was primarily electronics firms rather than traditional machine manufacturers which experimented with the numerical control technology in the 1950s. However, they disagree on whether or not this development contributed to the poor performance of the British machine tool industry. On one side of the argument, John Wilson stresses the difficulties of these pioneering companies such as Ferranti in finding buyers for its innovative machines.[27] On the other, Ross Hamilton criticises the newcomers for developing their own machine tools rather than pressing machine tool producers to integrate their control mechanisms in their products. As a

---

22 Frederic M. Scherer, *Innovation and Growth: Schumpeterian Perspectives* (Cambridge: MIT Press, 1984), 266-7.

23 Board of Trade, *Machine Tool Industry*, 16.

24 Economist Intelligence Unit, *Britain and Europe*, 103-6.

25 "Fourth Annual Conference on Problems of Aircraft Production: A Report on the Conference held in Southampton, 6 and 7 January 1956," *Aircraft Engineering* 28 (1956).

26 Board of Trade, *Machine Tool Industry*, 16-19.

27 John F. Wilson, *Ferranti: A History, Building a Family Business, 1882-1975* (Lancaster: Carnegie, 2000), 335-8.

consequence, he argues that electronics firms found it difficult to break into the market for machine tools due to a high degree of customer loyalty to their traditional suppliers.[28] In this sense, both sides of this particular argument ultimately blame conservatism on the part of traditional producers and consumers of machine tools for the fact that British manufacturing industry failed to exploit the potential of automating their production facilities. At the same time, British machine tool producers remained unconvinced that automation would provide the most fruitful direction for research and development.[29]

The faltering performance of the British machine tool industry led to repeated government inquiries about its specific difficulties. The report of a Ministry of Technology working party emphasised in 1966 that the cyclical nature of demand for British machine tools exacerbated the slower expansion of the market for capital goods due to a slower rate of productivity growth in the British economy than in continental economies. The report revealed inadequate investment by the machine tool industry in a new capacity as well as research and development. To stabilise the demand for machine tools, the working party called for increased government purchases of machine tools for use in Royal Ordnance Factories and Admiralty Dockyards.[30] Four years after the working party's report, the Machine Tool Expert Committee chaired by Sir Richard Way acknowledged in its report the welcome contribution of public purchasing of machine tools while pointing out the limited nature of such purchases.[31] If the cyclical nature of the demand for machine tools contributed to the decline of the British machine tool industry, then the defence programme reinforced the composition of machine tool production prior to 1950. As a consequence of Korean war rearmament, British machine tool production rose by over 60 per cent during the defence programme and remained well above its 1954 level for the remainder of the decade. At the same time, the shortage of skilled labour constrained the industry's research and development effort as well as the further expansion of output in this period.

While the British machine tool industry continued to export roughly 30 per cent of its output, the committee appointed to consider the Melman report

[28] Ross Hamilton, "Early British Machine Tool Automation: The Road to Numerical Control," *Journal of Industrial History* 2 (1999): 110-15.

[29] Roger Lloyd-Jones and M. J. Lewis, "Alfred Herbert and Co., The British Machine Tool Industry, and the 'Modernisation' of British Manufacturing in the 1950s and Early 1960s," paper presented at the Engineering Postwar Industries, Hagley Museum, Wilmington, 8-9 July 2001.

[30] Ministry of Technology, *Report of the Working Party on the Problems Arising from the Cyclical Patterns of Machine Tool Orders* (London: Her Majesty' Stationery Office, 1966).

[31] Department of Trade and Industry, *The Machine Tool Industry: Report of the Machine Tool Expert Committee under the chairmanship of Sir Richard Way KCB CBE* (London: Her Majesty's Stationery Office, 1970), 87-90.

warned that its share of the world market declined noticeably in the period from 1956 to 1959. The committee attributed the fall in the market share to the fact that the British industry produced primarily standard machine tools rather than specialised machinery as its main European competitor the West German machine tool industry.[32] In terms of exports, the West German industry overtook its British rival in 1956, even though it continued to produce significantly less in terms of output. While more than half of West German machinery exports went to other western European countries, the British machine tool industry exported primarily to countries outside the European Economic Community or European Free Trade Association (more than 75 per cent). Besides product quality, other factors became increasingly important in investment decisions such as technological leadership, reliability, after-sale service and availability of finance.[33] Since the early 1950s, the West German machine tool producers proved so successful, because they offered machines tailored to their customers' needs partly by utilising the emerging numeric control technology from an early stage.[34] Through specialisation, the West German machine tool industry had regained its pre-war share of the world market in machine tools by 1957. In his seminal study on *Industrial Growth and World Trade*, Alfred Maizels suggests that Korean war rearmament diverted British machine tool production from export production leading to the dramatic revival of West German capital goods exports in the 1950s. However, his own analysis shows that (West) German machine tool industry had traditionally been the largest exporter of metal-working machinery since 1913, losing its position briefly to the United States in the immediate post-war period.[35] Given this traditional strength, the British metal-working machine tool industry found it hard to exploit the post-war sellers' market to replace West Germany as premier producer in the European market particularly given the largely bilateral nature of intra-European trade prior to 1950. For a time, imports of American metal-working machinery largely filled the gap left by West German producers. However, British industry also failed to seize the potential opportunities arising from the temporary absence of West German manufacturing exports from the European market in the immediate post-war

---

32 Board of Trade, *Machine Tool Industry*, 20-23.

33 Egon Baumgart, "Die Maschinenbauindustrie der Bundesrepublik im europäischen Markt," *Vierteljahreshefte für Wirtschaftsforschung* (1962): 63-72. See also Stephen T. Parkinson, *New Product Development in Engineering: A Comparison of the British and West German Machine Tool Industries* (Cambridge: Cambridge University Press, 1984), 111-19.

34 Hartmut Hirsch-Kreinsen, "On the history of NC-technology - different paths of development," in *Technology and Work in German Industry*, eds. Norbert Altmann, Christoph Köhler, and Pamela Meil (London: Routledge, 1992), 63-76.

35 Alfred Maizels, *Industrial Growth and World Trade: An empirical study of trends in production, consumption and trade in manufactures from 1899-1959, with a discussion of probable future trends* (Cambridge: Cambridge University Press, 1963), 280-83.

period. Instead, British industrialists preferred to concentrate on safe Sterling Area markets leaving the European market to their West German rivals.[36]

The increased demand for machinery arising from the defence programme provided a much-needed boost to the manufacturers of metal-working machine tools. In response to this demand shock, the British machine tool industry failed to expand its production facilities and its research and development efforts. To some extent, the shortage of skilled labour constrained the potential of expansion in this period. In this respect, the industry potentially suffered from the hoarding of skilled engineers in the defence sector of the economy.[37] However, the industry did not mechanise its production processes in order to ease the labour constraint. This development suggests that most machine tool manufacturers believed that the expansion of demand would merely be temporary rather than sustained. Due to the defence programme, British machine tool producers reduced their exports of machinery, but even prior to this diversion the industry made little effort to increase its exports to western Europe. While most British manufacturers continued to buy primarily domestically produced machine tools, the British market for capital goods grew much more slowly than those of most its western European rivals for the greater part of the twentieth century. In other countries, the high investment level and rapid economic growth led to competitive pressure among machine tool producers to develop new machinery contributing to a virtuous cycle of expanding demand, rising productivity and technological progress.[38] Aside from the short-term boost to British metal-working machine tool production, the long-term impact of the defence programme on the industry is difficult to assess, particularly given Britain's long-standing weakness in this area. While it would be incorrect to attribute the disappointing performance of the industry solely to rearmament, the defence programme preserved the structure of machine tool output thus potentially harming international competitiveness by preventing a reorientation of output to more promising fields of capital goods production.

New investment in defence production and Scottish economic development

As this analysis underlines, increased defence expenditure may produce hidden, but largely negative long-term effects on the economic structure and development. These negative implications may arise even if the increase in the defence effort leads to the creation of additional employment in the short

[36] On this point, see Milward, *Rescue*, 396-406.
[37] Board of Trade, *Machine Tool Industry*, 26-7.
[38] Maizels, *Industrial Growth*, 258-70.; Milward, *Rescue*, 396-424.

term.[39] During Korean war rearmament, the Labour government initially aimed to restrict the expansion of defence production to a minimum, because of the severe labour market constraint hampering the conversion to a cold war economy. At the time, economic planners argued that if military requirements necessitated any new investment, then new defence factories should be established in areas of relatively high unemployment such as Scotland. The following section will explore to what extent rearmament contributed to or hampered local economic development in Scotland in the early 1950s.

To some extent, the need for renewed investment in defence production capacity revealed a fundamental flaw in the strategy of maintaining the war potential of the British economy. As the discussion of previous chapters shows, this war potential policy effectively conserved defence production facilities in the immediate post-war period. Without major production orders, defence contractors lacked the incentive to modernise the defence production facilities in line with new weapons technology in this period. The most striking example is the remarkable progress in the development of jet aircraft in the decade after the war. Leading the world in the development of jet engines, British aero-engine manufacturers lacked the production lines to mass-produce them.[40] As a consequence of this oversight, the government sought to enlarge the production capacity for jet-engines quickly.[41] Besides trying to interest a number of automobile manufacturers in building jet-engines, the government offered Rolls Royce several factories built under the Board of Trade scheme near Glasgow. Originally, these factories had been intended for American companies interested in locating in Europe.[42] While working hard to ensure Scotland would receive its share of rearmament contracts, the Scottish Council (Development and Industry) protested against the reallocation of the factory space in East Kilbride.[43] However, as Harold Wilson confirmed in a memorandum in December 1950, the needs of the defence programme had an over-riding priority:

---

[39] On this point, see the discussion in "Introduction," in *Defence expenditure, industrial conversion and local employment*, eds. Liba Paukert and Peter Richards (Geneva: International Labour Office, 1991), 1-6.

[40] See the discussion in chapters 4 and 5.

[41] PRO CAB 130/65: Minutes of an Ad hoc Meeting of Ministers in the Prime Minister's Room at the House of Commons, 23 November 1950.

[42] PRO BT 177/325: letter Oakley - Reading, 9 March 1951.; PRO BT 177/325: note "East Kilbride", undated, [18 March ?] 1951.

[43] Scottish Council (Development and Industry), Edinburgh (hereafter SCDI) SCDI SC 2/3/1/1: EC (50) 5th, Minutes of the 5th meeting of Executive Committee, 11 September 1950.; SCDI SC 2/3/1/2: EC (51) 3rd, Minutes of the 3rd meeting of Executive Committee, 13 April 1951.

> ... while we must regret this, [the case of Rolls Royce] is a clear case of defence needs taking a capacity priority over, presumably, less [...] essential [...] production.[44]

After months of bureaucratic wrangling, Rolls Royce together with the Ministry of Supply decided to locate its main Scottish production site in East Kilbride rather than in one of the unemployment black-spots around Glasgow such as Greenock which the Board of Trade would have preferred.[45] During the Second World War, Rolls Royce had produced aero-engines on the Hillington industrial estate in Glasgow. After the war, Rolls Royce took the Hillington factory over from the Ministry of Aircraft Production and reorganised the plant to service and repair Merlin engines. As a government report noted,

> [i]n this way the large organisation and the engineering skills built up at Hillington during the war were in considerable measure retained ready for rapid expansion if and when the need arose.

However, the Hillington site was deemed too small to accommodate the production of Avon jet engines in 1950.[46] Moving jet-engine production to East Kilbride necessitated the construction of new factory buildings. Moreover, this decision ignored the serious shortage of skilled labour and adequate housing in East Kilbride.[47]

At the same time, Korean war rearmament led to further cuts in the Labour government's regional development programme. Despite being a central plank in the Labour Party's economic policy, the regional development programme had been reduced after the convertibility crisis in summer 1947. The Attlee government's regional policy had been directed at employment creation rather than regional development.[48] Confronted with further cuts in its regional development budget, the Board of Trade tried to prevent the location of new defence production facilities in development areas and the allocation of already built government factories to defence contractors.[49] Instead, they suggested siting new factories in areas with high structural unemployment like

---

44 PRO BT 177/325: minute Wilson - Calder and Monier-Williams, 14 December 1950.

45 PRO BT 177/325: letter Oakley - Raffan, 1 December 1950.; PRO BT 177/325: letter Miller - Oakley, 22 December 1950.; PRO BT 177/325: letter Raffan - Oakley, 28 November 1950.

46 Scottish Record Office (hereafter SRO) SRO SEP 4/14: note "Rolls-Royce Limited: East Kilbride Factory Opening", 3 November 1953.

47 PRO BT 177/325: minute Monier-Williams - Calder, 7 December 1950.; see also note 45.

48 Peter Scott, "British regional policy 1945-51: a lost opportunity," *Twentieth Century British History* 8 (1997): 358-82.

49 PRO BT 177/331: Aide-Memoire (discussed at an informal meeting known as the Chancellor's group on 14 November 1950), undated, 1950.

Lanarkshire, the North East coast of Scotland, West Wales, Cumbria, Humberside, and Northern Ireland outside existing development areas.[50] In particular, Board of Trade officials argued for the establishment of large defence factories outside Edinburgh and on the Tullos estate in Aberdeen.[51] Treasury officials initially indicated support for the stance of the Board of Trade.[52] However, Shinwell insisted that defence needs would have to take priority.[53] Since the government relied on the co-operation of industry, important defence contractors had considerable bargaining power to influence the location of new armament factories.[54] In the case of East Kilbride, Rolls Royce, with the tacit approval of the Ministry of Supply controller for Scotland, confronted the Board of Trade with a *fait accompli*. Board of Trade officials remained concerned about Rolls Royce's decision which ignored the shortage of skilled labour and housing at East Kilbride.[55] Once the aero-engine factory opened in 1953, Rolls Royce raised this problem with the government demanding government action to overcome the problems. Originally, the local manager of Rolls Royce, Miller, complained to the chairman of the Scottish Council (Development and Industry), Lord Bilsland, about the housing shortage and the difficulties of retaining skilled labour.[56] Bilsland sought a meeting with government departments to discuss the problem of Rolls Royce and other firms in Dundee.[57] This meeting did not achieve any constructive results. While sympathetic to these demands, the Scottish Office found that the Treasury and the Board of Trade objected to the provision of new housing for key workers.[58]

---

[50] In January 1951, the Board of Trade wrote to its regional senior controllers inquiring about potential sites for new defence factories; see PRO BT 177/331: letter Reading - Robinson, 17 January 1951.

[51] Scottish Office officials argued hard for the fishing towns on the North East coast of Scotland, Orkney and Shetland; see PRO BT 177/331: letter Anderson - Reading, 17 January 1951. In response, the Board of Trade pointed out that the government was seeking a location for larger factories; see PRO BT 177/331: letter Reading - Anderson, 19 January 1951. However, Board of Trade officials did seriously discuss the possibility of siting smaller defence plants in the North East of Scotland; see PRO BT 177/331: letter Oakley - Reading, 20 January 1951.

[52] PRO BT 177/331: Suggested addition to brief for the President on PC(50)122, undated, 1951.; PRO BT 177/325: letter Raffan - Dobbie-Bateman, 10 January 1951.

[53] PRO BT 177/331: letter Shinwell - Gaitskell, 10 January 1951.

[54] Another example of the bargaining power is the Leyland tank factory; see Peter Burnham, "Rearming for the Korean War: the impact of government policy on Leyland Motors and the British car industry," *Contemporary record* 9 (1995): 343-67.

[55] PRO BT 177/325: letter Raffan - Chapman, 23 February 1951.; see also note 42.

[56] SRO SEP 4/14: copy of a letter Miller - Lord Bilsland, 23 July 1953.

[57] SRO SEP 4/14: "Houses for Skilled Workers", note of a meeting at St. Andrew's House, Edinburgh, 15 September 1953.

[58] SCDI SC 2/3/1/2: EC (53) 6th, Minutes of the 6th meeting of Executive Committee, 25 September 1953.; SRO SEP 4/14: letter Bannerman - Russell, 28 October

As the rearmament programme neared completion, Rolls Royce contemplated shifting the production of a new type of jet engine to Derby and winding down its Scottish operations. In the end, an American offshore procurement contract for Hunter jet fighters secured the continued production at the East Kilbride factory.[59] Given the continued problems, Rolls Royce applied to site part of its Scottish production facilities to Ashford in Kent, but the government turned the application down in October 1955.[60] The example of the Rolls Royce factories in Scotland demonstrates the ambivalent relationship between defence contractors, defence procurement agencies and other government departments. Creating additional aero-engine capacity in Scotland disrupted the efforts of the Board of Trade to attract American inward investment to Scotland. Rearmament empowered defence contractors to lobby for preferential access to economic resources and the location of new factories. The danger of such private bargaining between government departments and defence firms is that it might prevent the emergence of regional business networks and therefore hamper local economic development in the longer term.[61] Without the co-operation of Rolls Royce, the Ministry of Supply would not be able to meet the production targets for jet engines. Therefore, Rolls Royce effectively chose the location of their new factory against the opposition of a number of government departments. However, the defence programme arguably induced an over-expansion of jet engine capacity. Without American offshore procurement contracts for British jet fighters, Rolls Royce would have relocated its jet engine production south of the Scottish border just a year after the official opening of the East Kilbride plant.

Korean rearmament undermined the remnants of the government's regional development policy. Employment creation remained the major concern of the regional offices of the Board of Trade. Without the co-operation of the Ministry of Supply and the defence industry, the Board of Trade failed in its endeavour to attract a defence contractor to locate in Aberdeen.[62] At the same time, the Board of Trade lacked the financial resources to build advance factory units as suggested by a working party of the Scottish Council

---

1953.; SRO SEP 4/14: note of a conversation between the Minister of State and Mr Craig Mitchell, Mr Crow on 28 October 1953, 31 October 1953.

59 SRO SEP 10/16: "Industry, Employment and Economic Well-Being", brief for Estimates Debate, 14-15 July, 1953, 14 July 1953. Offshore procurement contracts are discussed in more detail in chapter 8.

60 SEP 4/14: note of a conversation between the Minister of State and Mr Craig Mitchell, Mr Crow on 28 October 1953.; SRO SEP 4/14: excerpt from minutes EPC (55) 9, 12 October 1955.

61 Mark Casson, *Enterprise and Leadership: Studies on firms, markets and networks* (Cheltenham: Edward Elgar, 2000), 161 and 180.

62 A large electronics firm, which had shown an interest in establishing a factory in Aberdeen, decided to locate in the Midlands due to the high transport cost; see SCDI SC 2/3/1/2: EC (51) 7th, Minutes of the 7th meeting of Executive Committee, 5 November 1951.

(Development and Industry).[63] During a meeting with the chairman of the Scottish Council (Development and Industry), the Minister of Supply, Duncan Sandys, promised that Scotland would receive a fair share of all new defence-related capacity. If additional capacity were needed, Aberdeen would be borne in mind as a possible site for any new development.[64] Despite government efforts to create employment, Aberdeen and the fishing ports in North East Scotland remained areas with high structural unemployment. Some defence procurement contracts were awarded to the local textile factories and fish canneries in the area.[65]

In sharp contrast to the government's failed attempts to develop a viable defence industry in Aberdeen, the defence programme assisted the electronics programme spearheaded by Jack Toothill of Ferranti. In an attempt to assure the future of Ferranti's wartime factories in Edinburgh, Toothill secured government support for establishing four research laboratories at its Crewe Tool site near Edinburgh. After several lean years, these laboratories benefited from substantial development contracts as part of the defence programme. However, this work did not lead to any major production contracts until firm developed a new monopulse radar system for the new Lightning fighter aircraft in the late 1950s. In the meantime, Ferranti gained valuable experience producing the latest standardised IFF aircraft recognition system for NATO under a subcontract from its American manufacturer Hazeltine in 1953.[66]

After the war, Toothill proposed to the Scottish Council (Development and Industry) the establishment of a joint laboratory for collaborative research to be shared by local electronics firms in order to create an electronics industrial cluster in Scotland. In this context, Toothill stressed the importance of overcoming the view commonly held by London-based civil servants "that Scotland was too distant for such work."[67] After he joined its Executive Committee, the Scottish Council (Development and Industry) put forward a proposal to government, which received a favourable first response from the Ministry of Supply. With the prospect of defence-related development contracts in the offing, several Scottish electronics and engineering firms created their own research and design teams in order to undertake such work. In this context, the Executive Committee noted with satisfaction the progress of

[63] SCDI SC 2/7/4/1: Miscellaneous Publications: copy of *Report of the Committee on Unemployment in Aberdeen and District*1952.

[64] SCDI SC 2/3/1/2: EC (52) 3rd, Minutes of the 3rd meeting of Executive Committee, 18 April 1952.

[65] SCDI SC 2/3/1/2: EC (53) 4th, Minutes of the 4th meeting of Executive Committee, 15 June 1953.; see note 59.

[66] Wilson, *Ferranti*, 322-32. IFF refers to Identification, Friend or Foe systems which aid the recognition of friendly military aircraft, ships, etc.

[67] SCDI SC 2/3/1/1: Minutes of meeting of Executive Committee, 2 June 1947.

its Electronics Group due to the rearmament programme.[68] Under the scheme, the government financed the building of a new laboratory opposite Ferranti's Crewe Tool site. Besides its important role facilitating collaborative research, the Council hoped that the new laboratory would become a training centre for skilled workers for the nascent Scottish electronics industry.[69] In order to achieve this objective, Ferranti managers applied to the government for their apprentice school to become the local examination centre for basic engineering qualifications.[70] After the Conservative government came to power, this Ferranti-based Scottish electronics scheme was partly thrown into doubt by the demand from the Treasury for a full review of the programme. This threat was removed by the reassurances of Duncan Sandys in April 1952 and the new laboratory was opened by the Duke of Edinburgh in 1954.[71]

With the end of the defence programme, the Scottish electronics programme withered away possibly because of its close links to Ferranti and its dependence on military research and development work. The need for secrecy severely limited the potential for technological spin-off and the emergence of an effective business network in the local electronics industry. Benefiting from further defence-related development contracts, the Scottish divisions of Ferranti did remain an important defence contractor. As Wilson highlights, incoming American electronics firms benefited hugely from the presence of a skilled labour force as a result of Toothill's electronics scheme.[72] Paradoxically, Toothill opposed the plans of the Marshall aid officials to finance the manufacture of American electronic equipment under licence by Scottish firms in September 1950, because they might compete with existing firms.[73]

Despite the visionary electronics scheme and the lobbying of the Scottish Council (Development and Industry), the Scottish economy benefited only temporarily from the increased defence spending of the Korean war rearmament programme. Besides the new defence production capacity at Rolls Royce in East Kilbride and at Ferranti in Edinburgh, Scotland received only limited new defence-related investment such as the new tank factory at the Royal Ordnance Factory in Dalmuir. After initial delays, the factory started producing tanks in 1953 only to be sold to Babcock & Wilcox following the

---

68 SC 2/3/1/2: EC (51) 7th, Minutes of the 7th meeting of Executive Committee.

69 SCDI SC 2/3/1/2: EC (51) 6th, Minutes of the 6th meeting of Executive Committee, 5 October 1951.

70 Wilson, *Ferranti*, 333.

71 SCDI SC 2/3/1/2: EC (51) 8th, Minutes of the 8th meeting of Executive Committee, 14 December 1951.; SCDI SC 2/3/1/2: EC (52) 4th, Minutes of the 4th meeting of Executive Committee, 27 May 1952.; SCDI SC 2/3/1/2: EC (54) 1st, Minutes of the 1st meeting of Executive Committee, 30 March 1954.

72 Wilson, *Ferranti*, 322-4.

73 SC 2/3/1/1: EC (50) 5th, Minutes of the 5th meeting of Executive Committee.

defence cuts announced in the 1957 Defence White Paper.[74] On balance, the increased military expenditure disrupted the government's regional development strategy exacerbating local housing and skill shortages, which were only partly offset by positive initiatives like the Scottish Council's electronics scheme. Indeed, a report compiled by the Local Development Committee of the Scottish Council (Development and Industry) criticised the government for refusing to support new industrial investment outside the development areas near the main industrial centres which were more attractive to inward investment. At the same time, the report urged the government to locate a defence factory in Aberdeen or along the North East coast, which could be converted to peace production when the defence demand subsided. However, the committee saw only limited scope for the rearmament programme to contribute to the longer term development of the Scottish economy.[75]

Conclusion

Undoubtedly, some industries such as defence-related industries and the metal-working and machine tool industries initially flourished due to the defence programme. To some extent, others such as the vehicle industry benefited indirectly from the construction of defence factories close to their existing plant.[76] In contrast to these relative gains, many consumer goods industries suffered due to falling consumer demands, rising raw material prices and increased shortages caused by the defence programme. As the government reviewed the defence programme, the short-term rapid expansion of production in the defence and metal-working machine tool industries came to an abrupt end in 1953. In the metal-working machine tool industry, the rapid expansion and contraction of demand contributed to the pronounced cyclical pattern of demand for machinery.[77] Due to the unusual demand of rearmament, British metal-working machine tool manufacturers concentrated on the defence-related orders and exports to Commonwealth countries rather than promoting their products on the rapidly expanding European market for machine tools.[78] As a consequence, British machine tool producers neglected to expand their research

---

[74] *ROF News*, October 1957.

[75] Scottish Council (Development and Industry), *Report of the Committee on Local Development in Scotland* (Edinburgh: Scottish Council (Development and Industry), 1952), 34-5.

[76] Burnham, "Rearming."

[77] On the cyclical pattern, see Ministry of Technology, *Report*, 9-14.

[78] On the pattern of exports and on the importance of the European market for the success of the West German machine tool industry, see Baumgart, "Maschinenbauindustrie."; Milward, "German Foreign Trade."

and development efforts and invest in modernising their plants. While the economic impact of rearmament on the defence sector is hard to assess, defence-related demand had a negligible multiplier effect on the wider economy in this period. Taking into account the longer term effects on the economy, rearmament undermined economic development and existing regional economic strategies due to its impact on the economic structure and the composition of industrial output.

In the case of defence-related industries, the additional capacity created under the defence programme only came on line towards the tail end of rearmament. Prior to the Korean war rearmament, procurement had concentrated on research and development rather than updating production facilities in line with technological progress. As chapter 5 shows, this neglect of the production side delayed the production of jet fighters and forced the British government to procure F-86 aircraft in Canada as a short-term stop-gap. As a consequence, this inadequacy in British jet engine production capacity prompted the government to expand this segment of the industry as rapidly as possible. The rush to make good this gap quite possibly led to an over-expansion of capacity.[79] In the case of Rolls Royce, the additional capacity enabled the company to become a successful exporter of jet engines. Nevertheless, continued production at Rolls Royce plants in Scotland came under threat in the mid-1950s due to the absence of sufficient orders. Indeed, the British aircraft industry did not contract in line with demand retaining a large number of highly skilled engineers and scientists. The resulting over-commitment of a research-intensive sector potentially affected economic growth.[80] Compared to other sectors such as consumer durables, motor cars, and office machinery, the market for both military and civil aircraft grew at a rather more sedate pace.[81] Despite heavy investment in the aircraft industry, the

---

[79] Staff of the American Military Assistance Advisory Group to the United Kingdom internally voiced some doubts about the scale and time-frame of the British aero-engine programme. In particular, American advisers were concerned about the knock-on effects for aircraft production; see National Archives and Record Administration, College Park (hereafter NARA) NARA RG 469. Defense Production. Box 1. Folder AMP Projects: Despatch Stofford - ISAC with 3 enclosures, 13 February 1951.

[80] Merton J. Peck, "Science and Technology," in *Britain's Economic Prospects*, eds. Richard E. Caves and Associates (Washington: Brookings Institution, 1968). Mary Kaldor has suggested that this process has led to the mummification of British industry since the end of the nineteenth century; see Mary Kaldor, *The Baroque Arsenal* (London: Abacus, 1983), 21-36.

[81] For an exposition of this argument, see Keith Smith, *The British Economic Crisis: Its Past and Future* (Harmondsworth: Penguin, 1985), 86-94.; Chris Freeman, "Technical Innovation and British Trade Performance," in *De-industrialisation*, ed. Frank Blackaby (London: Heinemann, 1978), 70.; Mary Kaldor, "Technical Change in the Defence Industry," in *Technical Innovation and British Economic Performance*, ed. Keith Pavitt (Basingstoke: Macmillan, 1980), 118-19.; Mary Kaldor, Margaret Sharp, and William Walker, "Industrial Competitiveness and Britain's Defence," *Lloyd's Bank Review* (1986): 31-49.

industry failed to develop dynamic economies of scale. To some extent, this failure reflected the disadvantage of a fairly small domestic market and limited international competition due to the national procurement policies. In this respect, the British defence procurement policy contributed to this failure through constant revisions of the specifications of weapons systems.[82] Overall, the Korean war rearmament exposed the absence of a coherent defence procurement policy or even an industrial development strategy on the part of the government.[83] Promising regional development projects were dropped to accommodate defence contractors. To a limited extent, the Ministry of Supply placed defence contracts in regions of high structural unemployment. However, the absence of an industrial or meso-economic and micro-economic policy contributed to the haphazard nature of the Korean war defence programme.

To summarise, Korean war rearmament disrupted the evolving patterns of accumulation by disproportionately increasing the demand for metal-working machine tools. In the defence sector, the defence programme induced an over-expansion of capacity leading to an over-commitment of resources to these industries. In the absence of a clear industrial strategy, government policy certainly exacerbated the economic impact of excess demand and in all probability prejudiced the chances of long-term economic development.

---

[82] See chapter 5.

[83] On the Attlee governments' efforts to modernise the British economy and their shortcomings, see Jim Tomlinson, "Mr. Attlee's supply-side socialism," *Economic History Review* 46 (1993): 1-22.

Conclusion

Britain and the economic problem of the first cold war: Reconsidering the political economy and economic impact of British defence expenditure, 1945–55

The nine case studies in this book examined different facets of the British defence effort during the first cold war. Most of these case studies used a previous interpretation of a particular aspect as their point of departure. The case studies then proceeded to re-examine the existing interpretation in light of the documentary evidence. This use of existing narratives to interrogate the past revealed that some previous studies attributed too much significance to certain decisions and thereby exaggerated their influence on British defence and foreign policy or their impact on post-war British economic development.

In the historical literature, two implied counterfactual assumptions predominate. First, some accounts argue that if the Attlee governments had pursued a different socialist foreign policy, then the cold war confrontation between the super-powers could have been prevented. The second cluster of studies suggests that if the second Attlee government had resisted American pressure more vigorously, then the Korean war rearmament programme would not have undermined the economic recovery boom. Both sets of analysis imply that alternative policy choices would have reduced the economic burden of the British defence effort in this period. As the case studies show, these accounts focus narrowly on these two key moments and therefore overlook the importance of previous decisions taken by other decision-makers. Moreover, these accounts conceive the state as a unitary actor rather than a complex set of different bureaucracies partly pursuing their departmental interests. In addition to these two dominant claims, a third explanation attributes slow economic growth to the fact that the British government spent more on defence than other European countries. These accounts imply either that British defence spending was excessive or that other countries failed to contribute their fair share of the Western defence burden. All three interpretations suggest the strong possibility of an alternative history without discussing the likelihood of such an outcome. As a consequence, previous authors frequently construct causal links supporting their argument, but these are difficult to substantiate with documentary or empirical evidence as the case studies show.[1] The first three sections of this concluding chapter will review the findings on the three counterfactual propositions. This brief review of the case studies reveals that the implicit assumptions of previous accounts in studies to date tend to exaggerate the potential for an alternative course of events.[2]

At the same time, the eclectic approach of this book has three limitations, because it confines itself to the re-examination of claims that the relatively high British defence expenditure contributed to relatively slow economic growth in this period. Firstly, the approach does not consider alternative arguments about the impact of the defence effort. Secondly, the foci of the case studies reflect the concerns of the original studies they analyse. And thirdly, the case studies raise a number of questions about the British defence effort, which are not further investigated here. The fourth section of this conclusion will examine these limitations, but argue that this approach is nevertheless justifiable in a study which aims to disentangle demonstrable historical fact from narrative emplotment in the declinist literature.

Despite these shortcomings, the case studies do provide the basis for a more complete and realistic assessment of the economic impact of the British defence effort. Taken together, the nine case studies reveal the contours of a new interpretation. The final section of this concluding chapter will draw on the findings of these nine studies to provide a more complex analysis of the economic impact of the British defence effort in this period.

1945: End of one war, beginning of the next?

This book has re-examined various suggestions of policy failure levied against British post-war governments in the literature. To some extent, the previous explanations have become so deeply embedded in British contemporary consciousness that their central proposition – excessive defence expenditure contributed to the relative British economic decline – is now widely accepted

---

[1] These problems are often associated with the use of counterfactual reasoning, see Peter D. McClelland, *Causal Explanation and Model Building in History, Economics and the New Economic History* (Ithaca: Cornell University Press, 1975), 146-68. For this reason, many historians are opposed to their use in historical writing.

[2] This is often the outcome of debates around counterfactual propositions. An example is the recent debate in German history on whether the rise of Hitler could have been prevented, if Chancellor Brüning had pursued Keynesian economic policies and reflated the German economy during the Great Depression or after the German banking crisis of 1931. On this point, see Niall Ferguson, "Introduction - Virtual History: Towards a 'chaotic' theory of the past," in *Virtual History: Alternatives and Counterfactuals*, ed. Niall Ferguson (London: Picador, 1997), 18.

without further questioning. Therefore, the case studies in this book have focused on the key moments and key aspects identified in previous studies. For many authors, the end of the Second World War in Europe represents one of these key moments when alternative policy choices could have prevented the calamity of slow economic growth.

While implying policy failure, previous studies normally fail to state under which conditions their implied alternative policy would have been adopted. Nevertheless, the literature is full of suggestions, as to how the cold war could have been avoided. One favoured suggestion seems to be that the cold war could have been prevented through a more conciliatory approach to the Soviet Union in the immediate post-war period.[3] In the British context, this speculative assumption has led to the suggestion that the appointment of a different Foreign Secretary, pursuing a "socialist foreign policy", would have averted the cold war. This speculation raises the question whether the Soviet leadership would have responded favourably to such overtures from the West. In a recent collection of essays, Niall Ferguson and his collaborators suggest that such a counterfactual can be investigated by openly examining the likelihood of such alternative histories.[4] For this collection, Jonathan Haslam analyses a slightly different proposition namely: under which conditions the cold war might not have occurred. Haslam investigates three different propositions raised in the literature on the origins of the cold war: firstly, what if the Americans had not had the atomic bomb; secondly, what if Soviet intelligence had not infiltrated western policy-making communities; and thirdly, what if Soviet Union had established a sphere of influence in Eastern Europe rather than imposing state socialism on these countries.[5] However, Haslam concludes that the Soviet leadership would have been unlikely to act differently, even if any of these three counterfactuals had come to pass. To some extent, he dismisses the importance of these factors by arguing that the

---

[3] Indeed, the revisionist school of thought on the origins of the cold war has argued that American universalism and expansionism were to blame for the emergence of the cold war; see for example William Appleman Williams, *The Tragedy of American Diplomacy* (New York: Delta Books, 1962).; and Joyce Kolko and Gabriel Kolko, *The Limits of Power: The World and United States Foreign Policy, 1945-1954* (New York: Harper and Row, 1972).

[4] See Niall Ferguson, ed., *Virtual History: Alternatives and Counterfactuals* (London: Picador, 1997). On the difference between Ferguson's approach and the one adopted in this book, see Introduction, 10–12.

[5] Jonathan Haslam, "Stalin's War and Peace: What if the Cold War had been Avoided?," in *Virtual History: Alternatives and Counterfactuals*, ed. Niall Ferguson (London: Picador, 1997), 348-67. Despite Ferguson's argument that counterfactuals should be based on historical and documented prognostication, Haslam resorts to using counterfactual propositions raised in the literature on the origins of the cold war. To some extent, this approach reflects the limited availability of Soviet records for this period (348-52). Moreover, he seems to share most of the reservations about such pure counterfactual speculation (348-9) discussed in the introduction. In this sense, Haslam's approach is in principle similar to the one adopted in this book on the question of the economic impact of British defence expenditure in this period.

Soviet leadership perceived the West as antagonistic to state socialism for ideological reasons.[6] Haslam's analysis highlights the fact that historical actors are often influenced by their own interpretation of contemporary history. Besides these perceptions drawn from experience, policy decisions are to some extent informed by expectations or aspirations for the future in situations of extreme uncertainty.[7] Therefore, perceptions of historical developments or dominant stories about the immediate past constrain the contingency of the historical situation.[8]

It is hard to imagine how else a historical actor would reach a policy decision in a situation of extreme uncertainty and therefore limited knowledge about the future. In these situations, the stories of past success or failure provide an indication of how to face the future. Therefore, ideology arguably offers clear guidance to policy-makers, because it induces the belief of having history on one's side. In this sense, Niall Ferguson may well be right when he suggests that determinist models of the past made military conflicts such as the cold war more likely.[9] But it does not follow that more open models of social development would ensure better policy decisions. Moreover, Haslam's analysis and Ferguson's statement are blind to the possibility that western observers might have been equally biased in their perceptions of Soviet foreign policy. Indeed, many contemporary western observers perceived the cold war as an ideological conflict between Soviet totalitarianism and western democracy. For example, Chester Wilmot reflected this sentiment in his acclaimed history of the Second World War published in 1951. Wilmot argued that the Soviet Union had been the real victor of the Second World War, because it had been able to extend its western border into central Europe. Indeed, he argues that this outcome could have been prevented, if the Americans had accepted Churchill's suggestion of attacking the German forces in Greece and the Balkans rather than attempting a cross-Channel invasion of northern France. Having misread Soviet intentions during the Second World War, Wilmot argued that the Americans were in the immediate post-war period paying for their mistake by having to rearm and maintain a global military presence. However, he wondered whether the Truman administration would have been less willing to offer economic and military aid to its European allies on such a massive scale if American policy-makers had not belatedly perceived their wartime policy towards the Soviet Union as a mistake.[10] In a sense,

---

[6] Haslam, "Stalin's war," 366-7.

[7] See chapter 1.

[8] On this point, see Edward P. Thompson, *The Poverty of Theory: or an orrery of errors* (London: Merlin Press, 1978), 18-68.

[9] Ferguson, "Introduction," 88-9.

[10] Chester Wilmot, *The Struggle for Europe* (originally published in 1951), (Ware: Wordsworth Editions, 1997), 715-17. In his introduction to the 1963 edition, Michael Howard suggested that if Wilmot had lived, he might have reconsidered his assessment of the Soviet

Wilmot's argument not only illustrates, how the contemporary perception of recent historical events might shape policy, but also how the supposed lessons of the past are emplotted into the writing of history. Given his argument, Wilmot traced the beginning of the cold war to the decision to prioritise the military preparations for a cross-Channel invasion in 1943.[11]

Using this model of decision-making under extreme uncertainty, chapter 1 shows that the particular British response to the problem of post-war defence was largely shaped by the experiences of the Second World War. Having come close to defeat in 1940, policy-makers were determined to improve the military capabilities of a post-war British state. For example, contemporary historians argued that the success in the Battle of Britain confirmed the wisdom of decisions to build up air power at the end of the previous war.[12] At the same time, many of the reforms tried to correct perceived weaknesses regarding weapons development and defence procurement, which became apparent during wartime mobilisation. Arguably, wartime experience prevented a critical appraisal of the defence equation which would have taken into account Britain's overall military and economic potential, the absolute minimal requirements for national security, the likely military threats, the potential for an international security arrangement, and the development of military technology. Several factors contributed to the failure to undertake a thorough review of British defence policy. Indeed, British policy-makers started to reform the British defence organisation to meet the challenges of the post-war period. Arguably, these reforms did not go far enough in centralising decision-making. Despite coming under the aegis of the newly created Ministry of Supply, individual services still exercised effective control over procurement decisions as the example of tank procurement in chapter 1 shows. One might speculate about the reason for Labour ministers' reticence to push reforms further. However, a key consideration must have been the opposition of British military leaders. Nevertheless, these reforms started the gradual centralisation of Britain's defence organisation.[13]

Arguably, the government faced more urgent problems than the reorganisation of the Britain's defence establishment such as the transition from war to peace. Nevertheless, politicians occasionally questioned the advice given by their foreign policy and military advisers. For example, Prime Minister Clement Attlee raised the question as to whether many of Britain's

---

contribution to the Allied victory; see "Introduction (originally published in 1963)," reprinted in *The Struggle for Europe* (1997). On Wilmot's book, see also John Keegan, *The Battle for History: Re-Fighting World War Two* (London: Hutchinson, 1995), 34-8.

[11] Wilmot, *Struggle*, 707-15.

[12] Wilmot, *Struggle*, 54-5.

[13] On this point, see also Adrian Smith, "Command and Control in Postwar Britain: Defence decision-making in the United Kingdom, 1945-1984," *Twentieth Century British History* 2 (1991): 299-309.

overseas bases were necessary in 1946, but the Foreign Secretary Ernest Bevin successfully pleaded the case of the military leadership for maintaining a military presence in the Mediterranean. After these initial battles, Attlee and successive chancellors tried to reduce the defence budget rather than to challenge individual military commitments. However, this focus on the overall budget meant that ministers never questioned the appropriateness of defence procurement policy in this period. As a consequence, the service departments enjoyed considerable latitude to implement their wartime plans for the post-war defence procurement strategy. This strategy implicitly rested on the assumption that a future global war would necessitate the total mobilisation of the economy as it had during the Second World War. To maintain this capability, the supply department regarded the existence of a large number of defence firms as instrumental. At the same time, the service departments severely pruned the military procurement budgets to maintain a global military presence. As a consequence of these cuts, large sections of the British defence industry remained under-employed in the post-war period. Some defence firms received repair and development contracts solely to maintain their military production capacity. Before the outbreak of the Korean war, the services lacked the funds to acquire new weaponry in significant quantities. As chapter 4 shows, the supply departments started on the eve of the Korean war to think about reducing the number of defence firms eligible to compete for development and procurement contracts. The requirements of rearmament delayed these attempts to merge defence production capacity until the late 1950s.

Moreover, chapter 1 shows that British policy-makers realised that as a consequence of the war the ability of the British economy to sustain another global war had been reduced significantly. Some simple economic comparisons illustrate this growing vulnerability. While British national income amounted to roughly 62 per cent of the national income of the United States in 1938, it had fallen to just over 41 per cent of the American national income in 1948. The reason for this deterioration is largely accounted for by the rapid expansion of the American economy during the Second World War from $29.03 billion in 1938 to $47.74 billion in 1948 at 1938 U.S. prices.[14] It is more difficult to find contemporary figures for the Soviet Union, which are comparable to western European estimates. In a paper published in 1951, the RAND analyst, Joseph Kershaw, estimated that Soviet GNP was roughly 40 per cent of the American Gross National Product (GNP) in 1950.[15] Therefore, Soviet national income

---

[14] The national income figures are taken and the percentage figures calculated from United Nations. Economic Commission for Europe. Research and Planning Division, *Economic Survey of Europe in 1948* (Geneva: United Nations. Department of Economic Affairs, 1949), 235, Table E.

[15] Joseph A. Kershaw, "The Economic War Potential of the U.S.S.R.," *American Economic Review* 41 (1951): 477-8. Kershaw's projection was based on projecting forward Baran's tentative calculation estimating that Soviet gross national product amounted to roughly

Table C.1

Mobilisation for the Cold War

Percentage of Gross Available Resources Allocated to Investment, National Defence, and Economic Mobilisation for the Cold War in the Soviet Union, the United States and the United Kingdom, 1948 and 1949

	1948			1949		
	Gross Investment	Defence	Cold War Mobilisation	Gross Investment	Defence	Cold War Mobilisation
Soviet Union	26.0	11.3	37.3	25.4	13.8	39.2
United States	19.3	6.0[a]	25.3	13.6	6.5[a]	20.1
United Kingdom	14.3	7.3	21.6	14.7	7.2	21.9

Notes: [a] includes foreign economic and military aid.

Source: Soviet Union and United States: *1948*: Abram Bergson and Hans Heymann, Jr., *Soviet National Income and Product, 1940–48* (New York: Columbia University Press, 1954), 107.; *1949*: "NSC 68: United States Objectives and Programs for National Security", 14 April 1950; reprinted in Thomas H. Etzold and John Lewis Gaddis, *Containment: Documents on American Policy and Strategy, 1945-1950* (New York: Columbia University Press, 1978), 405.; United Kingdom: Table 7.1.

probably just matched British national income in 1948, putting the country in a position similar to that of Germany relative to the Soviet Union prior to the Second World War.[16] Despite this parity in economic production, Britain was arguably more vulnerable than the Soviet Union for a number of reasons. If one adopts the American approach of measuring the mobilisation for cold war by adding investment and defence effort, then this vulnerability becomes even more apparent (see Table C.1). The British economy could not match the rate of mobilisation for the cold war by the other superpowers in both relative or absolute terms. However, these figures probably underestimate the extent of British vulnerability. To arrive at a more accurate picture, several other factors

$44.43 billion in 1940 dollars. Baran derived his estimate from a Russian national income estimate of $31.10 billion; see Paul A. Baran, "National Income and Product of the U.S.S.R. in 1948," *Review of Economic Statistics* 29 (1947): 230-31. An earlier estimate by Julius Wyler put the Soviet net national income in 1940 slightly higher at $45.1 billion; see Julius Wyler, "The national income of Soviet Russia," *Social Research* 13 (1946): 515-18.

[16] Maurice Dobb argued that on the eve of the Second World War, Soviet national income was slightly larger than that of Germany, but significantly less than that of Germany and all occupied countries combined; see Maurice Dobb, *Soviet Economic Development since 1917* (London: Routledge and Kegan, 1947), 294-5.

need to be taken into consideration. First, recent estimates suggest that the British war economy produced roughly $11 billion of munitions compared to $16 billion in the Soviet Union and $42 billion in the United States during the Second World War.[17] Second, American analysts argued at the time that the purchasing power of Soviet defence expenditure was much higher and therefore Soviet defence expenditure almost matched the American outlay on national security.[18] Thirdly, the Soviet Union and the United States were not similarly hampered by the burden of a large national debt.[19] Contemporary British estimates argued that the war potential of the British economy had fallen to 37 per cent of its GNP or by more than 10 per cent over its wartime peak.[20] In contrast to this decline in the national war potential, western analysts believed that the Soviet Union and the United States could probably mobilise up to 60 per cent of their national output in another global war.[21] Measured against the estimated maximum rates of mobilisation, Britain spent almost 20 per cent of its war potential on defence in 1948, more than either of the other superpowers. While the Soviet Union spent a similar proportion on defence (19 per cent of its estimated war potential), the United States spent only 7.1 per cent or 10 per cent if one takes foreign assistance into account.[22] However, this higher degree of mobilisation also entailed relatively higher opportunity cost for the British economy in terms of man-years of industrial labour.[23] Moreover, a fourth factor needs to be taken into account. In contrast to Britain, the Soviet Union was able to extract additional resources from the countries in Eastern Europe and its zone of occupation in Germany. The reparations from eastern Germany alone probably added an additional 10 per cent to the Soviet national income in the period 1945-47.[24] For Britain, its zone of occupation became an additional drain on resources in the immediate post-war period. At the same time, the existence of the Sterling Area allowed the British government to increase its international borrowing from its dependent areas. Arguably, this

---

17 The figures are in 1944 U.S. munitions prices and taken from Mark Harrison, "Resource Mobilisation for World War II: the U.S.A., U.K., U.S.S.R. and Germany, 1939-1945," *Economic History Review* 41 (1988): 172. Table 1.

18 Edward Ames, "The Economy of the Soviet Union: Discussion," *American Economic Review* 41 (1951): 489-93.; Abram Bergson and Hans Heymann, Jr., *Soviet National Income and Product, 1940-48* (New York: Columbia University Press, 1954), 103-5.

19 Britain's national debt amounted to £23,774 million in 1945 or roughly 2.7 times the GDP at the time. While debt continued to increase to £25,989 million in 1950, the debt/GDP ratio fell to 2.28; see N. F. R. Crafts, "Adjusting from War to Peace in 1940s Britain," *Economic and Social Review* 25 (1993): 4, Table 1.

20 R. C. Tress, "Defence and Public Finance," *London and Cambridge Economic Service* 27 (1949): 2-6.

21 Kershaw, "Economic war potential," 477.

22 Calculated from Table C.1.

23 See chapter 8, 253-6 and 253, Table 8.3.

24 On this point, see Alec Cairncross, *The Price of War: British policy on German reparations, 1941–1949* (Oxford: Basil Blackwell, 1986), 207-18.

ability to borrow came at the price of maintaining a military presence in distant places. The large sterling balances held by independent countries remained a constant headache for British policy-makers in this period. To solve its urgent balance of payments problem, Britain required additional financial assistance from the United States to maintain its military presence overseas, and prevent a collapse of the sterling area and finance imports from the dollar area.[25] Arguably, Britain therefore depended on American financial assistance to recover its war potential. To some extent, the American government bailed out the British government, because in the event of military confrontation between the superpowers, American strategic bombers required British bases in Britain and the Middle East to launch an attack on the Soviet Union. The experience of the Second World War demonstrated the vital importance of keeping the supply routes across the Atlantic open to maintain Britain's defence effort. Arguably, the foreign policy community perceived Britain's vulnerability and attempted to maintain Britain's status as a great power. The success of this strategy depended on the continued existence of the Empire, because without its colonies and the Commonwealth Britain increasingly looked like a declining power.

Chapter 1 shows that the higher postwar level of British defence expenditure reflected more the lessons of the Second World War than the projections of the future of warfare. In many ways, British defence planners tried to avoid the perceived mistakes of the past and therefore ruled out withdrawing from overseas bases, pruning the defence expenditure and postponing the procurement of new weapons. Policy-makers realised that the reduction in Britain's war potential made the country more vulnerable necessitating higher defence expenditure. To reduce Britain's military vulnerability, policy-makers argued for maintaining the domestic defence production base to prevent the armed forces being as unprepared for the next war as they were for the last one. By diverting resources from reconstruction, this policy potentially increased Britain's vulnerability. Moreover, British defence policy did not fully take into account the likely implications of the advent of nuclear weapons or the potential of missile technology. At the same time, there is some evidence that British defence expenditure helped to stabilise the economy during the transition from war to peace and encouraged investment and economic growth during the late 1940s.[26] However, it would be unfair to suggest that policy-makers could necessarily have done better given the high degree of uncertainty about the potential strength of the Soviet Union or the likely development of military technology. While far from flawless, British defence policy of this

---

[25] Thomas Balogh, "The International Aspect," in *The British Economy, 1945-1950*, eds. G. D. N. Worswick and P. H. Ady (Oxford: Oxford University Press, 1952), 476-510.

[26] See chapter 7.

period in the main addressed the security concerns as perceived by policy-makers at the time and can therefore hardly be faulted.

Nevertheless, this rather positive assessment might be rejected by those who believe that policy-makers should have realised the decline of British power and acted accordingly by prioritising economic reconstruction.[27] Those historians who believe in the power of counterfactual reasoning might be disappointed that this interpretation was not tested against counterfactual outcomes. However, it seems unlikely that an alternative post-war British government would have spent less on defence, given the relative importance of the wartime experience during the process of policy formulation. For example, most decisions regarding post-war British defence procurement policy were already taken during the Second World War. Therefore, it seems unlikely that if Churchill had won the 1945 General Election his Conservative government would have spent less on defence at least initially. Moreover, Churchill became a vociferous critic of the Attlee governments' foreign policy constantly suggesting that the government was not taking the Soviet threat seriously enough. Having declared that he would not preside over the dissolution of the Empire, he probably would have resisted demands for Indian independence in the immediate post-war period. Nevertheless, he might have been able to resist some demands of the armed forces given his prestige as wartime leader. In addition to this, after he returned to power, Churchill became instrumental in reducing the Korean war defence programme to a manageable scale. If Churchill had appointed Duncan Sandys as Minister of Supply, he might have pressed for the development of missile technology.[28] Alternatively, if the American government had honoured its wartime agreements and shared the information about the atomic bomb with British scientists, British defence planners might have adjusted their views about their weapons requirements earlier. The advent of nuclear warfare might have provided the opportunity to reconsider the need for preserving the nucleus of a future war economy. Given the rising costs of developing new weapons, policy-makers might have reorganised British defence industry to create a small number of firms, which could compete for the limited number of important weapons development projects. Indeed, the supply departments effectively allocated the important projects only to a number of major contractors, while maintaining a number of smaller firms to preserve their production capacity. Arguably, if Dalton had been appointed Foreign Secretary, he might have adopted a harsher policy towards Germany, which might have made an accommodation with the Soviet Union easier in the immediate post-war period. However, the Soviet leadership

[27] For example, see Correlli Barnett, *The Lost Victory: British dreams, British realities, 1945-1950* (Basingstoke: Macmillan, 1995), 7-120.

[28] On Duncan Sandys' fervent belief in missiles, see *English Electric Lightning*, prod. Prometheus Productions, (DD Video, 1993).

would still probably have regarded Britain as an imperialistic capitalist country and would not have been less antagonistic towards a more socialist Britain. On balance, there is little convincing evidence to suggest that an alternative British government would have spent less on defence, whether the cold war had occurred or not.

The Korean War and the British defence programme

In the literature, the second key policy decision, the Korean war rearmament programme, has attracted more attention than the first counterfactual proposition. While the development of post-war policy arguably reflected a fairly general consensus view among the policy-making elite, the Korean war defence programme led to a split within the Labour government, which had reverberations for the next decade. Arguably, the events triggered by the Korean war brought home to British policy-makers not only the frailty of the British economic recovery but also its weak military position. For many contemporary observers, the economic crisis in summer 1951 seemed at first glance to be directly caused by the rearmament programme. The decision of the newly elected Conservative government to scale down the defence programme reinforced this interpretation of events. Critics have interpreted the developments relating to the British rearmament programme as reducing Britain to the status of America's unsinkable aircraft carrier or the beginning of its economic decline brought about by the excessive drive to re-equip its armed forces. Several chapters examine different aspects of this interpretation. Chapter 3 concentrated on the question to what extent American pressure was responsible for the excessive nature of the British defence programme. Chapters 4 to 9 analysed the economic impact of the British rearmament programme from a number of different perspectives.

The case studies again show that the crucial policy decisions reflected previous choices and long-standing policy. Arguably, the Korean war throws a spanner in the carefully laid plans of the British government, which seemed to be bearing fruit in early 1950. As chapter 2 shows, the North Atlantic alliance agreed at its London meeting in May 1950 to create collective balanced forces and embark on a joint rearmament effort. Arguably, this decision might have allowed the Attlee government to scale down its own defence effort over the medium term. Indeed, the American government seemed for the first time willing to increase its own defence effort and to increase its military aid to its western European allies. At the same time, Whitehall started to reconsider its defence procurement policy in light of the changed requirements. Again, these reforms might have reduced the size of the defence sector and therefore freed resources for economic development. The Korean war clearly upset these plans, but the question remains did circumstances necessitate the Attlee government embarking on such a massive rearmament programme? To some extent, the debate has centred on this specific question. Policy-makers have defended the decision to rearm with reference to the considerable fears of another global war breaking out before the West had been able to build up its military strength. The critics have argued consistently that the policy-makers exaggerated this risk of another global war out all proportion. Arguably, this focus is not particularly helpful, because debate revolves around a counterfactual and in that we do not know whether a failure to rearm in 1950 would have led to a global war or indeed made it more likely.

However, if one treats the Korean war as a historical accident, then it can again be treated as a situation of decision-making under uncertainty. The case studies show that British policy-makers relied on interpretations of recent historical developments while adhering to previously formulated policy solutions for the perceived problem. In this context, the Anglo-American relationship came to be of prime importance for British policy-makers. From 1947 onwards, British policy-makers sought not only an American security guarantee to shore up Britain's relative weakness, but also a close partnership in organising western efforts in the cold war. At the same time, American policy-makers became convinced that western European countries required further economic aid to build up their military capabilities in order to resist the Soviet threat. While pursuing similar overall objectives, British and American views differed considerably over priorities and the required scale of the defence effort, which led to tensions after the outbreak of the Korean war.

Aware of their vulnerability, British foreign policy-makers devoted considerable efforts to establishing a special relationship with the American government in the immediate post-war period. The Truman administration, however, was at first reluctant to entertain such ideas still hoping to create a new international order under the aegis of the United Nations. In line with this policy, Truman opposed all contacts between American and British military planners. Nevertheless, military leaders on both sides of the Atlantic assumed that Britain and the United States would assist the other in a future global conflict. Despite some squabbles over oil concessions in the Middle East and the sharing of atomic secrets, policy-makers generally agreed on the broad policy objectives in the immediate post-war period. Under the containment doctrine, the Truman administration took over from Britain in 1947 the bankrolling of the Greek government's efforts to quell the Communist insurgency along its border with Yugoslavia and Albania. To some extent, American policy-makers hoped that the Marshall Plan would lead to the revitalisation of the western European economy. By building up economic strength, the Truman administration envisaged that western Europe would be able to resist any Communist advances. In contrast to European policy-makers, the American foreign policy-making community regarded economic recovery as more urgent than western rearmament. For this reason, American policy-makers initially rejected western European requests for military aid. After the announcement of the Marshall Plan, British policy-makers started a campaign to negotiate an American security guarantee for western Europe. These efforts eventually led to the signing of the North Atlantic Treaty changing the economics of the British defence effort. Having obtained an American security guarantee, it became less important to maintain the Empire as the basis of British military strength. Moreover, this arrangement increased Britain's military security and therefore would potentially have permitted a reduction in the national defence effort. However, the Truman administration was extremely reluctant to increase its own defence budget prior to the Korean war. After the creation of the alliance, western policy-makers tried to draw up plans for western defence and for financing rearmament. During these discussions, western European governments slightly inflated their military requirements in anticipation of receiving American military aid. For example, the British defence minister, Emmanuel Shinwell, committed the government in NATO discussions to the Medium Term Defence Plan (MTDP) entailing a £6,000 million defence programme much to the annoyance of the Chancellor, Stafford Cripps, who believed the country could not even afford a defence effort half that size. Without their finance having been secured, the Alliance's foreign ministers endorsed the MTDP at their meeting in London in May 1950. Nevertheless, British policy-makers managed at the same meeting to obtain an agreement on the establishment of collective balanced forces, which affirmed the principle of burden-sharing within the alliance and held out the promise of substantial American military aid to Britain.[29]

Following the invasion of South Korea by armed forces from the North, the United States spearheaded a United Nations intervention to repel the invasion and immediately sent American ground forces to South Korea. The British government reacted more slowly, but resolved to support the American action in the United Nations by sending some naval forces. In the month following the outbreak of the Korean war, officials hoped to attain a genuine partnership with the United States by responding positively to the American initiative in Korea as well as to its call for western rearmament. At the same time, the Truman administration adopted a more aggressive strategy for the cold war. In July 1950, the American government announced major increases in its military budget to meet a growing Soviet threat. This perception was partly based on a flawed analysis of the Soviet Union's economic war potential.[30] Having

---

29 See chapter 2.

30 Till Geiger, "Economic Growth and National Security: National income analysis, western rearmament, and cold war strategy, 1950-1952," *International History Review* (2004 forthcoming).

increased its military budget, American policy-makers exerted pressure on their western European allies to follow suit. Like other western European governments, the Attlee government proposed significant increases in its defence programme. Nevertheless, American policy-makers were disappointed by the British proposals, because American policy-makers believed that the increase fell short of the level the British economy could sustain. As a consequence, the American government rejected British requests for substantial financial aid and indeed insisted on ending Marshall aid to Britain. Over the following months, the British government increasingly found that its attempt to influence American policy over Korea and western rearmament led to increased American pressure for a further expansion of the British defence effort. Despite frequent trips to Washington, British policy-makers failed to convince American policy-makers of the seriousness of Britain's economic problems. As a consequence, British policy-makers became the victims of their own strategy. To influence the Americans, the Attlee government had to increase the rearmament programme further. However, this step increased the frictions within the government over foreign policy. At the same time, senior British politicians became concerned about the possibility that the use of atomic weapons in Korea would trigger another world war. Therefore, they argued that their ability to influence American policy-makers depended on expanding the defence effort. Together with the constant pressure, this concern about American policy led to the decision to increase the defence programme in January 1951. However, the increased £4,700 million defence programme still fell short of American expectation of what the British economy could sustain or the £6,000 million which was required under the MTDP.

From the start, Attlee and senior ministers stressed that the programme depended on the receipt of substantial amounts of American military aid. Despite British compliance with American wishes, American officials continued to argue that Britain failed to qualify for military aid, because of its growing balance of payments surpluses and currency reserves. Much to the annoyance of British policy-makers, the Truman administration continually treated Britain as just another European country rather than as a partner meriting special concessions over military aid. While the Attlee government had been able to cover up its internal disagreements, the differing views of ministers over rearmament came to the surface during the debate of the budget in April 1951. The Chancellor, Hugh Gaitskell, tried to balance the financial requirements of the defence programme against the social security budget. While he also succeeded in finding an acceptable compromise, the proposal to introduce prescription charges at some later date to curb the rising spending on the National Health Service led eventually to the resignation of Aneurin Bevan and Harold Wilson. In their respective resignation speeches, both former ministers accused the government of embarking on an unrealistically large defence programme and blamed American policy for Britain's economic woes. To some extent, their speeches established the interpretation that the unquestioned support of American policy imposed considerable additional economic costs on the British economy forcing the Labour government to abandon its socialist programme, which had always been a thorn in the side of American commentators. After the Labour Party lost the election in autumn 1951, the dispute about the Korean war rearmament programme rumbled on between various factions of the party. Arguably, the resignations fostered the myth that the decision to rearm had been forced on the Labour government by American pressure and led to its demise a year later.

After the resignations of Bevan and Wilson, Labour ministers resisted further American pressure for further increases in the British defence effort.[31] Indeed, American officials increasingly accepted that the rules governing aid distribution should be changed, if military assistance was to remain an effective policy tool.[32] The change in the British position isolated the Truman administration over further increases to western defence efforts within the alliance and led to the re-examination of the politico-economic capabilities of member states by the Temporary Council Committee (TCC).[33] As a result of this process, the Truman administration conceded a reduction in the British defence effort by phasing the rearmament programme over a longer period. The re-examination of national efforts led to Britain's receiving considerable American military aid to overcome the immediate balance of payments crisis and a large number of off-shore procurement contracts. This American aid eased the balance of payments constraint and helped the Conservative government to overcome the economic crisis. In this context, Churchill's prestige made it more difficult for American policy-makers to lean heavily on the British government. Nevertheless, the less co-operative stance adopted by Labour ministers in summer 1951 paved the way for this settlement, the benefits of which were reaped by the newly elected Conservative government. With the benefit of hindsight, this finding lends weight to the suggestion by Bevan and Wilson that the Attlee government might have been more successful in obtaining American military aid, if it had been more reluctant to rearm without firm American commitments over military aid. Moreover, if the Attlee government had soldiered on for another year, it might well have been able to reduce its defence programme with the American military aid promised by the

---

[31] See chapter 2.

[32] On these discussions, see also Till Geiger and Lorenza Sebesta, "A Self-Defeating Policy: American Offshore Procurement and Integration of Western European Defence Production, 1952-56," *Journal of European Integration History* 4 (1998): 55-9.

[33] Edwin Plowden, *An Industrialist in the Treasury: The post-war years* (London: Andre Deutsch, 1990), 125-33.; Till Geiger, "Studies in the political economy and economic impact of British defence expenditure and American military aid to Britain, 1945-1955," (Ph. D. Dissertation, University of Aberdeen, 1998), 209-15.

Americans as a result of the TCC report. Arguably, this episode shows that counterfactual reasoning was (and is) actually quite common in contemporary politics, but also illustrates how such suggestions become an element in contemporary politics and are eventually emplotted in the history of the period. On the other hand, the constant discourse of "what if", "if only" and "what might have been" marking contemporary politics also explains the reluctance of historians to indulge such counterfactual reasoning. In the end, historians can only analyse and therefore should be primarily concerned with how developments eventuated, not how they might have developed bar some historical contingency, such as for example the Korean war leading to another global war.[34]

For post-war British defence procurement policy, the Korean war became the first real test. On the one hand, the outbreak of the Korean war confirmed the wisdom of defence planners in maintaining a large domestic defence production capacity. Limited financial resources for military procurement meant that there was considerable excess capacity in the defence sector for expanding production of weapon systems currently in production. On the other hand, British defence procurement policy rested on the assumption that no global war would break out before 1955. By early 1950, western defence planners, however, became convinced that the Soviet Union might strike before the West had been able to build up its conventional capability to resist a Soviet attack in Europe or alternatively its nuclear arsenal to deter the Soviet leadership by threatening a nuclear holocaust.[35] At least initially, British defence planners seemed to regard the defence programme as a golden opportunity to increase service pay and the procurement of existing weapon systems. Due to the unexpected nature of the Korean war, British defence planners now faced the dilemma of whether to prepare for a global war breaking out in the immediate future or in several years' time. Moreover, the fighting in Korea revealed for example that even the newest types of British fighters were obsolete compared to the Soviet MIG-15 fighters deployed on the North Korean side. At the same time, British defence planners discovered that the country lacked the capacity to produce sufficient jet engines for the new generation of British jet fighters.[36] Therefore, the contingency of the Korean war forced British defence planners to make unexpected policy choices rapidly. As a consequence, the services pushed for interim procurement of F-86 fighters from Canada as well as arguing for the enlargement of the jet engine and tank

[34] Thompson, *Poverty of theory*, 64-8.

[35] Similar reasoning is employed in various RAND reports at the time, which have been recently released; see H. I. Ansoff et al., Outline of a Study for the Plans Analysis Section, RAND Report D-937 (10 May 1951 [cited 27 January 2002]); available from http://www.rand.org/publications/classics/wohlstetter/D937/D937.html.

[36] See Our Aviation Correspondent, "Aircraft and Defence," *The Times*, 18 August 1950.; and the analysis in chapter 4.

production capacity. As the analyses in chapters 1 and 4 document, the construction of new tank factories was not absolutely necessary, but reflected the original post-war plans which the supply departments had drawn up during the war. These two instances illustrate the fact that Treasury officials found it hard to block expenditure on items the economic planners did not regard as essential. Given the additional pressure from the American government, the service departments tended to win their battles with Treasury officials over the defence programme. For example, the Treasury could not prevent the construction of new defence plants in areas with extreme labour shortages. At the same time, the government persuaded a number of defence contractors to set up their new facilities in Scotland helping to reduce unemployment in certain depressed areas. In one case, such investment occurred at the expense of some inward investment by a large American firm. Despite contributing to regional development, the defence programme increased excess demand for labour and materials in the economy leading to regional shortages of skilled labour. Moreover, the enlargement of defence production capacity required a large number of new machine tools, which exceeded the existing capacity in the domestic machine tool industry. This sudden surge in demand crowded out civil and export demand for machine tools, but also damaged the long-term prospects of the machine tool industry. While not unequivocal, the empirical evidence suggests that the excess demand for machine tools potentially shifted the British economy onto a lower growth path.[37] However, the question arises whether the supply departments did not over-order new machinery to cope with the eventuality of another world war breaking out. Despite some revealed shortcomings, the war potential policy continued to guide the policy choices of the supply department in response to the immediate crisis of the Korean war.

The economic management of the rearmament programme reflected lessons from the Second World War and the heated debate over the merits and failings of economic planning in the late 1940s. At the time, most British economists agreed that while unavoidable during war, government should not attempt to direct production through direct intervention and controls in peace.[38] Given this consensus among economists, it is hardly surprising that British economic policy-makers preferred to rely on the market mechanism and "soft interventions" to steer the economy. For example, the Ministry of Supply tried to influence industry through moral persuasion to give priority to defence contractors in allocating vital materials and machine tools rather than re-introducing controls. At the same time, the British government urged industry

[37] See chapters 4, 7 and 9.

[38] On this debate, see Lionel Robbins, *The Economic Problem in Peace and War* (London: Macmillan, 1947).; James Edward Meade, *Planning and the Price Mechanism: The liberal-socialist solution* (London: George Allen and Unwin, 1948).; W. Arthur Lewis, *The Principles of Economic Planning* (London: George Allen and Unwin, 1948).

to restrain from panic-buying raw materials abroad in the hope that an international agreement for their allocation could be negotiated with the Truman administration. If such an agreement had been reached, it would undoubtedly have benefited the British economy. In its absence, the British economy faced having to restock its stockpiles of vital raw materials at highly inflated prices in spring 1951. From the start, British economic advisers had been concerned about the implications of the defence programme for the balance of payments and tried to minimise the effects. At the same time, the chief economic adviser, Robert Hall, counselled to start stockpiling raw materials immediately in the summer 1950. As the counterfactual in chapter 9 shows, if this advice had been followed, the balance of payments crisis would have occurred earlier thus making Britain eligible for American aid. Nevertheless, it seems by no means certain that Britain would have received such assistance as long as American remained convinced that the British economy could sustain a larger defence effort.

Besides soft interventions, the government primarily relied on macroeconomic policy measures to steer the economy. In autumn 1950, the newly appointed Chancellor, Hugh Gaitskell, decided to allow prices to rise, but attempted to compensate the income effects through increasing pension payments in his budget in April 1951. The increase in living costs led to demands for higher wages by the unions thereby undermining the government's incomes policy. Nevertheless, Gaitskell decided not to increase taxation massively, opting instead for a degree of continued inflation. At the same time, he announced the abolition of initial allowances for industrial investment from 1 April 1952. Andrew Shonfield has suggested that this measure led to a fall in investment causing a slow-down in British economic growth. However, investment started to fall before this measure took effect suggesting that industrialists postponed new investment, because of the looming economic crisis and the uncertainty about future economic development. Despite being much maligned, the case studies found little evidence that the Labour government's macroeconomic policies actually deepened the economic crisis. By not prioritising defence through overt controls, Labour ministers allowed the market mechanism to re-allocate resources. In contrast to this non-interventionist approach, chapter 4 suggested that the Conservative government inflicted substantial damage through the hitherto largely ignored super-priority scheme, which authorised defence contractors to requisition essential materials like steel.

Chapter 8 also examined another suggestion put forward by Andrew Shonfield that the Attlee government failed to take up the American offer of generous military aid and preferred to expand domestic armaments production. As already pointed out above, American officials not only rejected the British request for military aid and pressed for an early end to Marshall aid, but also leaned on their British counterparts to increase the defence programme. Despite constant pleading by British officials, America continued to argue that Britain did not qualify for American aid until summer 1951 when the economic crisis threatened to undermine the defence programme. Even then the American officials postponed a decision on military aid to Britain until after the completion of the TCC report. From 1952 onwards, the British government received substantial American financial aid. In addition, the American government placed large orders for military equipment in Britain for use by the British or other European armed forces. Arguably, these off-shore procurement contracts essentially facilitated a continuation of the war potential procurement strategy and therefore postponed a radical reappraisal of British defence strategy until 1957. When this source of American dollars dried up in the late 1950s, the British government decided to prune its weapons development programmes and rationalise its domestic defence industry. Therefore, this study found little evidence that British ministers were reluctant to accept American military aid in order to pursue an autarkic defence procurement policy. In contrast to Shonfield's insinuation, the British government won a major share of American off-shore orders due to its highly developed defence production base.

On balance, the case studies suggest that short of abandoning its previous foreign and security policy, the Attlee government had to respond to the historical contingency of the Korean war. Indeed, many British policy-makers saw this conflict as a golden opportunity to achieve their primary objective of a close partnership in security matters with the United States. In this context, the defence programme and most of the government's economic policies followed an established pattern. However, the supply department may have over-expanded defence production capacity, because officials rightly perceived that the defence sector needed to be re-equipped for the production of new advanced jet fighters in particular. Chapters 3, 8 and 9 revealed severe supply constraints such as the labour, material and machine tool shortages, which hampered the rapid adjustment of the British economy to the rearmament programme and were to some extent beyond the control of the government. Nevertheless, the handling of the defence programme arguably revealed some shortcomings in the government's decision-making structures, which prevented the thorough scrutiny of some aspects of the defence programme. During their stewardship of the defence programme, Labour ministers seemed to reach uneasy compromises in their attempt to balance the needs of the defence programme, to please the Americans and to prevent a split in the government. Given the potential pitfalls facing them, they managed remarkably well.

Limitations of the approach

The eclectic approach of this book has shed new light on specific aspects of the British defence effort during the period of the first cold war. As already stated at the beginning of this concluding chapter, this approach is overly concerned with the declinist interpretations of the economic impact of British defence expenditure. Therefore, the approach does not consider alternative theories and it studies predominantly established points of view. The pursuit of the new ones it raises falls largely outside the scope of the present study. The following section will briefly consider these three limitations.

As far as the first limitation is concerned, the book should possibly have considered the alternative theoretical argument that high defence expenditures promote wealth creation.[39] The empirical evidence presented in chapter 7 suggests that the British defence budget helped to stabilise economic demand in the late 1940s thus contributing to the speedy economic recovery in the immediate post-war period.[40] Moreover, the book does not extend to exploring whether large defence budgets are a precondition for the stability of capitalist societies in the post-war world.[41] While some Marxist analysts put forward

---

[39] Paul Kennedy has argued that Britain benefited from its military strength in accumulating wealth in the period 1660-1885. However, he argues that economic prosperity is more likely to translate into military power than military power to lead to greater prosperity; see Paul Kennedy, *The Rise and Fall of Great Powers: Economic change and military conflict from 1500 to 2000* (London: Fontana, 1989), 94-248. It is hard to find contemporary statements which support the notion that defence expenditure fosters economic growth. This may reflect the fact that economic growth was not yet a dominant concern of the economic policy-making community; see Jim Tomlinson, *British Macroeconomic Policy since 1940* (London: Croom Helm, 1985), 82-6. More typical was the argument put forward by Tony Crosland at the time that the Second World War had accelerated structural change in the British economy and therefore positively influenced post-war economic development; see C. A. R. Crosland, *Britain's Economic Problem* (London: Jonathan Cape, 1953), 14-22. However, the current consensus among economists is that defence expenditure is more likely to hamper economic growth than augment it; see Todd Sandler and Keith Hartley, *The Economics of Defense* (Cambridge: Cambridge University Press, 1995), 200-20. See also the discussion in the next section below.

[40] However, such additional demand may have been less important than the increased consumer demand; see Dudley Seers, "National Income, Production and Consumption," in *The British Economy, 1945-1950*, eds. G. D. N. Worswick and P. H. Ady (Oxford: Oxford University Press, 1952), 46. As Alan Milward has pointed out, the war effort created substantial consumer spending power, which became the major driving force of the post-war boom; see Alan S. Milward, *The Economic Effects of the Two World Wars on Britain*, 2nd ed. (Basingstoke: Macmillan, 1987), 16.

[41] This suggestion made principally by Marxist theorists is mainly rejected by western authors, who argue that policy-making communities in both East and West are interested in the continuation of the cold war arms race for different reasons; see John Kenneth Galbraith, *The New Industrial State*, 2nd. ed. (Harmondsworth: Penguin, 1972), 323-38.; François Perroux, *La coexistence pacifique* (Grenoble: Presses Universitaires de Grenobles,

similar positions in the early 1950s,[42] not even leftist historians have argued along similar lines more recently.[43] John Saville, for example, discusses the evolution of post-war British foreign policy exclusively in terms of Britain's relative decline.[44] Even authors who reject the declinist interpretation are primarily concerned with refuting these accounts without advancing the counter-argument that defence expenditure contributed to wealth creation.[45] Therefore, the focus on the declinist hypothesis seems on balance to be warranted.

The second limitation potentially has more far-reaching implications. To some extent, the concerns about Britain's economic decline have focused on the low British investment rate relative to other countries. As Jim Tomlinson has shown, these concerns emerged in the late 1950s at the same time as the government became increasingly worried about the economic impact of British defence expenditure.[46] This emphasis on investment reflected contemporary Keynesian economic growth theories, which aimed to balance labour supply and investment in order to achieve steady growth with full employment. These theories confined themselves essentially to two factors of production, labour and capital, assuming away other factors like technology, education or institutional factors.[47] Arguably, the historical contiguity of dominant economic thought and growing concern about the economic development in Britain is reflected in Andrew Shonfield's critique of British economic policy

---

1992), 437-40.; and Charles E. Lindblom, *Politics and Markets: the world's political economic systems* (New York: Basic Books, 1978), 184n.

42 These studies argue that monopoly capitalism supports high defence expenditure, because military production increases the profits of the large monopoly concerns; see for example John Eaton, *Economics of Peace and War: An analysis of Britain's Economic Problems* (London: Lawrence and Wishart, 1952).; and Sam Aaronovitch, *Monopoly: A Study of British Monopoly Capitalism* (London: Lawrence and Wishart, 1955).

43 The exception to this trend is Alan Milward, who argues that higher post-war defence expenditure may well have had a stabilising effect on the economy. However, he concedes that higher investment was a more important factor; see Alan S. Milward, *The Reconstruction of Western Europe, 1945-51* (London: Methuen, 1984), 490-91.

44 John Saville, *The Politics of Continuity: British foreign policy and the Labour government, 1945-46* (London: Verso, 1993).

45 For example, David Edgerton has argued that British governments used defence expenditure to promote economic and technological development. However, he concedes that the spin-offs of military technology were rather limited; see David Edgerton, *England and the Aeroplane: An Essay on a Militant and Technological Nation* (Basingstoke: Macmillan, 1991), 83-105.; David Edgerton, "Liberal Militarism and the British State," *New Left Review* 185 (1991): 138-69.

46 On the point regarding investment, see Jim Tomlinson, "Inventing 'decline': the falling behind of the British economy in the postwar years," *Economic History Review* 49 (1996): 731-57.

47 For an early critique of Keynesian growth models, see Moses Abramovitz, "Economics of Growth," in *Thinking About Growth and Other Essays On Economic Growth and Welfare* (Cambridge: Cambridge University Press, 1989), 80-124, particularly 109-10.

since the war. Despite its contextual contingency, this interpretation remained influential for later studies like Sidney Pollard's in the early 1980s. To some extent, these studies incorporated other contemporary concerns about Britain's economic position such as the balance of payments constraint, but the low investment rate remained the leitmotif of these studies. As a consequence, this book risked overemphasising the link between defence expenditure and investment. Indeed, chapters 7, 8 and 9 highlight the importance of other factors like the relative shortage of skilled labour, regional excess demand and the rise of raw material prices during the initial phase of Korean war rearmament. In this sense, a different theoretical approach might have been more productive in analysing the economic impact of British defence expenditure in this period. However, the aim of the case studies has been to re-examine the existing accounts in the light of empirical and documentary evidence, but essentially within the framework of those accounts. By using a similar theoretical framework, the case studies highlight the limitations of the original narratives, which rest on this discursive linkage between defence expenditure and investment.

As already pointed out, this book also raises some new questions about the impact of British defence procurement policy in this period. The explanation, offered in chapters 7 and 8, has relied on a dual sector model of the economy consisting of defence and non-defence industries. As chapter 4 shows, the defence sector remained under-employed in the immediate post-war period. Non-defence related production orders arguably smoothed the economic transition to a peace economy and therefore contributed to economic stability in this period. This positive contribution has to be weighed against the losses arising from the under-employment of the sector. Nevertheless, government policy fostered a degree of over-capacity in the research and development departments of defence contractors. During the initial phase of the Korean war, the government decided to expand the production capacity of the defence sector thus displacing the needs of the non-defence sector. These findings substantiate the claims that the defence sector obtained more than its share of resources and skilled workers. Therefore, the defence sector contributed to shortages and excess demand in the economy during the period of the first cold war. Compared to the economic cost, this book found little documentary evidence that the defence sector contributed to wealth creation in this period.

To some extent, this book suggests that a different defence procurement policy might have been less detrimental to the development of the British economy. This alternative history assumes that if the British government had adopted a capital-intensive defence posture in the immediate post-war period, then it would have been possible to rationalise the defence industries ten to fifteen years earlier. In this context, it would have been better if ministers had been prepared to reduce the number of key defence contractors to five for each of the services and to spend a larger proportion of the defence budget on the development of advanced weapons technology. A larger defence procurement budget, as called for by wartime planning, would have allowed a concentration of the development effort on a few key projects, while providing enough funding for limited production of new weapons to employ a smaller number of factories. Arguably, this counterfactual defence procurement policy would have led to less under-employment of the defence sector in the immediate post-war period, but would still have been sufficient to contribute to the stabilisation of the economy during the transition from a war to a peace economy. At the same time, this counterfactual policy would have required a reduction of overseas military expenditure, which would have entailed an early withdrawal from the Middle East and probably for all bases east of Suez. Arguably, these decisions would have reduced the economic burden of overseas military expenditure, which would have lessened the balance of payments constraint in the late 1940s. At first sight, this book provides no indication that any British politicians contemplated adopting such a radical policy despite the wishful thinking of some of the previous studies. This implied alternative history of this book possibly provides a potential basis for further examination or counterfactual speculation.

As the case studies show, one danger of counterfactual reasoning is that it may lead one to over-estimate the information available to decision-makers at the time, and the ability of governments to assess the information correctly and reach the most "sensible" decisions. To be realistic, counterfactuals or historical alternatives have to be based on reasonable assumptions. This applies equally to the assumptions about the decision-making process. For example, policy-makers in the immediate post-war period may have assessed the potential dangers of an inadequate defence effort differently than we would today. Even though they may have been aware of the potentially detrimental effects to the economy, they may not necessarily have made the connection between high defence expenditure and slow economic growth. The case studies in this book show that the British defence procurement policy regime institutionalised the lessons of wartime mobilisation during the Second World War. In the immediate post-war period, policy-makers remained justified in their cautious approach by the volatility of the international situation. Policy-makers started to reconsider their defence procurement strategy only after the economic crisis of 1951. This crisis also led to a reassessment of the economic impact of the British rearmament programme. As a result, policy-makers rethought British defence strategy in order to reduce the economic burden of defence. After the 1957 Defence White Paper, this reassessment led to the widespread conviction that the previous policy had been misguided and in the end costly. Arguably, these discussions contibuted to the emergence of the declinist thesis, which argued that the economic costs of this policy could have been prevented if this foolish policy had been abandoned earlier. However, this book shows that this change in the defence procurement regime resulted from a lengthy learning process. Throughout the period of the first cold war, British governments sought to develop their organisational capabilities for strengthening the defence of the realm.

The economic impact of British defence expenditure reconsidered

Since the primary theme of this book is the economic impact of British defence expenditure, this learning process has to be integrated as a prominent element into a new interpretation of how defence expenditure affected the British economic development during the first cold war. In this context, endogenous economic growth theory seems an attractive theoretical framework, because of its emphasis on institutional and organisational capability. Moreover, as Moses Abramovitz pointed out, endogenous economic growth theory conceptualises

> [...] organizational advance [as] to some extent, a matter of continuing exploration based on experience, a matter of learning by doing.[48]

However, organisational capability is only one of the factors contributing to the social capability of a country. Other important factors include capital formation, labour supply, institutional arrangements, industrial structure, education and technology. While admitting the difficulty of measuring social capability, Abramovitz has more recently stressed its importance for a country's ability to exploit growth potential arising from productivity levels between itself and the economic leader.[49] Drawing on endogenous growth theory, Nick Crafts has characterised Britain's economic growth performance as disappointing during the first decade after 1945. While Crafts concedes that endogenous growth theory cannot explain the shortfall in productivity growth in its entirety, he attributes this relative failure partly to the Labour government's policy of a gradual transition from war to peace and partly to the mishandling of microeconomic policies. Moreover, he argues "that the macropolicy framework effectively ruled out some productivity enhancing policies."[50] At the same time, Crafts rejects suggestions that the Welfare State contributed to the relatively slow growth in Britain. In this context, he also notes that the relatively high level of defence expenditure did not lead to higher

[48] Moses Abramovitz, "Manpower, capital and technology," in *Thinking About Growth and Other Essays On Economic Growth and Welfare* (Cambridge: Cambridge University Press, 1989), 184.

[49] Moses Abramovitz, "Catching Up, Forging Ahead, and Falling Behind," *Journal of Economic History* 46 (1986): 385-406.

[50] Crafts, "Adjusting from war to peace," 16.

government spending than in other countries and therefore rules it out as a cause of Britain's relative decline in this period.[51] In this sense, Crafts implies that the British state lacked to some extent the organisational capability to promote economic growth, but rejects the notion that the expansion of state activity was responsible for relatively slow growth in Britain. At first glance, these conclusions resonate with the findings in chapters 4, 7 and 9 that while the overall macroeconomic effect of defence expenditure was probably small or even slightly negative, the defence programme arguably induced structural changes which damaged Britain's prospects for rapid productivity growth in the 1950s.

Defence economists have suggested five ways in which defence expenditure might contribute to economic growth. First, defence expenditure may stimulate economic production in periods of severe unemployment. Secondly, defence expenditure may have technological spin-offs for civilian industry permitting further productivity growth. Thirdly, defence expenditure might induce improvements in the infrastructure of a country. Fourthly, defence expenditure may improve general levels of nutrition, training and education. Fifthly, defence expenditure may indirectly further growth by creating a stable and secure environment, which is conducive to economic growth and is attractive to foreign investors.[52] It is worth briefly exploring the potential contributions of these five sources of defence-induced economic growth to post-war British economic performance, before returning to the issue of the organisational capability of the British state.

As chapter 4 shows, British economic advisers were well aware of the potential of defence expenditure as a policy tool to stimulate economic activity and increase employment during a depression caused by under-consumption or under-investment. In the 1930s, British rearmament reduced unemployment by about 1 million, but the overall effect of employment creation was smaller than Keynes and other contemporary economists had hoped.[53] Moreover, the tremendous economic growth experienced by the American economy during the 1940s can be largely attributed to the economic stimulus of wartime mobilisation, which induced the massive expansion of industrial capacity and created millions of new jobs. Arguably, this experience led to the widespread perception in post-war America that military expenditure enhances economic prosperity.[54] However, the stimulative effect is confined to situations of under-employment, which did not apply in post-war Britain. Keynes and other

---

[51] Crafts, "Adjusting from war to peace," 9-10.

[52] Sandler and Hartley, *Economics of defense*, 201-3.

[53] George C. Peden, *Keynes, the Treasury and British Economic Policy* (Basingstoke: Macmillan, 1988), 32-3.

[54] Seymour Melman, *The Permanent War Economy: American Capitalism in Decline*, rev. ed. (New York: Touchstone, 1985), 15-26.

contemporary economic advisers realised that defence expenditure would be detrimental rather than conducive to economic growth in a situation of excess demand for labour. Nevertheless, they opposed the scrapping of military production and favoured the gradual transition to peace production. As the severity of labour and skill shortages became apparent, the Economic Section argued against any increases in defence expenditure on economic grounds using similar arguments. Arguably, the under-employment in the defence sector increased the excess demand for labour and therefore reduced the potential for productivity growth during the initial transition to a peace economy. The defence programme further enhanced this effect. Contemporary economists argued that the government should take measures to enhance labour mobility. In the late 1940s, the Labour government argued for moving industry away from London mainly for military reasons.[55] Indeed, the government used the defence programme to encourage military contractors, not always successfully, to locate new plants in deprived areas. This policy certainly created new employment opportunities in Scotland and may have enhanced the longer-term prospects of the Scottish economy by attracting the emerging electronics industry to the region. At the same time, these measures potentially reduced the labour mobility by essentially freezing the geographic distribution of the population.

Any assessment of the overall effect of defence expenditure on employment and potential for productivity growth depends crucially on one's assessment of the severity of the excess demand for labour in this period. Crafts argues that if the government had tolerated a higher level of unemployment in the 1940s, then productivity growth would have been more rapid. He assumes that a more Thatcherite economic policy approach might have induced the degree of short-term unemployment needed for a more rapid expansion of the economy.[56] However, this speculative analysis underestimates the excess demand for labour in this period. Demobilisation occurred rapidly during the first fifteen months after the end of the war without reducing the excess demand for labour significantly.[57] Two measures might potentially have increased the available labour force: reducing the size of the armed forces more drastically and retaining more women in industrial employment after the war. These measures would potentially have increased the labour force by roughly 1 to 1.5 million, which would have maintained the overall workforce roughly at its June 1945

55 Lewis, *Economic planning*, 75-86.
56 Crafts, "Adjusting from war to peace," 16.
57 On this point, see Peter Southwood, *Disarming Military Industries: Turning an outbreak of peace into an enduring legacy* (Basingstoke: Macmillan, 1991), 9-12.; and J. C. R. Dow, *The Management of the British Economy, 1945-60* (Cambridge: Cambridge University Press, 1964), 112-21.

level.[58] The potential increase in the active labour force would have absorbed most unfilled vacancies, but raised the level of unemployment from 282,000 to around 1 million in June 1948. This would have increased the unemployment rate from 1.3 per cent to 4.6 per cent.[59] Such a figure would significantly have exceeded the unemployment target of 3 per cent, which was first suggested in the Beveridge Report and adopted by the government in 1951.[60] However, this argument rests on the assumption that the active work force could have been increased by over 1 million in the immediate post-war period. With hindsight, this scenario seems highly unlikely. The government's economic advisers foresaw this problem in the 1944 White Paper on *Employment Policy* noting that during the transition period excess demand was likely to persist in the economy. This period might be prolonged by the need to maintain large armed forces for some time after the end of the war in Europe. Even after most shortages had disappeared, the White Paper argued that

> [Britain's] main problem for a considerable time to come may be, not to avert mass unemployment, but to secure with a limited labour force an adequate production of goods needed to improve our standard of living and to increase our exports. The immediate difficulties for our external trade will be serious. We may be struggling to restore our exports while we are still at war with Japan and liable to provide help to the liberated territories. We shall, therefore, be compelled during this period to regulate imports and to manage our exchange resources with great care.[61]

This quote highlights the fact that British economic policy-makers were far more concerned about the balance of payments constraint than the emergence of mass unemployment.[62] In this context, it is intriguing that Crafts' study does not consider the possibility that the balance of payments constraint in the immediate post-war period prevented the government from lifting controls on

---

58 The active labour force contracted by about 1.3 million between June 1945 and June 1948; see Treasury, *Economic Survey for 1951* (London: His Majesty's Stationery Office, 1951), 9.

59 This estimate is based on 490,000 unfilled vacancies in the months up to June 1948, which would have reduced the pool of additional workers on the job market to somewhere between 500,000 to 1 million; see Central Statistical Office, *Monthly Digest of Statistics*, vol. 87 (London: Her Majesty's Stationery Office, 1952), 22, Table 29. If one adds this figure to the average number of unemployed of 282,000 in June 1948, one arrives at a figure between 782,000 to 1,282,000. The figures for industrial unemployment and overall employment are taken from Treasury, *Economic Survey for 1951*, 11, Table 2.

60 Jim Tomlinson, *Employment Policy: The Crucial Years, 1939-1955* (Oxford: Clarendon Press, 1987), 71-2 and 122-41.

61 Ministry of Reconstruction, *Employment Policy*, Cmd. 8195 (London: His Majesty's Stationery Office, 1944), 6-10 (quote: 10).

62 Tomlinson, *Employment policy*, 122.

consumption and imports.[63] Crafts argues that the British economy would have benefited from early trade liberalisation and convertibility. However, this interpretation runs counter to the view among economic historians studying the immediate post-war period, that western European reconstruction required the maintenance of the discrimination against dollar goods due to the reduced competitiveness of European exports on the American market.[64] Besides their concern about the balance of payments, economic policy-makers were concerned that severe regional unemployment might emerge during the transition to a peace economy thus affecting the longer-term prospects for economic growth. Therefore, the government planned to phase out armaments production slowly depending on the regional employment situation while the war against Japan continued and during the initial transition period.[65] Arguably, this policy was on the whole successful in preventing regional unemployment from again becoming a serious problem in post-war Britain. In the immediate post-war period, defence expenditure is unlikely to have stimulated employment, while arguably contributing to the excess demand in the economy by sustaining a significant degree of under-employment in the defence sector. During the Korean war defence programme, the expansion of defence production further increased the excess demand for labour, but mitigated the employment effects of the sudden collapse in textile production during the economic crisis of 1951 and encouraged the creation of new jobs in Scotland. On balance, defence expenditure might overall have had a slightly dampening effect on economic growth.[66]

As the case studies show, British post-war governments were determined to maintain the domestic defence industrial base by encouraging the development of new weapons incorporating the most advanced military technology. In this sense, the British warfare state strove to be a developmental state. As Edgerton concedes, the massive military research and development effort did not necessarily result in spin-offs into civilian applications.[67] A perturbing aspect of this story is that the British aircraft industry probably led the world in the development of jet aircraft at the end of the Second World War only to lose this lead by the late 1950s.[68] Analysts have attributed this decline to the structure of the British aircraft industry, because it consisted of a large number of medium size firms which could not compete with the larger more efficient

[63] A. P. Thirwall, "The Balance of Payments Constraint as an Explanation of International Growth Rate Differences," *Banca Nazionale del Lavoro Quarterly Review* (1979): 45-53.

[64] John Killick, *The United States and European Reconstruction, 1945 - 1960* (Edinburgh: Keele University Press, 1997), 14-22.

[65] Ministry of Reconstruction, *Employment policy*, 6-10.

[66] See chapters 4, 7 and 9.

[67] Edgerton, *England and the aeroplane*, 83-105.

[68] See chapter 5.

French and American manufacturers.[69] Despite government support, aircraft manufacturers remained fairly risk adverse concentrating on obtaining development orders rather than on the production of aircraft. The war potential policy emphasised maintaining the largest possible number of aircraft design teams, because the supply departments believed successful aircraft production depended on the existence of a design capability within firms. However, most firms found it difficult to attract and retain qualified staff for their design departments. During this period, the reputation of the aircraft industry suffered severely from spectacular project failures, numerous cancellations, and delays in the production of new aircraft.[70] Productivity levels in the industry declined steadily after 1954 due to a lack of new large production orders.

At the beginning of the Korean war, the jet engine shortage highlighted the outmoded production methods of the industry. For the most part, the British aircraft engine industry could not produce sufficient blades of a high enough standard for the latest type of jets with axial compressors. Despite the acknowledged superior performance of axial flow engines, some aircraft engineers argued for building engines with centrifugal compressors, because of their higher resistance to damage from blade failure.[71] Throughout this period, officials and industry reproached each other for the failures in the procurement of military aircraft. The Select Committee on Estimates repeatedly criticised the Ministry of Supply's management of defence procurement in this period, while not totally exempting the defence industry from blame.[72] As Ely Devons pointed out in 1958, the experience of the British aircraft industry highlighted the considerable risks and uncertainties involved in the development and production of modern aircraft. Therefore, government policy in this period aimed to reduce the likelihood of failure as far as possible. The irony is that this policy of "insuring against failure" tried to redress the lack of state support, which had plagued the development of the British aircraft industry between the

[69] Andrew Moravcsik, "Arms and Autarky in Modern European History," *Dædalus* 120 (1991): 33-4.

[70] Ely Devons, "The Aircraft Industry," in *The Structure of British Industry: A Symposium*, ed. Duncan Burn (Cambridge: Cambridge University Press, 1958), 42-92.

[71] On this point, see "Aero Engines," *The Economist*, 28 July 1951.; "The New Aircraft," *The Economist*, 15 September 1951.; Our Air Correspondent, "Aircraft Output Hampered," *Financial Times*, 23 October 1951.; and "The Relative Merits of Centrifugal and Axial Compressors for Aircraft Gas Turbines: A Discussion led by E. S. Moult and H. Pearson," *Journal of the Royal Aeronautical Society* 55, March (1951): 129-52.

[72] House of Commons, *Second Report from the Select Committee on Estimates, Session 1956-57: The Supply of Military Aircraft*, Parliamentary Papers (London: Her Majesty's Stationery Office, 1956). On this point, see also Roy Fedden's speech at the fourth Conference on problems of Aircraft Production in January 1956; "Fourth Annual Conference on Problems of Aircraft Production: A Report on the Conference held in Southampton, 6 and 7 January 1956," *Aircraft Engineering* 28 (1956): 88-96.

wars.[73] However, the more air-minded policies of post-war governments may well have contributed to the difficulties of the industry by spreading resources too thinly over too many projects.[74] As a consequence, the technological gap between the British and American aircraft industry widened during this period. On balance, there is little evidence to suggest that defence expenditure contributed to economic growth through advancing either military or civilian technology in this period.

The case studies do not shed much light on the third and fourth growth enhancing effect of defence expenditure and require further investigation. However, defence economists suggest that these two potential benefits of military expenditure mainly occur in less developed countries. Since Britain was a highly developed country at the end of the Second World War, it seems unlikely that defence expenditure contributed to economic growth in this period through military infrastructure investment. Nevertheless, the existence of large army camps helped to alleviate the post-war housing shortage.[75] Another example of such indirect effects is that consumer rationing improved nutrition of the British population during the war and the immediate post-war period.[76] Arguably, national service offered an opportunity to increase the skills of individual servicemen, which might have benefited economic growth in this period. This book has found no prima facie evidence to support this proposition, which raises the question whether this should be regarded as a failure of government policy. Crafts certainly attributes a large proportion of slower growth in Britain to an inadequate skills base due to a lack of appropriate training programmes.[77]

It is similarly hard to assess whether British defence expenditure indirectly contributed to economic growth by maintaining international security. Despite the impossibility of quantifying this factor, it should be considered. Chapter 1 presented some evidence that British policy-makers regarded continued high defence expenditure as a precondition for economic recovery. The answer to this question depends on whether the prospect of another world war made investors and consumers more risk adverse and therefore less likely to invest in new industrial capacity or to save a major share of their income. If the answer

[73] On this point, see the debate between Peter Fearon and Alex Robertson: Peter Fearon, "The British Airframe Industry and the State, 1918-35," *Economic History Review* 27 (1974): 236-51.; and A. J. Robertson, "The British Airframe Industry and the State in the Interwar Period: A Comment," *Economic History Review* 28 (1974): 648-57.

[74] Devons, "Aircraft industry," 58-65.

[75] Many of these army camps were occupied by squatters in the immediate post-war period; see James Hinton, "Self-help and Socialism: the Squatters' Movement of 1946," *History Workshop* 25 (1988): 100-26.

[76] Alan S. Milward, *War, Economy and Society, 1939-1945* (Harmondsworth: Penguin, 1977), 285-6.

[77] Crafts, "Adjusting from war to peace," 11-12.

is yes, then the increased defence expenditure contributed to the stabilisation of the economy in the immediate post-war period. The analysis in chapter 8 reveals some not very strong empirical evidence to support this proposition. Another possible indication might be the drop in industrial investment during the Korean war, which might reflect the increased uncertainty about the future.[78] At the same time, policy-makers were aware that the continued production of tanks and atomic bombs potentially postponed improvements in living standards offered by post-war economic growth. Therefore, the question is whether the arms race or further economic growth contributed more to the happiness of the British people.[79] In this context, it is important to remember that any assessment will reflect one's personal beliefs about whether increased defence expenditure delivers more security or whether the growth of national income indeed makes everyone happier as economic theory assumes.[80] Even before the cold war began, British policy-makers cited the uncertainties about the international situation to justify maintaining Britain's defence effort. As the cold war began, this justificatory discourse established the necessity of ever more weapons, while continually affirming the wisdom of post-war defence policies and making it more difficult to disengage from the arms race.[81]

In summary, the case studies in this book provide considerable evidence that British post-war defence procurement strategy led to an over-commitment of resources to defence production, which contributed to excess demand in the economy and thereby prolonged the transition to a peace economy. The persistence of excess demand probably hampered British economic recovery in the late 1940s. At the same time, there is some evidence that continued defence expenditure stabilised economic demand during this period. These two effects may well have cancelled each other out. Korean war rearmament entailed massive increases in defence expenditure inducing large shifts in economic demand. The expansion of military production led to further increases in the size of the defence sector. There is considerable evidence that the defence programme absorbed a large proportion of British machine tool production. However, this finding does not prove that the defence programme prevented profitable investment elsewhere in the economy. Overall, industrial investment in Britain fell slightly, but noticeably, in 1951 and 1952, possibly due to the increased uncertainty about the international situation and the economic future. The stagnation in industrial investment led to a loss of momentum, which might have slowed the pace of economic development. In this context, the key question is whether the slowdown or the changes in capital formation had a

---

[78] See chapter 8, Table 8.1.

[79] Henri Lefebvre, *Critique of Everyday Life* (London: Verso, 1991), 48-9.

[80] Thompson, *Poverty of theory*, 49.; and Seers, "National income," 61.

[81] Edward P. Thompson, "Notes on Exterminism, the Last Stage of Civilisation," in *Exterminism and the Cold War*, ed. New Left Review (London: Verso, 1982), 1-33.

lasting impact on the rate of British economic development during the Great Boom from 1950 to 1973. Chapters 7 and 8 rely on traditional models of economic growth to argue that the structural break in the trend growth of the investment rate may have shifted the British economy on to a lower (sub-optimal) growth path. However, this argument should not be pushed too far. All things considered, there is enough evidence to suggest that defence expenditure hampered economic development during the period of the first cold war.

This assessment of the economic impact of British defence expenditure provides no conclusive evidence that defence expenditure actually caused slow economic growth in the post-war period. Following the suggestion of the declinist accounts, the discussion has so far assumed that defence expenditure influences economic growth (investment). Moreover, these accounts emplot a negative relationship between defence expenditure and economic growth. However, the discussion in chapter 7 pointed out that while the proportion of national income spent on defence fell continually between 1953 and 1960, the rate of investment increased faster than the fall in defence expenditure. Based on observation, chapter 7 proposed that the cuts in the defence effort after 1952 led to an increase in the investment rate or that resources released from the defence budget crowded in investment. However, the higher investment rate did not lead to faster economic growth in Britain due to the relatively high incremental capital-output ratio. Therefore, there is no reason to presume that the British economy would have grown faster, if British governments had spent less on fighting the cold war.[82] As Crafts notes,

> ... the most striking feature of this period is not that British investment spending was low but that the British incremental capital to output ratio was high.[83]

While British defence procurement policy may have contributed to the rising capital-output ratio in the aircraft industry, this book found no evidence to suggest that defence expenditure could explain the overall high capital-output ratio in the remainder of the economy. Indeed, neither traditional nor endogenous growth theory can offer a satisfactory explanation for the high incremental capital-out ratio.[84] Therefore, the findings in the case studies do strongly suggest that the British defence effort did not cause Britain's relative economic decline.

---

[82] See chapter 7, particularly Tables 7.2 and 7.3.

[83] Crafts, "Adjusting from war to peace," 14.

[84] R. C. O. Matthews, Charles H. Feinstein, and J. C. Odling-Smee, *British Economic Growth, 1856-1973* (Oxford: Oxford University Press, 1982), 393.; and Crafts, "Adjusting from war to peace," 14.

Nevertheless, the case studies have repeatedly highlighted certain weaknesses in the organisational capability of the British warfare state. The discussion of British defence procurement policy showed that the government lacked structures and policies to exercise effective control over the weapons acquisition process. Arguably, the government could have adopted the American model of hiring consultants to provide an independent assessment of weapons development projects. Moreover, the discussion of the defence programme revealed the problem of control defence expenditure. Given the urgency of rearmament, the Treasury did not have the information or power to effectively question the expansion of British defence production capacity. Therefore, the armed services and the supply departments used the defence programme as a golden opportunity to push through projects, which they had not been able to implement due to a lack of finance in the late 1940s. This informal approach to managing the defence sector dates back to the Second World War, when the government had more economists to co-ordinate the allocation of resources.[85] Arguably, these organisational weaknesses may partly explain why the British defence effort did not promote economic growth more strongly in some instances and did hamper it in others. On balance, the government's handling of the macro- and meso-economic aspects of the defence programme proved to be more successful than its micro-economic management of defence procurement policy.

In reconsidering previous explanations of the economic impact of the British defence effort during the first cold war, this book suggests that British foreign policy-makers argued for retaining a relatively large defence effort, because of the increased vulnerability of the country. Britain's relative vulnerability arose largely from the reduction in its economic strength due to the war effort. Therefore, British policy-makers opted to maintain the country's military power to exercise a degree of influence over the emerging international settlement after 1945. Arguably, the large defence effort hampered post-war recovery slightly, but did not precipitate the relative economic decline of the British economy in the post-war period. In this sense, the interpretation here confirms Paul Kennedy's argument that economic strength can be translated into military power, but military power tends to reflect the balance of economic strength.[86] In this sense, the decline of British economic strength and military power had already begun much earlier in the outgoing nineteenth century. Therefore, it is hard to see how a different economic strategy or foreign policy could have increased Britain's economic strength sufficiently for it to return to the dominant position it held in the middle of the nineteenth century.

---

[85] Peter Howlett, "New light through old windows: a new perspective on the British economy in the Second World War," *Journal of Contemporary History* 28 (1993): 361-79.

[86] Kennedy, *Rise and fall*, 565-76.

All things considered, this analysis found that the British defence effort reflected a prudent response by a group of battle-weary policy-makers to the historical contingencies of the first cold war. While their policies have been much maligned, the policies proposed in alternative histories would have involved considerably greater risks while exaggerating their potential benefits. Short of isolating its economy from the outside world, there was probably no real alternative solution in 1945 to cautious integration into a new international economic order. Therefore, Britain needed American financial support to regain its economic strength just as the United States would come to rely on British (and European) military strength as the cold war intensified. Maybe British policy-makers should have realised earlier the limits the country's weakened state imposed on their foreign and defence policy, but they certainly learned this lesson during the trials and tribulations of the first cold war.

Bibliography

Archives

Government archives

Great Britain

Public Record Office, London (PRO)
- Air Ministry (AIR)
- Board of Trade (BT)
- Cabinet Office (CAB)
- Ministry of Defence (DEFE)
- Treasury (T)
- War Office (WO)

Scottish Record Office, Edinburgh (SRO)

United States

National Archive and Record Administration, Washington (NARA)
- National Archives, Civil Reference Branch
  - Records of International Conferences, Commissions and Expositions (Record Group [hereafter RG] 43)
  - Department of State, Central Decimal Files (RG 59)
  - National Security Council (RG273)
- National Archives, Military Reference Branch
  - Joint Chiefs of Staff (RG 218)
  - Records of the Army Chief of Staff (RG319)
  - Secretary of Defense (RG 330)
  - Interservice Agencies (RG 334)
- National Record Centre, Suitland, Maryland
  - European Cooperation Administration (RG 469)

Other collections

British Library, London
- India Office Library and Records
  - India Office Records (IOR)

Imperial War Museum, London (IWM)

Department of Documents
Papers of Field Marshall Viscount Montgomery of Alamein, PP/MCR/C30 (BLM)
Lieutenant L. G. G. Smith, 86/61

John Rylands University Library, Manchester (JRULM)

Labour Party Archive (LPA)

Communist Party of Great Britain Archive (CP)

Scottish Council (Development and Industry), Edinburgh

Scottish Council (Development and Industry) (SCDI)

University of Sussex, Falmer, Brighton

Tom Harrison Mass-Observation Archive (MOA)

University of Warwick, Coventry

Modern Record Centre
CBI Predessor Archives (MSS 200)
Standard Motor Co. Ltd. (MSS 226)

Published Documents

R. J. Bullen and M. E. Pelley, eds., *Documents on British Policy Overseas, series 1, volume 3: Britain and America: Negotiations of the United States loan, 3 August-7 December 1945*, (London: Her Majesty's Stationery Office, 1986).

R. J. Bullen and M. E. Pelley, eds., *Documents on British Policy Overseas, series 2, volume 3: German Rearmament, September-December 1950*, (London: Her Majesty's Stationery Office, 1989).

Department of State, ed., *Foreign Relations of the United States, 1950, volume iii: Western Europe*, (Washington: Government Printing Office, 1977).

Department of State, ed., *Foreign Relations of the United States, 1952-1954, volume ii: National Security Affairs*, (Washington: Government Printing Office, 1984).

Department of State, ed., *Foreign Relations of the United States, 1951, volume iv: Europe: Political and Economic Developments*, (Washington: Government Printing Office, 1985).

T. H. Etzold and J. L. Gaddis, eds., *Containment: Documents on American policy and strategy, 1945-1950*, (New York: Columbia University Press, 1978).

L. Galambos, ed., *The Papers of Dwight David Eisenhower: The Chief of Staff*, (Baltimore: Johns Hopkins University Press, 1978).

G. Ross, ed., *The Foreign Office and the Kremlin: British Documents on Anglo-Soviet Relations, 1941-45*, (Cambridge: Cambridge University Press, 1984).

H. J. Yasamee and K. H. Hamil, eds., *Documents on British Policy Overseas, series 2, volume 4: Korea, June 1950 - April 1951*, (London: Her Majesty's Stationery Office, 1991).

Official Publications

Great Britain

Air Estimates 1951/1952, Cmd. 8162 (London: His Majesty's Stationery Office, 1951).

Army Estimates 1951/1952, Cmd. 8161 (London: His Majesty's Stationery Office, 1951).

Navy Estimates 1951/1952, Cmd. 8160 (London: His Majesty's Stationery Office, 1951).

Revised Estimates of the Sums Required in the Year Ending 31 March 1952 for Board of Trade and Ministry of Supply Services (London: His Majesty's Stationery Office, 1951).

Board of Trade, *The Machine Tool Industry: A Report by the Sub-Committee of the Machine Tool Advisory Council appointed to consider Professor Melman's Report to the European Productivity Agency* (London: Board of Trade, 1960).

Business Statistics Office, *Historical Record of the Census of Production, 1907 to 1970* (London: Her Majesty's Stationery Office, 1978).

Cabinet Office, *Defence Programme: Statement made by the Prime Minister in the House of Commons on Monday, 29th January, 1951* (London: His Majesty's Stationery Office, 1951).

Central Statistical Office, *Monthly Digest of Statistics* (London: Her Majesty's Stationery Office, 1952).

Central Statistical Office, *National Income and Expenditure 1958* (London: Her Majesty's Stationery Office, 1958).

Central Statistical Office, *Annual Abstract of Statistics* (London: Her Majesty's Stationery Office, 1959).

Central Statistical Office, *National Income and Expenditure 1968* (London: Her Majesty's Stationery Office, 1968).

Central Statistical Office, *Fighting with Figures: A Statistical Digest of the Second World War* (London: Her Majesty's Stationery Office, 1995).

Department of Trade and Industry, *The Machine Tool Industry: Report of the Machine Tool Expert Committee under the chairmanship of Sir Richard Way KCB CBE* (London: Her Majesty's Stationery Office, 1970).

House of Commons, *War-Time Tank Production: Reports by the Select Committee on National Expenditure and the Replies to these Reports by the Government of the day* (London: His Majesty's Stationery Office, 1946).

House of Commons, *Official Report* (London: His Majesty's Stationery Office, various years).

House of Commons, *Seventh Report from the Select Committee on Estimates, Session 1947-48: Royal Ordnance Factories* (London: Her Majesty's Stationery Office, 1948).

House of Commons, *Tenth Report from the Select Committee on Estimates, Session 1951-52: Rearmament* (London: Her Majesty's Stationery Office, 1952).

House of Commons, *Twelfth Report from the Select Committee on Estimates, Session 1951-52: Royal Ordnance Factories* (London: Her Majesty's Stationery Office, 1952).

House of Commons, *Second Report from the Select Committee on Estimates, Session 1956-57: The Supply of Military Aircraft* (London: Her Majesty's Stationery Office, 1956).

Ministry of Aircraft Production, *The Aircraft Builders: An Account of British Aircraft Production, 1935-1945* (London: His Majesty's Stationery Office, 1947).

Ministry of Aviation, *Report of the Committee of Inquiry into the Aircraft Industry* (London: Her Majesty's Stationery Office, 1965).

Ministry of Defence, *Central Organisation for Defence* (London: His Majesty's Stationery Office, 1946).

Ministry of Defence, *Statement relating to Defence* (London: His Majesty's Stationery Office, 1946).

Ministry of Defence, *Statement relating to Defence 1947* (London: His Majesty's Stationery Office, 1947).

Ministry of Defence, *Statement related to Defence 1948* (London: His Majesty's Stationery Office, 1948).

Ministry of Defence, *Estimates 1951-1952* (London: His Majesty's Stationery Office, 1951).

Ministry of Defence, *Statement on Defence 1952* (London: Her Majesty's Stationery Office, 1952).

Ministry of Defence, *Statement on Defence 1953* (London: Her Majesty's Stationery Office, 1953).

Ministry of Defence, *Statement on Defence 1954* (London: Her Majesty's Stationery Office, 1954).

Ministry of Defence, *The Supply of Military Aircraft* (London: Her Majesty's Stationery Office, 1955).

Ministry of Defence, *Defence: Outline of future policy* (London: Her Majesty's Stationery Office, 1957).

Ministry of Labour, *Ministry of Labour Gazette* (London: Her Majesty's Stationery Office, various dates).

Ministry of Reconstruction, *Employment Policy* (London: His Majesty's Stationery Office, 1944).

Ministry of Supply. Directorate of Royal Ordnance Factories. Explosives, *Industrial Experimentation* (London: His Majesty's Stationery Office, 1946).

Ministry of Technology, *Report of the Working Party on the Problems Arising from the Cyclical Patterns of Machine Tool Orders* (London: Her Majesty' Stationery Office, 1966).

Treasury, *Statistical Material Presented During the Washington Negotiations* (London: His Majesty's Stationery Office, 1945).

Treasury, *Economic Survey for 1951* (London: His Majesty's Stationery Office, 1951).

Treasury, *Financial Statement* (London: His Majesty's Stationery Office, 1951).

Treasury, *United Kingdom Balance of Payments, 1948 to 1951* (London: His Majesty's Stationery Office, 1951).

Treasury, *Economic Survey for 1952* (London: Her Majesty's Stationery Office, 1952).

Treasury, *Economic Survey for 1953* (London: Her Majesty's Stationery Office, 1953).

Treasury, *Economic Survey 1954* (London: Her Majesty's Stationery Office, 1954).

Treasury, *Economic Survey 1955* (London: Her Majesty's Stationery Office, 1955).

Treasury, *United Kingdom Balance of Payments, 1946-1957* (London: Her Majesty's Stationery Office, 1959).

India

Defence Science Organisation, *Nuclear Explosions and their Effects* (Delhi: Ministry of Information and Broadcasting, Publications Division, 1958).

United States

Bureau of the Census, *The Statistical History of the United States: From Colonial Times to the Present* (New York: Basic Books, 1976).

International organisations

Organisation for European Economic Co-operation

Organisation for European Economic Co-operation, *Financial Stability and the Fight against Inflation* (Paris: Organisation for European Economic Co-operation, 1951).

Organisation for European Economic Co-operation, *Statistics of National Product and Expenditure, 1938 and 1947 to 1955* (Paris: Organisation for European Economic Co-operation, 1957).

United Nations

United Nations. Economic Commission for Europe. Research and Planning Division, *Economic Survey of Europe in 1948* (Geneva: United Nations. Department of Economic Affairs, 1949).

United Nations. Economic Commission for Europe. Research and Planning Division, *Economic Survey of Europe in 1951* (Geneva: United Nations. Department of Economic Affairs, 1952).

United Nations. Economic Commission for Europe. Research and Planning Division, *Economic Survey of Europe since the War: A Reappraisal of Problems and Prospects* (Geneva: United Nations. Department of Economic Affairs, 1953).

Newspapers

British Library

ROF News

John Rylands University Library of Manchester, Manchester

Labour Party Newspaper Cutting Archive

Daily Express
Daily Herald
Daily Mail
The Daily Telegraph
Daily Worker
Financial Times
Manchester Guardian
The Observer
Recorder
Reynold's News
Sunday Express
The Economist
The Times
West Lancashire Evening Gazette

Manchester Central Library, Manchester

Social Science Library

Manchester Evening News
Manchester Guardian
New York Times
The Observer
The Daily Telegraph

Queen's University Main Library, Belfast

The Economist

The Statist

Books, articles and other secondary material

The First of the Few, dir. L. Howard (British Aviation Pictures, 1942).

One Way Only: A Socialist Analysis of the Present World Crisis (London: Tribune Publications, 1951).

"Problems of Aircraft Production: A Report on the Second Conference by the Southern Section of the Institution of Production Engineers and held at the University of Southampton on December 18 and 19, 1953," *Aircraft Engineering* 26 (1954) 300, 46-50.

"Fourth Annual Conference on Problems of Aircraft Production: A Report on the Conference held in Southampton, 6 and 7 January 1956," *Aircraft Engineering* 28 (1956) 325, 88-96.

"Introduction," in *Defence expenditure, industrial conversion and local employment*, eds. L. Paukert and P. Richards, (Geneva: International Labour Office, 1991), 1-10.

English Electric Lightning, prod. Prometheus Productions, (DD Video, 1993).

The Myth of the Few, Secret History, prod. S. T. Productions, (Channel 4, 25 July 2000).

S. Aaronovitch, *Monopoly: A Study of British Monopoly Capitalism* (London: Lawrence and Wishart, 1955).

W. Abelshauser, *Wirtschaftsgeschichte der Bundesrepublik Deutschland, 1945-1980* (Frankfurt am Main: Suhrkamp, 1983).

M. Abramovitz, "Catching Up, Forging Ahead, and Falling Behind," *Journal of Economic History* 46 (1986) 2, 385-406.

M. Abramovitz, "Economics of Growth," in *Thinking About Growth and Other Essays On Economic Growth and Welfare*, (Cambridge: Cambridge University Press, 1989), 80-124.

M. Abramovitz, "Manpower, capital and technology," in *Thinking About Growth and Other Essays On Economic Growth and Welfare*, (Cambridge: Cambridge University Press, 1989), 173-186.

D. Acheson, *Present at the Creation: My Years in the State Department* (New York: W. W. Norton and Company, 1969).

P. Addison, *The Road to 1945: British Politics and the Second World War* (London: Quartet Books, 1982).

G. A. Akerlof, "The economics of caste and of the rat race and other woeful tales," in *An Economist's Book of Tales*, (Cambridge: Cambridge University Press, 1984), 23-44.

D. K. Allison, "U.S. Navy Research and Development since World War II," in *Military Enterprise and Technological Change: Perpectives on the American Experience*, ed. M. R. Smith, (Cambridge: MIT Press, 1985), 289-328.

E. Ames, "The Economy of the Soviet Union-Discussion," *American Economic Review* 41 (1951) 2, 489-493.

P. Anderson, "The Figures of Descent," in *English Questions*, (London: Verso, 1992), 121-192.

Anglo-American Council on Productivity, *Final Report of the Anglo-American Council on Productivity* (London: Anglo-American Council on Productivity, 1952).

H. I. Ansoff, W. W. Baldwin, D. J. Davis, N. Kaplan, P. Kecskemeti and A. Wohlstetter, Outline of a Study for the Plans Analysis Section, RAND Report D-937 (10 May 1951 [cited 27 January 2002]); available from http://www.rand.org/publications/classics /wohlstetter/D937/D937.html.

R. E. Asher, *Grants, Loans and Local Currencies: Their Role in Foreign Aid* (Washington: Brookings Institution, 1961).

T. S. Ashton, "The Relation of Economic History to Economic Theory," *Economica* 13 (1946), 81-96.

N. Balchin, *Darkness Falls From the Air* (originally published in 1942), (London: Sphere, 1969).

T. Balogh, "The International Aspect," in *The British Economy, 1945-1950*, eds. G. D. N. Worswick and P. H. Ady, (Oxford: Oxford University Press, 1952), 476-510.

P. A. Baran, "National Income and Product of the U.S.S.R. in 1948," *Review of Economic Statistics* 29 (1947) 4, 227-234.

E. Barker, *Britain between the Superpowers* (Basingstoke: Macmillan, 1983).

J. Barnes and D. Nicholson, eds., *The Empire at Bay: The Leo Amery Diaries, 1929-1945*, (London: Hutchinson, 1988).

C. Barnett, *The Collapse of British Power* (Gloucester: Alan Sutton, 1984).

C. Barnett, *The Audit of War: The illusion and reality of Britain as a great nation* (Basingstoke: Macmillan, 1986).

C. Barnett, *The Lost Victory: British dreams, British realities, 1945-1950* (Basingstoke: Macmillan, 1995).

E. Baumgart, "Die Maschinenbauindustrie der Bundesrepublik im europäischen Markt," *Vierteljahreshefte für Wirtschaftsforschung* (1962), 63-72.

J. Baylis, *British Defence Policy: Striking the Right Balance* (Basingstoke: London, 1989).

J. Baylis, *The Diplomacy of Pragmatism: Britain and the Formation of NATO, 1942-1949* (Basingstoke: Macmillan, 1993).

W. Beckerman, *An Introduction to National Income Analysis* (London: Weidenfeld and Nicholson, 1980).

N. Beloff, *The General Says No: Britain's exclusion from Europe* (Harmondsworth: Penguin Books, 1963).

T. Benn, *Years of Hope: Diaries, Papers and Letters, 1940-1960* (London: Arrow Books, 1994).

A. Bergson and H. Heymann, Jr., *Soviet National Income and Product, 1940–48* (New York: Columbia University Press, 1954).

F. Beswick, *Plan for the Aircraft Industry* (London: Fabian Society, 1955).

W. Beveridge, *The Price of Peace* (London: Pilot Press, 1945).

A. J. Birtle, *Rearming the Phoenix: U.S. Military Assistance to the Federal Republic of Germany, 1950-1960* (New York: Garland, 1991).

A. Boltho, "Growth," in *European Economy: Growth and Crisis*, ed. A. Boltho, (Oxford: Oxford University Press, 1982), 9-37.

B. Bond, *War and Society in Europe, 1870-1970* (London: Fontana, 1984).

T. Brett, S. Gilliatt and A. Pople, "Planned Trade, Labour Party policy and US intervention: the successes and failures of post-war reconstruction," *History Workshop* 13 (1982), 130-142.

British Productivity Council, *Ammunition: Report of a British Productivity Team on Ammunition which visited the United States in 1952* (London: British Productivity Council, 1953).

S. Brittan, *Steering the Economy: The Role of the Treasury* (Harmondsworth: Penguin, 1971).

B. Brivati, *Hugh Gaitskell* (London: Richard Cohen, 1996).

S. Broadberry and P. Howlett, "The United Kingdom: 'Victory at all costs'," in *The Economics of World War II: Six great powers in international comparison*, ed. M. Harrison, (Cambridge: Cambridge University Press, 1998), 43-80.

B. Brodie, "Strategy as a Science," *World Politics* 1 (1949) 4, 467-488.

H. Brooks, "The Military Innovation System and the Qualitative Arms Race," in *Arms, Defense Policy, and Arms Control*, eds. F. A. Long and G. W. Rathjens, (New York: W. W. Norton & Company, 1976), 75-98.

W. A. Brown, Jr. and R. Opie, *American Foreign Assistance* (Washington: Brookings Institution, 1953).

A. Bullock, *Ernest Bevin: Foreign Secretary, 1945-51* (Oxford: Oxford University Press, 1985).

P. Burnham, *Political Economy of Postwar Reconstruction* (Basingstoke: Macmillan, 1990).

P. Burnham, "Rearming for the Korean War: the impact of government policy on Leyland Motors and the British car industry," *Contemporary Record* 9 (1995) 2, 343-367.

A. Cairncross, *Years of Recovery: British Economic Policy, 1945-51* (London: Methuen, 1985).

A. Cairncross, *The Price of War: British policy on German reparations, 1941–1949* (Oxford: Basil Blackwell, 1986).

A. Cairncross, *The British Economy since 1945* (Oxford: Blackwell, 1992).

A. Cairncross, ed., *The Robert Hall Diaries, 1947-53*, (London: Unwin Hyman, 1989).

A. Cairncross and N. Watts, *The Economic Section: A Study in Economic Advising* (London: Routledge, 1989).

J. Callaghan, *Time and Change* (Glasgow: Collins/Fontana, 1988).

E. Cambi, "Les Répercussions du Réarmement sur l'Italie," *Public Finance / Finances Publiques* 7 (1952) 1/2, 83-99.

E. H. Carr, *Conditions of Peace* (New York: Macmillan, 1944).

C. F. Carter, "The Impact of the Rearmament on Britain," *Public Finance / Finances Publiques* 7 (1952) 1/2, 35-51.

M. Casson, *Enterprise and Leadership: Studies on firms, markets and networks* (Cheltenham: Edward Elgar, 2000).

S. Chan, "The impact of defence spending on economic performance: A survey of evidence and problems," *Orbis* 29 (1985), 403-434.

R. Chartier, *On the Edge of the Cliff: History, language, and practices* (Baltimore: Johns Hopkins University Press, 1997).

M. Chick, *Industrial Policy in Britain, 1945-51: economic planning, nationalisation and the Labour governments* (Cambridge: Cambridge University Press, 1998).

R. Clarke, *Anglo-American Economic Collaboration in War and Peace, 1942-1949* (Oxford: Clarendon Press, 1982).

A. Clayton, "'Deceptive Might': Imperial Defence and Security, 1900-1968," in *The Oxford History of the British Empire, volume 4: The Twentieth Century*, eds. J. M. Brown and W. R. Louis, (Oxford: Oxford University Press, 1999), 280-305.

G. D. H. Cole, *The Intelligent Man's Guide to the Post-War World* (London: Victor Gollancz, 1947).

E. Conze, "Konfrontation und Détente: Überlegungen zur historischen Analyse des Ost-West-Konflikts," *Vierteljahreshefte für Zeitgeschichte* 46 (1998) 2, 269-282.

W. M. Corden, "The Control of Imports: A Case Study," *Manchester School of Economic and Social Studies* 26 (1958) 3, 181-221.

R. W. Cox, "Towards a post-hegemonic conceptualization of world order: reflections on the relevancy of Ibn Khaldun," in *Governance without Government: Order and Change in World Politics*, eds. J. N. Rosenau and E.-O. Czempiel, (Cambridge: Cambridge University Press, 1992), 132-159.

N. Crafts and G. Toniolo, "Postwar Growth: an overview," in *Economic growth in Europe since 1945*, eds. N. Crafts and G. Toniolo, (Cambridge: Cambridge University Press, 1996), 1-37.

N. F. R. Crafts, "Adjusting from War to Peace in 1940s Britain," *Economic and Social Review* 25 (1993) 1, 1-20.

C. A. R. Crosland, *Britain's Economic Problem* (London: Jonathan Cape, 1953).

E. Dell, *The Schuman Plan and the British Abdication of Leadership in Europe* (Oxford: Clarendon Press, 1995).

E. Devons, "The Aircraft Industry," in *The Structure of British Industry: A Symposium*, ed. D. Burn, (Cambridge: Cambridge University Press, 1958), 42-92.

A. DiFilippo, *Military Spending and Industrial Decline: A Study of the American Machine Tool Industry* (New York: Greenwood Press, 1986).

R. Dingman, "Atomic Diplomacy during the Korean War," *International Security* 13 (1988) 3, 50-91.

M. Djilas, *Conversations with Stalin* (Harmondsworth: Penguin, 1963).

M. Dobb, *Soviet Economic Development since 1917* (London: Routledge and Kegan, 1947).

M. Dockrill, *British Defence Policy since 1945* (Oxford: Basil Blackwell, 1988).

M. J. Dockrill, "The Foreign Office, Anglo-American relations and the Korean War, June 1950-June 1951," *International Affairs* 62 (1986), 459-476.

W. K. Domke, R. C. Eichenberg and C. M. Kelleher, "The Illusion of Choice: Defense and Welfare in Advanced Democracies, 1948-1978," *American Political Science Review* 77 (1983) 1, 19-35.

J. C. R. Dow, *The Management of the British Economy, 1945-60* (Cambridge: Cambridge University Press, 1964).

J. C. R. Dow and L. A. Dicks-Mireaux, "Excess Demand for Labour: A Study of Conditions in Great Britain, 1946-56," *Oxford Economic Papers* 10 (1958) 1, 1-33.

T. Driberg, *The Best of Both Worlds: A personal diary* (London: Phoenix House, 1953).

P. Dukes, *The Last Great Game: USA versus USSR: Events, conjectures, structures* (London: Pinter, 1989).

S. Dunston, *Modern Combat Vehicles 2: Centurion* (Shepperton: Ian Allan, 1980).

J. Eaton, *Economics of Peace and War: An analysis of Britain's Economic Problems* (London: Lawrence and Wishart, 1952).

Economist Intelligence Unit, *Britain and Europe: A Study of the Effects on British Manufacturing Industry of a Free Trade Area and the Common Market* (London: Economist Intelligence Unit, 1957).

D. Edgerton, *England and the Aeroplane: An Essay on a Militant and Technological Nation* (Basingstoke: Macmillan, 1991).

D. Edgerton, "Liberal Militarism and the British State," *New Left Review* 185 (1991), 138-169.

D. Edgerton, "The Prophet Militant and Industrial: The Peculiarities of Correlli Barnett," *Twentieth Century British History* 2 (1991) 3, 360-379.

D. Edgerton, "Whatever happened to the British warfare state? The Ministry of Supply, 1945-1951," in *Labour Governments and Private Industry: The Experience of 1945-1951*, eds. H. Mercer, N. Rollings and J. Tomlinson, (Edinburgh: Edinburgh University Press, 1992), 91-116.

D. Edgerton, "Public ownership and the British arms industry, 1920-50," in *The Political Economy of Nationalisation in Britain, 1920-50*, eds. R. Millward and J. Singleton, (Cambridge: Cambridge University Press, 1995), 164-188.

R. Edmonds, *Setting the Mould: The United States and Britain, 1945-1950* (Oxford: Clarendon Press, 1986).

W. Y. Elliott, F. Altschul, R. M. Bissell, Jr., C. C. Brown, H. v. B. Cleveland, T. Geiger, H. D. Gideonse, E. S. Mason and D. K. Price, *The Political Economy of American Foreign Policy: Its Concepts, Strategy, and Limits* (New York: Henry Holt and Company, 1955).

H. S. Ellis, *The Economics of Freedom: The Progress and Future of Aid to Europe* (New York: Harper & Brothers, 1950).

D. Ellwood, *Rebuilding Europe: Western Europe, America and postwar reconstruction* (London: Longman, 1992).

M. A. Evangelista, "Stalin's Postwar Army Reappraised," *International Security* 7 (1982) 3, 110-138.

P. Fearon, "The British Airframe Industry and the State, 1918-35," *Economic History Review* 27 (1974) 2, 236-251.

C. H. Feinstein, *National Income, Expenditure and Output of the United Kingdom, 1855-1965* (Cambridge: Cambridge University Press, 1972).

N. Ferguson, "Introduction - Virtual History: Towards a 'chaotic' theory of the past," in *Virtual History: Alternatives and Counterfactuals*, ed. N. Ferguson, (London: Picador, 1997), 1-90.

N. Ferguson, ed., *Virtual History: Alternatives and Counterfactuals*, (London: Picador, 1997).

S. Fielding, "What did 'The People' want? The meaning of the 1945 General Election," *Historical Journal* 35 (1992), 623-639.

M. F. Fogarty, *Prospects of the Industrial Areas of Great Britain* (London: Methuen, 1945).

C. Freeman, "Technical Innovation and British Trade Performance," in *De-industrialisation*, ed. F. Blackaby, (London: Heinemann, 1978), 56-77.

J. F. C. Fuller, "The Tank in Future Warfare," *Brassey's Annual* 63 (1952), 262-272.

J. L. Gaddis, *Strategies of Containment: A critical appraisal of post-war American national security policy* (New York: Oxford University Press, 1982).

J. L. Gaddis, *We Now Know: Rethinking cold war history* (New York: Oxford University Press, 1997).

J. K. Galbraith, *The New Industrial State* (Harmondsworth: Penguin, 1972).

A. Gamble, *Britain in Decline: Economic policy, political strategy and the British state* (Basingstoke: Macmillan, 1994).

L. C. Gardner, *Approaching Vietnam: From World War II through Dienbienphu* (New York: W. W. Norton, 1988).

T. Geiger, "Opposition in the Shadows of an Emerging Conflict: The Aberdeen Trades Council, government policy and voicing dissent in the cold war, 1945-1955," *Northern Scotland* 13 (1993), 103-135.

T. Geiger, "Embracing Good Neighbourliness: Multilateralism, *Pax Americana*, and European integration, 1945-58," in *Regional Trade Blocs, Multilateralism, and the GATT: Complementary Paths to Free Trade?*, eds. T. Geiger and D. Kennedy, (London: Pinter, 1996), 56-78.

T. Geiger, "Believing in the Miracle Cure: Economic transition in Germany and East-Central Europe," in *Germany Since Unification: The Domestic and External Consequences*, ed. K. Larres, (Basingstoke: Macmillan, 1998), 174-202.

T. Geiger, "Why Ireland needed the Marshall Plan but did not want it: Ireland, the Sterling Area and the European Recovery Program, 1947 - 1948," *Irish Studies in International Affairs* 11 (2000), 193-215.

T. Geiger, "A false dawn? Military procurement and Manchester industrial district, 1935-1960," in *Clusters and Networks in English Industrial Districts, 1750-1970*, eds. A. Popp and J. F. Wilson, (Aldershot: Ashgate, 2003), 251-270.

T. Geiger, "Economic Growth and National Security: National income analysis, western rearmament, and cold war strategy, 1950-1952," *International History Review* (2004 forthcoming).

T. Geiger and D. M. Ross, "Banks, institutional constraints and the limits of central banking: Monetary policy in Britain and West Germany, 1950-52," *Business History* 33 (1991) 3, 138-156.

T. Geiger and L. Sebesta, "National Defense Policies and the Failure of Military Integration in NATO: American Military Assistance and Western European Rearmament, 1949-54," in *The United States and the Integration of Europe: Legacies for the Postwar Era*, eds. F. H. Heller and J. R. Gillingham, (New York: St. Martin's Press, 1996), 253-279.

T. Geiger and L. Sebesta, "A Self-Defeating Policy: American Offshore Procurement and Integration of Western European Defence Production, 1952-56," *Journal of European Integration History* 4 (1998) 1, 55-73.

M. Geyer, *Deutsche Rüstungspolitik, 1860-1980* (Frankfurt/Main: Suhrkamp, 1984).

A. Ghosh, *Experiments with Input-Output Models: An application to the economy of the United Kingdom, 1948-55* (Cambridge: Cambridge University Press, 1964).

M. Gilbert and I. B. Kravis, *An International Comparison of National Products and the Purchasing Power of Currencies: A Study of the United States, The United Kingdom, France, Germany and Italy* (Paris: Organisation for European Economic Co-operation, 1954).

R. W. Goldsmith, "The Power of Victory: Munitions Output in World War II," *Military Affairs* 10 (1946) 1, 69-80.

P. Gordon Walker, *The Cabinet* (London: Jonathan Cape, 1970).

M. H. Gorn, *Harnessing the Genie: Science and Technology Forecasting for the Air Force, 1944-1986* (Washington: Office of Air Force History, 1988).

A. Gorst, "British military planning for post-war defence, 1943-1945," in *Britain and the First Cold War*, ed. A. Deighton, (Basingstoke: Macmillan, 1990), 91-108.

A. Gorst, "Facing Facts?: The Labour Government and defence policy 1945-1950," in *The Attlee Years*, ed. N. Tiratsoo, (London: Pinter, 1991), 190-209.

A. Gorst, "'We must cut our coat according to our cloth': the making of British defence policy 1945-1948," in *British Intelligence, Strategy and the Cold War*, ed. R. Aldrich, (London: Routledge, 1992), 143-165.

M. Gowing, *Independence and Deterrence: Britain and atomic energy, 1945-1952, vol. 2: policy execution* (Basingstoke: Macmillan, 1974).

D. Greenwood, "Defence and National Priorities since 1945," in *British Defence Policy in a Changing World*, ed. J. Baylis, (London: Croom Helm, 1977), 174-207.

R. Hamilton, "Early British Machine Tool Automation: The Road to Numerical Control," *Journal of Industrial History* 2 (1999) 1, 96-121.

W. Hamilton, *Blood on the Walls* (London: Bloomsbury, 1992).

C. J. E. Harlow, *The European Armaments Base: A Survey. Part 2: National Procurement Policies* (London: Institute of Strategic Studies, 1967).

A. Harris, *Bomber Offensive* (London: Collins, 1947).

K. Harris, *Attlee* (London: Weidenfeld and Nicholson, 1982).

M. Harrison, "Resource Mobilisation for World War II: the U.S.A., U.K., U.S.S.R. and Germany, 1939-1945," *Economic History Review* 41 (1988) 2, 171-192.

M. Harrison, ed., *The Economics of World War II: Six great powers in international comparison*, (Cambridge: Cambridge University Press, 1998).

T. Harrison, *Living through the Blitz* (Harmondsworth: Penguin, 1976).

R. Harrod, *Are these Hardships Necessary?* (London: Rupert Hart-Davis, 1947).

R. Harrod and J. Jewkes, "The Impact of rearmament on the British economy," in *Defense, Controls, and Inflation*, ed. A. Director, (Chicago: Chicago University Press, 1952), 254-284.

J. Harsanyi, "The dimension and measurement of social power," in *Power in Economics*, ed. K. W. Rothschild, (Harmondsworth: Penguin, 1971), 77-96.

J. Haslam, "Stalin's War and Peace: What if the Cold War had been Avoided?," in *Virtual History: Alternatives and Counterfactuals*, ed. N. Ferguson, (London: Picador, 1997), 348-367.

M. Hastings, *Bomber Command* (London: Pan Books, 1999).

C. Hay, "The Structural and Ideological Contradictions of Britain's Post-War Reconstruction," *Capital and Class* 34 (1994), 25-59.

I. Hay, *R.O.F: The Story of the Royal Ordnance Factories, 1939-1948* (London: His Majesty's Stationery Office, 1949).

D. Healey, *The Time of my Life* (Harmondsworth: Penguin, 1990).

G. D. H. Henderson, "Government and Industry," in *The British economy in the nineteen-fifties*, eds. G. D. N. Worswick and P. H. Ady, (Oxford: Clarendon Press, 1962), 326-377.

P. D. Henderson, D. G. Holland and D. Seers, "The Crisis of 1951," *Bulletin of the Institute of Statistics Oxford* 13 (1951) 10, 305-338.

P. Hennessy, *Whitehall* (London: Fontana, 1990).

P. Hennessy, *Never Again: Britain, 1945-1951* (London: Vintage Books, 1993).

T. A. Heppenheimer, *Turbulent Skies: The history of commercial aviation* (New York: John Wiley and Sons, 1995).

J. R. Hicks, "World Recovery After War: A theoretical analysis," *Economic Journal* 57 (1947) 226, 151-164.

J. Hinton, "Self-help and Socialism: the Squatters' Movement of 1946," *History Workshop* 25 (1988), 100-126.

H. Hirsch-Kreinsen, "On the history of NC-technology - different paths of development," in *Technology and Work in German Industry*, eds. N. Altmann, C. Köhler and P. Meil, (London: Routledge, 1992), 63-76.

A. O. Hirschman, *The Rhetoric of Reaction: Perversity, futility, jeopardy* (Cambridge: Harvard University Press, 1991).

C. Hitch, "Economics and Military Operations Research," *Review of Economics and Statistics* 40 (1958) 3, 199-209.

C. J. Hitch and R. M. McKean, *Economics of Defense in the Nuclear Age* (Cambridge: Harvard University Press, 1960).

M. W. Hoag, "What Interdependence for NATO?," *World Politics* 12 (1960) 3, 369-390.

W. G. Hoffmann, "Der Anteil der Verteidigungsausgaben am Bruttosozialprodukt - Ein internationaler und intertemporaler Vergleich," *Kyklos* 23 (1970) 1, 80-97.

M. J. Hogan, *The Marshall Plan: America, Britain, and the reconstruction of Western Europe* (Cambridge: Cambridge University Press, 1987).

M. Howard, "Introduction," in *The Struggle for Europe*, ed. C. Wilmot (Ware: Wordsworth Editions, 1997), Cited no page numbers.

P. Howlett, "New light through old windows: a new perspective on the British economy in the Second World War," *Journal of Contemporary History* 28 (1993), 361-379.

S. Howson, "The problem of monetary control in Britain, 1948-51," *Journal of European Economic History* 20 (1991) 1, 59-92.

S. Howson, *British Monetary Policy, 1945-51* (Oxford: Clarendon Press, 1993).

T. W. Hutchison, *Economics and Economic Policy in Britain, 1946-1966: Some aspects of their inter-relations* (London: George Allen and Unwin, 1968).

G. Hutton, *We Too Can Prosper: The promise of productivity* (London: George Allen and Unwin, 1953).

G. J. Ikenberry, *After Victory: Institutions, strategic restraint and the rebuilding of order after major wars* (Princeton: Princeton University Press, 2001).

H. A. Innes, "Great Britain, the United States and Canada," in *Essays in Canadian Economic History*, (Toronto: Toronto University Press, 1956), 394-412.

H. L. Ismay, *NATO: The first five years, 1949-1954* (Paris: North Atlantic Treaty Organisation, 1954).

W. Jackson, *Britain's Defence Dilemma: An inside view* (London: B. T. Batsford, 1990).

H. James, "The IMF and the Creation of the Bretton Woods System," in *Europe's Post-War Recovery*, ed. B. Eichengreen, (Cambridge: Cambridge University Press, 1995), 93-126.

B. Jessop, *State Theory: Putting Capitalist States in their Place* (University Park: Pennsylvania State University Press, 1990).

W. A. Jöhr, *Theoretischen Grundlagen der Wirtschaftspolitik: Die Konjunkturschwankungen* (Tübingen: J.C.B. Mohr (Paul Siebeck), 1952).

H. Joly, "Sociology of the members of the French productivity missions to the USA, 1949-1954," in *Catching up with America: Productivity missions and the diffusion of American economic and technological influence after the second world war*, ed. D. Barjot, (Paris: Presses de l'Université de Paris-Sarbonne, 2002), 183-196.

H. Jones, "New tricks for an old dog?: The Conservatives and social policy, 1951-5," in *Contemporary British History, 1931-61: Politics and the limits of policy*, eds. A. Gorst, L. Johnman and W. S. Lucas, (London: Pinter, 1991), 33-43.

R. Jong-yil, "Special relationship at war: The Anglo-American relationship during the Korean War," *Journal of Strategic Studies* 7 (1984) 4, 301-317.

M. Kaldor, "Technical Change in the Defence Industry," in *Technical Innovation and British Economic Performance*, ed. K. Pavitt, (Basingstoke: Macmillan, 1980), 100-121.

M. Kaldor, *The Baroque Arsenal* (London: Abacus, 1983).

M. Kaldor, M. Sharp and W. Walker, "Industrial Competitiveness and Britain's Defence," *Lloyd's Bank Review* (1986) 162, 31-49.

M. Kalecki, "Political Aspects of Full Employment," *Political Quarterly* 14 (1943), 322-331.

M. Kalecki, "The Minimum Essentials for Democratic Planning," in *Socialism: Functioning and Long-Run Planning (Collected Works of Michal Kalecki, vol. 3)*, ed. J. Osiatynski, (Oxford: Clarendon Press, 1992), 269-274.

M. I. Kamien and N. L. Schwartz, *Market Structure and Innovation* (Cambridge: Cambridge University Press, 1982).

T. Kampmann, *Vom Werkzeughandel zum Maschinenbau: Der Aufstieg des Familienunternehmens W. Ferd. Klingelnberg Söhne, 1900-1950* (Stuttgart: Franz Steiner, 1994).

J. Kaplan and G. Schleiminger, *The European Payments Union: Financial Diplomacy in the 1950s* (Oxford: Clarendon Press, 1989).

L. Kaplan, *A Community of Interests: NATO and the Military Assistance Program, 1948-1951* (Washington: Government Printing Office, 1980).

J. Keegan, *The Battle for History: Re-Fighting World War Two* (London: Hutchinson, 1995).

S. Kelly, "Ministers Matter: Gaitskell and Butler at odds over convertibility, 1950-52," *British Contemporary History* 14 (2000) 4, 27-53.

G. Kennedy, *Defense Economics* (London: Duckworth, 1983).

P. Kennedy, *The Rise and Fall of Great Powers: Economic change and military conflict from 1500 to 2000* (London: Fontana, 1989).

P. M. Kennedy, *Realities behind Diplomacy: Background influences on British external policy* (London: Fontana, 1985).

R. O. Keohane, *After Hegemony: Cooperation and Discord in the World Political Economy* (Princeton: Princeton University Press, 1984).

J. A. Kershaw, "The Economic War Potential of the U.S.S.R.," *American Economic Review* 41 (1951) 2, 475-482.

J. M. Keynes, *The General Theory of Employment, Interest and Money* (London: Macmillan, 1974).

J. M. Keynes, "How to Pay for the War," in *Essays in Persuasion*, ed. Royal Economic Society, (Basingstoke: Macmillan, 1984), 367-439.

J. Killick, *The United States and European Reconstruction, 1945 - 1960* (Edinburgh: Keele University Press, 1997).

P. King, *Knights of the Air: The life and times of the extraordinary pioneers who first built British aeroplanes* (London: Constable, 1989).

K. Knorr, *The War Potential of Nations* (Princeton: Princeton University Press, 1956).

T. L. Knutsen, *A History of International Relations Theory* (Manchester: Manchester University Press, 1997).

J. Kolko and G. Kolko, *The Limits of Power: The World and United States Foreign Policy, 1945-1954* (New York: Harper and Row, 1972).

J. Kornai, *Economics of Shortage* (Amsterdam: North-Holland, 1980).

J. Kornai, *Growth, Shortage and Efficiency* (Oxford: Basil Blackwell, 1982).

R. Koselleck, "'Erfahrungsraum' und 'Erwartungshorizont' - zwei historische Kategorien," in *Vergangene Zukunft: Zur Semantik geschichtlicher Zeiten*, (Frankfurt/Main: Suhrkamp, 1979), 349-375.

R. Koselleck, "Standortbindung und Zeitlichkeit: Ein Beitrag zur historiographischen Erschließung der geschichtlichen Welt," in *Vergangene Zukunft: Zur Semantik geschichtlicher Zeiten*, (Frankfurt/Main: Suhrkamp, 1979), 176-207.

S. Kuznets, "National Income: A New Version," *Review of Economics and Statistics* 30 (1948) 3, 151-179.

E. Laclau, *New Reflections on the Revolution of Our Time* (London: Verso, 1990).

H. Laski, *Reflections on the Revolution of our Time* (London: George Allen and Unwin, 1943).

H. Lefebvre, *Critique of Everyday Life* (London: Verso, 1991).

M. P. Leffler, *A Preponderance of Power: National security, the Truman administration, and the cold war* (Stanford: Stanford University Press, 1992).

H. Leigh-Phippard, *Congress and US Military Aid to Britain: Interdependence and dependence, 1949-56* (Basingstoke: Macmillan, 1995).

S. W. Leslie, *The Cold War and American Science: The military-industrial-academic complex at MIT and Stanford* (New York: Columbia University Press, 1993).

J. Lewis, *Changing Direction: British military planning for post-war strategic defence, 1942-1947* (London: Sherwood Press, 1988).

W. A. Lewis, *The Principles of Economic Planning* (London: George Allen and Unwin, 1948).

C. E. Lindblom, *Politics and Markets: the world's political economic systems* (New York: Basic Books, 1978).

W. Lippmann, *Cold War: A Study in American Foreign Policy* (London: Hamish Hamilton, 1947).

I. M. D. Little, "Fiscal Policy," in *The British economy in the nineteen-fifties*, eds. G. D. N. Worswick and P. H. Ady, (Oxford: Clarendon Press, 1962), 231-300.

W. Loth, *Die Teilung der Welt: Die Geschichte des Kalten Kriegs, 1941-1955* (München: Deutscher Taschenbuch Verlag, 1989).

W. R. Louis, "American anti-colonialism and the dissolution of the British Empire," *International Affairs* 61 (1985), 395-420.

J. Lovering, "Defence expenditure and the regions: The case of Bristol," in *Defence Expenditure and Regional Development*, ed. M. Breheny, (London: Mansell, 1988), 122-137.

J. Lovering, "Military expenditure and the restructuring of capitalism: the military industry in Britain," *Cambridge Journal of Economics* 14 (1990) 4, 453-467.

R. Luxemburg, *Die Akkumulation des Kapitals: Ein Beitrag zur ökonomischen Erklärung des Imperialismus* (originally published in 1923), (Frankfurt am Main: Verlag Neue Kritik, 1970).

D. MacDougall, *Don and Mandarin: Memoirs of an Economist* (London: John Murray, 1987).

K. Macksey, *The Tanks: The History of the Royal Tank Regiment, 1945-1975* (London: Arms and Armour Press, 1979).

C. S. Maier, "Finance and Defense: Implications of Military Integration, 1950-1952," in *NATO: The Founding of the Atlantic Alliance and the integration of Europe*, eds. F. H. Heller and J. R. Gillingham, (London: Macmillan, 1992), 335-351.

A. Maizels, *Industrial Growth and World Trade: An empirical study of trends in production, consumption and trade in manufactures from 1899-1959, with a discussion of probable future trends* (Cambridge: Cambridge University Press, 1963).

K. Mannheim, "The Crisis of Culture in the Era of Mass-Democracies and Autarchies," *Sociological Review* 26 (1934) 2, 105-129.

W. A. P. Manser, *Britain in Balance: The Myth of Failure* (Harmondsworth: Penguin, 1973).

N. Mansergh, "Britain, the Commonwealth and Western Union," *International Affairs* 24 (1948) 4, 491-504.

N. Mansergh, *Survey of Commonwealth Affairs: Problems of wartime co-operation and post-war change, 1939-1952* (London: Oxford University Press, 1958).

R. Marjolin, *Architect of European Unity: Memoirs, 1911-1986* (London: Weidenfeld and Nicolson, 1989).

A. Marwick, *Britain in the Century of Total War: War, peace and social change, 1900-1967* (Harmondsworth: Penguin, 1970).

Mass-Observation, *Peace and the Public* (London: Longmans, Green & Co., 1947).

R. C. O. Matthews, C. H. Feinstein and J. C. Odling-Smee, *British Economic Growth, 1856-1973* (Oxford: Oxford University Press, 1982).

P. D. McClelland, *Causal Explanation and Model Building in History, Economics and the New Economic History* (Ithaca: Cornell University Press, 1975).

J. McGlade, "The US Technical Assistance Program: From revolutionary vision to productivity drive," in *Catching up with America: Productivity missions and the diffusion of American economic and technological influence after the second world war*, ed. D. Barjot, (Paris: Presses de l'Université de Paris-Sarbonne, 2002), 67-86.

D. McLachlan, A. H. Head, R. G. Jessel, H. G. Martin, O. Sargent and H. G. Thursfield, *Defence in the Cold War: The Task for the Free World* (London: Royal Institute of International Affairs, 1950).

J. E. Meade, *Planning and the Price Mechanism: The liberal-socialist solution* (London: George Allen and Unwin, 1948).

S. Melman, *The Permanent War Economy: American Capitalism in Decline* (New York: Touchstone, 1985).

M. Middlebrook, *The Battle of Hamburg: The Firestorm Raid* (Harmondsworth: Penguin Books, 1984).

R. Middleton, *Government versus the Market: Growth of the public sector, economic management and British economic performance* (Cheltenham: Edward Elgar, 1996).

I. Mikardo, *Back-Bencher* (London: Weidenfeld and Nicolson, 1988).

A. S. Milward, *War, Economy and Society, 1939-1945* (Harmondsworth: Penguin, 1977).

A. S. Milward, *The Reconstruction of Western Europe, 1945-51* (London: Methuen, 1984).

A. S. Milward, *The Economic Effects of the Two World Wars on Britain* (Basingstoke: Macmillan, 1987).

A. S. Milward, "The Marshall Plan and German Foreign Trade," in *The Marshall Plan and Germany*, eds. C. S. Maier and G. Bischof, (New York: Berg Publishers, 1991), 452-487.

A. S. Milward, *The European Rescue of the Nation-State* (London: Routledge, 1992).

J. Mitchell, *Crisis in Britain 1951* (London: Secker & Warburg, 1963).

B. L. Montgomery, *The Memoirs of Field-Marshal the Viscount Montgomery of Alamein, K.G.* (London: William Collins, Sons & Co., 1958).

A. Moravcsik, "Arms and Autarky in Modern European History," *Dædalus* 120 (1991) 4, 23-45.

K. O. Morgan, *Labour in Power, 1945-1951* (Oxford: Oxford University Press, 1985).

J. U. Nef, "War and Economic progress, 1540-1640," *Economic History Review* 12 (1943) 1, 13-38.

R. R. Nelson, "Uncertainty, learning and the economics of parallel research and development efforts," *Review of Economic and Statistics* 43 (1961) 4, 351-364.

M. Newman, *John Strachey* (Manchester: Manchester University Press, 1989).

D. F. Noble, "Command Performance: A Perspective on Military Enterprise and Technological Change," in *Military Enterprise and Technological Change: Prespectives on the American Experience*, ed. M. R. Smith, (Cambridge: MIT Press, 1985), 329-426.

R. M. Ogorkiewicz, *Design and Development of Fighting Vehicles* (London: Macdonald, 1968).

G. Orwell, "You and the Atom Bomb," in *Collected Essays, Journalism and Letters of George Orwell: volume 4: In Front of Your Nose, 1945-1950*, eds. S. Orwell and I. Angus, (London: Secker and Warburg, 1968), 6-10.

R. Ovendale, *The English-Speaking Alliance: Britain, the United States, the Dominions and the Cold War, 1945-51* (London: George Allen and Unwin, 1985).

R. J. Overy, *The Air War, 1939-1945* (New York: Stein and Day, 1981).

C. Paddock, "Future Wars and the Use of Armour," *Brassey's Annual* 67 (1956), 107-120.

D. Paige and G. Bombach, *A Comparison of National Output and Productivity of the United Kingdom and the United States* (Paris: Organisation for European Economic Co-operation, 1959).

S. T. Parkinson, *New Product Development in Engineering: A Comparison of the British and West German Machine Tool Industries* (Cambridge: Cambridge University Press, 1984).

M. J. Peck, "Science and Technology," in *Britain's Economic Prospects*, eds. R. E. Caves and Associates, (Washington: Brookings Institution, 1968), 448-484.

M. J. Peck and F. M. Scherer, *The Weapons Acquisition Process: An Economic Analysis* (Boston: Graduate School of Business Administration, Harvard University, 1962).

G. C. Peden, "Economic Aspects of British Perceptions of Power on the Eve of the Cold War," in *Power in Europe? Great Britain, France, Italy and Germany in a Postwar World, 1945-1950*, eds. J. Becker and F. Knipping, (Berlin: Walter de Gruyter, 1986), 237-260.

G. C. Peden, *Keynes, the Treasury and British Economic Policy* (Basingstoke: Macmillan, 1988).

F. Perroux, *La coexistence pacifique* (Grenoble: Presses Universitaires de Grenobles, 1992).

A. Piatier, "The Economics of the Rearmament and its Effects on the Western Economics: A theoretical synthesis," *Public Finance / Finances Publiques* 7 (1952) 1/2, 176-192.

B. Pimlott, *Harold Wilson* (London: HarperCollins, 1992).

B. Pimlott, ed., *The Political Diary of Hugh Dalton, 1918-40, 1945-60*, (London: Jonathan Cape, 1986).

M. Pinto-Duschinsky, "Bread and Circuses? The Conservatives in Office, 1951-1964," in *The Age of Affluence, 1951-1964*, eds. V. Bogdanor and R. Skidelsky, (London: Macmillan, 1970), 55-77.

L. Pliatzky, *Getting and Spending: Public expenditure, employment and inflation* (Oxford: Basil Blackwell, 1982).

E. Plowden, *An Industrialist in the Treasury: The post-war years* (London: Andre Deutsch, 1990).

R. A. Pollard, *Economic Security and the Origins of the Cold War, 1945-1950* (New York: Columbia University Press, 1985).

S. Pollard, *The Development of the British Economy, 1914-1967* (London: Edward Arnold, 1969).

S. Pollard, *Wasting of the British Economy: British economic policy, 1945 to the Present* (London: Croom Helm, 1984).

S. Pollard, "Economic Policies and Traditions," in *Government and economies in the postwar World: Economic policies and comparative performance, 1945-85*, eds. A. Graham and A. Seldon, (London: Routledge, 1990), 294-302.

H.-J. Puhle, "Theorien in der Praxis des vergleichenden Historikers," in *Theorie und Erzählung in der Geschichte*, eds. J. Kocka and T. Nipperdey, (München: Deutscher Taschenbuchverlag, 1979), 119-136.

R. D. Putnam, "Diplomacy and domestic politics: the logic of two-level games," *International Organization* 42 (1988) 3, 427-460.

G. Raudzens, "War-Winning Weapons: The Measurement of Technological Determinism in Military History," *Journal of Military History* 54 (1990) 4, 403-434.

E. Reid, *Time of Fear and Hope: The making of the North Atlantic Treaty, 1947-1949* (Toronto: McClelland and Stewart, 1977).

J. Reppy, "On the economics of national security," in *Security and Arms Control, volume 1: A guide to national policymaking*, eds. E. A. Kolodziej and P. M. Morgan, (New York: Greenwood Press, 1989).

P. Ricœur, "Narrative Time," *Critical Inquiry* 7 (1980) 1, 169-190.

L. Robbins, *The Economic Problem in Peace and War* (London: Macmillan, 1947).

L. Robbins, "Towards the Atlantic Community," *Lloyds Bank Review* New Series (1950) 17, 1-24.

F. K. Roberts, "Ernest Bevin as Foreign Secretary," in *The Foreign Policy of the British Labour Governments, 1945-1951*, ed. R. Ovendale, (Leicester: Leicester University Press, 1984), 21-42.

A. J. Robertson, "The British Airframe Industry and the State in the Interwar Period: A Comment," *Economic History Review* 28 (1974) 4, 648-657.

E. A. G. Robinson, "The Overall Allocation of Resources," in *Lessons of the British War Economy*, ed. D. N. Chester, (Cambridge: Cambridge University Press, 1951), 34-57.

J. Robinson, *The Generalisation of the General Theory and other Essays* (Basingstoke: Macmillan, 1979).

W. P. Rogerson, "Economic Incentives and the Defense Procurement Process," *Journal of Economic Perspectives* 8 (1994) 4, 65-90.

N. Rollings, "British budgetary policy, 1945-54: a Keynesian revolution?," *Economic History Review* 41 (1988) 2, 283-298.

D. Romer, *Advanced Macroeconomics* (Boston: McGraw-Hill, 2001).

T. Rooth, "Britain's Other Dollar Problem: Economic Relations with Canada, 1945-50," *Journal of Imperial and Commonwealth History* 27 (1999) 1, 81-108.

G. M. Ross, *The Business of Tanks: 1933 to 1945* (Elms Court: Arthur H. Stockwell, 1976).

L. Rostas, *Comparative Productivity in British and American Industry* (Cambridge: Cambridge University Press, 1948).

T. Sandler and K. Hartley, *The Economics of Defense* (Cambridge: Cambridge University Press, 1995).

J. Saville, *The Politics of Continuity: British foreign policy and the Labour government, 1945-46* (London: Verso, 1993).

W. M. Scammell, "Rearmament: The First Year," *Westminister Bank Review* (November 1951), 1-8.

F. M. Scherer, *Innovation and Growth: Schumpeterian Perspectives* (Cambridge: MIT Press, 1984).

W. R. Schilling, "The Politics of National Defense: Fiscal 1950," in *Strategy, Politics and Defense Budgets*, eds. W. R. Schilling, P. Y. Hammond and G. H. Snyder, (New York: Columbia University Press, 1962), 1-266.

G. Schmölders, "The Impact of Rearmament on Western Germany," *Public Finance / Finances Publiques* 7 (1952) 1/2, 100-112.

J. A. Schumpeter, *Capitalism, Socialism and Democracy* (originally published in 1943), (London: Unwin Hyman, 1987).

J. D. Scott, *Vickers: A History* (London: Weidenfeld and Nicolson, 1962).

J. D. Scott and R. Hughes, *The Administration of War Production* (London: Her Majesty's Stationery Office, 1955).

M. F. Scott, "The Balance of Payments Crises," in *The British Economy in the Nineteen-Fifties*, eds. G. D. N. Worswick and P. H. Ady, (Oxford: Clarendon Press, 1962), 205-30.

P. Scott, "British regional policy 1945-51: a lost opportunity," *Twentieth Century British History* 8 (1997) 3, 358-382.

Scottish Council (Development and Industry), *Report of the Committee on Local Development in Scotland* (Edinburgh: Scottish Council (Development and Industry), 1952).

D. Seers, "National Income, Production and Consumption," in *The British Economy, 1945-1950*, eds. G. D. N. Worswick and P. H. Ady, (Oxford: Oxford University Press, 1952), 35-61.

G. L. S. Shackle, *The Years of High Theory: Invention and Tradition in Economic Thought, 1926-1939* (Cambridge: Cambridge University Press, 1967).

D. Sheridan, ed., *Among You Taking Notes ...: The wartime diary of Naomi Mitchison, 1939-1945*, (Oxford: Oxford University Press, 1986).

A. Shonfield, *British Economic Policy since the War* (Harmondsworth: Penguin, 1958).

O. Šik, *Der dritte Weg: Die Marxistisch-leninistische Theorie und die moderne Industriegesellschaft* (Hamburg: Hoffmann und Campe, 1972).

E. S. Simpson, "Inflation, Deflation and Employment in Italy," *Review of Economic Studies* 17 (1950) 3, 203-225.

J. A. Simpson and E. S. C. Weiner, *The Oxford English Dictionary* (Oxford: Clarendon Press, 1989).

J. D. Singer and F. Diehl Paul, eds., *Measuring the Correlates of War*, (Ann Arbor: University of Michigan Press, 1990).

J. Singleton, "Lancashire's last stand: Declining employment in the British cotton industry, 1950-1970," *Economic History Review* 39 (1986) 1, 92-107.

A. Smith, "Command and Control in Postwar Britain: Defence decision-making in the United Kingdom, 1945-1984," *Twentieth Century British History* 2 (1991) 3, 291-327.

H. L. Smith, "The effect of the war on the status of women," in *War and Social Change: British Society in the Second World War*, ed. H. L. Smith, (Manchester: Manchester University Press, 1986), 208-229.

K. Smith, *The British Economic Crisis: Its Past and Future* (Harmondsworth: Penguin, 1985).

M. R. Smith, "Introduction," in *Military Enterprise and Technological Change: Perspectives on the American Experience*, ed. M. R. Smith, (Cambridge: MIT Press, 1985), 1-37.

R. Smith, "Military Expenditure and Investment in OECD Countries, 1954-1973," *Journal of Comparative Economics* 4 (1980) 1, 19-32.

A. J. Smithers, *Rude Mechanicals: An account of tank maturity during the Second World War* (London: Grafton, 1989).

W. Sombart, *Krieg und Kapitalismus* (München: Duncker und Humblot, 1913).

P. Southwood, *Disarming Military Industries: Turning an outbreak of peace into an enduring legacy* (Basingstoke: Macmillan, 1991).

R. H. Spector, *Advice and Support: The Early Years of the U.S. Army in Vietnam, 1941-1960* (New York: Free Press, 1985).

C. Steedman, *Dust* (Manchester: Manchester University Press, 2001).

Stockholm International Peace Research Institute, *SIPRI Yearbook of World Armaments and Disarmament, 1968/69* (Stockholm: Almqvist & Wiksell, 1970).

W. Stueck, *The Korean War: An International History* (Princeton: Princeton University Press, 1995).

P. Summerfield, *Women Workers in the Second World War: Production and patriarchy in conflict* (London: Routledge, 1989).

R. H. Tawney, "The Abolition of Economic Controls, 1918-1921," *Economic History Review* 8 (1943), 1-30.

P. Temin, "The 'Koreaboom' in West Germany: fact or fiction," *Economic History Review* 48 (1995) 4, 737-753.

G. Thayer, *The War Business: The International Trade in Armaments* (London: Weidenfeld and Nicolson, 1969).

A. P. Thirwall, "The Balance of Payments Constraint as an Explanation of International Growth Rate Differences," *Banca Nazionale del Lavoro Quarterly Review* (1979) 128, 45-53.

E. P. Thompson, *The Poverty of Theory: or an orrery of errors* (London: Merlin Press, 1978).

E. P. Thompson, "Notes on Exterminism, the Last Stage of Civilisation," in *Exterminism and the Cold War*, ed. New Left Review, (London: Verso, 1982), 1-33.

A. P. Thornton, *The Imperial Idea and its Enemies: A study in British power* (Basingstoke: Macmillan, 1985).

J. Tinbergen, "The Impact of the Rearmament on the Netherlands," *Public Finance / Finances Publiques* 7 (1952) 1/2, 133-145.

N. Tiratsoo, *Reconstruction, Affluence and Labour Politics: Coventry, 1945-60* (London: Routledge, 1990).

H. T. Tizard, "Science and the Services," *Journal of the Royal United Service Institution* 91 (1946) 563, 333-346.

J. Tomlinson, *British Macroeconomic Policy since 1940* (London: Croom Helm, 1985).

J. Tomlinson, *Employment Policy: The Crucial Years, 1939-1955* (Oxford: Clarendon Press, 1987).

J. Tomlinson, "Labour's management of the national economy, 1945-51: Survey and Speculations," *Economy and Society* 18 (1989) 1, 1-24.

J. Tomlinson, "The Attlee Government and the Balance of Payments, 1945-1951," *Twentieth Century British History* 2 (1991) 1, 47-66.

J. Tomlinson, "The Failure of the Anglo-American Council on Productivity," *Business History* 33 (1991) 1, 82-92.

J. Tomlinson, "Mr. Attlee's supply-side socialism," *Economic History Review* 46 (1993) 1, 1-22.

J. Tomlinson, "Inventing 'decline': the falling behind of the British economy in the postwar years," *Economic History Review* 49 (1996) 4, 731-757.

J. Tomlinson, "Correlli Barnett's History: The case of Marshall aid," *Twentieth Century British History* 8 (1997) 2, 222-238.

J. Tomlinson, "Marshall Aid and the 'Shortage Economy' in Britain in the 1940s," *Contemporary European History* 9 (2000) 1, 137-155.

R. Toye, "Gosplanners versus Thermostatters: Whitehall planning debates and their political consequences, 1945-49," *British Contemporary History* 14 (2000) 4, 81-106.

R. Toye, "The Labour Party's External Economic Policy in the 1940s," *The Historical Journal* 43 (2000) 1, 189-215.

R. Toye, "The Attlee government, the Imperial Preference System, and the creation of GATT," *English Historical Review* (forthcoming).

R. C. Tress, "Defence and Public Finance," *London and Cambridge Economic Service* 27 (1949) 1, 2-6.

R. C. Tress, "The Armed Economy," *London and Cambridge Economic Service* 29 (1951) 1, 2-7.

A. Tusa and J. Tusa, *The Berlin Blockade* (London: Coronet, 1989).

W. Wallace, "World Status without Tears," in *The Age of Affluence, 1951-1964*, eds. V. Bogdanor and R. Skidelsky, (London: Macmillan, 1970), 192-220.

B. Ward, *Policy for the West* (Harmondsworth: Penguin, 1951).

D. C. Watt, "Britain, the United States and the opening of the cold war," in *The Foreign Policy of the British Labour Governments, 1945-1951*, ed. R. Ovendale, (Leicester: Leicester University Press, 1984), 43-60.

C. Webster, I. Jacob and A. Robinson, *United Kingdom Policy: Foreign, strategic, economic* (London: Royal Institute of International Affairs, 1950).

H. White, *Metahistory: The historical imagination in nineteenth-century Europe* (Baltimore: Johns Hopkins University Press, 1973).

H. White, "The Politics of Historical Interpretation: Discipline and de-Sublimation," in *Content of the Form: Narrative Discourse and Historical Interpretation*, (Baltimore: Johns Hopkins University Press, 1987), 58-82.

C. Wiebes and B. Zeeman, "Eine Lehrstunde in Machtpolitik: Die Vereinigten Staaten und ihre Partner am Vorabend der NATO-Gründung," *Vierteljahrshefte für Zeitgeschichte* 40 (1992) 3, 413-423.

S. Willet, "The impact of defence procurement on the electronics sector: a London case study," in *Defence Expenditure and Regional Development*, ed. M. Breheny, (London: Mansell, 1988), 140-172.

B. R. Williams, *International Report on Factors in Investment Behaviour* (Paris: Organisation for Economic Co-operation and Development, 1962).

J. H. Williams, *Economic Stability in a Changing World: Essays in economic theory and policy* (New York: Oxford University Press, 1953).

P. M. Williams, *Hugh Gaitskell: a political biography* (London: Jonathan Cape, 1979).

P. M. Williams, ed., *The Diary of Hugh Gaitskell, 1945-1956*, (London: Jonathan Cape, 1983).

W. A. Williams, *The Tragedy of American Diplomacy* (New York: Delta Books, 1962).

C. Wilmot, *The Struggle for Europe* (originally published in 1951), (Ware: Wordsworth Editions, 1997).

A. J. Wilson, "The future of armour as the arm of mobility," *Royal United Services Institute Journal* 91 (1946), 396-400.

J. F. Wilson, *Ferranti: A History, Building a Family Business, 1882-1975* (Lancaster: Carnegie, 2000).

J. M. Winter, "Introduction: The economic and social history of war," in *War and Economic Development: Essays in the memory of David Joslin*, ed. J. M. Winter, (Cambridge: Cambridge University Press, 1975), 1-10.

T. W. Wolfe, *Soviet Power and Europe, 1945-1970* (Baltimore: Johns Hopkins University Press, 1970).

H.-W. Würzler, "Die Anfänge kanadischer Militärhilfe für die europäischen NATO-Partner: Probleme und Motivationen (1948/49-1951/52)," in *Das Nordatlantische Bündnis, 1949-1956*, eds. K. A. Maier and N. Wiggershaus, (München: R. Oldenbourg Verlag, 1993), 109-129.

J. Wyler, "The national income of Soviet Russia," *Social Research* 13 (1946), 501-518.

B. Zeeman, "Der Brüsseler Pakt und die Diskussion um einen westdeutschen Militärbeitrag," in *Vom Marshallplan zur EWG: Die Eingliederung der Bundesrepublik Deutschland in die westliche Welt*, eds. L. Herbst, W. Bührer and H. Sowade, (München: R. Oldenbourg, 1990), 399-426.

J. Zeitlin, "Americanizing British Engineering?: Strategic debate, selective adaptation and hybrid innovation in post-war reconstruction, 1945-1960," in *Americanization and its Limits: Reworking US technology and management in post-war Europe and Japan*, eds. J. Zeitlin and G. Herrigel, (Oxford: Oxford University Press, 2000), 123-154.

K. Zilliacus, *I Choose Peace* (Harmondsworth: Penguin, 1949).

Theses, working papers and other unpublished material

N. W. Boorer, "Barnes Wallis, Designer (1887-1979): A memorial lecture," paper presented at the British Aerospace Factory, Weybridge, 4 March 1981.

M. Chick, "Economic Planning, Managerial Decision-Making and the Role of Fixed Capital Investment in the Economic Recovery of the United Kingdom, 1945-55," (Ph.D. thesis, University of London, 1986).

B. Cros, "Statistical information - Les donnés d'équipement dans le total des dépenses de défense et le pourcentage des forces armées dans la population active, 1949-1987," (NATO Communication, Ref.: SAS(87)151, 1987).

P. Foot, "Defence Burden-Sharing in the Atlantic Community, 1945-1954," Aberdeen Studies in Defence Economics (Aberdeen Centre for Defence Economics, 1981).

T. Geiger, "Studies in the political economy and economic impact of British defence expenditure and American military aid to Britain, 1945–1955," (Ph. D. Dissertation, University of Aberdeen, 1998).

T. Geiger and R. Toye, "Britain, America and the origins of the European Payments Union: A reassessment," (unpublished manuscript, 2003).

W. P. Howlett, "Towards a model of the central decision-making process in a war economy," in *Discussion Paper in Economics*, (Department of Economics, University of Stirling, 1989).

M. W. Kirby and R. Capey, "The origins and diffusion of operational research in the UK," paper presented at the Annual Conference of the Economic History Society, Lancaster University, 29-31 March 1996.

R. Lloyd-Jones and M. J. Lewis, "Alfred Herbert and Co., The British Machine Tool Industry, and the 'Modernisation' of British Manufacturing in the 1950s and early 1960s," paper presented at the Engineering Postwar Industries, Hagley Museum, Wilmington, 8-9 July 2001.

G. Mayer, "Le Conseguenze Economiche e Finanziarie dovute al Programma di Riarmo del Regno Unito," (unpublished manuscript, 1952).

P. A. Winston, "The British Government and Defence Production, 1943-50," (Ph.D., University of Cambridge, 1982).

Index